SEMINOLES!
The First Forty Years

Bill McGrotha

Published by the Tallahassee Democrat

Edited by Ron Hartung

Designed by Jane Houle

Photos courtesy of the Tallahassee Democrat photo staff (Phil Coale, Mike Ewen, George Kochaniec, Bruce Mellinger, Phil Sears and Mark Wallheiser, with research by Chris Norman); the Tallahassee Democrat library; Florida State University Sports Information (with research by Lisa Franson).

Also contributing photos were: The Associated Press; Jerry Blankenship; Charley Durbin; Florida State Archives; Florida State University/Special Collections; Darryl Kochaniec; Ryals Lee; J. Barry Mittan; Courtland Richards; Dan Stainer; Ray Stanyard; Sage Thigpen; and Earl Warren.

Statistics pages courtesy of FSU Sports Information

Published by the
TALLAHASSEE DEMOCRAT
P.O. Box 990
Tallahassee, Florida 32302

First edition

Manufactured in the United States of America

LC 87-51238
ISBN 0-9613040-1-4

contents

To the legions of *good* football fans who came to cheer. And to Irma and the kids — June, Mike, Molly, Rosemary, Hank — who did, too.

Battle Cry

Introducing a big cheer, eight coaches and a program that climbed ever higher

Florida State football was born of war.

And it was nurtured, against huge odds, in an enduring atmosphere of combat.

Many would-have-been students had answered the demanding call of World War II. When that war ended in 1945 they looked to higher education. For a great number, though, there was no room at the inn.

Moving swiftly, the nation sought to create room. At Florida State College for Women in 1946, a satellite facility was formed — the Tallahassee Branch of the University of Florida. But that was short-lived. By 1947 FSCW, with its TBUF appendage, had become Florida State University. The clamor that had started in 1946 — for a men's athletic program, and for football — grew louder.

Virtually overnight, it all became a reality. In 1947, football was born.

From Day One, Florida State football was an underdog. Surely that first team, with its many men who had been to war, was an unruly underdog, and one of uncommon spirit.

Personifying that spirit — moving and shaking that spirit — was one of those veterans, perhaps the smallest warrior of them all.

Doug Bonifay never played the game, not at Florida State anyway, but at the beginning he was a compelling part.

"An agitator and an aggravator," said an associate of those first days. "To the team, he was like a mascot — and everybody's friend."

At 5-foot-4 and 125 pounds, Bonifay was about as big as Florida State football at the time. And about as proud. He could do 100 push-ups without stopping, and frequently obliged at the drop of a hint.

He read Shakespeare, and would often quote. " 'I am the mightiest man of all men,' " he would proclaim, paraphrasing a line from "Macbeth." " 'I fear no one of woman born.' "

Bonifay was quick to accept — and extend — a physical challenge, and it was sometimes

fortunate that he had such seconds as big tackle D.L. Middlebrooks, who had grown up with him in Pensacola.

Like some others among those veterans, Bonifay had a degree of familiarity with the grape.

" 'O God, that men should put an enemy into their mouth that should steal away their brain,' " Bonifay was fond of quoting from "Othello" at times that seemed appropriate, and perhaps otherwise.

A cheer is born

One evening, at a place east of town called the Edgewood Club, there was a convivial gathering of these warriors.

"It was after a game," said Bonifay. "I don't remember what game."

At one point in the evening, Bonifay was moved to climb upon a table. Possibly he was assisted.

"FSU one time!" he hollered. His pals responded with cheers.

"FSU two times!" he bellowed, now encouraged by the response, and waving an arm. More cheers.

"FSU three times!" he yelled, throwing up both arms. Louder cheers.

"FSU *all* the damn time!" screamed Bonifay. And the place was bedlam.

Years later, he would say: "I don't know what motivated me. Everybody started yelling after the first one. Then they yelled more. And it kind of got going."

Rapidly, the cheer grew, and when FSU's third season rolled around, the cheer rang out all over — including, according to a newspaper account, the table tops in the lobby of Jacksonville's Mayflower Hotel before and after the game there with Stetson.

One who helped spread the cheer was Ed "Daddy Rabbit" Dilsaver, a guard on that first team.

"It kind of roused everybody up," said Dilsaver of the yell. "I think I first led it at a basketball game in that old gym over on West

"FSU two times!" That's part of the cheer Doug Bonifay concocted back in FSU's infancy.

3

Campus. You had everybody in close there and could get people riled up in a hurry."

Dilsaver picked up the name Daddy Rabbit following a minor accident with a carload of teammates. "Come to your daddy rabbit," he had said after the accident, as he tried to assemble the group around him to contemplate their next move.

"I was never timid, you know," said Dilsaver. "And when things got to going kind of slow at a game, I would jump up and give the FSU-one-time yell. If we were going to become a real university, we had to get something going.

"But it was Doug who came up with the yell that night at the old Edgewood Club. He was a powerful little individual — cheerful, a showman in his own right, the type of fellow who never had any enemies anywhere."

Bonifay became somewhat more than the father of an original yell. He was sometimes caught, literally, in the grip of the spirit at games.

"They would pick me up and pass me around — up and down the stands, around and around," he said.

Through it all, the cheer rang out: *"FSU all the damn time!"*

Don Veller, the second among eight coaches of those first 40 years who would hear the cheer so often, remembered it well.

"Always, it would send cold chills down your back," he said.

A bit of luck, a lot of work

Like Bonifay in the stands, Florida State football would go up and down, around and around its amazing success story over those first 40 years. From an 0-5 start, Florida State moved to an unbeaten season three years later. In the first five years, the teams won 30 of their 39 games.

"There was, from the beginning, a kind of indefinable spirit about FSU — a boldness to innovate," said Pat Hogan, Florida State vice president for public affairs, who was a student in those early years and, later, sports-information director.

Part of the phenomenal development, Hogan thought, was by accident rather than design. But much of it was sweat.

"The athletic program sort of carved things out of granite — going against large odds," said Hogan. "The people quotient is what pulled it up.

"I have thought of writing a book, and I might call it 'The Granite Glory' or, somewhat cornily, 'The Miracle on Pensacola Street.'

"It was a kind of spartan work effort. People of high energy worked harder, with less. There were very few lazy folks. Florida State had, I think, these robust people around who needed something big to do."

Florida State, from the start, was different.

"It was a place that had a circus," Hogan said, "and a colorful showman for a football coach named Tom Nugent — who everybody thought, if he was not crazy, was at least partially so."

Nugent was the third of Florida State's eight head football coaches through the first 40 seasons. And if indeed he was thought of as a little crazy at times, so at times were the seven other coaches.

"We had to swim upstream against either the lethargy or the non-objectivity of the media," recalled Hogan. "How very difficult it was to get anything into some newspapers."

How very difficult it was for so much.

Most of the attention went to the University of Florida. And the rival school was always blocking the path — when Florida State wanted to go coeducational, when it wanted to begin a football program, when it wanted to play Florida, when it wanted to play Florida in Tallahassee as well as Gainesville, when it wanted to play by NCAA rules rather than ones peculiar to the Southeastern Conference.

Eight coaches, eight eras

This is a story of the pride and the passion of Florida State football, and of what some do not well comprehend — the why. A story of granite glory — a story of garnet glory.

This is a story told extensively by the eight coaches, all of whom talked with patience, and at considerable length, of the good times and the bad.

There was the gentlemanly, benevolent Ed Williamson, called by his players "Mr. Nice Guy." He never sought the job, and agreed to take it for one year only.

There was the scholarly Veller, wise student of football and many other things, who produced a dramatic early turnaround that headed the game in a splendid direction.

There was Nugent, the imaginative showman who attracted unusual attention off the field, and on it with the likes of a memorable first victory over a Southeastern Conference opponent, Tennessee in Knoxville.

There was Perry Moss, well acquainted with the tactics of the game and with road maps. He dropped in for a cup of coffee in 1959 before moving on and on in a career that had him in 20 coaching jobs by the time he was 60.

There was the energy-charged Bill Peterson — a tireless worker and fighter who casually turned out malapropisms and future head coaches while taking Florida State to unprecedented heights that included a first victory over Florida.

There was Larry Jones, a good guy who often spoke of love for his players, who surely, to a degree, was the victim of the quicksand of circumstances.

There was Darrell Mudra, a different breed of man and coach who sat in the pressbox during games. Over 25 years, he succeeded virtually everywhere he coached except Florida State, and there is some thought he would have here, too, with more time than he was granted.

Then there was Bobby Bowden, who seemed more than any other before him a man for all Florida State seasons — a coach with a gift of relating to most all people while winning games to spectacular degree.

The old yell still echoes

This, too, is a story of Bob Harbison, the canny line coach who served with the last seven of those eight coaches, through 37 seasons.

This is a story of people like cinematographer/equipment man/bus driver Charley Durbin, who saw more games in those first 40 seasons than any other person, who drove FSU athletic teams close to 2 million miles — who perhaps came as close to being indispensable as anyone Florida State knew.

This is not a game-by-game story, not a play-by-play of those 40 years. For a greatly detailed account read "FSU One Time" and "The Bowden Years," so well documented by Dr. James Jones, the ardent student of all Florida State athletics and head of the school's history department. From his extensive earlier research, this endeavor has benefited liberally, shamelessly — and gratefully.

This is a story of the reverberations of an original cheer. Bill Bunker, once a player and later FSU's sports-information director, painted this word picture:

"On autumn Saturdays, the Seminoles play football. On all of these Saturdays — win or lose, in stadiums in Tallahassee, in Gainesville or Blacksburg, Va. — a familiar scene evolves. At points in time, following the first arrival and last departure, a figure will rise from the faceless crowd. He may be young or he may be old, and he may be

short or he may be tall, and he may or may not be wearing a hat or Seminole jacket. Whatever, he will be instantly recognized by his action, when one arm shoots skyward, the index finger extended as he shouts: 'FSU one time!' Those around him will respond with a loud cheer. The arm goes up again, this time with two fingers outlined against the sky: 'FSU two times!' More voices join the acclaim. And it becomes three fingers extended as the volume rises: 'FSU three times!' The chorus of voices swells. Then the supremely climactic moment, as the extended fingers become a clenched fist or both arms are spread wide: 'FSU all the damn time!' The deafening noise subsides. The crowd settles back in its seat. And waits for the next impromptu cheerleader to stand and identify himself with the words that are at once a cry of camaraderie and a shout of defiance, typifying a dauntless, exultant and absolutely unique spirit."

On a golden night before one of those garnet Tallahassee Saturdays, the first team of 1947 gathers in annual reunion, and more than once during the evening, Doug Bonifay will rise, much as he did the first time on that long-ago evening at the Edgewood Club, to lead the old warriors in the yell:

"... *FSU all the damn time!*"

SOUVENIR
FOOTBALL
PROGRAM

INAUGURAL GAME-FLORIDA STATE UNIVERSITY

FLORIDA STATE UNIVERSITY

vs

JOHN B. STETSON UNIVERSITY

PRICE 15 CENTS

KICK-OFF
4:00 P.M

CENTENNIAL FIELD
TALLAHASSEE, FLORIDA

SATURDAY
OCT. 18
1947

The Williamson Year

A football team emerges from nowhere and makes an 0-5 start to somewhere

No players. No coach. No schedule. No equipment. No stadium.

Three months later, on Oct. 18, 1947, Florida State fielded a football team — it had no name, either — that almost beat Stetson in an opening game before 7,165 people at Tallahassee's Centennial Field. The losing score was 14-6.

Zip and zap.

So quickly, Florida State gained a name — Seminoles — and a respected football reputation. So swiftly, also, it established the University of Florida as a primary rival.

It was all interwoven. The long road from football's Nowhereland was, indeed, a winding one, some of it shadowed now by the cobwebs of time.

Overnight, in 1947, Florida State University had evolved from Florida State College for Women — just one of the names the Tallahassee school had known.

It had all started nearly a century before. Some say it started even before with an institution east of town that folks called simply "the school on the hill."

On Jan. 24, 1851, a legislative act called for two seminaries of higher learning, meant primarily to be teacher-training schools — one east of the Suwannee River, one west. East Florida Seminary was awarded to Ocala in 1853 — the same year, incidentally, that the town of Gainesville was founded. Tallahassee won West Florida Seminary in 1857, following a bitter legislative battle with Marianna and Quincy. One year later, the "school

0 wins, 5 losses

Ed Williamson in 1987.

on the hill" became part of West Florida Seminary. So it was that Florida State turned coeducational early, while it took some people about a century to catch up.

In 1865, the school was briefly called Florida Military and Collegiate Institute. In March of that year, the cadets of the school were called into emergency action for the Confederate States of America. With outmanned forces at the Battle of Natural Bridge, not far from the school, they played a vital role in repulsing invading Federals — and Tallahassee stands as the only Confederate capital east of the Mississippi never captured by Union forces. Quickly, though, the name reverted to West Florida Seminary.

A little-known detail seems to be that among names West Florida Seminary later had was "The University of Florida" — by legislative decree in 1885. Interestingly, West Florida Seminary, which some saw as a school well ahead of its time, ignored the name, never officially using or adopting it.

In 1901 West Florida Seminary became Florida State College, and in 1903 the Legislature transferred "The University of Florida" title that nobody in Tallahassee seemed to want to the state's agricultural college at Lake City.

1902 and 1903: The games begin

Florida State College did, in fact, play football, and very well indeed.

The first action came Nov. 21, 1902, when South Georgia Military rolled into town — on

Here's the cover of the program from Florida State University's first football game, in 1947.

two-horse wagons, perhaps — from Bainbridge amid whispers that the team was loaded with ringers who had played the game for Georgia's Bulldogs.

In a time when a touchdown was worth 5 points, Florida State won 5-0. A celebration followed, according to a school yearbook, and "staid old people, awakened from placid dreams, were glad, no doubt, that football comes but once a year."

The noise included an ancestral cheer of "FSU One Time."

> Boom, get a rat trap,
> bigger than a cat trap
> Boom, get a rat trap,
> bigger than a cat trap
> Boom-er-bang, boom-er-bang.
> Sis boom bah,
> Florida State College — rah, rah, rah!

Two other games were played in 1902 — both against the University of Florida, each team winning by 6-0 scores.

After that 2-1 start in 1902, Florida State played an ambitious six-game schedule and finished 3-2-1 in 1903.

Two games with South Georgia Military saw that foe fall 22-0 at Tallahassee and 5-0 in Bainbridge. Then East Florida Seminary, in Gainesville, prevailed 16-0 in Tallahassee on Halloween Day.

Soon after, Georgia Tech won in Atlanta 17-0.

Then Florida State topped the University of Florida on a Friday the 13th in Tallahassee, 12-0. After the game, the Lake City school protested that Florida State had used professionals — a charge Stetson also made that year against East Florida Seminary.

(At most schools in those early days, all manner of cheating went on. Little of it was challenged. There was no authority to do so.)

If this was, as some said, the first controversy between FSU and Florida, it would hardly be the last.

In a game played in DeLand for the Florida

More than 40 years before Florida State University was born, Florida State College played football. These unsmiling lads played in 1902.

Times-Union's state-championship College Cup, Stetson and Florida State tied 5-5. Because Stetson had earlier beaten East Florida Seminary, the cup stayed with Stetson.

1904: 'The finest article of football'

The year 1904 would bring Florida State's last football for 43 years. Despite a 2-3 record, the team made it a memorable one by winning that state championship it had narrowly missed the year prior.

The season started with a 33-0 blowout in Atlanta at the hands of a Georgia Tech team coached by John Heisman, the man after whom the Heisman Trophy symbolizing the nation's best collegiate player would be named.

Two weeks later, at Lake City, Florida State whipped the University of Florida 23-0. The record showed a Florida State lineup of Charles Puleston and J.K. Johnson at the ends, Moses Liddell and Guyte McCord at the tackles, David Cook and Fritz Bucholz at the guards, Dan Williams at center, and a back-field of Jack "Pee Wee" Forsythe — who was also the coach — plus Ed Watson, Lawrence Murray and Church Whitner.

An account of that victory over Florida ran in Lake City's Florida Index on Oct. 28, 1904. Excerpts from that story:

> For the second time in two years the Florida State College has blanked the university, and this time by a decisive score of 23-0. The University of Florida team is the weakest in the history of the institution. . . .
>
> On the part of the State College team, we can say — aside from fumbling, which they did on many occasions, and their off-sides plays — they put up the finest article of football ever seen on the local gridiron.
>
> On the part of the home team we can say they put up the weakest promise of football ever witnessed here.
>
> After the kickoff, Florida had the ball on the visitors' 21, only to kick to the State College 11 . . . from then on the FSC team had a walk-over, the university team putting up a game of ping-pong variety.

Florida State fell to two non-collegiate foes, the Savannah Athletic Club and Jacksonville Consolidated — both on the road, both by 6-0 scores.

On Thanksgiving Day in Tallahassee, Florida State clipped Stetson 19-6. Because Stetson had twice beaten East Florida Seminary, and Florida State had decisively whipped the University of Florida, the outcome meant the

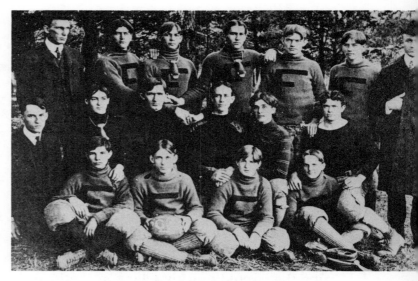

The 1903 team, rumored to have professionals.

The 1904 team, which won a state championship.

state championship and the Times-Union cup for Florida State.

The 1904 record was 2-1, if you count only college competition. It stands 2-3 if you also include the encounters in Savannah and Jacksonville.

A war ends; a team begins

Football at Florida State College ceased — and so did Florida State College — with the state's big fruitbasket-turnover of 1905. The Legislature, with something called the Buckman Act, abolished, among others, Florida State College in Tallahassee and the University of Florida at Lake City. (The father of Tallahassee's Rainey Cawthon — who later would become a Florida football hero, and later still play a prominent role in FSU football's development — rode shotgun on a wagon as they moved the school's facilities out of Lake City.)

The act created instead the University of

the State of Florida for men in Gainesville, and the Florida Female College for women (changed the following year to Florida State College for Women) in Tallahassee.

FSCW became a school of academic distinction.

"Florida State University, as we know it, did not start from scratch," said Coyle Moore, longtime dean of the School of Social Welfare. "We started with a very fine heritage. FSCW, for example, had the first Phi Beta Kappa chapter in this state."

The University of Florida, still an all-male school, pushed the Legislature for decades to let it become coeducational, and to keep FSCW all-female. FSCW alumni strongly objected. This was one of the first in a series of rubs that would quickly follow in the historical rivalry between the two schools — rivalry that has involved far more than football.

What changed everything was World War II. In 1945, millions of returning veterans had priorities to pursue their college education. Demand quickly exceeded supply — too many veterans, not enough colleges.

Interest in Florida becoming coed temporarily subsided; no room.

In early September of 1946, Florida had 2,200 more applicants than it could accommodate. In an emergency context, Florida State agreed to provide instruction for some of them. They would be housed in the vacated barracks of Tallahassee's Dale Mabry Field, an Air Force training facility for pilots during the war — which would be known as the Tallahassee Branch of the University of Florida (TBUF).

At a Cabinet meeting, the state's attorney general declared that this development was not to be construed as making the school coeducational. Doak Campbell, the school's president, disagreed, pointing out that, whatever the technicalities, the school had in fact become coeducational with its enrollment of men.

'Like you were in a harem'

Tallahassee stirred with movement to make Florida State coeducational through legislative action. State Sen. LeRoy Collins drew primary responsibility for drawing up the bill for presentation. Florida loyalists fought it, and more seeds of rivalry were sown.

On May 7, 1947, Collins and a number of able allies succeeded in getting the bill passed. The coeducational Florida State University was born.

Forty years later, Bill "Bull" Bentz, a back-

up center from Jacksonville, would recall the atmosphere fondly: "When you walked through that school, it was like — well, like you were in a harem, and that's the truth. There was a ratio of about 35 females to one male for a while, and maybe I should have stayed at Jacksonville State, where I was making fairly good grades. My wardrobe was more for pleasure than for school, and my mother couldn't understand why I was buying dinner jackets, or something like that, all the time, and I just played that one year."

Ed Dilsaver, a guard from St. Augustine, echoed Bentz on how it was for males at a school so recently all-female:

"In history class, I was the only male. I must say I enjoyed that. Males got a lot of preference there at the beginning. Instructors seemed so glad to see something other than females, it seemed to me. You would stand in a line, and an instructor would move you up to register *ahead* of the girls.

"Ah, it was a great school!"

The town asks: What about football?

The first football kickoff for Florida State since 1904 was about five months away.

"As I recall, after the bill to make Florida State coed, we had a planning council," said Ed Williamson. "We were to set up a program for the coed institution, and I was given the assignment of working up a curriculum for men's physical education."

A longtime Tallahasseean with a sense of humor — "I was born in Atlanta, but as soon as I found out where I was, I moved to Tallahassee" — Williamson had been named an instructor in physical education for TBUF in September of 1946. He was on terminal leave from the Navy, where he had served as a gunnery officer on the Murmansk Run. Soon Williamson would, in fact, serve as director of intramurals at TBUF.

His versatile sports background included playing end for Tallahassee's Leon High and for the University of Florida. He also had served as a high-school football coach in Lake City, St. Augustine, Hastings and Newberry.

"At some point," said Williamson, "we were going to have to address the matter of intercollegiate athletics."

That time came sooner than anyone dreamed.

"Some of the people on the planning council were members of Tallahassee civic clubs," said Williamson. "Members of the club were all asking the question of when we were going to start football.

"There was talk all over town, and all over campus. You couldn't ignore it.

"The planning council was concerned about attracting men with a curriculum that had been designed for women. We knew we had to have a College of Education offering that would attract men — and physical education turned out to be a prominent part of that.

"To help attract men, a decision was made that the P.E. department would be staffed only by coaches — but by coaches who would not just be coaches, but teachers as well. Football was seen as fitting in well in this quest to attract men.

"Things kind of worked up to a point of such a public clamor that we had to make a decision."

An instant coach

President Campbell called together a committee. Faculty members included Ralph Eyman and Moore.

Eyman argued that he never knew of any great university that had a great football program. "And I said," recalled Moore, "that I never knew one that didn't have."

That was one of the first moves Moore made in football's favor. There would be hundreds more for a man destined to become far more involved in FSU's game than any other faculty person of those first 40 seasons, and for whom the current athletic center is named.

Campbell indicated he favored a well-rounded athletic program that included football.

"And a decision was made," recalled Williamson, "that we were going to have football."

Williamson himself was handed the assignment of finding a coach. At least three people he proposed — Nash Higgins, Crockett Farnell, Ed Manning — were interviewed for the job.

Florida State's academic sights for a coach, it turned out, were aimed high.

"The decision was that none of them would do," said Williamson, "because none had doctorates."

With a decision to field a football team that year — and no players, no coach, no stadium, no schedule, no equipment on hand — the situation grew a little more binding.

It was made more acute, perhaps, by the absence of an athletic director. Howard Danford had been hired as the school's first, but he would not be on campus for another month or so.

Broward Culpepper, then dean of FSU stu-

In 1947 — when shrimp were 49 cents a pound, coffee 39 cents a pound, Florida State's best football ticket $2 — Henry Edward Williamson drew a salary of $4,200 for coaching FSU's first football team while also teaching four physical-education classes. And the legalization of face masks for players was still four seasons away.

dent affairs (he was later to distinguish himself as chancellor of the state's entire university system), called Williamson in.

"I knew him well," said Williamson. "We had gone to the University of Florida at the same time, played pool together over at the YMCA, and he knew I had some football background.

"It was just his realization that we didn't have any longer to wait for a Ph.D. to come in as coach.

"He asked if I would take the job.

"I reminded him that I had only high-school coaching experience. And with that said, I told him I would take the job for one year. No more."

It was July, and the first kickoff would come in three months.

Rumblings from Gainesville

Threads of orange and blue were strongly interwoven in FSU's football beginning. Culpepper — whose sons Blair and Bruce would later be fine football players for the Gators — and Williamson were two of the first with UF backgrounds. There would be several others.

But Williamson's identity with his alma mater was short, indeed, after his selection as coach.

"I had enough bad experience with Florida in my early time at Florida State," said Williamson years later, "to hope that they not only would not beat Florida State, but also nobody else."

In essence, he came to view Florida as persistently trying to head off Florida State — and its football program — at every pass.

Florida had sought, in early 1947, full control over virtually every aspect of Florida State's athletic program:

In January, President Campbell had received a letter from his Florida counterpart, John J. Tigert.

The text appears in Campbell's book "A University in Transition."

Excerpts follow:

Dear Dr. Campbell:

This memorandum will confirm the agreements ... concerning athletic relations between the University of Florida and the Tallahassee Branch.

1. The program will be operated in the name of The University of Florida, Tallahassee Branch, and activities will be carried on in the interest of the University.

2. The following policies were agreed upon with reference to the control and supervision of activities:

(a) Personnel of the coaching staff will be chosen for appointment with the approval of the Athletic authority at the University of Florida.

(b) The matter of fees, salaries, and budgets will be handled in the same way that these matters are handled in other relations, i.e., the same as published in the University catalog.

(c) The University of Florida will furnish as quickly as possible rules, regulations and policies which will govern the making of schedules....

(d) Competition in the following sports only is recommended: basketball, tennis, swimming, golf, and track.

(e) The status of all athletics shall have that of a 'B' team of the University of Florida, and no official University of Florida monograms will be awarded....

(f) The program shall be operated under the same scholastic eligibility rules as the University of Florida. This means that eligibility blanks of the Southeastern Conference will be made out and forwarded to the Committee on Athletics at the University of Florida, who will in turn forward them to the Commissioner of the Southeastern Conference.

Cordially yours,
John J. Tigert,
President

There were those who viewed the Tigert letter as tantamount to a declaration of war, and apparently Williamson was among them.

Milton Carothers, director of TBUF, asked Williamson if he had thought of a response to a similar letter received from Dutch Stanley, the Florida athletic director.

Williamson's suggested response was: "Tell 'em to 'go to hell — you run your program, and we'll run ours.'"

Carothers, said Williamson, replied to Stanley far more diplomatically. He said his school was unaware of any agreement such as Tigert had addressed in his letter, and pointed out that if existing schedules for basketball and other sports were canceled, the press would want to know why.

"Stanley quickly backed down," said Williamson.

Finally, football becomes official

For Florida State to have football, approval was necessary from the Board of Control, which later evolved into the Board of Regents.

J. Thomas Gurney, chairman of the board, recalled a matter at Jacksonville's George Washington Hotel — one in which UF partisans again tried to head off Florida State football at the pass. The date: July 12, less than three months before the first kickoff.

UF graduates Tom Bryant of Lakeland and J. Henson Markham of Jacksonville opposed a proposal that Florida State play football.

"I remember Bryant as one of the finest members the board ever had," said Gurney. "Both men, of course, were very sincere in their position. At that time, their feeling was the state offered a limited supply of football material — and in view of the fact Florida was having considerable difficulty at that time, as far as winning goes, perhaps it would be wise to restrict the game.

"Probably, under the circumstances, their position was not difficult to understand. However, other members of the board did not agree."

N.B. Jordan of Quincy and Luther Marchon of Miami supported the Florida State proposal. That brought a 2-2 deadlock.

"As chairman, I had the obligation to break the tie," said Gurney. He voted affirmatively.

Gurney — born and educated in Mississippi but a Florida resident for 25 years when he cast that tie-breaking vote — spoke 40 years later of the reasons for his action.

"I felt an athletic program, more or less, was an essential part of any university's agenda," he said. "I thought, secondly, any university had a moral right to play football if it wanted to do so.

"Thirdly, I felt it was not a disservice to the University of Florida, because of a view that competition breeds excellence. And, in my judgment, that has proven correct — most certainly in the football area, and perhaps in other areas.

"I would say that what I did was the right thing."

Gurney said it all reminded him of an old story. In 1925, when there was a large migration of Georgians to Florida, the governor of Georgia was asked what he thought of the fact.

"And the governor said he thought it a good thing — because it raised the IQ of both states," said Gurney. "And I think that story is consistent with the welfare of both Florida and Florida State."

Adopting a far gentler interpretation of that line than Georgia's governor obviously intended, Gurney was suggesting that the decision that day genuinely elevated the quality of both schools.

In the board minutes of that meeting is this wording: ". . . the board authorized the president of the Florida State University to establish such policies for athletics . . . as in his judgment and discretion he feels best suited." There was no specific mention of football.

"That was like revising the Constitution," said Gurney of the phraseology on the action. "It gave the people who objected to it some substance for their position, and gave the other side what it wanted — gave the president free rein.

"Football was what they were talking about, no question about that."

Piecing together a schedule

What they were talking about in Tallahassee was ways and means.

Williamson recalled a story of 1947 swimming competition that had included Tallahassee action against Miami. Katie Montgomery, director of women's athletics, had a firm rule for years that no one could use the pool without a cap. And there was the interesting sight of two men's swimming teams competing with bathing caps on their heads. "It was a successful season," he said of that first-year swimming endeavor. "Nobody drowned."

Nor did anybody go under as Williamson addressed the formidable tasks of assembling a football team out of very thin air.

Looking for a schedule, he got down an NCAA handbook.

"I would thumb through the book to see who had open dates, and I would call them," he said.

One he called was Ben Clemons, the head coach at Stetson — who, like Williamson, was a Tallahasseean and had played football at Florida.

"He was an old friend, and when I called he was receptive," said Williamson. " 'Great idea — we'll pay you $300 to bring your team down here,' " Clemons said.

Williamson thought quickly.

"Ben, we'll give you $750 if you come up here and play," said Williamson, not knowing whether in fact Florida State could give such a guarantee.

After a slight pause, Clemons said: "Well, OK."

Williamson would soon put in a travel request to scout Stetson in a game at Jacksonville. He was summoned to President Campbell's office.

"Do you mean," asked a shocked Campbell, "that you actually want to go over there and *spy* on this team?"

To the president who later would develop an uncommon tie with players from those early teams, Williamson gently explained that scouting was accepted procedure at all levels of football.

Not acceptable was playing the game without equipment.

"It was really hard to get," said Williamson. "Because of World War II, there was a considerable shortage of many things, including athletic equipment. We had to go to several sources to get what we needed, and old friendships helped. We had to go to Tampa, to Jacksonville and to Gainesville to get enough. There was no choice.

"But we even got garnet and gold uniforms" — the colors FSCW had long favored. "The manufacturers all complained about the garnet, saying it was the hardest color to make, and that it would fade."

Jack Haskin was designated the single assistant coach, and he and Williamson would become the warmest of personal friends. Williamson remembered the first time he heard Haskin's name. Still selecting FSU's next coach at the time, Williamson recalled talking to Dean Eyman about Howard Danford, the new athletic director.

"Can he coach football?" Williamson asked.

"No, his specialties are horseshoes and volleyball," said Eyman. "But he's bringing with him another guy. His name is Jack Haskin."

"Oh," said Williamson, "he's going to be the new football coach."

"No," replied Eyman. "He's the circus coach."

Indeed, Haskin did become the extraordinary director of a unique student circus that would receive world acclaim. Danford, when he arrived, decided that Haskin also would become Williamson's assistant.

Williamson would coach the linemen, Haskin the backs. They would do lots more.

Practice, practice, practice: "It was just full-going the whole time."

Wes Carter, left, and D.L. Middlebrooks in '47.

'Band-Aids and Mercurochrome'

Among the many things that first team did not have was a trainer. "Jack and I had to move out about three hours before a game and tape everybody," said Williamson. "It worked out to about 30 men for each of us."

Originally, there had been many more football candidates. About one-fourth of the entire 1947 male enrollment of 500 had initially come out.

"At first we had a 125-man team that was unmanageable for two coaches," said Williamson. "We figured if we worked 'em hard, they would probably drop out."

Some did, and the squad became more manageable for two.

"Attrition took care of the size of the squad," said Williamson. "We never cut anybody.

"Oh, yeah, there was one guy we cut. Came out to practice smoking a long black cigar."

The squad shaped up perhaps as well as it could, given circumstances that included players washing their own uniforms.

"We apparently had the boys in pretty good condition," said Williamson, "for nobody had a serious injury all year.

"If we had had these players longer — had there been spring practice — I think we could have had a successful team. But when you get two men working that many fellows in such a short time before the season opens, it is damned difficult."

A first practice that year was held Sept. 15, barely a month before the team would start the five-game schedule Williamson had hastily assembled.

Four of the games would be at home, with Cumberland the lone road game.

By Oct. 2, attrition had reduced the original group of eager candidates to an 85-player squad that gradually became smaller still. Williamson soon announced a squad scrimmage under lights one week before the Stetson opener, and 3,000 people showed up.

Jack Tully, a Tallahasseean who would start at guard, was selected as captain for the opener in downtown Centennial Field — just a long block from the state Capitol.

"But we had to dress for the game in that old fieldhouse out at Dale Mabry," recalled Tully.

"There were no real facilities whatsoever out at Mabry. No lockers. You just hung your clothes up wherever you could.

"There were no breaks in our practices out there. It was just full-going the whole time.

"The grass was deep — what grass there was on that old drill field we practiced on. There was just one field, and we practiced on it day in and day out."

There was no scholarship, no aid of any kind.

"We didn't get one thing," said Tully. "But we were having a good time, and didn't ask for anything."

Sandspurs on the practice field didn't bother Jack McMillan. "It was typical of a lot of fields back then," he said. "I played on many that had sandspurs."

Ken MacLean remembered one plus at those early practices. A big running back, native of Quincy, MacLean had been a starter in 1944 at Florida, scoring on a 91-yarder as he skipped for more than 180 yards against Georgia, but came to FSU after time in military service.

"We had as many girls watching those first workouts as we did players on the field," he said. "They routinely lined the field, and it wasn't uncommon to stop a bit and talk to them while you were doing sprints."

In the absence of a trainer, team managers tended to injuries the best they could.

"Band-Aids and Mercurochrome," said Lonnie Burt, one of the managers on that first team. "That was about all we put on 'em. If somebody was really hurt, we hollered for the coach."

McMillan, who along with Phil Rountree would be named permanent captain for the 1947 season, remembered hurting his knee the Monday before the first game.

"What I did was to shower and run a lot of hot water over that knee every day for a while," said McMillan. "That was it."

A bunch of hungry veterans

Though it had had no scholarships, no trainer, no training table, Florida State did have some financial resources to start a program properly.

"A lot of people had the impression there was no money," said Williamson. "That wasn't true. The state had not been able to spend a lot of money during the war years. It could not build roads, for example. You couldn't buy an automobile. There was plenty of money in 1947, and I never got turned down.

"Of course, you couldn't buy a whole lot of things. The crunch was still around."

At least half the squad members, estimated Williamson, were World War II veterans, all on the GI Bill that provided government assistance for veterans who went to college. But the small government ration of spending money went fast with the free-wheeling veterans.

"Those checks were sometimes late, and there were players who actually went hungry," said the coach. "There were a lot of pecan trees over there on West Campus, and some of 'em used to eat pecans and drink powdered milk."

Tully was one of several who once held scholarships at other schools. A handful had been at Florida, Wes Carter at Georgia, and Tully at Miami on scholarship.

This, too, fueled the budding rivalry with Florida.

"I'm gonna tell you this, the very first squad out there — from the very first day — wanted some of the Gators," said Tully. "Those that transferred from Florida didn't care much for 'em. From my little time at Miami, I didn't like 'em.

"And those feelings just got worse."

The first game of the first season

The feeling was pretty good shortly before 8 p.m. on Oct. 18, 1947, when Captain Tully won the coin toss and advised the referee that his no-name team would receive.

It would be a month before Florida State was christened "Seminoles." Meanwhile, there were press references to the Garnet and Gold.

On that football-inaugural evening, there was a Chamber of Commerce-sponsored pep rally, highlighted by a snake dance through downtown Tallahassee. With extra seats added to Centennial Field — prompting some to dub this the "Bleacher Bowl" — a standing-room-only crowd showed up. It went down in the records as 7,165 people, but some estimates reckoned 8,000 or more.

With the exception of Bill Fannin — a freshman from Raceland, Ky. — every player on that 1947 squad was from Florida. The first-game program listed a Florida State roster that included 11 Tallahasseeans, seven

Pensacolans and five players each from Quincy and Panama City.

The starters for Florida State that evening, in an era that demanded both defensive and offensive action from all:

Ends Jim Costello of Miami and Chris Banakas (Pensacola), tackles D.L. Middlebrooks (Pensacola) and Leonard Gilberg (Tallahassee), guards Jack Tully (Tallahassee) and Bill Quigley (Panama City), center Buddy Bryant (Perry), quarterback Don Grant (Perry), lefthalf Ralph Chaudron (Pensacola), righthalf Wyatt "Red" Parrish (Chipley), fullback Jack Watson (Pensacola).

Grant returned the opening kickoff to the 31, then lined up behind center in the split-T formation.

"We used this split-T that I had used earlier when I coached at Lake City," said Williamson. "Later, for the last game of the season, we added the single wing. We had two defenses, the 7-diamond and the 6-2-2-1, and on the latter we sometimes had a man who amounted to a roving center — who operated at his own discretion."

Williamson recalled that Jake Gaither, the great coach of Florida A&M, was also using the split-T at the time.

"We learned a lot about it from him," said Williamson. "But there was a pass Gaither used that we never could get right.

"He had this quarterback who was a crackerjack at jumping once, faking, then coming down before going up again and throwing. We tried that, but I guess we didn't have the skilled players to do it."

Florida State came out running that first night, Parrish soon ripping off an 18-yard run.

(Years later, Williamson and Haskin would call Parrish their most memorable player. "He was certainly the best," said Williamson. "He was a left-handed passer, and he created the most threats," said Haskin.)

Shortly after the Parrish run, a Grant pass was intercepted and Stetson drove to the 1 — where Florida State waged its first successful goal-line stand. Soon Florida State repulsed another attack, at its 25, but a fumble provided the Hatters with a third opportunity and Stetson scored. A holding penalty wiped it out,

however, and Florida State held for a third time.

From the Stetson 24, Grant whipped a pass to Quincy's Charles McMillan, and a spectacular end-zone catch put FSU up 6-0.

Holding the second-half option, Stetson chose to kick again — and Grant returned this one 48 yards to Stetson's 48. Stetson held, marched 85 yards and scored as Jim Olson's end-zone fumble was recovered by teammate George Douglas for a touchdown that, with an extra point, provided a 7-6 lead.

On a Charles McMillan interception and return for more than 65 yards to the Stetson 15, FSU threatened. It came to naught as Stetson intercepted. A fourth-quarter Stetson touchdown brought the final score to 14-6.

"Seldom has a team won so many supporters in defeat," wrote Fred Pettijohn, sports editor of the Tallahassee Democrat. "FSU's garnet-and-gold gridders — untested, untried and undaunted — shocked a seasoned Stetson eleven...."

With striking perception after the Stetson game, Pettijohn also wrote of all the historic firsts:

This is a sports writer's report to the far-flung football future.

It's written particularly for the intra-space sports series of the supersonic

School spirit, circa 1947.

Opposite page: This is it — FSU's first touchdown, scored by Charles McMillan on a pass from Don Grant. It happened against Stetson, at Centennial Field in Tallahassee, in 1947.

Here is Florida State University's 1947 football team, as pictured in a yearbook. First row, left to right: George Cave, Don Grant, Red Parrish, Billy Bishop, Addison Meade, Harold Conrad, Wendall Barns, Jack Watson, Harry Hughey, Phil Rountree, Ralph Chaudron, Howard Stephens, Bo Manuel. Second row: Ed Dilsaver, Lem Davis, Bill Quigley, Ed Quigley, Chris Kalfas, C.E. Silas, Bill Bentz, Joe Crona, Ken MacLean, Jack McMillan, Jim DeCosmo, Leonard Melton. Third row: Earl Payne, Bill Kratzert, D.L. Middlebrooks, Bill Fannin, J.P. Love, Al Tharpe, Sam Harris, Clice Yancey, Jack Tully, Charles Hospodar, Ronnie Melton, Chris Banakas. Fourth row: Fred Boris, C.N. Procter, Charles McMillan, John Fisher, Buddy Bryant, Bob Browning, Dick Williams, Jim Costello, Fred Schneider, Billy Osteen.

1970's and 1980's, who some day are going to dig back in the files in search of information on the "old gaffers" who played in Florida State University's first football game against Stetson back in 1947.

They'll enjoy looking this far into the past. The quaint old ads with the funny '47 model automobiles, silly old medicines like radium and sulfa, and the old fashioned football uniforms — Wow! Only the women's hats, now at a fantastic peak, will appear up to date.

Some day when they have a big intra-planet game coming up and want some background and historical material they can run these plays as "Famous FSU Firsts":

The honor of handing the first FSU play, and receiving the first kickoff, went to Don Grant ... who took a Stetson kickoff on his own three and returned it to the 31.

The first running play from scrimmage was by Wyatt (Red) Parrish ... who broke over his right tackle and moved from the 31 to the 49, almost breaking into the clear for a score. Parrish also racked up the initial FSU first down on the play.

Don Grant threw the first FSU pass — and had it intercepted when Byron Brasington grabbed the ball at the Stetson 33.

Jim Costello made the first FSU tackle. Grant's pass was intended for him, and when Brasington plucked it out of the air

in front of him, he promptly flopped the safety on the Stetson 35.

Gerry (Bo) Manuel, who came in at fullback to replace Jack Watson after the ninth play, was the first substitute.

The first goal-line stand was put up midway the first quarter, when they rose up to halt the Hatters in their tracks ... after first-and-goal from the one. FSU took over on the 4½.

Leonard Gilberg, former Leon High star, got off the first punt. The big tackle, kicking from his own end zone, booted out on the 38.

Wes Carter, another ex-Leon ace, committed the first fumble ... at his own 20.

Chris Banakas ... recovered the first fumble ... when he jumped on a bad pass from center that got away from the Hatters at the FSU 39.

Phil Rountree of Chipley, lefthalf and one of the student-body presidents, hit fullback Ken MacLean of Quincy with the first completed pass ... early in the second period.

Harry Hughey, tiny Pensacola quarterback, made the first punt return, taking Brasington's boot at his 48 and moving just over into Stetson territory.

Ralph Chaudron ... made the first pass interception when he nabbed Brasington's stray toss on the three and ran it up to the 11.

FSU's first lateral went from Charley

McMillan to Chris Banakas on the Stetson 41, with Banakas battling his way to the 24.

McMillan scored the first touchdown with a leaping miracle catch in the east corner of the southern end zone.

Gilberg attempted the first point-after from placement, and missed.

Florida State wasted no time breaking into the penalty column. On the second play of the game, it drew a 5-yard assessment from the backfield being illegally in motion.

The first block? A man next to me said he didn't see 5 cents' worth all night — and with prices the way they are now, it sounds too cheap to mention.

No longer the no-name team

Blocking or not, a football team had to have a name.

Between the first game and the second — a month later against Cumberland at Lebanon, Tenn. — Florida State got its Seminole name.

The name did not come easy, and the full story is not etched in stone.

The most accurate account seems to be that students balloted on the name, and that one week after the first game, a list of suggestions had been narrowed to six: "Golden Falcons," "Statesmen," "Crackers," "Senators," "Indians," "Seminoles." Other proposals had included "Sandpipers," "Fleas," "Gold Diggers," "Tallywhackers," "Pinheads," "Tarpons."

At the conclusion of student balloting, following further consideration of choices, "Seminoles" had won. The Florida Flambeau reported that, in final balloting, "Seminoles" won by 110 votes over "Statesmen," and that following, in order, were "Rebels," "Tarpons," "Fighting Warriors" and "Crackers."

Jim Crabtree, a student from Pensacola, remembered "Tarpons" as the chief challenger, and suggests it took a whole lot of vigorous campaigning to keep that name from winning.

"The women's swim team was named 'Tarpons,'" said Crabtree. "That name was submitted, and it just about overwhelmed some of us. Only other thing that seemed strong in the running was the name 'Seminoles.'

"A bunch of us got together and decided it would be a whole lot better to have an Indian name than a *fish*.

"We got a group of girls to go around knocking on doors. And that thing was turned around, just enough for 'Seminoles' to make it. To me the name could not have worked out better."

Williamson remembered the choice as a little controversial at the time.

"I think the name caught on primarily because of the things that go with it," he said. "There were so many things — fancy dress, the war dances."

Bill Bentz recalled "Falcons" and "Tallywhackers" were heavy challengers, insisted it took more than campaigning for "Seminoles" to emerge on top.

"I watched every damn ballot that went through, and a whole lot of 'em that didn't have 'Seminole' on them, I threw away," said Bentz at a 1986 reunion of the first team.

Later, he elaborated.

"I was a bigmouth in those days — still am," he said. "At the time, doctoring those ballots seemed the thing to do. When you played football there then, you were actually bigger than you were, you know, and you could get by with a lot."

The Flambeau perhaps well reflected campus thinking on the new name:

> The selection certainly gives FSU a distinct title. There are no college teams that bear the name....
>
> New nicknames ... are apt to appear ill-fitting, but they take on polish with constant usage — and are mellowed, aged and honored with time.
>
> The name Seminoles will be just as good a name as Florida State University makes it in the years to come....
>
> Okay, Seminoles, take over from here!

Ed Dilsaver remembered the name being affixed to the bus en route to that game at Cumberland.

"Never will forget, our bus stopped at this place, and ol' Slick (Don Grant) went in there and came back with lipstick and painted 'Florida State Seminoles' on the side of the bus.

"But first he wanted to know, I remember, how to spell 'Seminoles.'"

A game full of stories

The Cumberland game is one of the more storied in FSU history. Williamson said it was surely the most memorable of his single season as coach.

"We got $600 for going up there, and they put us up in this boiler room," said Williamson. "Back then, it was kind of like you were in high school — you accommodated the other team the best way you could.

"We slept on cots. Everybody had war-surplus cots back then. Water pipes in that boiler room were just over our heads."

One of the strangest Cumberland-game stories was of several players drawing straws to see who would make the trip.

When word, rather inevitably distorted, later got around on campus, there was considerable rumbling. The Flambeau reported:

"From the Sweet Shop to the barracks out on Dale Mabry Field could be heard the loudest gripes ever voiced on this campus," one student said in a letter to the editor that appeared in The Flambeau. "... This drawing deal ... if the coach had announced that he was taking 33 husky females from the campus to represent FSU, this move would have brought less criticism."

"The truth of that old straw-drawing story is that Coach Williamson picked his first 22 men, and the rest drew straws," said Tully.

"I don't think we had more than 35 players, total, on that trip — all on that old piece of bus, along with our equipment.

"Coach had wanted to be fair, and he said there wasn't that much difference in the ones, beyond the top 22, who would draw."

Those who made the trip found a messy field awaiting them.

"It rained the whole game, and I don't mean *sprinkled*," Williamson said. "I remember Bo Manuel kicked a punt, and it hit a pool of water, and just spun around down there in the water. The field lights that night were not protected, and in the rain they just kept popping out.

"We had officials that were honest, but not knowledgeable.

"We had three touchdowns called back.

Cumberland completed one pass, and got 6 points out of it."

Dilsaver said officials could place the ball only on certain parts of the field that rainy night at Lebanon.

"It was the only way to keep it from floating away," he said. "Red Parrish slid out of bounds once, and he looked like somebody on a surf board coming through that water."

Said Jack Tully: "When you tackled somebody on the sidelines, you damn near drowned."

Bull Bentz said it was not just the rain. "There were rocks on that field big as loaves of bread," he said.

Final score: Cumberland 6-0, as Florida State lost five of its 11 fumbles. With the miserable conditions, fewer than a dozen people turned out for the game, some Seminoles said.

"But their president wrote our president praising our sportsmanship," said Williamson, "and he said he thought we should have won."

The arrival of Satchmo Martin

The most dramatic story from the game involved the Cumberland player who, after extended conversation in the heat of combat, became intrigued with Florida State possibilities — and months later transferred to play for the Seminoles.

Ted "Satchmo" Martin, a Cumberland center out of Gadsden, Ala., and a former paratrooper who had seen action in Belgium, has been variously described as a non-stop talker, a fellow who kept everybody laughing, and a character.

"The game wasn't two minutes old when Martin, playing across from me, started that

First-team starters, most of them throughout the season, included (from left): Front — tackle D.L. Middlebrooks, guard Jack Tully, center Buddy Bryant, guard Bill Quigley, tackle Leonard Gilberg, quarterback Jack McMillan. Back — end Chris Banakas, halfback Leonard Melton, fullback Jack Watson, halfback Wes Carter, end Jim Costello.

talking," recalled Tully. "He wanted to know what the school was like, how many women there were in relation to men, and things like that.

"Before the half, he wanted to know if he could get on the bus with us and go back to Tallahassee and join up with the team.

"He kept up conversation the whole game about going back with us. And when the game was over, I'll never know how he showed up so quick, but he was already dressed and in our locker room before *we* got there."

Martin was told there was no room on the bus, but a few months later he made it to Tallahassee on his own.

"Ah, it was a bitter-cold night, and that rain was blowing in," recalled Martin. "I wanted to get out of that place.

"One thing I remember was that at halftime my girl gave me a half a cup of Southern Comfort whiskey so I could make it out there in that weather — I'm serious, it happened!

Ted "Satchmo" Martin, who played against the Seminoles in their first road game, soon decided he wanted to BE a Seminole. He's shown here in a Cumberland uniform before he got around to the switch.

"That ball game ought never to have been played, it was so bad."

The girlfriend was a Florida native and would graduate within a month and go home. Martin said that was a primary reason he wanted to get to Florida.

"Oh, she dumped me," said Martin when asked the result of the relationship. "My girlfriend was, you know, a debutante. It was a case there of me looking at four or five generations of money and breeding — and a mule ain't gonna never win the Kentucky Derby!"

But determined to get to Florida he was that dreary evening.

"I'm talking all night, back and forth to them, during the game. But I'm paying attention to what's going on, too. I remember FSU's pass receivers that night had different-colored helmets."

During the summer that followed, Martin got to Florida on his own. "I remember bumming around all over the state," he said. "And I hitchhiked to Tallahassee, caught me a ride on a Tropical Ale truck."

He got off at the main drag, Tennessee and Monroe streets, and walked less than two blocks before spotting a group of FSU players emerging from the Florida Theatre.

"I told you," said Martin, "that I was coming."

The theater story was confirmed by tackle D.L. Middlebrooks, who later would become a federal judge.

"They took me home with 'em, and I stayed," said Martin.

Perhaps because of a loose style that some reckoned much like that of Satchel Paige, the great pitcher, or perhaps because he arrived with his few belongings in a satchel, Martin soon picked up the nickname "Satchmo" from teammate Ralph Chaudron.

"Oh, it was a good bunch," said Martin. "I

Ed Williamson, head coach

Jack Haskin, backfield coach

remember we used to drink a little Spearman Ale. You can't find it anymore, but the danged stuff had an ace of diamonds on the front, went for 15 cents a bottle, and out-sold Budweiser.

"Another thing I remember was that bunch had some of the best poker players in the country down there, and what you might call some of the best developing poker players."

Martin would be with the Florida State squad in 1948 and 1949 as a reserve center.

"They had what they called the Red Team, which was more or less a scout team," said Martin, laughing. "And that was where I played best.

"I was around down there four years, but never did get a degree. I didn't study that hard, and I changed majors — and then that money from the GI Bill ran out."

The tales of Martin's antics would become legend among both players and coaches in those early days.

A helmet, to Martin, was a ball cap.

"He would say, 'Coach, hold on, until I get my ball cap,'" said Tully. "And he just kept everybody laughing with stuff like that."

Don Veller, who came as coach in 1948, remembered a favorite running play.

"We would, on this play, trap the opposing tackle, and we gained an awful lot of yards on this play," said Veller.

"One day in practice we did this, and suddenly there was no one between fullback Mike Sellars and the goal line. Except Martin.

"Well, Martin just stepped aside and — like a traffic cop — waved Sellars on through!"

Veller, like players of the time, remembered Martin favorably. "He kept us all laughing, and was definitely a big plus for team morale."

"A hundred pounds of mean"

Dilsaver recalled a prayer meeting before the second game.

"Cumberland was a Baptist school, and we were invited to this gathering, which was like a prayer meeting," he said. "And I think it was about the only time some among us ever went to anything like church.

"Ah, but it was a fine group. I don't think we ever really got any bad apples until Florida State started offering scholarships.

"Everybody out there played because he *wanted* to play. When I was in the service, hell, I took care of myself and did the thing I thought was right — and that was the kind of people I associated with. This first team was that kind."

It was surely true that fighting was not foreign to several prideful, rambunctious and absolutely tough war-tested veterans. There are many stories.

Some feature Tully. One recounted his fight, outside a Tallahassee nightspot called the Seminole Club, with an athlete from the University of Illinois, in town for a baseball series with Florida State.

"I had a good go at it," said Tully, declining to elaborate.

One eyewitness, Lewis Sutton, said Tully got much the better of it that long-ago night when his opponent was Ray Nitschke, whose later image as a linebacker with the Green Bay Packers was that of one of the tougher men in the National Football League. "Jack knocked him down three times," said Sutton.

Martin also witnessed the fight.

"It was after our playing days. Tully was moonlighting as a bouncer at the club," said Martin. "Nitschke got real loud in there.

"Jack showed him the way out the door. They got into it outside, and Nitschke got his butt whipped."

Not that big at the time, listed at an even 6 feet and 185 pounds, Tully's look was apparently deceptive.

"He's got a hundred pounds of *mean* that don't show," said Martin.

No wins, but some promise

One of the toughest teams Florida State faced that first year was Tennessee Tech, a 42-0 victor over Cumberland. In Tallahassee, on a muddy field before 5,436 fans, Florida State got just 5 yards rushing as it fell 27-6.

The crowd dropped to 2,942 in Tallahassee on Thanksgiving Day as Troy (Ala.) State won 36-6, with Tallahasseean Leonard Melton scoring FSU's second touchdown of the season, from the 1 following a Jack McMillan interception that placed the Seminoles at Troy's 25.

Then Jacksonville (Ala.) State brought its unbeaten (8-0) Gamecocks to town for the final game of Florida State's difficult first season, with 3,700 fans present for what most reckoned would be a blowout.

In a splendid effort, the Seminoles allowed Jacksonville a quick touchdown — and nothing else. The visitors spent much of the rest of the game fighting for their lives, as FSU drove to the foe's 1, then later the 6 — only to fail. Jacksonville escaped the trap in an evenly played game, 7-0.

In that winless five-game season, Florida

State struggled for 687 total yards — 400 of that passing, on 32 completions of 87 attempts.

"We were not much of a football team," Red Parrish once said, with a sly dig at circus-coach Haskin, "but when we lined up in three rings for those pregame warm-ups, we were the best in the world."

Just a few years later, Parrish's record on the battlefields of Korea was as distinguished as it had been on the football fields of Florida State. A tank commander, wounded in action, Parrish received the Silver Star for extraordinary bravery.

In extraordinary circumstances that first Florida State football year, the two coaches, Williamson and Haskin, had taught a full load of classes while trying to pull a rabbit from a hat — putting together in weeks a team that had no players, no equipment, no schedule and no name.

Thereupon Williamson, who had accepted the job for one year, retired from the game, as did Haskin.

They left the great respect of a group of tough men — so obvious at reunions 40 years later, and beyond.

They also left seeds that, far more than those two or anyone else dreamed, would not be long producing great fruit.

The Veller Years

After his first 34 games he'd won 30 and chalked up an unbeaten season

"Hang in there, Uncle Benny!"

It was an exhortation that Alfred Veller, a machine operator in a coal mine, favored at football games when his son was playing. The son never knew who Uncle Benny was, never knew the precise meaning or the story behind the yell.

But over many years, long after his dad was gone, the words would ring in Don Veller's head and inspire him to keep on keeping on.

Perhaps he heard the words many times in 1948, when he became head coach of a school that had just turned coed, just started football, and just lost every game of its inaugural season.

"Hang in there, Uncle Benny!"

Indeed, Veller's men did. And in one of college football's more amazing transformations, fledgling Florida State shook off its short and dismal past and pronounced that the future is now. Over the next three years — the first three of Veller's five — the Seminoles lost only twice.

Twenty lettermen returned from that 0-5 team of 1947, but only 12 would again letter in 1948.

Don Veller, the astonishing architect of change, was a low-key student of not only football but whatever else was out there, and a man with great concentration for vital detail.

Remarkably, Florida State went 7-1 in 1948 even though it was August before Veller moved to Tallahassee. And two years later

He was nicknamed "Doleful Don," but Veller had little to cry about during his time as FSU's football coach.

---

31 wins, 12 losses, 1 tie

Don Veller in the mid-1980s.

Florida State would go unbeaten (8-0) even though Veller was away during the summer burning midnight oil in pursuit of a doctorate.

If, in FSU's pursuit of football heights, there was a significant University of Florida connection — and there was — an Indiana connection is also notable.

Don Loucks, who in 1947 would become Florida State's first basketball and tennis coach, had been associated with Indiana since 1936.

To Howard Danford, FSU's first athletic director, Loucks mentioned Veller as a possibility to succeed Ed Williamson. Loucks and Veller hailed from Bicknell, Ind., their homes three blocks apart.

An Indiana University backfield hero, Veller had, among other things, run 82 yards to spur an upset over rival Purdue and been a teammate of Michigan center Gerald Ford — later the nation's president — in the East-West Shrine game. In seven years as coach of Elkhart (Ind.) High, Veller had fielded two unbeaten teams and won 80 percent of his games. After four years of wartime service in the Air Force that saw him attain rank as a major, he served Hanover College briefly as head football coach in 1946. Then he left to work on his doctorate at alma mater Indiana, while also assisting his old coach, the great Bo McMillan.

Just after the Christmas holidays of 1947, Veller came to Tallahassee for an interview and accepted the Florida State job. It would not be until August of 1948 that he assumed a full role in his new job — remaining at Indiana until that time to continue working on his doctorate.

'48: The arrival of Bob Harbison

But even before he arrived at Florida State, Veller began accentuating the Indiana connection, assembling a small coaching band of "Hoosier Hot Shots." Later would come a number of players from the state, including some from Indiana University.

Veller would hire three assistants — each a former Indiana University football player, each from Evansville.

The Armstrong brothers, Charley and Bill, would come right away, to hold a January spring practice.

(Charley Armstrong would move immediately from football that January to another sport. Designated as Florida State's first baseball coach, he put together a team that finished 9-8 — inaugurating a tradition of Florida State never having a losing season in that sport. Over their first four seasons, Armstrong baseball teams would finish 49-29.)

Bob Harbison, just finishing his work for a degree, would come later. Back in hometown Evansville, he had played for a different high school from the Armstrongs. Then he became a teammate of Bill's at Indiana.

Harbison drove down to Tallahassee with Eddie Kwesterowski, who would become Florida State's first athletic trainer and soon shorten his name to Eddie Kwest.

"I knew I wasn't too interested in being a coal miner, and I knew I wasn't too interested in working on a farm," said Harbison. "So when the opportunity came to coach in college, I grabbed it."

Through 37 of Florida State's first 40 seasons, Harbison would serve seven coaches as a valued line coach, and more.

His football insight, his candor and his droll humor became part of a legend. He would coach one of FSU's most celebrated units — "The Seven Magnificents" of 1964 (the seven linemen and linebackers) — and would recruit such all-time Seminole greats as receiver Ron Sellers and punter Rohn Stark.

He had not been around, while still playing the game at Indiana, for the first season of 1947. And he would not be around for the all-losing season of 1973 — fired just after the 1972 season by Coach Larry Jones.

"He ought to have fired me," Harbison would quietly say years later. "I was addicted to alcohol."

Darrell Mudra rehired him in 1974, and he would remain on the staff until retirement just prior to the 1986 season. He had come to grips with the problem of alcohol during his two years with Mudra, and he had won.

In 1948 — when a 10-pound bag of potatoes was 35 cents, 100 aspirin 19 cents, Florida State's best football ticket $2 — Donald Arld Veller drew a salary of $5,200 for coaching FSU's second football team while also teaching classes, including two during the season. And unlimited substitution was permitted with each team's change of possession.

The practice-field blues

The Hoosier Hot Shots worked well together.

"All of us, as coaches at Florida State, were moving in the same direction," Charley Armstrong said. "It wasn't like you had coaches coming in there from semi-different backgrounds.

"The system we had — essentially Bo McMillan's system — well, Veller had coached it, Bill and I had played it, and so had Bob.

"I think each of us firmly believed in what he was doing. There was never any controversy about how we were going to do things."

Veller saw basic tenets of the game as an early key.

"We were all big on fundamentals," he said.

"We believed in blocking and tackling — I mean, if we had a theme song, that was it."

Veller had little tolerance for the likes of brush blocking; a blocked opponent was supposed to be knocked on his rear.

When they arrived, the Armstrongs found what other FSU coaches for many years to come would find — a shortage of facilities.

"The practice field, over there on Dale Mabry Field, was the site of an old outdoor theater the airmen had used," said Charley Armstrong. "There was no dressing room — no place to shower. The old dressing room in the Mabry gym was simply not big enough.

"We looked around, and the only structure adaptable was an elevated place with a concrete floor — a kind of stage or bandstand, it was — there at that old outdoor theater. With the help of a school engineer, we turned that into a dressing room and called it our fieldhouse.

"On that old, hard field, we found a lot of

sandspurs — but also a lot of enthusiasm. We were fairly well impressed with people like Red Parrish, and Bo Manuel — a little old tough bowling ball. We worked hard that spring."

Veller remembered the dust.

"The practice field was not normally watered," he said. "The dust became terrible, and at times it was impossible to practice because of it — until we got somebody out there to sprinkle it down."

The Cockeyed T

The facilities, or lack of them, did not much bother Harbison.

"My salary was $3,200 that first year," said Harbison. "And I always said back then if I could just make $100 a week, I was going to be rich.

"It was a beginning program and you couldn't really expect much, you know. Facilities, and things like that, I really wasn't concerned about."

The Armstrongs familiarized players in that first-ever spring football practice with a system riveted around the Cockeyed T that McMillan had employed so successfully at Indiana.

"You used an unbalanced line, lining up the quarterback underneath center — and either the wingback on the wing, or back in a three-back set that was similar to the straight T-formation," said Charley Armstrong. "But, with the wing out, you would also shift the quarterback from underneath center to set for a direct snap."

Simply put, the Cockeyed T was a combination of the T, new then, and the old single wing. With quick shifts, the team moved from one to the other.

"It was a new system — with that Cockeyed T kind of a mystery to most opponents," said Veller.

"But a big thing was we had those young coaches working their heads off. We had a lot of spirit.

"We also had some players there at the start — particularly Parrish as a backfield threat, and Middlebrooks at tackle."

Quickly, more players would flock to Florida State — many of them transfers from other schools, Indiana included. With no scholarships, there were also few of the binding eligibility rules involving transfers; they could play immediately.

A '48 season and a '42 bus

In 1948, Veller's team opened with Cumberland in Tallahassee — and Florida State won its first football game since 1904. It shut out the Bulldogs 30-0 with a ground game that ate up 426 yards as Ken MacLean and Parrish each scored twice.

But the Flying Fleet of Erskine College clipped the Seminoles 14-6, with a strong passing game. Like the Cumberland trip the year prior, the one to Erskine in Due West, S.C., spawned many a story.

It was the first trip for the team in "Old Ironsides" — a 1942-model bus (Beck Motor Coach) that had been newly painted and upholstered in an FSU shop.

Charley Durbin was FSU's bus driver then, as he would be for most of the school's first 40 football seasons. The versatile Durbin served in 1948 as equipment man and was also in general charge of the practice field.

Later he would add a variety of duties — including a key role as cinematographer — while driving FSU teams more than 1.8 million miles through the summer of 1987. His bus trips included four to faraway Omaha, with the baseball team for the College World Series.

"That old bus had been used all during the war years by somebody, and in a time of shortage had been put to heavy use," said Durbin. "So you can imagine how many miles it had on it. About 200,000 when we got it.

"But we got a lot more miles out of it for 13 years. We went to our first bowl game in it.

Behold "Old Ironsides," the 1942 Beck Motor Coach that hauled the Seminoles up hill and down. Well, better down than up; sometimes the players had to push.

"And well, really, it never left us stranded but three times."

En route to Erskine, the team stopped overnight in Athens, Ga. The clutch went out, and players were obliged to get out and push "Old Ironsides." It would not be the last time.

"I remember one time getting behind that thing with other players and pushing it up a mountain," said Chris Kalfas, a lineman. "That old bus was always giving us problems."

Once they arrived at Erskine, the players had more work to do.

"There were so many rocks on that field when we played Erskine, it was unbelievable," said Veller. "Working out there the night before, we had players line up and walk from goal line to goal line, picking up rocks on the way."

As was the custom then, Erskine provided Florida State with a place to stay the night before the game.

"It was so very cold in those old military barracks they put us in, and all the players were shivering under one blanket apiece — all we had," said Veller. "And I will always remember there was one toilet for all of us — and one cracked mirror, about 4 inches square, for everybody to use to shave.

"Which is not an excuse. They had a good team, and we didn't play well."

At last, an extra point

But soon Florida State would hang up another first. No extra-point attempts had been successful in 1947, nor in the first two games of 1948. And the first good one — by Joe Crona — would be the margin of victory in a 7-6 triumph over Millsaps.

So poor was Florida State at kicking extra points that there had been no warm-up practice. Veller had decided Florida State's best chance was to run for the point. A "chance hunch," Veller called his sideline decision to send Crona in for a kicking try.

"Teammates called him 'The Toe' after that," recalled Veller. "And Crona would leave with a 1.000 percentage in extra-point kicking. That was the only one he ever tried."

Veller remembered Dave McIntosh, whose 40-yard run brought a Millsaps touchdown. "A little guy who was about as good a runner as I've ever known," said Veller. "He could have played on any team anywhere."

And Bill Armstrong remembered that on McIntosh's big run, an official had brought his handkerchief out, with apparent intent to call a penalty. But as McIntosh scored, the official returned it to his pocket "like a tired farmer after a hard day's work," said Armstrong.

In the Tallahassee Democrat, Fred Pettijohn wrote of a football team "with no more background than a photograph of a blank wall," but of growing campus support. He wrote of Jack Watson, a fullback on the first team who had been forced to quit the game because he needed to work if he was to continue in college. Watson led a school-cafeteria rally of 500 students before the Stetson game. "It is a healthy sign," typed Pettijohn, "when a former squad member who is forced to remain on the sidelines will stand as a rallying point for his teammates."

En route to Stetson for the next game, "Old Ironsides" broke down — and a player who got left behind hitchhiked and actually beat his teammates to the destination!

"I was very strict about departure times, and Karl Vogtretter — a good-looking kid who never played very much — didn't show up," said Veller. "Somebody said he had gone to get a haircut.

"My memory is that as we sat there waiting for that daggone bus to get fixed, Vogtretter stopped with whoever he had caught a ride with, said hello, and kept on going."

In his frustration, Veller said if he had a match he would set "Old Ironsides" afire. Whereupon, receiver Norm Eubanks struck a match and moved toward the busted bus. Veller rushed to restrain him.

A 7-1 season comes to a close

Stetson fell 18-7, but had Ted Hewitt, a sophomore back, done what was expected of him on a certain play, Florida State might not have won.

"Hewitt had never played football when he got to Florida State, but he was a competitor," said Veller. "He had come to Florida State with a basketball player he had met in the service. Hewitt's game was golf."

Stetson was threatening at the FSU 2 after blocking a quick kick.

Gambling big that Stetson would throw, after initially failing on runs, Hewitt was "completely out of position" for the next play, according to Veller.

But he was in perfect position to intercept the pass that did come, and he raced 99 yards to a Florida State touchdown.

Had Stetson not thrown, Hewitt might not have played again. Because Stetson did throw, Hewitt found himself a spot in Florida State record books.

"It was one of those things where you

would have wanted to kill him if it had not worked," said Veller.

Another newcomer who would find a place in the record books was Buddy Strauss, a Tallahasseean who, unlike Hewitt, had extensive football experience. During his Navy time, he had played service football at Georgia Pre-Flight. Upon his discharge, Duke awarded him a scholarship, but he yearned to come home after so much time away, and soon found his way to Florida State.

"Buddy ran over people," said Veller. "He also had a jump pass he was very good at."

Florida State rolled on, closing its 7-1 season with a 33-12 thumping of Tampa at a festive homecoming — FSU's first as a coeducational school — that included a couple of U.S. senators (Claude Pepper, Spessard Holland), a congressman (Bob Sikes) and a governor-elect (Fuller Warren).

Pettijohn wrote, after the Tampa game, of the running of Strauss and Ken MacLean: "Neither of the pair has any more deception than a bull, and they can do as much damage to an enemy line as any he-cow can to a china shop."

In a season that saw halfback MacLean lead in both rushing (463 yards) and passing (216), FSU also won the Dixie Conference championship.

The Dixie Conference was the simon-pure brainchild of Danford, who had become FSU athletic director in August of 1947. In May of 1948 the league was formed. Its original nine members were Florida State, Stetson, Tampa, Mississippi College, Millsaps, Mercer, Howard, Lambuth and Oglethorpe. Only six of the nine played football, however. League bylaws stipulated that freshmen could play on the varsity, that transfers could play immediately, and that there would be no scholarships.

Danford's approach to sports was seen by many as overly idealistic, impractical. The new athletic director spoke of the equality of sports and indicated resentment that the press gave little attention to the likes of volleyball while playing football prominently.

Danford seemed quite opposed to big-time football, as well as the stance of the press.

"There will be a special place in hell reserved for head football coaches — and sportswriters!" he once proclaimed.

Danford was a particularly sturdy supporter of volleyball and gymnastics — and Florida State would soon have national champions in both sports. A tall and articulate man with an authoritative manner, Danford seems primarily responsible for establishing such a solid all-round athletic foundation. But football's growth evolved in spite of him.

"Over my dead body!"

Danford's football stance was not without some faculty support.

There have been many — including Veller and perhaps all of those early players — who felt President Doak Campbell was notably responsible for football's growth. A special bond of respect and affection developed between Campbell and players from those teams.

"Had it not been for Dr. Campbell, I would have resigned within my first three years," said Veller.

He remembered the time the president received a letter of protest from a faculty member. Veller had asked for a preliminary report on players' grades, to better stay abreast of their classroom progress and eligibility. The teacher chose to view this as an improper and outrageous request.

Buddy Strauss, who "ran over people" during the Veller era.

Campbell called Veller to his office. The coach explained. Campbell said he understood. "But if anybody asks you about this," said the smiling president, "you tell 'em I gave you heck."

With Veller losing only two games those first three years, interest mushroomed — and so did general demand from townspeople and other supporters that a stadium be built and the general status of the game at Florida State improved.

"You incite those people!" accused Danford, demanding that Veller do something to stop it.

One thing supporters sought was scholarships for football players.

"There won't be any scholarships at FSU," said Ralph Eyman, dean of the School of Education. "Never — over my dead body!"

Dean Eyman lived until he was 100. He lived to see not only scholarships but also a Florida State football team that would be ranked among the nation's best while, among other things, playing in two consecutive Orange Bowl games.

"Dean Eyman was a very fine person," said Coyle Moore, who so long reigned as dean of the School of Social Welfare while consistently supporting a strong football program. "He was incapable of animosity.

"But he could take your hide off in a discussion. You could, however, take his hide off, too."

Doak Campbell and wife Edna, two favorites of early players.

'49 starts with a blowout

Florida State took a few hides off in 1949, including Whiting Field at the start of a 9-1 campaign.

In World War II years, a number of fine service teams had blossomed. They were free to use any service men, and if these men had played professionally or, say, four years of college football, so much the better. Often these teams beat college opponents that included the best. Great Lakes Navy ranked among the better of those teams. In 1944, four service teams — Randolph Field, Bainbridge Navy, Iowa Pre-Flight, 4th Air Force — had finished in The Associated Press top 10.

But one mark of those teams was inconsistency.

Whiting Field, near Pensacola, fell to the Seminoles in that 1949 opener by 74-0, which would stand 40 years later as Florida State's biggest margin of triumph ever.

It was 48-0 at halftime, and Veller is said to have admonished his Seminoles in the dressing room not to let down.

"In those days, those service teams shipped those All-Americans in and out," said Veller. "I don't know what happened to Whiting Field.

"I know the next week they beat Great Lakes Navy."

The Great Lakes coach had called Veller prior, seeking scouting information. "I told him I didn't have the guts to tell him anything — that they were so bad, it wouldn't be fair." Later, Veller heard that Whiting Field had suddenly moved in three or four college stars to bolster the team before playing Great Lakes.

Never one to dig his own graves, Veller often accentuated the negative in quest of positive results. It is a style hardly foreign to coaching. In football, there had been the great Gil "Gloomy Gil" Dobie at the University of Washington, and the passmaster Wally "Weeping Wally" Butts, at Georgia.

And FSU had its "Doleful Don," as Pettijohn dubbed Veller.

Veller invoked a no-swearing rule with a team that included so many crusty veterans.

"It was a rule I picked up playing for Bo McMillan," said Veller. "I myself had learned a few choice words. Bo's rule was that anyone that swore had to take a lap around the practice field.

"It wasn't so much the lap as the embarrassment."

The rule eliminated his swearing for all time, said Veller.

"The rule worked just great at Florida State, and I was real proud of it," said Veller. "That first year we had a lot of laps run. Then each year the laps decreased until there were practically none.

"I think the rule sort of set the pace for other favorable things, training generally."

As McMillan had broken his own swearing habit, Veller was detoured from another habit by his dad. His father smoked two packs of cigarettes daily. Once he gave his son a puff.

"Let that be your last," said his father.

It was.

A loss to "a bunch of roughnecks"

For the 1949 season, Veller had all of his top players back. Additionally, the squad had two notable Indiana transfers, linemen Duke Maltby and Jerry Morrical.

"We had a tall, fast — great — receiver in Norm Eubanks, though contact was not his forte," said Veller. "I think Eubanks might have been the first 'lonesome end' in football. We would flank him way out there, reasoning that since he couldn't block anybody, he could at least keep one guy busy covering him.

"But Eubanks surely could catch that ball, and we had a good thing going with the left-handed Parrish passing to him off a reverse.

"Eubanks was always wrapped up. No telling how many yards of tape we'd use wrapping him before practices. I remember he had designed — had made for him somewhere — the first nose protector I ever saw."

Florida State's lone loss was 13-6 on the road to Livingston (Ala.) State. The team was coached by Vaughn Mancha, the former Alabama All-American whom Veller would soon hire as an assistant, and who later would become FSU athletic director. The loss terminated an 11-game FSU winning streak.

"Vaughn had corraled a bunch of roughnecks — guys who had been kicked out or had flunked out at colleges around the Southeast," said Veller. "And if you talk to him, he'll tell you that.

"We played the game in Selma, and it was sponsored by, I believe, the Lions Club. They had a good crowd."

A slight oversight — no game officials

Just before the teams got ready to kick off, Mancha approached Veller.

"You know, they (the Lions Club sponsors) tell me they don't have any officials," Mancha said, according to Veller. "They told me they thought I was going to obtain the officials, and I thought they were."

The game was delayed approximately an hour while an emergency search for officials went on.

"I took our players over to our bus — there was no locker room — and they were upset," said Veller. "They kept saying, 'Coach, it's a setup,' and I could not convince them it was an honest mistake.

"Then we went out there and played *terrible*.

"Now, I never did feel that those high-school officials they had rounded up cheated that night, but they didn't call *anything*!"

Just after the game, Mancha proclaimed it "by far our best game of the season." Veller said: "We just got licked."

The Seminoles rode roughshod over every other opponent, except Sewanee. In a bad-weather game — punts literally sailed out of sight in the fog that hung low in those Tennessee mountains — FSU escaped 6-0.

Players had been reluctant to travel in "Old Ironsides" to Sewanee. Thinking of having to push the old bus up those mountains, they went to the fraternity houses in a quest for contributions to rent a Greyhound bus. The mission was successful.

"I got accused of lobbying for them to do that," said Veller. "It was something I had not known about until they had been to all the fraternity houses."

For the second-half kickoff, Florida State had only 10 men on the field. "Jerry Morrical was tying his shoe and, because of the fog, he was not aware the rest of the unit had gone out on the field," said Veller. "You couldn't see that kickoff in the fog, and that was sure one we never ran back."

Stetson, 3-1-1 going in, fell to FSU in Jacksonville 33-14. Its coach, Bob Trocolor, had been most optimistic with his preliminary quotes, while Veller had, characteristically, been gloomy, weeping and doleful with his pronouncements.

"Psychological warfare," Veller would later say of his style.

Surely the most remarkable fact involving that game, however, was its entering the books as Florida State's first on any kind of television — with WMBR-TV airing it in Jacksonville. The date: Oct. 20, 1949.

A 34-7 thumping of the University of Tampa in the next-to-last game of an 8-1 regular season brought FSU's first postseason bid — to Tampa's Cigar Bowl. That bowl had backed off Florida State's 7-1 team the prior year after indicating strong consideration, but the stunning rise of the Seminoles three years from nowhere had now intrigued many.

Fifteen hundred people showed up for a "Seminole Appreciation Party" co-sponsored by the Tallahassee Democrat and the city's Quarterback Club. Gifts worth more than $1,300 were distributed to players — gifts that might have placed FSU in NCAA jeopardy years later. But FSU was not then an NCAA member, and, moreover, that organization's rules were not as strict as they later would be.

Five Seminoles were chosen to the Dixie Conference all-star team — center Joe Marcus plus Eubanks, Parrish, Morrical and, by unanimous choice, Strauss.

President Campbell mentioned plans for a 15,000-seat stadium. At about the same time he also said: "We don't know what the future holds, but we are determined to give amateur football every chance."

But the days of no football scholarships — and the Dixie Conference — were fast running out.

Players, staying over during the holidays to practice for the bowl, had to pay their own way. Townspeople wanted to provide them with free room and board, but Danford vetoed such.

Wofford, unbeaten through 23 straight games, would be the opponent for the Jan. 2 Cigar Bowl. In national ratings at the time, Wofford was ahead of such big-time teams as

Colorado, Maryland, Mississippi State and Arizona. The Terriers had stirred fans in South Carolina, and more than 2,000 would make the pilgrimage to Tampa — among them Gov. Strom Thurmond.

"A powerhouse, with a tailback that had averaged about 9 yards per carry throughout the season," described Veller.

Veller planned a defense based on team and individual statistics he culled out of the Greenville News.

"We noticed that the wingback on the team averaged only about 1 yard per carry," said Veller. "So we overshifted defensively to concentrate on the tailback.

"On every defensive play, the job of Buddy Strauss would be to crash from left end, into that Wofford backfield, and knock bodies up into the air.

"He did that. I think that All-American tailback of theirs averaged about 1 yard.

"And we beat that team that could perhaps have beaten most big teams."

Strauss played not only a spectacular defensive game but an extraordinary offensive one as well, gaining 132 yards as FSU — the underdog by two touchdowns — sprung a 19-6 upset. Eubanks had made a sensational catch between two defenders to pave a touchdown that put Florida State ahead to stay.

"A better team beat the hell out of us," said Wofford coach Phil Dickens.

Pete Norton typed in his Tampa Tribune column: "Wofford had better press relation and publicity men than football players. No small-college team has ever been boomed as high. . . ."

It was the first bowl victory by any Florida college team since Jan. 1, 1933, when Miami topped Manhattan 7-0 in the Palm Festival, a forerunner of the Orange Bowl.

Something of a sour aftertaste

Veller views the triumph over Wofford as the most memorable of his five seasons, and as one of the great victories in FSU history.

But the players, promised watches by the Tampa people for playing in the game, felt not so good when, at the awards ceremony, they were instead presented miniature rubber footballs — the likes of which Strauss and some teammates had seen priced in a downtown store at 39 cents each.

Because of that distasteful memory, players would nix bowl opportunities the following season when they finished unbeaten.

"We had at first an invitation from the

Tangerine Bowl in Orlando, and then one from the Cigar Bowl," said Veller. "The Refrigerator Bowl in Evansville, Ind., also wanted us.

"I called a team meeting, and I told the players I was going to get out of there and let them decide.

"They voted it down."

Students and supporters initiated a campaign to obtain a Gator Bowl bid, but the Jacksonville group said FSU was not big enough. Whereupon, the Gator Bowl passed on unbeaten Florida State. Instead it invited Washington and Lee — which would fall 20-7 to Wyoming.

Veller noted there were contributing reasons, beyond the little-footballs factor, that players spurned the Cigar, Tangerine and Refrigerator. "Remember, it was a time of no scholarships," said Veller. "A lot of 'em felt they had to go home and work — go somewhere and get a job during the holidays."

Like the players, Veller had found something irritating.

"Well, like we lost that close game to Erskine the first year," he said. "The Flambeau wrote that there was dissension on the team. I called the guy and asked the source. He said it was just what somebody said. I asked him who, and he said he didn't know — just somebody.

"The squad was out looking for that somebody."

The dean of women called to say that fullback Mike Sellars had shown up at a formal campus dance wearing a sweatshirt. A check disclosed that Sellars was not in town that weekend. Veller later recalled that when he advised the dean, she replied, "Well, it must have been somebody else."

In a day when all members of the football staff also taught classes, Veller also recalled having to pay a substitute teacher one year whenever he left on a recruiting mission.

Sometimes prospects just showed up, wanting to play football.

"This big old Georgia boy came down for the first time and went out for practice," said Veller. "He just about killed everybody."

Veller put his arm around him after practice and said he wanted him to get his transcript right away.

"What's a transcript?" asked the boy.

Veller told him the school would have to have his high-school transcript — the record of his classes and grades.

"I just went to the eighth grade," said the player.

But there was a growing perception that Florida State had players aplenty.

"It is almost as bad having a winning team as a losing one," Danford said. "We can't get some coaches and athletic directors to answer our letters."

Following the 1949 season, Florida had hired Bob Woodruff as its football coach for $17,000 annually — a princely sum at that time. Veller was then making $6,500.

Frances Veller asked her husband: "Is Woodruff a good coach?"

"He must be," replied Veller.

"Is he better than you?" she asked.

"He must be," he said.

"Is he *three* times better than you?" she asked.

Silence.

The guys who powered the team

After watching 17 seniors graduate from the Cigar Bowl team, and unable to corral talented Georgia walk-ons minus transcript, Veller was particularly doleful entering the 1950 season.

But the arrival of Mike Sellars — latest in a long line of Indiana transfers — helped. So did that of Tommy Brown, something of a Tallahassee legend, who had starred on some of Army's best teams. Veller also rounded up one of his own second cousins — Dwight Osha, a tackle who played very well that year.

It was a team that still had Bill Dawkins, a linebacker-guard who was an exceptional blocker. Along with Hugh Adams, the Little All-American tackle of the previous year, Dawkins would rank as the best two-way lineman of Veller's time.

Later an assistant coach, Adams would earn a doctorate and become president of Broward Junior College. Veller remembered Adams, while still a player, debating Athletic Director Danford on the question of subsidization for football at a campus hall.

"Danford was smart, very articulate — but so was Adams," said Veller. "I sat in the back and listened.

"Adams was a great leader for our team. And he could play position.

"But Dawkins — with some exceptions for Adams — was absolutely the best player we had. Off the field, he was a nice guy, but on it he was not. He had the ability of meeting the play that nobody could teach — never waiting for the other people to get to him."

Veller found it hard to choose the most memorable player of his time.

"But," he said, "it would have to be either Dawkins or Adams."

The two were a big part of an uncommonly spirited corps.

Fights on the practice field, at one point, seemed to be getting out of hand. "Trying to control it, I made a very unwise threat," said Veller. "I said the next guy who started something would be kicked off the squad for good."

Suddenly, a player was laid out cold on the field. Unconscious. Adams had been responsible. In a quandary, Veller hesitated.

"Then the guy who was out cold woke up," said Veller. "He said Adams had hit him — but had hit him fair.

"I was never so relieved in my life."

1950: A stadium is born

The 1950 team, despite those heavy graduation losses, had indeed returned a superb nucleus.

In its first season in Campbell Stadium, this was the team that would go unbeaten, then thumb its nose at bowl bids. (That unbeaten run followed a summer when Veller was away, working final extreme hours toward his doctorate at the home of his wife's parents in Madison, Ind. In qualifying tests, the studious Veller had posted the second-highest grade in the history of Indiana's doctoral program.)

The team shook off the dust of old Centennial Field, where all home games of the first three seasons were played — the last a 20-0 trimming of Troy State on Nov. 25, 1949.

"Centennial Field was made for baseball," said Veller, "and the lights were always poor. There were parts where you could not see — where players were just about in the dark. Then, too, we never had any dressing-room facilities there." Star running back Nelson Italiano said of Centennial: "I always felt like we were playing in a hole in the ground."

Initially, Campbell Stadium was hardly ideal.

"The turf that first year had not had time to grow properly," recalled Veller. "They put down sod from the university's dairy farm, and that stuff just got harder and harder. There were several injuries. I remember Dub Kendricks, a fine tackle, broke his leg just falling on that hard ground — it wasn't a blow that caused it, just the ground. And the further the season went on, the harder that ground got."

But soon that turf would become the manicured envy of many — as fine a playing surface as was possible on natural grass.

The steel structure — 7,500 seats on each side — had another early liability. "There were no dressing rooms at first, and before the game and at halftime we would huddle the team underneath those stands," said Veller. "There would be people running around those steel stands up above while you were trying to talk to the team. The noise was terrible — sometimes really deafening."

But compared with all previous home facilities, the new stadium, despite its early bugs, was like heaven to the Seminoles.

A memorable wheelbarrow ride

The building of Campbell Stadium had been a prideful and astonishingly quick endeavor. President Campbell, in his 1964 book "A University in Transition," put it this way: "The response to the need by the people of Tallahassee was prompt and efficient."

To finance the project, two prominent Tallahassee businessmen, Rainey Cawthon and Charley Rosenberg, had conceived the idea of selling five-year season tickets for $50 each.

The Chamber of Commerce took the initiative, and on Feb. 6, 1950, the Tallahassee Athletic Council was chartered with membership that included representation of the city, the county, the state, the chamber and the Quarterback Club. Cawthon, representing the Chamber, was named chairman of the stadium project.

A considerable football hero as a halfback for the University of Florida in the late '20s, Tallahasseean Cawthon would contribute greatly not only to the building of a stadium but also to later fund-raising endeavors for the football Seminoles.

Under his relentless leadership, 506 season tickets were sold in two weeks. In less than four weeks the figure climbed to 814, and within six weeks 1,000 had been sold and the money turned over to Florida State. On April 20, the Board of Control approved the awarding of a building contract, and on July 5 the first steel was moved into the old pasture where the stadium would rise.

Still driving, Cawthon challenged the stadium builder, Red Coleman, to complete it on schedule. The terms of a wager stipulated that the loser would ride the other down Monroe Street in a wheelbarrow.

Coleman lost the bet by two days. On a rickety wheelbarrow with a lopsided wheel, Coleman gave Cawthon a ride down the city's main street as hundreds turned out to watch.

After his bumpy ride, Cawthon would always insist that he got the worst of the bet.

That's Rainey Cawthon in the wheelbarrow, and Red Coleman resting after pushing it. The two men had a wager in 1950: If Coleman didn't finish his work on the new Campbell Stadium in time, he'd have to roll Cawthon down Monroe Street. He lost the wager. In a sense, so did Cawthon: That wheel was wooden, and flat on one side.

This is what the construction site looked like. Off in the distance, you'll see the Pensacola Street overpass.

Players helped paint the stadium, working for $1 an hour.

The name of the game — defense

The first game at Campbell would follow a road opener at Troy State, where the Seminoles romped 26-7.

That Campbell inaugural came on Oct. 7, under lights, with Randolph Macon falling 40-7 before a crowd of 9,676. On Oct. 28, at the homecoming game with Sewanee, the stadium would be formally dedicated and its namesake, President Campbell, honored.

Veller seems to have been primarily responsible for getting the stadium named after Campbell.

"I have always said he did as much for Florida State football as any other person ever," said Veller. "I know that it was because of him that I stayed — he kept me from leaving."

Only two games were close in that unbeaten run of 8-0.

Howard, out of Birmingham with Bobby Bowden — the same — playing quarterback, put up a brisk battle in Tallahassee before falling 20-6.

And Sewanee, which played outstanding defense at the time, held Florida State to 14-8 in a memorable first homecoming.

Defense, too, was much the name of Veller's game. Only Tampa — a 35-19 loser in a closing game — scored more than a touchdown on that 1950 team. "I always loved defense, and devoted more time to it," said Veller. "Some members of our staff, wanting more offensive time, used to complain of too much attention to defense. And I would say, 'Well, how are we doing winning and losing?'

"The fun of the game was defense. I loved to screw up offenses."

The fun of the game, for many, included Charley Spivak playing for that inaugural homecoming dance after Sewanee fell. One among the celebrating many was Reubin Askew, president of the student body, later governor of Florida.

A name — "The Marching Chiefs" — was announced for Florida State's band following a campus contest, and Tommy Wright, ardent fan and a member of the School of Music

faculty, introduced his "FSU Fight Song" to the crowd at the Sewanee game.

> We're gonna fight, fight, fight for FSU
> We're gonna scalp 'em Seminoles
> We're gonna win, win, win, win, win
>   this game
> We're gonna go out and get some goals
> For FSU is on the warpath now
> And at the battle's end we're great
> So fight, fight, fight to victory
> The Seminoles of Florida State

Wright, perturbed that the Seminoles had been using the music of the "Notre Dame Victory March" and "On Wisconsin" as spirit rousers, had set to music a poem by Doug Alley that appeared in The Flambeau.

Reassessments after a season of triumph

That unbeaten season ended on a frigid note, with that 35-19 victory in Campbell Stadium over Tampa.

"The game was played in the afternoon," said Veller. "There was ice everywhere. I remember an old water tower, by the railroad tracks down there near the stadium, had huge icicles hanging down."

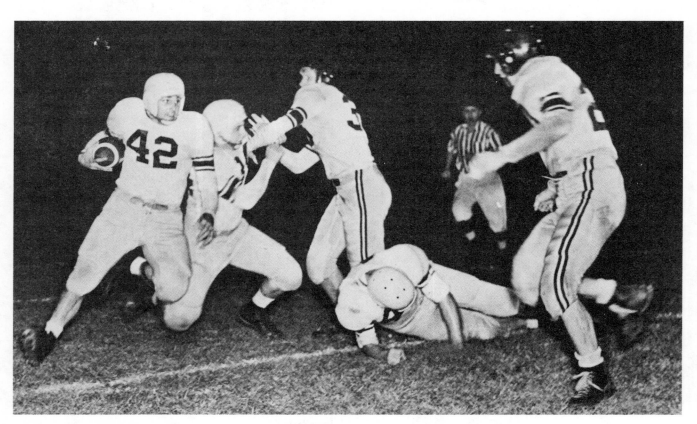

Halfback Nelson Italiano (42) carries the ball against Randolph Macon on Oct. 8, 1950, in the first game ever played in Doak Campbell Stadium. A total of 9,676 fans attended that game.

The temperature was 16 degrees.

Tampa coach Frankie Sinkwich, a Heisman Trophy winner as a running back for Georgia, proposed that the game be canceled and shifted to Tampa.

"At halftime, we went to our bus — because it was warm," said Veller. "We had the bus there to go over to old West Campus later, where we still dressed."

One of the highlights of that chilly game was provided by Tommy Brown. He boomed the longest punt in Florida State history — an 84-yarder, from the FSU 16 to Tampa's end zone.

Another bell-ringer was Nelson Italiano's two touchdown passes to Harry Bringger. All season long, Italiano threw just five times to Bringger — and the fellow back caught all five for touchdowns!

And it was the last of those five touchdowns, covering 34 yards, that early in the last quarter snapped a 13-13 tie. It was the first of three touchdowns that enabled FSU to pull away in a span of 4 minutes and 8 seconds.

It was a season in which Italiano checked in as FSU's most productive offensive player up until that time — 883 yards, 424 of it running and 459 passing. Among his eight touchdown passes, his five to Bringger averaged an incredible 49.1 yards.

Tackle Jerry Morrical was selected to the Little All-American team, as Hugh Adams had been each of the two prior years.

The success of those first four years precipitated what Veller would describe as "a tug from both ends."

On one side was a tug from university elements, led by Danford, to keep football "in its place" — as it was, and notably including no scholarships. On the other side was a tug from football's many supporters to upgrade the schedule, provide scholarships for players as other schools did — and play the University of Florida.

At the Howard game in 1950, students had raised Campbell Stadium banners: "Bring on Florida."

Upgrading the schedule was not simple. Many larger schools with more football tradition — including Florida — had little interest in playing Florida State. The problem of an independent seeking a more desirable schedule was one that would plague Florida State for a few decades.

The first major school to agree to play Florida State was the University of Miami. In late November of 1950, the Seminoles announced a date in the Orange Bowl with the Hurricanes for the following year.

"I was not one that wanted to play Florida at that time," said Veller. "But I really think our 1949 team could have whipped them — the team Florida had then. I would think that the 1949 team was better than the unbeaten one of 1950, though they were pretty close."

Florida was beginning to get under Veller's skin a bit, however. He said he grew weary of hearing Florida referred to as "the university," as though there were none other.

In December of 1950, Florida State announced that it would award football scholarships the following year, perhaps as many as 65.

It was a move that doomed the Dixie Conference, whose bylaws excluded athletic scholarships. Probably the conference was already doomed. Stetson and Tampa had earlier pulled out.

In three years, Florida State never lost a game to a Dixie Conference foe; in three years, Veller had posted an overall 24-2 record.

"Danford had said the conference was going to be the greatest experiment in athletics," said Veller. "But that 'Garden of Eden' just plain didn't work out."

A movement would start to obtain membership in the Southern Conference. It was a bid Veller opposed, and Florida State would operate as a football independent through the remainder of its first 40 seasons.

Florida State, however, did soon seek Southeastern Conference membership, and there would come a time when the University of Florida would propose Florida State as a member. But the Seminoles never really came close. A mounting factor was economics. With a shared pool of TV and bowl money eventually reaching into the millions, the SEC found no reason to bring any outsider in on the split.

After FSU decided to grant scholarships and pull out of the Dixie Conference, FSU scheduling would change. "A game with Florida still looks pretty far in the future," Veller advised hopeful fans, "but not nearly as far as it once did." That game would be eight years down the road.

A career that might have been

Newcomers on Veller's 1951 team included someone once described as Florida State's "best player never."

Roy Thompson was a handsome young man — a running back, 5-foot-10 and 173, an uncommon talent from Wrightsville, the small

FLORIDA STATE UNIVERSITY

THE 1950 FSU FOOTBALL SQUAD AND COACHING STAFF

19 50

Florida's First Undefeated and Untied College Football Team

The 1950 team — Florida State's first to go undefeated.

Georgia town that later spawned Heisman Trophy winner Herschel Walker. He had transferred from Georgia Tech, perhaps guided by a strong developing bond between Tech coach Bobby Dodd and Veller. The word was that Thompson was "a problem" Tech could not resolve, and perhaps a change in scenery would be beneficial.

"He would not practice, and he would not block," said Veller. "All he wanted to do was carry the football. Indeed, he could carry the ball.

"He was so fast on his start he made divots in the ground — honestly — the way he pushed off."

But Thompson ran his way.

"Once, against Stetson, he had a touchdown going up the middle," said Veller. "Everybody had been knocked down. But he spun out, went wide — and lost 5 yards."

As films were later shown, coaches asked Thompson why he hadn't gone up the middle.

"Gosh, it was no fun doing that — nobody was there," retorted Thompson.

Fun, and doing things his way, seemed a Thompson priority.

"We had a play on kickoff returns where we just threw the ball to him," said Veller, "and let him run where he wanted to run."

Such an athlete, Thompson picked up pocket money betting $1 that he could jump over the hood of a car. "He could do it," said Veller.

He skipped spring practice, and Veller asked him why.

"Oh, I'm out for the circus," replied Thompson. "I catch girls. It's more fun than football."

Because he would not practice, Thompson sat on the bench most of his final season — and Veller's final — in 1952, when the Seminoles won once, tied once and lost eight times. The coach said it would not have been fair to the other players to play him.

"I believe he was probably the best I ever saw," said Veller.

He said he understood that Thompson had joined the Marines and "got straightened out," but what might have been a spectacular football career was gone.

The '51 season: 6 wins, 2 losses

In 1951 Florida State started with a 40-0 thumping of Troy State. Italiano ran for 83 yards and passed for 88.

Then Florida State moved into Miami for that first major game. Before 38,278 fans on Oct. 6, the Seminoles fell 35-13.

"Miami had a great team and was ranked high," said Veller. "Our kids were *frozen* before those 38,000 people — by far the biggest crowd they'd ever played in front of.

"But Miami was plain faster, had us outmanned."

Florida State managed 275 yards to Miami's 400, and Coach Andy Gustafson described the losing effort as "a gutty performance."

FSU followed with five straight victories. All came with relative ease, save Stetson in an Oct. 27 homecoming game that celebrated the 100th anniversary of the founding of Florida State. With the help of a 76-yard Roy Thompson run, the Seminoles struggled from behind in the last half and won 13-10.

One victory in the stretch had come over Sul Ross State 33-13 in a Campbell Stadium downpour. Perhaps the single fact most recalled was that the Texas team had at one tackle Dan Blocker, later famed as the beloved Hoss Cartwright on the long-running TV series "Bonanza."

Florida State lost its last game — to Tampa, on a cold night in Campbell, 14-6. There were 235 penalty yards walked off on the two teams, and one Seminole would later call it "a slugfest."

A 70-yard run by speedster Vince Chico brought Tampa's first touchdown.

"Chico was a great running back who played four years at Purdue before going on to Tampa," said Veller. "Tampa's winning touchdown the next year was scored by a sergeant at McDill Field down there. We later learned he was enrolled for one hour at Tampa in a physical-education course. That made him a student."

Initially, a ninth game had been scheduled for the 1951 team — a closing one in Tallahassee on Nov. 24 against Bradley.

But in October came word of the game's cancellation — because Bradley had three black players in its lineup.

Board of Control policy at that time prohibited any state university from competing against blacks.

"As I recall, when the contract with Bradley was signed, they had said they had no blacks," said Veller. "But in the meantime they had recruited one or more. I don't remember the number.

"We said it was all right with us, but we were told it was not all right with the Board of Control — that it was against the law."

Part of the contract called for Florida State to play at Bradley in 1952, but the game in Peoria was canceled, too.

It was a different era, one of widespread segregation. Though Florida State would soon play teams with blacks on the road, it was not until the mid-1960s that Florida State — and other Deep South schools — started recruiting blacks for athletics, and very gingerly at the start.

'52: the beginning of a slide

Veller, in four years, had lost only four games. He had won an even 30 at that point.

But there was sound advice from Bobby Dodd, head coach of Georgia Tech and friend of Veller's, when he spoke in Tallahassee in January of 1952.

"Don't get your sights too high," said Dodd. "You're going to have to take some lickings.

"I don't care how good a coach you have, or how fine a school, you've got to have the boys. And it takes time to get the right kind of boys."

Veller would win only one more game.

The tested men of war — the veterans — were beginning to run out. One who departed after the 1951 season was Mike Sellars, the big, tough fullback. He had problems in his playing time at Indiana, and Veller had told him one false move at Florida State would mean goodbye. Sellars became a model individual.

"We never had any problem with the veterans — we got 'em so wrapped up in the team," said Veller.

"One thing I recall is that panty raids were big on campuses in those days. Sellars took the lead in quelling one at Florida State."

Also running out were immediately eligible transfers, like Sellars. After dropping out of the Dixie Conference, FSU instituted a policy that barred such. Henceforth, transfers would have to be in residence for a year before gaining athletic eligibility.

"And we started upgrading our schedule without really enough time to adjust," said Veller. "We needed more time to get the right players."

The schedule toughens up

The arm of coincidence also played a role. For example, Louisville came to Tallahassee in early 1952 with a quarterback named Johnny Unitas.

"Unitas had the greatest day of any passer I've ever seen," said Veller. "He was just phenomenal. No way he couldn't play for anybody anywhere anytime.

"Louisville also had an extraordinary fullback (Jim Williams) who graduated that year."

As Williams ran for 143 yards, Unitas passed for 195 and three touchdowns — completing 15 of 21 efforts. After the 41-14 whipping, Veller prophetically said of Unitas: "He is out of this world."

Virginia Military Institute came in and administered a 28-7 defeat. The next year its coach, Tom Nugent, would succeed Veller at Florida State — whereupon, he would quickly coach the Seminoles to a 12-7 triumph over VMI.

"You gotta watch a fellow," Frank Howard, the down-home coach of Clemson, said of Nugent, "who takes his'n and beats your'n, then takes your'n and beats his'n."

After four games of his fifth year, Veller would lose as many games as he had in the 34 of his previous four seasons. With a 6-6 tie of Stetson in the fifth game, brief brakes were applied.

Suddenly, Florida State was playing a schedule beyond comparison with the earlier ones. This one had not only Louisville and

VMI for the first time, but also N.C. State, Mississippi Southern, Furman and Georgia Tech for the first time.

"Of the 22 men we started against one of Georgia Tech's great teams, 17 were freshmen," said Veller.

Florida State played Tech tough — much closer than the final 30-0 score suggests. Stan Dobosz, one of those freshmen, ran for 87 yards — more than any other individual had gained on Tech all season.

Tommy Brown intercepted two passes to help blunt Tech bids.

"He was one of the great pass defenders of all time," said Veller. "A great competitor with fine ability, who could really leap. They just didn't complete any passes around Tommy Brown."

At the conclusion of that vintage season, Georgia Tech saluted Brown by selecting him on its all-opponent team.

"When some of those freshmen mature a bit," said Tech's Dodd, "they are going to be a tough combination to beat."

Coach Veller steps down

Only nine seniors lined up on that 1952 team — among them Italiano, Brown, Curt Campbell, Earl O'Neill and Thompson.

One thing remained the same — the Seminoles' hold on Wofford. Florida State had beaten good Wofford teams two years running, and would again for the lone victory of 1952. Playing at Wofford, the Seminoles terminated a 13-game home winning streak for the Terriers. Score: 27-13.

Item: That trip to Spartanburg, S.C., was the Seminoles' first ever by plane.

On Dec. 4 in Campbell, Florida State's long season ended with a 39-6 loss to Tampa as the well-experienced Chico ran wild.

Veller, who had strongly considered stepping out of coaching before that season's start, did not immediately bow out at the conclusion of that disappointing run.

"There was no pressure," he said. "When I resigned, it was completely of my own volition."

Under a condition of his original employment, Veller was given the right to step down any time he chose — and remain in the physical-education department. Veller had the tenure of an associate professor, and when he had received his doctorate, President Campbell had promised he would automatically have the rank of a full professor when he stepped down.

It would be a few weeks after the season

Coach Veller watches a nail-biter of a game from the sidelines.

Crowned by feather headdresses, Florida State majorettes practice their routines in 1950.

before Veller made up his mind to act. A distaste for recruiting, said Veller, was a major factor in his decision to get out of coaching — much as it has been for other coaches who got out on their own initiative.

"I kept hearing from the high-school players, 'What are you offering?'" said Veller. "I would say 'Nothing,' and tell them that was the truth.

"And they would keep asking 'What else,' beyond the scholarship and what the NCAA allowed."

He recalled a visit to campus of five junior-college prospects. When they asked the 'What else' question, Veller suggested, it was the last straw.

"I was so mad I got up out of my chair and told them to get out," said Veller. "I had got so sick of hearing that 'And what else' stuff. I was fed up."

The letter to Danford was dated Jan. 16, 1953. It requested release from the duties of football coach "as soon as convenient." On the same date, Danford sent a letter to President Campbell recommending the resignation be granted, and expressing "my deep appreciation of the excellent work."

Very soon after the announcement of his decision, Florida State football supporters signified their own appreciation.

The coach who in his final season had won just one game was handed the keys to a new blue Chrysler convertible.

After becoming a Florida State physical-education professor who wrote many articles in the field, Veller would also serve for a time as associate athletic director, then later as an exceptional golf coach. For many years, on past retirement, he wrote a golf column for the Tallahassee Democrat.

Veller left much to FSU football when he stepped out following that 1952 season.

The list included a number of promising freshmen, plus some red-shirted talent that included Al MacKowiecki, who would become one of Florida State's top all-time tackles.

He left Bob Harbison, whom at least five of the following six head coaches would, at one time or another, call their most valuable aide.

"I had always felt, when he played at Indiana, he was physically not a great player — but he *played* well," said Veller. "Which meant he had something else.

"He was smart in football — and, oh, he loved it! He would work hours and hours, mostly with film stuff.

"He was a great scout. If you sent him out to get information on a team, he came back with it. And he had this innate ability to analyze a situation."

Veller left a heritage that Harbison, as much as any single individual, would help preserve through all the change that would follow over the next three decades.

Harbison, too, would often hear the equivalent of an old cry that Veller knew from his dad.

Like few others in Florida State athletic history, Harbison and Veller were the personification of persistence.

"Hang in there, Uncle Benny!"

The Nugent Years

An era of showmanship, innovation, Burt Reynolds and, at last, Florida!

He stood 5-foot-8 and weighed 168, and while a college sophomore during the Depression years he had fought a few club fights, for $25 or so, under the name of Danny Morgan.

He got paired against an over-the-hill veteran of ring wars.

"I found out I couldn't beat that old pug if I lived to be 100," said Tom Nugent, "so I decided to go into another business."

Florida State's third football coach was many things.

A talker, with a degree of appreciation for what his Irish ancestors called blarney, he would stand on a street corner or in a hotel lobby for hours and talk to an acquaintance about football or Broadway musicals.

An innovator who popularized the I-formation that so many coaches would later favor, who utilized the typewriter huddle, double quarterbacks and more.

A dreamer of extensive imagination.

A driving taskmaster who conducted some of the hardest practices that Florida State football ever knew.

A showman with great flair, who surely was the best-dressed FSU coach of them all — a prideful man who in his seventies would look better than most men 20 years younger.

And a fighter — always a fighter seeking a way, an opening.

34 wins, 28 losses, 1 tie

Tom Nugent in 1970.

Painted up in preparation for the '54 Sun Bowl are end Tom Feamster, center Bob Crenshaw and tackle Don Powell. Four years later Crenshaw died in the crash of an Air Force jet — and every year since, the Crenshaw Award has gone to a player voted "the Seminole with the fightingest heart" by his teammates.

"When you were in sports, as I was growing up, you had a peculiar feeling if you went near the music school or a drama class," said Nugent. "But I used to go over to those things, watch and listen."

At Ithaca (N.Y.) College, where he earned 10 letters competing in four sports, Nugent sometimes literally sang for his supper. "In my junior year, I sang with a band at the Colonial Restaurant," he said. "Never was paid anything. I sang eight songs for my dinner."

His identity with athletics was always foremost, but a feel for show business — as an Army captain during World War II, his duties included staging entertainment for the troops — was always around.

"I always figured whatever you do, you gotta work at it, do it right," said Nugent, "but I never saw any reason why you shouldn't throw in a little show business."

Part of his quest for a lighter side may have been related to the fact Tom Nugent was also a worrier.

He came to Florida State in 1953 with a duodenal ulcer and a spastic colon.

But he quit smoking, adjusted his diet and brought it under control. Pat Hogan, the school's sports-information director then, used to bring Nugent a glass of chocolate milk on the practice field. And in the dressing room after practice, Hogan would sometimes join Nugent in song. "Ragtime Cowboy Joe" was one favorite, and "Shine" another. Nugent liked to sing, and he appreciated another good voice.

But sometimes the frustrations of a coach — the pressure — built up so in Nugent that

45

neither song nor dance provided a reasonable outlet.

It is fact that he would, on occasion, go bass-fishing alone and seek to relieve the pressure.

He would find the most isolated spot possible on vast Lake Talquin, not so far from campus.

Whereupon, he would stand up in the boat and let it all out.

"Kiss my *bleep*, kiss my *bleep*, kiss my *bleep*!" he would yell to the world out there. To his heart's content, and to the point he felt he had gotten his message across.

And never mind if he scared all the fish away.

The magic of believing

Nugent, native of Lawrence, Mass., had gone 19-18-2 in four seasons at Virginia Military Institute, including a memorable upset of Georgia Tech in Atlanta, and a 28-7 triumph over the Seminoles in Tallahassee the prior year that got the attention of FSU administrators.

Soon after accepting the FSU job, Nugent was sure he had made a mistake.

"The facilities looked to me like they were out in the woods," he said, speaking of old Dale Mabry Field buildings that FSU referred to as West Campus. "The only offices they had were in those old barracks."

One area he found no problem with was the playing surface of Campbell Stadium. "Oh, that field was always nice," he said. "They used to manicure that field so, and I used to say I would like to have a football team to match that field."

Nugent looked around at the players he had inherited.

"I counted 67 players on scholarship," he said, "and I interviewed every single one."

He soon would bring in several junior-college players, notably including quarterback Harry Massey.

One newcomer that year was guard Vince Gibson, a Birmingham native and transfer from Howard, where in one game he had caught three touchdown passes from a quarterback named Bobby Bowden. After sitting out a year of ineligibility, he would play for the Seminoles in 1954 and 1955. Later, Gibson would become head coach at Kansas State, Louisville and Tulane. When serving as an assistant on Bill Peterson's FSU staff, Gibson would remember an old Birmingham friend, and persuade Peterson to hire Bowden — thereby initiating a relationship that would

In 1953 — when a loaf of bread was 17 cents, T-bone steaks 79 cents a pound and Florida State's best football ticket $4 — Thomas Norman Nugent drew a starting salary of $8,000 as FSU's third head football coach. And unlimited substitution was abolished, with players allowed to enter a game only once each quarter.

work out so well for the Seminoles many years later.

At the beginning, Nugent radiated great optimism, as he almost always would.

"I had read a book ('The Magic of Believing') by Norman Vincent Peale the year before coming to Florida State," said Nugent. "In my first talk to FSU's student body I told them of the magic in believing.

"The positive approach we had — the band, the cheerleaders, the students, the team — was a big key to our success."

From Veller's staff Nugent retained two assistants, Bob Harbison and Vaughn Mancha. Among new assistants was Mike Long, who soon would become the highly successful track coach.

Nugent's association with Harbison would be particularly good.

"Boy, when I had something to talk over, I always went to Harbie," he said. "Of all the guys I had, he was the one guy who fit into my plans best.

"We came up with the most difficult drills ever devised. It was one of the wildest, hardest spring practices anywhere.

"And out of the 67 we ended with 13 guys who played for me in the fall."

Practices that only a Marine could love

Many players, including Burt Reynolds, would testify to the extremely difficult Nugent practices that would continue.

It was a day, long gone, when many coaches permitted no water — no liquid of any kind — at practices. It was considered less than spartan; you were not *tough* if you required such.

"Nugent practices were the toughest thing I ever went through, including all my years in the Marine Corps — boot camp and everything," said one player who came along later, then for several years was a Marine Corps officer.

Interestingly, some journalists observed the precise drill-team-like shifts that Nugent favored throughout his time and called it all "Tom Nugent's Dancing School."

It was no dancing school.

On occasion the team would move, as darkness approached, from its regular practice site to one on a nearby, lighted softball field.

"We'd turn on those lights and practice on that clay over there," said Vic Prinzi, who came aboard as a freshman quarterback in Nugent's second year. "I can remember lying in our beds at night, and a couple of guys would be hurting so bad they would just quietly cry."

In the fall, Nugent held *six* game-like scrimmages — including ones with squads of Troy State and Navy squads from Jacksonville and Pensacola — before the '53 opener at Miami.

With the advent of Nugent came a key national rule change drastically restricting substitution. Previously, free substitution had been permitted, but Florida State was never able to take full advantage because of a lack of depth.

Lee Corso, one of the more versatile stars of the Nugent era, is shown here as coach of the USFL Orlando Renegades, in 1984.

Lee Corso, a pure freshman from Miami listed at 5-foot-9 and 142 pounds, would start at quarterback against Miami — because Nugent, as a condition of recruiting this highly sought prospect, had promised he would start his first game before the home folks.

Corso would be possibly the most valuable player of Nugent's years at Florida State — excelling as a defensive back and running back, as well as a quarterback — and later be an assistant under Nugent before becoming head coach of Louisville, Indiana and the pro Orlando Renegades of the ill-fated United States Football League.

But he did not have the experience to quarterback that Friday night in Miami. Possibly, it little mattered: Miami utilized three teams and romped 27-0.

Tough practices seemed to produce dividends, however. Louisville — with the great Johnny Unitas still at quarterback but nursing a bum ankle that night — fell 59-0 in Nugent's first home game.

Abilene Christian College brought FSU back to earth with a 20-7 upset in Tallahassee. (ACC would duplicate the feat, 13-0, in Tallahassee the following year.)

About this time, Florida State learned that, come 1955, it would qualify under NCAA guidelines as a major school in football. Those guidelines required three successive seasons of competition against a majority of opponents already considered major. Florida State had already lined up such schedules through 1955 and would maintain them.

"I'm pleased," said Nugent when that news was announced, "but I hope we're not moving too fast."

Florida State was not.

A big victory over VMI in '53

The Seminoles, after a road loss to Louisiana Tech, stood 1-3 when VMI came to town that first Nugent year. There was a bit of ill feeling between Nugent and his VMI successor, John McKenna, who had referred to Nugent shifts and other maneuvers as "veneer."

Nugent wanted to beat VMI perhaps more than any other opponent of his time at Florida State.

"Probably the Tennessee game was the most memorable one of my Florida State years," Nugent said 30 years later of that game in his last year, when Tennessee fell in Knoxville 10-0. "But, from a very personal standpoint, the VMI game of 1953 meant the most to me."

VMI came with college football's leading

Substitution rules used to forbid players to go back into the game during the same quarter they had left it. So Coach Nugent devised a sideline area called "The Reservation" for those players. Shown here are (front, from left) George Boyer, Stan Dobosz, Buddy Bryant, Al Mackowiecki, and (rear, from left) Steve Kalenich, Bobby Fiveash, Al Pacifico.

rusher of the moment, Johnny Mapp. A Florida State open date the week prior helped, with Nugent able to scout VMI against West Virginia personally.

Fullback John Griner would recall that Nugent had tears in his eyes as he addressed the squad before the kickoff.

Capitalizing on VMI first-half fumbles, including two by Mapp, FSU cut out a 12-0 halftime lead behind the running of Buck Metts. VMI cut it to 12-7 in the third quarter and threatened late before a Griner interception cemented the upset. Metts ran up 111 yards in just nine carries. Mapp, checked at every turn, managed 28 for the evening.

"We gave them a little veneer," Nugent would say later, applying the needle to McKenna.

The record fell to 2-5 as Southern Mississippi — a power at the time — shut out the Seminoles 21-0 and Furman won 14-7.

"Always leave 'em smiling," Nugent would often say, alluding to the importance of winning late-season games.

He did.

The team finished 5-5 with triumphs in the final three — Stetson, N.C. State, Tampa. A 41-6 triumph at Tampa, with Bobby Fiveash running for 141 yards, whetted hopes for next year.

Fiveash, bound for graduation and a fine career in the Canadian Football League, would

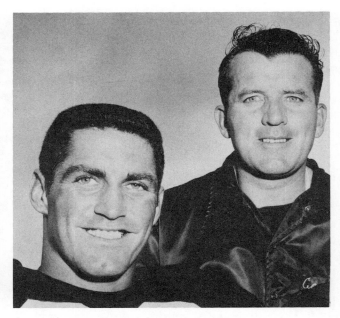

Tough end Ron Schomburger with Nugent.

soon become the first Seminole saluted as the state's top college player after leading FSU in rushing (455 yards, 6.6 average), scoring (48 points) and kickoff returns (22.5 average).

Nugent would beat Tampa four times — every time he played that foe, and each time in Tampa.

The coach recalls Syde Deeb, a Tallahassee millionaire and notable supporter of Florida State football, telling him before one of those Tampa games — perhaps the first — that if the Seminoles won, he would treat Nugent and whatever friends he chose to bring at Tampa's famed Columbia Restaurant.

FSU won. Whereupon, Nugent took his entire team to the Columbia Restaurant.

"I figured," he said, "the whole team was my friends."

New faces for '54

Expectations soared for 1954, with 20 top lettermen returning, with so many promising new recruits, with more than 100 candidates showing up for fall workouts.

Among the new players:

• Ted Rodrigue, a heralded quarterback from Lynn, Mass., just out of the Air Force, where he had excelled in football and also reigned as a Far East boxing champion.

• Ron Schomburger, a Pennsylvanian who would become an outstanding end.

• Tom Feamster, a 6-foot-7, 250-pound transfer from William and Mary, who would become eligible that fall and evolve into one of the top ends in FSU history. Later he would become an Episcopal priest.

Vic Prinzi, pal of Burt Reynolds, quarterbacked FSU's fine 1958 team.

• Gene Cox, a 5-foot-6, 180-pound former All-Southern halfback from Lake City who had previously played at Vanderbilt and South Georgia Junior College, destined to achieve later fame as the winningest coach in Florida prep history while serving at Tallahassee Leon.

• Burton Leon Reynolds, an all-state back, a freshman from West Palm Beach, listed at 5-10 and 180. Fast and elusive, he was called Buddy then. Later, the world would know him as Burt Reynolds.

• Vic Prinzi, a heralded quarterback out of Waverly, N.Y., whose coach (Frank Toomey) would join the FSU staff at the same time.

Also aboard for 1954 was a new trainer. Don "Rooster" Fauls, like Nugent a graduate of Ithaca College, would become one of Florida State's more popular athletic figures. He served as trainer for 29 of FSU's first 40 years in athletics — missing three years during the 1970s while in private business, then returning and finally retiring in early 1986.

Georgia came in for a Sept. 18 opener. No out-of-state team at that time — and, indeed, perhaps none within — had a bigger image among Floridians than the Bulldogs. The coming of Georgia was an unprecedented *happening* for Florida State and Tallahassee, and a record 19,401 fans would pack Campbell Stadium.

Georgia won 14-0, somewhat as anticipated, but Rodrigue had heightened hope with his late passing, including a 33-yarder to Reynolds.

After which, pesky Abilene Christian came to town and again startled the Seminoles, this time 13-0, in the rain.

"They had a linebacker who just kept running everybody down," Prinzi recalled.

He ran everybody down, too, in the 1956 Olympics at Melbourne, and suddenly the whole world knew about Bobby Morrow, that Abilene Christian linebacker.

The Seminoles started to roll at Louisville (47-6), as Reynolds scored one of the touchdowns, then returned home to throttle Villanova (52-13).

A revised offense helped. Harry Massey, the quarterback, was beginning to click with a roll-out option pass.

Another first had come at Louisville. It was the Seminoles' first engagement against black players. Louisville had three, including Lenny Lyles, who later would start with the Baltimore Colts.

After a 13-7 victory at N.C. State, the string was severed 33-0 by Auburn, a team that would become a nemesis.

Reynolds provided Florida State with its biggest moment as he broke on a 54-yard run before Bobby Freeman ran him down. Many years later Reynolds would recall that it was Fob James who tackled him on that run. "It was me," said Freeman, chuckling at the recollection more than 30 years later, "but I don't know that it makes a whole lot of difference to the hundreds of millions of Chinese out there."

But James, later governor of Alabama, did ample damage, scoring on a 37-yarder as the Tigers ran for 499. Reynolds got more on that single run than the Seminoles' whole-game net of 44.

FSU moved from that stinger to five straight zingers — tripping VMI, Furman, Stetson, Southern Mississippi and Tampa.

Of these, the 19-18 decision over rugged Southern Miss ranked easily as the biggest. A tie was averted when fullback Joe Holt blocked a Southern extra-point attempt following a late touchdown.

Massey passes brought 10 touchdowns — a high figure for the time — during a season that saw him hit 50 of 90 for 750 yards, and the tall Feamster snaring a school-record 24. The versatile Corso ran for 273 yards, caught 20 passes for 240 more and led the team in scoring (39 points) and interceptions (six).

"This was a team," said Nugent, "that just got better and better."

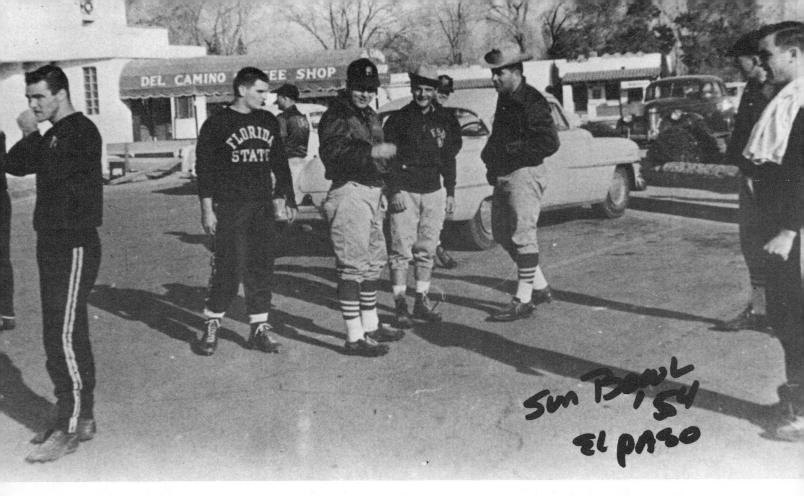

Sun Bowl '54
El Paso

Here we are in lovely El Paso, just before the '54 Sun Bowl. Recognize that brooding fellow to the left?
None other than Burt "Buddy" Reynolds, a freshman halfback that year.

A place in the Sun

With an 8-3 record in the school's first 11-game season, Florida State earned a bid to the faraway Sun Bowl, where the opponent would be hometown Texas Western.

Meanwhile Nugent, well before the season expired, had publicly urged the inauguration of a football series with Florida.

In December, Bob Woodruff, the University of Florida coach who also doubled as athletic director, advised Howard Danford, the FSU athletic director, that the Gators were not interested in playing FSU — ever.

As part of what he would later tell The Associated Press was a liberal offer, Woodruff advised Danford that Florida might be interested in minor-sports relations with Florida State — but only if the Seminoles agreed to stop all this talk about a football series.

"I was shocked," said Danford.

The state's newspapers were beginning to pick up the beat, most suggesting that the schools should, indeed, play in football. Charley Johns, acting governor, and members of the Board of Control indicated interest in a football series.

But Woodruff, for a long while, would re-main firm, and Morris McLemore, sports editor of The Miami News, wrote that his "never" stance was "bull-headed."

Florida State partisans would soon identify Woodruff as the object of their frustration, and Florida fans — many resenting the rising pressure — would become bitter toward Nugent and his expressions in favor of the game. "Anywhere — any time," Nugent was fond of saying.

When the series was inaugurated four years later, and Florida succeeded in getting the first six games played on its home field, the Gators reminded Florida State of that "Anywhere-any time" stance.

Three days after Christmas, the Seminoles flew away on a chartered plane to El Paso, and possibly the most enjoyable Florida State football excursion of all time.

FSU found the Sun Bowl at El Paso — just across the Rio Grande from Mexico and festive Juarez — most hospitable, most entertaining. There were daily trips across the river for shopping, bull fights, dining and partying. Bowl events that included a "Sheriff's Posse Breakfast" were also fun.

In the game itself, Florida State proved no

match for Texas Western. The score was 47-20. It might have been worse.

"After all these years, I plan to ask them today what really happened out there," Nugent would say 30 years later at a reunion of that Sun Bowl team — including Reynolds, Corso and pals.

Corso had been injured in the game. "He was supposed to have had a broken leg," Nugent said, laughing. "But my information is he was dancing in Juarez after the game."

Said Schomburger: "They showed us such a good time, we forgot to play football."

Some thought El Paso's high altitude adversely affected FSU, and a few thought a sinking sun that blazed in Seminole eyes the last half contributed a bit. Much of the truth was that Texas Western, playing at home, was a very fine football team that afternoon. Jesse Whittendon, the Miners' tough quarterback, would play for many years in the defensive backfield of the Green Bay Packers.

The typewriter huddle

Though Nugent, like most coaches, believed greatly in fundamentals, his imaginative touch and the precise maneuvering of his players sometimes conveyed a different impression.

Bill Bunker, a journalist who became sports-information director of the Seminoles in the mid-1960s, reflected both sides as he later recalled his own brief time as a Florida State football candidate in 1955 under Nugent.

Side one:

"During the first of what must have been a million head-on tackling drills performed that year, I received a severe charley horse on a blow delivered by a muscular 130-pounder from somewhere in Alabama, and found myself peering through the ear hole of my shiny golf helmet after attempting to deliver a similar blow to a 3-legged monster from Eastern Pennsylvania. Although my face was on the ground, my identifying piece of tape was spotted by Coach Vince Ragunas.

" 'Bunker, where are you from?'

" 'Madison, Florida.'

" 'You're going to get killed out here!' "

Side two:

"I was chosen as one end on a team picked to demonstrate the 'Typewriter Huddle' to our peers.

"The interior linemen formed the first row, with hands on knees. Backs and ends stood straight and tall on the second row. The quarterback stood a few yards in front looking downfield to size up the defense, which in those days was pretty standard.

"As he wheeled sharply and came toward the huddle, the two ends executed a smart left or right face, and came to a position of parade rest. Then the second row leaned forward in unison to hear the plays.

"It took timing, and we practiced about 15 minutes before our demonstration.

"I have never quite figured the value of this little wrinkle. But I was pretty good at it."

Setting the Reynolds record straight

As the 1955 season rolled around, Reynolds soon rolled out — and on to Hollywood.

Many stories of Reynolds' FSU football past circulated with his increasing fame as a movie actor in a career that eventually made him the world's No. 1 box-office attraction. Some of the stories ridiculed the notion he was ever any kind of *real* football player.

In fact, Reynolds was a fine athlete who might have become an exceptional running back. He was fast, with a gliding and elusive style. He had the good shoulders, the big neck of a player.

While some of the tales put him down, others built him up — suggesting he was the team's fastest, and had a neck size of 19½.

In a lengthy 1986 interview, Reynolds sought to set the record straight.

"I was 5-foot-11 and I got up to about 190 between my freshman and sophomore year," he said. "I'm not sure my neck was ever as big as 19½. I think it must have been about size 17. I do remember that I couldn't find a shirt anywhere, and borrowed from Leo Baggett."

A stocky guard, and a good one, Baggett surely had a big neck.

"I don't think I was ever the fastest man on the team," said Reynolds. "Billy Odom was. But I sure wasn't the slowest.

"I had pretty good peripheral vision, and I used to hit the line — and slide whichever way I could go. A lot of time my hand would hit the ground, for balance. A lot of guys were doing that kind of running back then. I think it was a kind of glide."

A little-known fact is that Reynolds initially signed with the University of Miami. It was a day when players could change their minds without penalty.

"I was going to Miami, but I was enjoying all those recruiting trips," said Reynolds. "They were like a fraternity rush party. I went to Duke, to Kentucky — places like that.

"I came up to FSU with three or four of my

friends. I had no intention of signing. But Tom Nugent was the slickest talker I've ever run up against — and I've run up against some pretty good ones. If there was a class in charm, he would get an A.

"Before I got out of that room with him, I was coming to Florida State."

During all of his Florida State time, he was known as Buddy Reynolds. "My dad was big Burt, and I was a junior but Dad refused to call me Junior," said Burt. "So I came to be called Buddy."

An uncommon bond would evolve between Reynolds, the players of that time and the school, though he played only one season and part of another.

"It was too bad I had not seen a lot of those guys earlier," said Reynolds following the 1985 reunion. "I think they realized how important they are to my life — how close to my heart that school is."

Reynolds suggested the special bond evolved because he and his teammates went through some very hard times together.

"That year I was a freshman, there were an awful lot of football players out there," he said. "It was a question of who was standing after those first four or five weeks.

"A lot of really good players were run off."

It was a day of tryouts, of partial scholarships, of a big numbers game. Some players left, apparently, with less than a good look. There is the story of Bob Harbison, at some point during the Nugent era, bringing to campus a stocky lineman from the Midwest. Nugent did not much like what he saw. He called Harbison aside.

"Get that fat slob out of here," Nugent said, according to Harbison's recollection.

So it was that Alex Karras left, soon to matriculate at Iowa, where he earned All-American acclaim, and thence to the Detroit Lions, where he was All-Pro.

"I guess that's why I remember those who stayed," said Reynolds. "We had gone through really a tough, tough time. It was like going through a war together."

Prinzi, the quarterback who was a Reynolds roommate, would remain particularly close to Reynolds in the years that followed.

"Vic tells me it was never again as tough as that first year," said Reynolds.

A fateful knee injury

Off a promising freshman season, Reynolds figured to be a starter in 1955.

"I was running No. 1," he said. "During the second week of fall practice, my knee went out.

"I didn't know what to do. I decided to go back home, to West Palm Beach. There I would make a mistake I would regret the rest of my life. I went to a surgeon, and he said the knee needed surgery."

Years later a famed specialist would operate on the damaged knee and suggest that the previous work looked like that of a butcher.

Active in little theater while home in West Palm Beach, Reynolds went to New York and embarked on an acting career. Soon he was in Hollywood, his foot in the door but little more.

Away two seasons, he returned to Florida State football in 1957. He had stopped in town to see a girl and had decided to go by Nugent's home. The coach suggested he come back out for football.

Writing about Reynolds in 1954, I had been intrigued by his running style. When he returned in 1957, he dropped by the Tallahassee Democrat. He told me he could not get football out of his system. Moreover, he said, he was tired of those Hollywood phonies.

Off to a 1-2 start in 1957, the Seminoles

That's the way Burt Reynolds looked in his Seminole uniform, on the opposite page. Above, Reynolds visits the FSU sideline in 1970, after his Hollywood star was on the rise.

knew the pressure was rising as they came home to face a good N.C. State team.

"I was now, after that knee operation, about two or three steps too slow," said Reynolds. "I had been running around, trying to be an actor, but I hadn't done anything to stay in shape.

"It would be a year I would like to forget. The guys when I came back thought differently than the earlier ones I had known. It would have been better had I never come back."

Florida State was playing N.C. State's two-touchdown favorites evenly when, suddenly, Dick Christy broke free with a pass reception and scored on a 47-yard play.

The halfback got behind Reynolds on the play.

Christy also, films would clearly show, got behind the sideline boundaries on the play. He went out of bounds — a move that made him an illegal receiver — and came back in, undetected by officials, for the big catch.

The play accounted for the only scoring. N.C. State won 7-0.

"At halftime, Nugent gave this speech to the team — and if we lost this game, he said, it would be Buddy Reynolds' fault," recalled Reynolds.

"No one could feel as bad as I felt. In the last half, I sat on the bench with no one within 20 yards of me. The guys stayed away from me.

"When it was over, I was devastated.

"And I thought, 'To hell with it.' I was not the football player I was, and never will be. So I would just move on."

'I was so enormously proud of the school'

There is a story of Reynolds being demoted to the B team before his departure. "It was lower than the B team," said the actor. "I would have been thrilled to be on the B team."

He recalls leaving for California with $80 in his pocket.

First he said goodbye to teammates who included Prinzi, Corso and Carmen Battaglia.

Reynolds recalls one among them saying: "Well, we'll see you in the movies."

After millions had seen him in the movies, Reynolds would look back at Florida State.

"The bad part is far outdistanced by the good memories," he said. "I am so enormous-

Burt Reynolds chuckles with FSU President Bernie Sliger in 1981, when he received an honorary degree...

... and cavorts with one of his leading ladies, Farrah Fawcett.

ly proud of the school and so many things it has done.

"When I see Terry Donahue (UCLA coach), he introduces me as 'This is the guy who played at Florida State — where they have one of the best coaches (Bobby Bowden),' and I am very proud of that."

He had, he said, some trepidations about seeing Nugent again at that 1985 reunion.

"But when I saw him," he said, "he was the same guy I saw that very first day when I knew I was coming to Florida State though I had signed with Miami."

The two threw their arms around each other.

"There were things about Nugent that were just unbelievable, in terms of his being ahead of his time," said Reynolds. "Throwing the ball the way he did, for one thing.

"And I remember the white shoes. We had white shoes when nobody else did."

Reynolds' notable identity with football never wavered.

"I never dreamed about Academy Awards or things like that," he said. "I always dreamed about scoring touchdowns, or coaching.

"Every dream I ever had — I guess you could call it a real fantasy — has always been in sports."

In his last football fling in 1957, Reynolds handled the ball on offense only five times — three runs, two pass receptions. Including his 1954 figures, his career statistics were 19 runs for 146 yards and a 7.7 average, six receptions for 76 yards, two touchdowns (both on runs). On defense, he had one interception.

Meanwhile, back in '55 . . .

In the third and fourth years of Nugent's time, 1955 and 1956, Florida State went 5-5 and 5-4-1 but closed each of those campaigns on hopeful notes.

It opened in 1955 with a 7-0 trimming of N.C. State. The huge Feamster scored on a 49-yard pass after quarterback Len Swantic faked brilliantly before throwing. Feamster also sparkled defensively, along with Corso (two interceptions).

Whereupon, the Seminoles lost four straight as toughening schedules started exacting a price. Only one of the four setbacks was close, Virginia Tech winning 24-20 in the inaugural of a long and lively series that often saw strange happenings hindering the Seminoles.

An odd development in this one saw Flori-

da State, trailing 21-7, attempt an onside kick — and Bill Proctor, a fine tackle who also kicked, miss the ball with his toe.

Three heavyweights — Miami, Georgia, Georgia Tech — romped over the Seminoles.

Corso particularly remembered a big Georgia fullback romping over him as the Bulldogs came to Campbell Stadium for the second straight year. Then a 5-9, 142-pound defensive back, Corso had tried to stop him. "He broke my nose, chipped my teeth, blackened both eyes, and left size-24 cleat marks on my chest." Final score: 47-14.

A merciful open date followed as a 1-4 team licked its wounds.

"And then we threw that get-right party," Nugent recalled.

On the Monday following the open date — the Monday just before the game with Villanova in Campbell on Saturday — the players were dressed in sweatsuits as coaches huddled them into buses. Anticipating a workout someplace in secluded woods that would perhaps make any previous practices pale by comparison, they were silent as the buses drove away.

The destination indeed was secluded — the Silver Lake area outside of town. Upon arrival, players were marched into a building.

Thereupon, a band from crosstown Florida A&M, Larry Smith and his Knights of Swing, cut loose with "Shake, Rattle and Roll." And for two hours, players and coaches cut it all loose as the band rocked on and a feast of barbecue and all the trimmings was devoured.

"It humanized the coaching staff," said Corso, who years later as a coach would on occasion use the same psychological ploy.

Florida State then won four of its last five, starting with a 16-13 decision over Villanova — a rocking defensive struggle.

Vince Gibson emerged as a considerable hero.

With Villanova leading 13-9 as the last quarter started, Gibson fell on a foe fumble at the Villanova 4. But four FSU offensive endeavors had been futile, and Villanova took over at its 1.

Thereupon, Gibson knocked the ball loose as quarterback Bill Magee tried to squirm through the line — with Leo Baggett covering the fumble in the end zone for the touchdown that won it.

"They had a big split in their line," recalled Gibson. "I jumped in that gap, hit the quarterback clean and knocked the ball out of his hands.

"With that ball rolling there in the end

zone, Baggett and I jumped on it at the same time for the touchdown.

"But after the touchdown, I let Baggett have the ball. He jumped up, waving the ball.

"And a sorry sports writer I know gave Baggett all the credit."

Said sorry sports writer quickly followed up with a correction in the Tallahassee Democrat, but Gibson never forgot the original error. Perhaps the most incredible part of all that was Gibson permitting Baggett to have the ball, for Bowden's old Birmingham buddy was never shy about drawing attention to himself.

In the mud at Hattiesburg, strong Southern Mississippi mashed FSU 21-6, the only loss in the last five starts. But again FSU fans were left smiling after a closing 26-7 road victory over a Tampa team that had gone into the game with a 7-1 record.

It was the last game for Bob Crenshaw, a spirited and inspirational leader, a 155-pounder who played center and, along with Don Powell, served as a captain of that 1955 team.

Three years later, Crenshaw died in a crash of an Air Force jet he piloted. Every year since his death, a trophy — the Crenshaw Award — has gone to a player voted by his teammates "the Seminole with the fightingest heart."

By virtue of the Tampa victory, Florida State had broken even in its first season of NCAA recognition as a major school in football.

And by virtue of extensive, varied maneuvering, it had been the year in which football with the University of Florida was finally ordained.

The pressure mounts: Schedule Florida!

"The game was going to happen sooner or later," said Coyle Moore, the FSU dean. "Some of us just made it happen sooner."

Precisely who made it happen, in a day when the Sunshine Law was not a Florida statute, is difficult to say. Clearly, many played a role. The many included Gov. LeRoy Collins, Wilson Carraway (powerful and effective state senator from Tallahassee), Coyle Moore Jr. (president of the FSU student body, son of the dean), the two university presidents (Florida's J. Wayne Reitz and FSU's Doak Campbell), and Fred Kent (chairman of the Board of Control).

Surely, the *threat* of legislative action that would force the series was a compelling factor.

In February of 1955 the Board of Control unanimously approved a report that became policy, directing the two schools to "initiate and maintain" relations in all sports. But there was no immediate football activity.

In April, a bill was introduced by Sen. Nick Connor of Inverness, entitled "an act to establish intercollegiate athletic relations between University of Florida and Florida State University in all major and minor sports."

The Senate, on April 26, voted down the bill 19-15, after two amendments — both advantageous to Florida — were tacked on.

But the handwriting was on the wall. Next time the vote might not be so close, and the bill might not be so disadvantageous to Florida State.

Gov. Collins became concerned. Though a firm Florida State fan, he did not perceive legislative action as a proper answer.

"I had heard the rumblings in the Legislature and always had discouraged them," he said, "because I felt it was not anything we should be passing laws to achieve.

"But the rumbles got so strong I felt something had to be done."

When Reitz, the Florida president, visited him on another matter, Collins spoke to him of his views.

"I told him I did not favor that sort of thing in the Legislature," he said. "I told him I thought the schools should work it out — and if they could not, to take it to the Board of Control for resolution.

"And I said I wanted it all resolved — the sooner the better.

"Dr. Reitz said he would consult some of his people back in Gainesville — that he would consider it.

"And the next thing I heard was that he had talked to Dr. Campbell and worked out an agreement that would be presented to the Board of Control.

"I was happy about that, and I expressed my appreciation."

Years later, said Collins, someone wrote that he had called Reitz to Tallahassee and demanded that he get the series started, and had made Reitz "toe the line."

Said Collins: "That was not at all the way it was."

In a letter to the Gainesville Sun many years later, Reitz recalled the conversation with Collins. The letter was written in reply to the suggestion that Collins had called Reitz in and "persuaded" him to inaugurate action.

"It was not his manner," wrote Reitz, "to call university presidents in his office and suggest how they should administer a university. Because of our friendship and his great interest in higher education, we visited from time to time when I would be in Tallahassee.

"I do recall his mentioning a bill which had been proposed by someone in the legislature — which would have required the University of Florida and Florida State University to play football. Governor Collins felt this was not an appropriate function for the legislature. I agree. But he made no request of me.

"What did happen was soon thereafter a member of the Board of Control suggested that it would be desirable for President Doak Campbell of Florida State University and me to discuss the possibility of the universities playing a game of football.

"In due course, we did discuss the issues and decided that a contest would be desirable and accordingly asked the two athletic directors to work out a contract."

Fred Kent recalled the mounting pressure.

"Both student bodies wanted the game," said the board chairman. "Alumni were after us on both sides. I was getting 10 phone calls a day. It was a very hot subject."

Collins suggested later that the board became involved late at the instigation of the two presidents.

"My guess is that the presidents got together and decided to play the game," he said. "But that they felt a decision of such broad and deep consequence should be made with the Board of Control. That gave the sense of a united front. Had there not been such a furor, I'm sure the presidents would have scheduled the game by themselves."

The details were worked out by the two athletic directors, Woodruff and Danford. Contracts would eventually find Florida State visiting Gainesville for the first six games. Woodruff would drive a hard bargain that included a minimal financial guarantee for the Seminoles, and stipulation that they play by the rules of the Southeastern Conference — and not just those of the NCAA.

1956: Year of the Renn

FSU fans awaited the 1956 season with great hope, primarily because of the advent of Bobby Renn.

Out of Henderson, N.C., he was cut out of the classic triple-threat pattern — a back who could run, pass and kick extremely well.

Renn could also play defense spectacularly well. As a Davidson freshman, he had tied an NCAA record for interceptions. After that single year, Renn had gone into the military and had played the game in Europe. Upon his dis-

charge in 1955, he transferred to Florida State and had put in the required year of residence before becoming eligible for FSU action in 1956.

With Corso now back at quarterback — and starting — following strong contribution as a halfback, FSU slammed Ohio University 47-7 in an opener as Renn ran for 90 yards.

At Georgia, a short Renn pass to Bob Nellums for a touchdown was rubbed out by a penalty as FSU fell 3-0. With 1:30 remaining in the game, Georgia won on a Ken Cooper field goal of 43 yards — a distance then considered prohibitive.

"Cooper's was a field goal you simply did not kick in those days," said Nugent years later.

On rib injuries received at Georgia, Renn was out for three games.

Corso heroics beat N.C. State 14-0. He scored on a 35-yard run and set up a second touchdown with a 60-yard punt return. Throughout his time, Corso was a particularly dangerous punt returner.

But what might have been a big season tailed off to a final 5-4-1 as only Villanova (20-13), Furman (42-7) and Southern Mississippi (20-19) fell the remainder of the way.

Southern Mississippi had come to Tallahassee with a 7-0 record and 13 straight victories.

Buck Metts, a fine halfback of that era, had sent Florida State winging toward an upset with a 40-yard scoring run with an interception. Doug Barfield — later head coach of Auburn — scored twice for Southern, tying the game at 13-13. After Renn reached behind himself for a scoring catch of a Swantic pass to make it 20-13, Southern drove and scored but an extra-point try was muffed on a high snap — and a 20-19 FSU victory was preserved.

Auburn, in a closing game, edged an injury-riddled FSU team 13-7 despite Renn's 104 rushing yards.

A haunting play evolved when Auburn, leading in the first half 7-0, kicked off after its touchdown. Billy Odom, possibly the fastest Seminole of the first 10 years, fielded the ball at the 4 — and suddenly seemed free for a scoring run.

Troy Barnes, a center who had moved downfield, found no one in front of him, and suddenly wheeled around, apparently looking for someone to block. As he did so, he moved right into Odom's path. The collision knocked Odom almost unconscious.

Few FSU fans liked that finish, but Nugent

Just as many would acclaim Bobby Renn (right) the Seminoles' best all-round back through Florida State's first three decades of modern football, so would many view Fred Pickard (above) the best runner.

liked the overall look of his Seminoles that year. "This was a good football team," he said. "It had heart."

1957: Call it a rebuilding year

Not such a good football team was the one of 1957. "This could be the year of upsets," said Nugent then, looking to a schedule that would include the first-ever Tallahassee visits of Auburn and Miami, but upsets eluded the Seminoles.

Before the 1957 season, Florida State had made the unique move of designating a "Department of Football," and Nugent had been given the additional title of "Director of Football."

The short-lived concept seems to have been viewed as a way to avoid historic friction between athletic directors and head football coaches. Don Veller recalled an afternoon tea, with Dean Ralph Eiman the host, where he had mentioned, in jest, the possibility of a separate football department.

"They took it seriously," he said. "The next

week, they had such a department, and named Nugent its director."

Plans were announced in the fall for Campbell Stadium expansion to 30,000 seats.

On the field, there was a shortage of depth — and experienced quarterbacks. It was to be a building year, with a shift of Renn to quarterback not working out.

On FSU's first football play of 1957, Renn swept around end against Furman and scored on a 37-yard run — but, alas, the play had been flagged. And though FSU bounced Furman 27-7, it was much as though the season had been flagged.

Three straight losses followed — Boston College, Villanova, N.C. State — the latter that memorable 7-0 game that saw Dick Christy go out of bounds, then streak by Burt Reynolds for the game's only touchdown.

FSU rallied, knocking off Abilene Christian 34-7 as Renn ran for 150 yards, and Virginia Tech 20-7, with Fred Pickard running 81 yards for the last touchdown.

"On Monday, we'll put the tutors on that

58

Meet the I-formation. First the quarterback (Bobby Renn), then the fullback (Eddie Johnson), then the righthalf (Billy Weaver), and the lefthalf (Stan Dobosz).

boy," said a smiling Nugent of Pickard, a sophomore who was having grade problems.

As Renn would be acclaimed by many the Seminoles' best all-round back through Florida State's first three decades of modern football, Pickard would be viewed the best runner.

At 5-foot-8 and 165 pounds, Pickard had unusual balance. Florida State had initially given him a scholarship only because a coveted lineman — long ago forgotten — from Columbia, Tenn., had insisted on his "little buddy" getting one as a condition of his coming.

But Pickard's sophomore development was hardly enough. After Virginia Tech, the Seminoles lost three straight — to Miami, Southern Mississippi, and an 8-0 Auburn team ranked No. 2 nationally that won in Tallahassee 29-7.

Florida State salvaged a 21-7 victory at Tampa and waited for 1958 and a first game with Florida.

A big win: Tennessee in '58

Vic Prinzi, sidelined for 13 straight games after requiring surgery for a damaged spleen, would return for a senior year at quarterback and be a considerable key in a vintage season.

At the start, Tennessee Tech fell 22-7 and Furman 42-6 before Georgia Tech brought FSU up short 17-3. FSU was 3-1 following a 27-24 triumph over Wake Forest.

At Jacksonville, Georgia dealt a second loss, 28-13, before Florida State embarked on one of its brightest stretches.

On Oct. 18 one of Virginia Tech's better teams got lashed 28-0 in Tallahassee.

On Oct. 25 in Knoxville, Florida State registered one of its biggest victories of all time, a stunning 10-0 upset of Tennessee.

It would be the only meeting between these two in FSU's first 40 years of modern-day football, and Nugent's recollection is that Florida State was a late replacement for Maryland.

"But because of a black player that was on Maryland's roster, Tennessee called off the game in the spring of 1957 when it found out about it," said Nugent. "That was how we ended up on their schedule."

It had been billed as a quarterbacking duel of the Majors brothers — FSU's Joe, a transfer from Alabama, and Tennessee's Billy. Joe held up his part, but Billy was sidelined after a first-quarter injury. All members of the famed Majors football family were on hand, save father Shirley, busy as coach of Sewanee.

And Florida State had been billed, by a Knoxville Journal columnist, as a "second-rate gridiron power."

After a scoreless first half, Florida State

marched from its 11, Pickard getting 51 on one burst up the middle, and Johnny Sheppard booting a 26-yard field goal for 3-0.

An interception by linebacker Al Ulmer soon set up FSU at the Tennessee 28. Following a Joe Majors pass to Tony Romeo near the goal, Renn scored. A Prinzi interception canceled Tennessee's only real threat thereafter. The hard running of Pickard — 133 yards on 22 carries — had exceeded Tennessee's entire offensive total, by 22 yards.

"And you let that little son-of-a-*bleep* run all over you!" shouted Coach Bowden Wyatt to his Vols in the dressing room just after.

But Wyatt was gracious in his more formal postgame utterances, praising the quality of Florida State players and their effort.

Thousands of welcoming fans — among them Gov. LeRoy Collins — swarmed Tallahassee's old airport at Dale Mabry Field as FSU's chartered flight returned from what some still consider the Seminoles' biggest victory of all time. Estimated at 3,000, that crowd would dwarf most such in the years that followed.

"The Tennessee game, really, has to be No. 1 during my time at Florida State," said Nugent. "It meant so much to the school and to the fans."

It is questionable whether Florida writers chronicled that Seminole all-timer as well as they might have.

Most had been well entertained until 4 a.m. the night prior by Gus Manning, the Tennessee sports-information director. They nursed headaches, to say the least, as the early-afternoon game rolled around all too soon. One Florida writer, from one of the state's larger newspapers, was in particularly bad shape as he sat in the pressbox about an hour before the kickoff. A member of Florida State's official group suggested to Manning that a little "hair of the dog" might assist him through the game.

Manning got the attention of a nearby security officer.

"See that fellow with the hat on about 20 rows down?" asked Manning, pointing for the benefit of the officer. "Well, he's got a bottle in his coat pocket, and that's illegal in this stadium."

The officer nodded, walked 20 rows down, and relieved the startled fan of the bottle. Then he brought it to Manning, who continued his extraordinarily hospitable role as he walked over and tapped the afflicted writer on the shoulder.

At homecoming, FSU whammed Tampa 43-0. Renn, in his final home game, checked in with two touchdowns that brought his point total to 99, making him the Seminoles' leading all-time scorer up to that point.

First Miami, then ... the Gators

Miami was 5-0 against Florida State, but the 1958 game was one in which many things would go right for the Seminoles.

Not long after the kickoff, Renn had gone back to punt on third down — in a day when third-down punts were sometimes considered smart. The snap sailed over his head, Renn covering the ball at the 2. On fourth down, he punted again — and Miami fumbled it away to the Seminoles.

A 42-yard Majors run on an interception off George McIntyre — later head coach of Vanderbilt — gave FSU a 7-0 lead.

One thing that did not go FSU's way was a brilliant bootleg run by Prinzi for a touchdown run that wasn't. On the play, Prinzi had faked out not only the defense, and pressbox viewers, but officials as well. The referee had blown the play dead as Prinzi sprinted toward the goal line.

That official walked over to Nugent, told him he had made a mistake that he could not change, and apologized.

Nugent told him to forget it — and the way things started going FSU's way again, he could surely afford to be gracious.

A second touchdown came on a Prinzi pass to Romeo — the ball bouncing off the big end's hands and into the eager mitts of Pickard, who scored. And in a game that saw Miami lead in first downs, 20 to 9, and in yardage, 309 to 176, Florida State beat the Hurricanes 17-6, and for the first time.

Four straight victories, unusually impressive, propelled Florida State toward Gainesville and an inaugural date with Florida, ranked No. 12 nationally.

Just before FSU, the Gators had a date with Arkansas State, coached by former FSU assistant Hugh "Bones" Taylor. The Gators bristled when a wire-service story said Nugent suggested Florida had made a deal with Taylor to run FSU plays. Actually, Nugent said, what he had told a quarterback club in DeLand was that UF coach Bob Woodruff had probably scheduled Arkansas State because it might run from the I-formation FSU favored. Florida racked Arkansas State 51-7.

At a campus barbecue before the first FSU-Florida game, a Gator adaptation of a popular ditty ("Hang Down Your Head, Tom Dooley") rang out a few times:

Hang down your head, Tom Nugent
Hang down your head and cry
Hang down your head, Tom Nugent
Good boy, you're going to die

Florida State would have 10,000 fans among the packed 42,000 in Florida Field.

Renn won the coin toss, and Florida State chose to receive.

Surely, no athletic rivalry ever had a more dramatic beginning.

Final score: Florida 21, Florida State 7

Jack Espenship gathered in the kickoff and then, according to plan, quickly handed the ball to Renn. Almost immediately, Renn broke free with a blocker — tackle Bob Swoszowski — in front of him.

As Renn ran, writers in the pressbox rose to their feet. Bill Beck, sports editor of The St. Petersburg Times, led an alarmed corps of Gator partisans with a cry: "Stop him — stop him!"

After a 78-yard run, Renn was stopped at the 15 by quarterback Jimmy Dunn.

"The play was return left," said Renn, years later. "Espenship was running full speed. His handoff almost knocked the wind out of me.

"I had wanted Swoszowski to commit himself — lunge right or left, or fall down. Anything to foul up Dunn."

But the tackle never committed and Dunn, as Renn said, played it perfectly.

Five plays later Pickard scored from the 1, and FSU led 7-0.

One of the game's big plays was not so obvious — a planned quick kick by Renn on which quarterback Prinzi was hurt. Suddenly, Prinzi was playing with a torn thigh muscle.

"I took the snap and was going to pitch back in the flat to Renn for the quick kick," said Prinzi. "But somebody was coming through over there, so I just ate the ball — and I took a shot on the thigh."

Prinzi stayed in the game. On the next play Dave Hudson, a big end, tore in to block a Renn punt, picked up the ball at the FSU 5 and scored easily, tying the game 7-7.

"The snap from center was a little high," recalled Prinzi. "But it could have worked out all right. I was supposed to block a man up the middle on the play. I feel like, if my leg had been right I could have done that and got back in time to throw Hudson off track as he rushed through. When I made contact with the guy up the middle, I could not push off. My leg wasn't hurting then, but I couldn't move right."

Three decades later, Prinzi and Nugent felt Florida State would have won had the quarterback remained healthy. FSU outgained Florida, 286 yards to 219, but five turnovers — three fumbles, two interceptions — were costly.

"I tried to come back in the second quarter, but I couldn't go," said Prinzi. "A lot of the game plan was built around what I could do. If I had not got hurt, I feel we could have scored two or three more touchdowns, and won."

Not long after Florida's first touchdown, Hudson intercepted a pass, blunting a deep FSU drive. Florida drove 89 yards, Dunn scoring from the 9 on fourth down. A fumble paved another Florida touchdown, Dunn getting this one from the 11, as Florida won 21-7.

Dunn was properly proclaimed the game's most valuable performer. A stringbean 142-pounder out of Tampa but a gifted athlete, Dunn had originally signed a Florida State scholarship. He said that FSU offered him

In the first play of the 1958 FSU-Florida game, Bobby Renn returned the kickoff 78 yards to the Gator 15-yard line, after . . .

only a partial one, and that when Florida later extended a full scholarship he took it.

As Florida went to the Gator Bowl — the winner of the FSU-Florida game would go to that bowl five of the first 10 years of the series — the Seminoles, now 7-3, accepted an invitation to the Bluegrass Bowl.

Nugent wanted to go to the Louisville bowl, but FSU's administration had opposed it, questioning the chance of breaking even financially on the venture. Florida State did not break even, and there were those who thought the decision hurt Nugent with FSU President Bob Strozier.

It was one more first for Florida State, however, as FSU went to Louisville to play Oklahoma State — the first FSU game televised nationally (ABC). Harry Wismer handled the play-by-play, with a totally unknown assistant named Howard Cosell doing the color.

One of the worst-weather bowls of all time, the ill-fated Bluegrass Bowl was played on a rock-hard field in sub-freezing weather with a high wind increasing the chill factor.

"Unbelievably cold," said Pickard.

Both teams wore tennis shoes, for better footing. Oklahoma State won easily, 15-6, and

it might have been by a bigger score. Just before halftime, end Ron Hinson on fourth down stopped a Cowboys runner a foot short of the goal.

Less than a month later, Nugent accepted Maryland's head-coaching job.

It was a strange development.

Farewell to Nugent

Nugent in 1958 had become athletic director, as well as head football coach, following the sudden, surprising resignation of Danford for personal reasons. Nugent's identity with the Florida climate seemed pronounced, and his large family well settled and happy in Tallahassee.

It seems probable that he had not intended to leave — at least, not at the time of the announcement, in Tallahassee, of his departure.

From a national coaches' convention, Nugent had advised Florida State by phone of Maryland's interest, and of his interest in that possibility.

One oft-repeated story was that Strozier announced Nugent was going to Maryland before the coach had actually accepted. There had been a brief movement in Nugent's behalf back in Tallahassee to turn things around, but it was too late.

The Tallahassee announcement by Strozier seems to have forced Nugent's decision. Soon there came another announcement — this time from Maryland. Nugent had accepted the job.

Years later, Nugent would return to Florida and the climate he so loved — first to Miami, later back to Tallahassee, and then to Indian Harbour Beach. Always, he seemed to look back fondly on Florida State and Tallahassee.

"They were the happiest of my 25 years in coaching," said Nugent of his six Florida State seasons.

"My last team there was a good one. They put it on the line."

The most memorable players of his time were Renn and Corso. When Renn died tragically several years later, he was generally hailed as FSU's best.

"Renn was one real polished football player," said Nugent, "and he was a good football player before we ever saw him.

"Corso played a lot of everything for us, and so well."

Nugent had brought a lot of things to Florida State, but notably a flamboyance that many would consider particularly significant

. . . Jack Espenship received the kickoff and slipped the ball to Renn.

Two Doaks: Doak Walker and Doak Campbell. One of the game's all-time backs, first with SMU and later in the NFL, Walker was a lecturer at one of Coach Nugent's acclaimed clinics.

as a young school sought a spot in the football sun.

"He brought to Florida State the greatest coaching clinics that ever existed anywhere — in the world!" said Harbison.

Vince Lombardi came to lecture. So did Bear Bryant, Bud Wilkinson, Bobby Dodd, Gen. Bob Neyland. And Blanton Collier, Bowden Wyatt, Bob Woodruff, Duffy Daugherty, Eddie Erdelatz, Sid Gillman, Murray Warmath.

Plus such NFL stars as Sammy Baugh, Otto Graham, Doak Walker.

Moving away would not be simple for the Nugent family. There were nine children. Their mother, Peggy, a former journalist, said their dairy delivery man would probably make the most fuss.

"I guess," she said, "he is crying in his milk right now."

The children, she said, were looking forward to the snow. "Me? I'm looking forward to a fur coat."

But the Nugents liked Tallahassee — liked Florida — and would one day return to the state.

"When Daddy says move, you move," said Peg Nugent in January of 1959.

"*C'est la guerre.*"

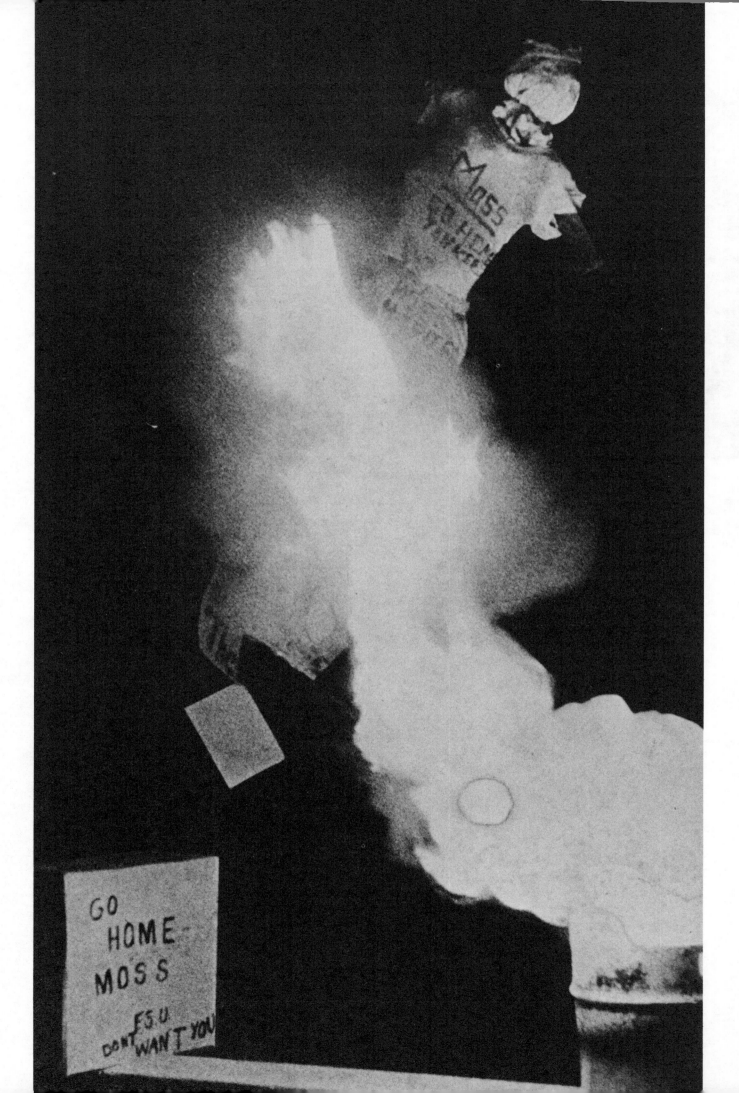

The Moss Year

A wandering coach stops for a season, raises hopes, falls short and moves on

He recalled a Thanksgiving Day when there was no food in the house.

A neighbor brought over what was left of the family's turkey, and it was not much, but they were glad to get it.

Perry Moss, in the clutches of the Great Depression and the Dust Bowl of his native Oklahoma, was as well acquainted with hunger early as he would be with football later.

"We were very poor," he said. "Many times there was no food. No electricity. My dad, like millions of others, could not get work."

To help the family survive, Perry and his brother delivered newspapers there in Tulsa, and with cloth bags slung over their shoulders sold Liberty magazines for a nickel apiece.

Perhaps the hunger — the insecurity of those early days — stayed with the two brothers.

Les Moss quit school at 16 to go into professional baseball, and he was a major-league catcher (St. Louis Browns) by the time he was 19. He would catch in the majors for many years, then coach and manage all over. He managed the Detroit Tigers prior to Sparky Anderson.

Perry Moss, by 1987, had held 20 coaching jobs in football — surely a record.

In 1959 he became Florida State's fourth head coach.

---

4 wins, 6 losses

Perry Moss in 1959.

Already he had been an assistant at five schools — Illinois, Washington, LSU, Miami, Wisconsin.

As a player, he had quarterbacked Tulsa to an Orange Bowl victory, then entered military service and played more, after which he transferred to Illinois and quarterbacked that team to a Big Ten title and the Rose Bowl. He played in the College All-Star game, and he played one year with the Green Bay Packers.

His time with the Seminoles was short indeed. One troubled season. But many years later the memory of Florida State haunted him.

"I should have stayed," he said. "I believe we could have had great success. FSU was on the verge. I regret leaving.

"Fate, or whatever, changes your whole life."

Indeed. Fate had played an interesting role in getting the Florida State job for Moss in the first place.

Ray Graves could have been Florida State's head football coach in 1959. Then a well-regarded first lieutenant to Bobby Dodd at Georgia Tech, Graves was interviewed in Jacksonville, and some FSU committeemen had the impression he was definitely coming. But he turned it down. A year later, he became Florida's coach.

Bill Peterson also could have been Florida State's head football coach in 1959. Then one of Paul Dietzel's top aides at LSU, which had just finished a national-championship season, Peterson was off recruiting when contacted and could not come for an interview. A year later, he became Florida State's coach.

A warm welcome: This is the reception Coach Moss got on the FSU campus right after the Seminoles lost 42-0 at Georgia in 1959.

At the time, however, Moss seemed just about ideal for Florida State.

He was young, with a versatile and enormously successful background. He had the reputation then, as years later, of a brilliant tactician.

Success had been associated with every Moss move.

And there was more.

At Illinois, he had won the Swede Nelson Award, a national trophy for sportsmanship. Quarterbacking against Iowa in a 0-0 tie, Moss had Illinois driving. Suddenly, just before the snap of the ball, an Iowa guard fainted. Instead of taking advantage of the situation, Moss called a timeout.

'I guarantee you'

He was 33 when he came to Florida State.

"Wanting to win, and that sort of thing, I was probably too impatient," said Moss. "And I had some lack of coaching expertise."

Moss was very quick on the trigger. His decisions often seemed lightning-like, without due care. His impatience was pronounced.

He was confident, and sometimes too swift to express that, too.

"We could have the finest record that a Florida State team has ever had," said Moss during the summer of '59, though he suggested luck and injuries could alter that possibility.

"We shall start spring practice on Sept. 1 expecting to win 10 games."

He would win four — The Citadel, Virginia Tech, Richmond, Tampa — in a luckless season of many injuries.

For years after his departure, fans would recall a Moss declaration at the traditional Kickoff Luncheon. Held for many years on the Wednesday before FSU's opening game, the luncheon always attracted hundreds of fans. Part of the tradition called for the coach to introduce players, and to offer hopeful opinion on the season ahead.

"I guarantee you," Moss told that luncheon, in praise of his secondary, "no one will get behind these guys all season long."

And then, in the first game — before an aroused Campbell Stadium crowd — Norm Snead threw two touchdown passes on those scintillating defenders. Wake Forest, down 20-9, rallied to win 22-20 as an FSU fumble at its 20 presented splendid opportunity for the visitors — one that quickly brought a decisive touchdown.

Moss had assembled coaches he later would say constituted "the best young staff"

In 1959 — when bananas were 10 cents a pound, a four-bedroom house $18,650, Florida State's best football ticket $4 — Perry Lee Moss drew a salary of $14,000 as FSU's fourth head football coach. And the introduction of the 2-point conversion was one year old.

he was ever around in all his many years at the game.

The staff included Don James, John Coatta and Vince Gibson. Later, James would be head coach at Kent State and the University of Washington, Coatta head coach of Wisconsin and Mankato State, Gibson head coach of Kansas State, Louisville and Tulane. Another Moss aide, Ken Shipp, was later head coach of the New York Jets.

But in 1959 these men were relative beginners in the profession. Surely they were not as good then as they would be.

Harbison was the lone coach Moss retained off Nugent's staff. For a time he appeared headed to Maryland with Nugent, who had extended an offer, but Harbison decided to remain for family reasons.

"I've said it many times — Harbison was one of the best football coaches I've ever been around," said Moss.

Years later, Harbison would recall the workouts of that single Moss year as the most demanding he had ever been around

"We held the toughest spring practice I've ever experienced," Moss himself had said during the summer of '59.

But high expectations that year were perhaps never realistic.

The first 1-point loss

Only seven seniors lined up in September. Among them were Al Ulmer, an extraordinary but small (5-10, 178) guard; quarterback Joe Majors, who would check in as the school's all-time leading passer through that year; and Fred Pickard, the small but superb runner.

"One helluva football player," said Moss of Pickard, identifying him as the most memorable one of his single season. "A great runner. Totally dedicated. Always kept on going. Pickard was something else.

"He was one of those guys who had no real

talent. Out of high school, you would not have signed him.

"But, ah, he could run well enough to win games for you. He had the concentration, the determination — the basic things that only come out when it gets to the point you've got to get the job done."

A good start was imperative in 1959, if Florida State was to have the good year. Five of the final seven games were on the road, but the first three — Wake Forest, The Citadel, Miami — would be at home.

The Seminoles might well have won all three, but in fact won only one — Citadel.

A pair of 7-6 games, back to back, proved to be crushers.

Oddly, a 7-6 loss to Miami in Tallahassee seemed to some less depressing than a 7-6 victory over Virginia Tech in Blacksburg.

After the latter game, it was as though, for the first time, this team stared reality in the face — and blinked.

Reality included mounting injuries on a team that had been short of depth in the first place.

Moss considered the Miami game particularly pivotal.

"We should have — and could have — won it," said Moss, "and it would have put a different outlook on everything."

Moss wanted to beat Miami in the worst way, having coached there. Don James felt similarly, having quarterbacked there.

At center Miami lined up Jim Otto, who would be all-pro so many years with the Oakland Raiders, and at quarterback Fran Curci, later head coach of Tampa, Miami and Kentucky.

Miami dominated the first half — notably on defense — but led only 7-0. In the waning minutes of the fourth quarter, FSU drove from midfield to a touchdown that Pickard scored from 8 yards out.

Florida State went for 2 points — and the victory. Pickard swept wide on a run and was stopped at the goal line by defender Jim Crawford. FSU fans would long insist that Pickard had gone over the line, had scored the 2-pointer. Years later, Pickard would say it was close and might have been called either way. In retrospect, Pickard said that it might have been better to play for the 7-7 tie, that the resulting downer adversely affected him — and the team — for a long while.

"We had worked several weeks on that specific 2-point situation, and that play," said Moss.

"Pickard had worked long and hard in the game, and he was tired. If he had not been tired, he may have scored standing up."

It was the first 1-point loss in Florida State history, and for Moss it was surely the most memorable game of his short time.

"As long as I live, I'll never forget that loss," said Moss almost 30 years later.

"I had worked on Andy Gustafson's staff at Miami. He and I respected each other, though I'm not sure he liked me too much.

"Probably, we prepared too hard for Miami — over prepared, put all our eggs in one basket.

"But we almost did it."

Clearly, the loss deflated Florida State. And soon, injuries deflated many players.

"A game or two after that," recalled Moss, "we lost all our linebackers."

From bad to worse

At Virginia Tech's homecoming, the Seminoles won in a striking parallel to the manner of their loss to Miami. Trailing 7-0, Virginia Tech scored late — and failed on a 2-point try, as Tony Romeo and Bill Brown smothered the runner.

Bud Whitehead, the versatile Marianna native who later would have a long NFL career as a cornerback, intercepted three Virginia Tech passes on an afternoon that saw FSU defenders swipe seven.

Despite the victory, the mood was melancholy on the team's return flight to Tallahassee. A triumph over a difficult opponent — always, in Blacksburg, Virginia Tech seemed among the toughest of teams — seemed somehow like a loss.

Perhaps the awareness that the offense had netted only 106 yards, and no defense could come up with seven interceptions every game, accounted for part of the depression.

In the remaining six games, FSU would be scoreless in two and get only one touchdown in two others. Richmond fell 22-6 midway, and in a final game Tampa went down 33-0.

Moss noted, prior to a date at Georgia, his decimated ranks. "We have so few players — probably less than any major school in the country." And at Georgia, the Seminoles would utilize only 24 players — about half Georgia's 46.

In desperation, Moss had closed practices while installing elements of a new offense — the split-line T attack devised by the great Jake Gaither at Florida A&M. But FSU had neither the time nor the personnel to make something new go.

Georgia romped 42-0 with a lineup that

included Fran Tarkenton, soon to achieve far bigger fame as the scrambling quarterback of the Minnesota Vikings.

"Really, despite the circumstances, I had thought we could play with Georgia," said Moss, "but I underestimated Georgia.

"I never will forget we played our first team for nine minutes, then took our first team out to rest — it was so hot up there — and they scored two quick touchdowns on us. That changed the ball game.

"Looking back on it, I could have done a lot of things differently that year."

After Georgia, things went from bad to much worse.

An open date preceded homecoming against William and Mary. Extra time, it seemed, for the wounded to mend.

But nothing helped.

During this period Moss received — and accepted — an offer, incredible for the time, to coach the Montreal Alouettes in the Canadian Football League. Announcement would be made at the end of the season.

"Montreal gave me an offer triple my $14,000 FSU salary," said Moss years later. "They gave me a 5-year contract, with the titles of managing director and general manager, as well as coach. Also, they gave me 5-percent ownership of the team.

"I wasn't really interested in going to Canada. But they came up with an awful lot. It was the only way I would have gone up there."

Though Moss and Montreal were mum at the time, word got around. The city and the state were awash with rumors.

'No comment' meant Moss was long gone

Whatever the faults of Moss, he had always seemed extraordinarily candid, completely open.

He was asked about the reports concerning Montreal.

"No comment," said Moss.

It was, in my view, the equivalent of acknowledging that he was bound for Montreal, and that was reflected in the Tallahassee Democrat. On the day before the homecoming game, the Democrat reported he was definitely going.

On campus, Moss was hung in effigy before homecoming — and after homecoming. The actions reflected more than disappointment in a losing season — they were also the symbol of outrage that Moss had accepted a new position with three games to go, including the big one with Florida.

The homecoming game itself was surely among the most depressing FSU would ever know.

William and Mary came in 3-5, a two-touchdown underdog. William and Mary won 9-0.

The following week in Gainesville, Florida was more than a two-touchdown favorite.

But Florida, ahead 18-0 at one point, won only 18-8 in Bob Woodruff's last game as coach. Some said later that failure to whip Florida State's depleted team by more than 10 points contributed significantly to the decision to terminate Woodruff's contract.

Under the circumstances, Florida State's effort that day may rank with its all-time best.

"We went down to Florida with 27 players, I think," said Moss.

Pickard was not one who would play. He had damaged an ankle and a knee in practice.

"We didn't warm up because we had so few players," said Moss. "Well, we did warm up our quarterbacks and our snapper in the dressing room.

"But part of that was a psychological thing — to stress we were saving everything for a total effort in the game.

"We did not go out on that field until it was time to play."

Florida took an early 6-0 lead, and that remained the halftime score after a Florida State tying touchdown was rubbed out on a holding penalty. Majors had provided an opportunity with a 39-yard run, then passed to Whitehead for the 6-pointer that was nullified. Soon after, a Ken Cone interception at Florida's 20 provided another chance, but nothing came of that either.

An interception off Majors precipitated a 12-0 game in the third quarter, and Florida made it 18-0 with less than five minutes left in the game. Majors passed and ran the Seminoles to a touchdown and 2-pointer.

Florida State perhaps had played as well as it possibly could, under the circumstances, and the press applauded "courageous cripples."

As quickly as it reasonably could, Florida State moved to replace Moss.

Like Nugent in his final season, Moss had served as athletic director and football coach. Before the Florida game, FSU announced that Vaughn Mancha — then an assistant coach on the Columbia University staff — would be FSU's new athletic director.

Too late, FSU's offense came alive. In the last game, Majors passed for 313 yards — Whitehead catching nine of his 20 completions — as the Seminoles totaled 503 yards in a 33-0 conquest of Tampa.

"It was a good football team," said Moss many years later, "but we had no depth. And it was a disappointing season.

"I thought we got some things headed in the right direction, including the coaching staff."

Moss went on in many directions.

After three years in Montreal, his football-coaching pilgrimage found him at Green Bay as an assistant, thence to Charleston (W. Va.) in the Continental League as head coach, to head coach of the Orlando Panthers in the Continental League, to head coach of Marshall University, to assistant with the Chicago Bears, to assistant at Green Bay again, to the San Antonio Wings in the World Football League as head coach, to assistant at Kentucky, to assistant with the Ottawa Roughriders, to assistant with the Buffalo Bills, to assistant with the Orlando Renegades of the United States Football League and to assistant at Central Florida. In the summer of 1987, Moss was also an assistant with the Pittsburgh Gladiators of the Arena Football League.

Perhaps a rolling Moss gathers no stones. Or, at least, fewer stones.

But Moss, for all his travels, had found a home, and the same one for 20 years. It was near Orlando, not so far from the home his brother Les — his only surviving relative from that Oklahoma family — had known for 35 years. "I'm sure I'm settled now," he said in 1987.

Swiftly, after that closing 1959 game in Tampa, Moss left for Canada, and swiftly Florida State named a successor.

His name was Bill Peterson.

But it would be a little while before there was any dancing in the streets.

Bud Whitehead intercepted three passes in a 7-6 victory at Virginia Tech. A versatile back, he starred under three coaches — Nugent, Moss and Peterson — and played for several years in the NFL.

The Peterson Years

A passy flashing game — uh, a flashy passing game — puts FSU on the map

After the first three games of 1962, Florida State was not only unbeaten but also unscored upon.

During all of this season, the team would lose only 11 fumbles.

But on the night of Oct. 5 in the Orange Bowl, the Seminoles would lose six fumbles — all in Miami territory — and the toughest kind of game, 7-6.

In the dressing room, Bill Peterson spoke a few quiet words, trying to calm his distraught players, endeavoring to get their chins off their chests.

And then, wrapping up: "Let's say our prayer, and get out of this place."

He told someone to turn out the lights, which was unusual, and there was total quiet in the somber dressing room as the team awaited the familiar Lord's Prayer.

Peterson began:

"Now I lay me down to sleep. . . ."

Realizing he had reverted to the bedroom-darkened prayer of his childhood, Peterson turned toward his quarterback: "You take it, Feely."

And Eddie Feely started anew: "Our Father, who art in heaven. . . ."

For 11 seasons, Florida State fans laughed and cried with Bill Peterson, perhaps as with no other. He had a high talent for mixing up words and phrases while challenging individuals — players, coaches, politicians, fans, col-

62 wins, 42 losses, 11 ties

Bill Peterson at FSU.

lege presidents — to produce more than they thought they reasonably could.

While the "Now I lay me down to sleep" story has become a classic of a kind, not so many tell the story of that being the last team of Peterson's ever to lose to Miami. His Seminoles would beat the Hurricanes five straight times thereafter — and each time in the Orange Bowl.

He would also beat the Georgia Bulldogs four straight times — every time he played them. The last time, in 1965, was ample for Coach Vince Dooley, who would decline repeated overtures thereafter to schedule Florida State.

Just because he mixed up words — sometimes much in the manner of an endearing character, Mrs. Malaprop, in an 18th-century play called "The Rivals" — surely did not mean Peterson was unaware.

"Florida State is two years ahead of everybody else in college, the way it does things," praised Al Davis, the shrewd coach and general manager of the NFL's Raiders, in a Sports Illustrated story of 1965.

But writers sometimes compared Peterson to baseball's great and wise Casey Stengel, who also had a memorable way of putting language in a blender and turning the thing on full speed. "Petersonisms" or "Petersonese" became the stuff of stories that his former assistants spread through the land. One of these coaches — Bobby Jackson, an assistant with the San Diego Chargers in 1987 — collected them and considered writing a book.

Peterson was hardly non-stop with his classic utterances. You might be around him for weeks and not pick up one. Many, though

Those bald heads are a dead giveaway: These are the Seven Magnificents, defensive stars from Peterson's era. From left, they're end George D'Alessandro, tackle Frank Pennie, linebacker Dick Hermann, middle guard Jack Shinholser, linebacker Bill McDowell, tackle Avery Sumner and end Terry Garvin.

not all, seemed to come in stressful and excited circumstances.

Some he tended to repeat. FSU's Doak Campbell Stadium was sometimes Doak *Walker* Stadium, and there were frequent references to the *Atlantic* Falcons and the *Biltmore* Colts.

You could, indeed, write a book. And if a few of the many tales are not precise in documentation, if a couple perchance are the uncut gems of others, then surely many Peterson originals have been credited to others or fallen through the cracks of time, and let us pray it all evens up.

But, for most of the stories, some among us were there to hear, to enjoy, to remember and maybe to pass on to our grandchildren.

Hang loose, as away we go with 50 such.

A pocketful of Petersonisms

• Admonishing players before a game at Kentucky: "I didn't bring you guys up here on a two-plane engine for nothing."

• "Fred Biletnikoff's limitations are limitless. He's footsure and fancy free."

• Talking to a pro scout about the limitations of another receiver: "He hears footprints."

• Summation of a close, winning game: "Whew, this was the cliffdweller to end all cliffdwellers!"

• On favorable crowd reaction to a speech he made: "They gave me a standing observation."

• Talking sternly to his team of the intense approach to practice prior to a Florida game: "I guarantee you they are down there just blocking their chips — uh, chopping their lock. I mean, licking their chops."

• "I've always had a great repertoire with my players."

• Doing color on radio broadcast of FSU-Pittsburgh game that matched Hugh Green and Ron Simmons: "It's going to be a great football game, fans, for tonight we got the two nations' greatest linemen." And in later game: "Florida State lost all of its minimum just before halftime." Similarly, he once spoke of a Final Four basketball game: "North Carolina blew it when Dean Smith went to that five-corner offense too soon, and they lost all their minimum."

• "The greatest thing just happened. I got indicted into the Florida Sports Hall of Fame."

• "Let a dead horse rest."

• Excited and angered, making a point on his authority: "I'm the football around here — and don't you remember it!"

In 1960 — when a six-pack of frozen orange juice was 89 cents, 10 pieces of take-out chicken $1.99, Florida State's best football ticket $5 — William Edward Peterson drew a starting salary of $14,000 as FSU's fifth head football coach. And the return to unlimited substitution was five years away.

• Using a David-and-Goliath analogy to make a point with his squad, according to Jackson, before workouts the week of a Florida game: "David needed some help, and he went out and got this sling and some rocks. And he practiced. Just like you guys, he didn't like to practice, but he kept at it so he could be good. You gotta practice. David just went out there and practiced and practiced and practiced — slinging those rocks at tin cans and old beer bottles for days and days and days."

• "Nobody goes to the Silver Slipper anymore. It's too crowded."

• "She played tennis, you know, at Wilmington."

• Dressing down Jackson, during his time on the FSU staff, for the nature of his recruiting in his native Georgia: "How in the world could you sign that guy — he doesn't even assemble a football player! I know what you've been doing. You've been hanging around with your crownies up there, and not recruiting like you should."

• "You guys pair off in groups of threes, then line up in a circle."

• Painting a glowing picture to his not-greatly-enthusiastic team before the trip to the 1966 Sun Bowl at El Paso, a city within sprinting distance of the border and the attractions of Juarez: "Each of you players will receive a nice piece of Seminite luggage. We're going to have a grand time but I don't want you guys getting in trouble over there in Warsaw."

• "He has one of those naggravating injuries that just seem to hang on."

• "Let's nip this thing in the butt."

• Trying to fire up the team by citing a historic precedent prior to a big game: "Just remember the words of Henry Patrick — 'Kill me, or let me live.'"

- "Don't look a sawhorse in the mouth."
- Always upset when an assistant left for another school, Peterson admonished one: "Just remember, buddy, our crosses will path again!"
- "Like two ships that crash in the night."
- At halftime: "Things are not going good out there, and they've got our walls to the back. But we've got to keep our cools."
- After gallant but losing effort: "We can hang our heads high."
- Angrily talking to his team after a disappointing, costly 1969 loss to Memphis State, Peterson abruptly stops. Then he softly tells the team to "hit a knee" (kneel). Turning to end Ronnie Wallace, an aspiring minister, he says: "Lead us in a few words of silent prayer."
- Describing versatile quarterback Tommy Warren: "He's a trick of all trades."
- "Fools fall in where angels fear to tread."
- Hearing that players were stuffing themselves on doughnuts at the school cafeteria during a period when the training table was inactive, Peterson assembled the squad and said: "I've talked to a nutritionist, and I wanta tell you guys something. Three things are bad for you. I can't remember the first two, but the third is doughnuts."
- "He has a chronicle knee injury."
- Helping a photographer on press day: "You guys line up alphabetically by height."
- To an assistant who had been exercising during lunch hour: "Where have you been — out bogging?"
- Pregame instructions: "When the coins go out for the toss of the captains. . . ."
- On his wife's new endeavor to lose weight: "She's joined one of those Night Watchers Clubs."
- Preseason words to new freshmen: "You can't become a football overnight — you've got to work at it!"
- "It's cold outside, and be sure to put your ear muffins on."
- To players, on taboo items in dormitory: "No guns at any time in the dorm — we don't want any huntermen around here!"
- "Don't burn your bridges at both ends."
- When someone asked if he thought it would rain: "What do you think I am — a geologist!"
- "Recruiting top football players — that's the crutch of the problem."
- On playing style: "We're going to throw the football, come high or hell water. We're not gonna be any three-clouds-and-a-yard-of-dust kind of team."

- "In this game of football, you've got to pipe the payer."
- To players before a key game: "We can beat this team. All we have to do is capitalize on our mistakes."
- "You guys have to run a little more than full-speed out there."
- "You can observe a lot by just watching."
- On a hospitalized friend: "They gave him one of those E.G.G.s, and they got him in extensive care."
- "Let sleeping bags lie."
- Speaking of pursuing a grievance in the courts: "I'm seeing my lawyer, and this is gonna be a suit case."
- "Don't kill the goose that lays the deviled egg."
- "This is the greatest country in America."

A somewhat shocking transposition came on Peterson's television show following a 14-14 tie with Auburn in 1962.

Auburn's Tucker Frederickson had mishandled a punt, the ball bouncing off his shoulder pads, and Peterson was narrating the highlight play on his show.

Only thing, he reversed the first letters of "Tucker" and "Frederickson." Then, trying to make amends, he made the same highly embarrassing — and equally hilarious — mistake.

Whereupon, "Stop Tucker Frederickson" banners appeared around campus — the names' first letters also transposed.

Some stories are associated with Peterson's time with the Houston Oilers:
- "Men, I want you thinking of one word all season — just one word. That one word is 'Super Bowl.' "
- On proper decorum as the national anthem is played: "I want you men standing on your helmets with the sidelines under your arms."
- "We're not gonna take this standing down!"
- "That Oakland is tough. They *timidate* your offense, they *timidate* your defense, they even *timidate* the officials!"

The Peterson style sometimes seemed contagious. Very soon after Bud Adams hired him as coach of the Oilers, I saw him and his wife at a Super Bowl party in New Orleans.

"You've just got to meet this owner of the Oilers," said Marge Peterson. "Ad Budam is really something."

A story for every occasion

Peterson had a lively sense of humor that sometimes softened a demanding manner, and he often played games with sportswriters who kidded him about his malapropisms. On occasion, he deliberately misused words to twit them — as he did with the word "indicted" upon his induction into the Florida Sports Hall of Fame.

"You know, I kinda mess with those sport writers," he would say, grinning. "I used to have this slight speech *implement* and couldn't remember things before I took that Sam Carnegie course."

Peterson thinks it may all have evolved from a quick, careless habit of thinking ahead to something else while talking. "Never could break myself of that thing," he said. "But I've sure given you sport writers a lot to write about."

He firmly disclaims perhaps four or five of the Petersonisms.

"I know I didn't say it that way," he said of one, "because I had it written down."

Then, laughing: "As for that Henry Patrick story — heck, I didn't know who Patrick Henry was."

Humor is perceived differently. Texas writers, when Peterson was coach of Rice and then the Houston Oilers, appeared to laugh at him. In Florida, the writers laughed with him, and he reigned as one of the most popular of coaches.

The Peterson stories involve far more than his mixed-up words and lively humor.

A favorite of Dan Henning and Don Breaux, two assistants of the late 1960s, was of the time they drove to Peterson's house in late afternoon to pick him up for a fishing trip.

They saw his wife on a ladder outside the house, a paint brush in hand. Peterson sat inside, reading a paper. He yelled that he would be with them as soon as he got his "reeling rod."

Just before they drove away, wife Marge said some men were coming out to see about a problem with the pool, and what should she tell them?

"My gosh, Marge, do I have to do everything around here!" shouted Pete as he got into the car.

Bobby Jackson recalled a first year on Peterson's staff when he served as a volunteer coach, receiving no form of compensation at all.

Near the end of the year, Peterson called him aside. "Bobby, you're doing such a good job," he said, a twinkle in his eye, "that I'm going to double your salary."

His wit was often both quick and incisive. There was the time Congressman Don Fuqua, a graduate of the University of Florida, sought his support for the approaching election day.

"Pete, I want you to know that I really like you," said Fuqua, "and I'm always for you and Florida State every day except one."

As the conversation wound down, the two men shook hands.

"Don, I want you to know I like you also," said Peterson. "And I'm going to be for you.

"Every day except one."

Thriving on crises

Away from football, Peterson was an uncommonly friendly man who frequently stopped to converse with the likes of doormen and street cleaners. He had a wide range of friends, highly placed and otherwise. Despite some detractors, he surely ranks as one of the most popular FSU coaches of them all.

Detractors sometimes included members of his own coaching staff.

The fact was understandable, given the atmosphere of crisis he generated and the degree of challenge to each.

Peterson seemed to thrive on crises, and it was said if there was no crisis handy he would create one — the better to challenge his assistants and players.

"Let me tell you one thing, the more problems you have the more alive you are," Peterson said. "I just feel so much more vital when I have problems — when I can solve 'em, when I can do it, instead of being out playing golf."

He got on his coaches. Daily. His staff was not always a happy family, but it was always an effective family — and sometimes to extraordinary degree.

During his 11 years, Peterson produced far more head-coaching material than any other Florida coach, college or pro.

The list:

Don James (Kent State, Washington), Bobby Bowden (West Virginia, Florida State), Vince Gibson (Kansas State, Louisville, Tulane), Al Conover (Rice), Gene McDowell (Central Florida), Joe Avezzano (Oregon State), Y.C. McNease (Idaho), John Coatta (Wisconsin, Mankato State), Joe Gibbs (Washington Redskins), Dan Henning (Atlanta Falcons), Bill Parcells (New York Giants), Ken Meyer (San Francisco 49ers).

Twelve head coaches — eight college, four pro — for his 11 Florida State years. Additionally, Peterson, while head coach at Mansfield (Ohio) High, gave Earle Bruce (Ohio State) his first coaching job, and he gave Kay Stephenson (Buffalo Bills) his first coaching job while

Three looks at Peterson: Above, with his feet propped up in his office; below, with Alabama's legendary Bear Bryant; and left, at Campbell Stadium.

Coach Peterson and one season's staff. In the front row, from left, are John Coatta, Peterson, Don James, Bobby Bowden and Don Powell. In the back row, Bill Crutchfield, Bob Vogt, Steve Medwick and Bob Harbison.

serving as head coach of Rice. Bobby Ross, later head coach of Maryland and Georgia Tech, was also on his Rice staff. Moreover, Bill Crutchfield was head coach at Presbyterian after serving on Peterson's Mansfield staff, but before the time he was on Peterson's Florida State staff.

There are two schools of thought on such unusual production.

One holds that Peterson was plain lucky.

The other says Peterson, with extreme demands on staff members, made candidates far better coaches than they otherwise would have been — that Peterson took men off the street, so to speak, and turned them into coaches when they had little background.

"I think a couple of things," said Peterson. "First thing, almost all were young when they were on my staff. I kept my eyes open for the young coach. I went to pro camps — picked up on players that were about to get out that might make good coaches. I just always had somebody in mind, talking to people. Joe Madro, for example, told me about Gibbs.

"I didn't want any more old coaches. I wanted the young ones.

"The second thing, I made 'em work. I worked them, and I worked with them. It was the only chance we had. They had to do a lot of extra stuff. All the things we did — so much. I remember I didn't have Thanksgiving dinner with my family because I was off recruiting. I remember one Christmas Eve I couldn't have dinner with friends because I had to get a game plan ready for Oklahoma in the Gator Bowl. I worked like that, and my assistants worked like that.

"They deserve a place in heaven for all the

things they did. And I wish I had enough money to call 'em all together and throw a party."

A place for coaches to grow

To Bob Harbison, the heavy demands of Peterson were alleviated by other factors.

"When I coached defense under Pete — those were the favorite of my 37 seasons at Florida State," he said. "Really, the freedom he allowed was great.

"He would let you switch around. Give you the opportunity to do some things other people wouldn't at the time, and I enjoyed that.

"You don't go around in football getting your butt kicked, then turn around and do the same thing. And I think that is true in life."

Don James said that when he moved on to the University of Michigan after several years with Peterson, he thought himself far better prepared than other assistants on the Wolverine staff.

"Better prepared in overall concepts — tying everything together," said the University of Washington coach. "I learned from Bill, I think, the total and complete football program.

"He would challenge you now, and you had to be prepared to support your position. Presenting your case on the blackboard, there would be fights — we threw chalk and erasers — but once a decision was made, it was over. He backed you all the way. I might not forget one of those fights for a day, but he had forgotten it 10 minutes later.

"One year he came back from visiting the San Diego Chargers, talking of this weight program Sid Gillman had introduced during the season. He wanted to put it in. We on the staff said 'No way' — our players were busy enough already.

"Pete had two of us go out to San Diego with him, to better see how Gillman did it. We became sold, and put it in.

"Of all the things I picked up wherever I've been in my career, I got more from him. He wanted, always, to change — not to stand still, to learn something new.

"I remember when pro scouts walked in, he'd call us all together, and we'd have a clinic. And we'd find something we could use."

James delighted perhaps more than most in the many "Petersonisms" but thought some perhaps came out of the mouths of others. Any person, he thought, comes up with an occasional one.

"One time when I was on the Michigan staff, we were playing Purdue," said James, "and I said, 'Purdue is gonna fill that football with air.'

"I had not realized what I said. We all do that sort of thing — but maybe Pete much more."

Not an ideal job interview

Surely, Peterson was much more attuned to the pro passing game than other coaches of his era. Florida State's game was significantly patterned after that of the Chargers during the coaching time of Gillman. The San Diego connection was pronounced, and several FSU assistants were hired via that connection, though only Henning (a Chargers quarterback) and Gibbs (a player at San Diego State) became head coaches.

"I never fired a coach I hired," Peterson said.

But he threatened to fire one and all countless times. Peterson often barked, loud and long, but his bite was hardly terminal.

If many times he found the names of players — and coaches — beyond his quick recall, there was a tough FSU running back from the early 1960s whose name he would never forget.

"That time I was hung in effigy, and Dave Snyder went up there in front of the Westcott Building — and it was him that cut me down, buddy!" said Peterson.

Things happened to him, and it sometimes seemed everything he did involved a story. A good story.

He had not been interviewed for the Florida State job in 1959, when he might have gotten it, because he was off recruiting for LSU and could not come at the time.

One year later he got it, partly because Charlie Waller, a Clemson assistant, would not agree to come to Tallahassee before the Tigers' game in the Bluebonnet Bowl. Robert Strozier, the FSU president, grew impatient and gave instructions to "call that fellow at LSU."

When Peterson came for an interview, no one met him at the airport.

"But they had told me to go to the Duval Hotel," he said. "So I did. There was nobody there either."

Finally, a couple of committeemen came by. He was advised that the interview the following day had been moved from 9 to 7 a.m.

"So I got up and ate breakfast at 6," he said. "Nobody came by. Nobody called. I was starting not to want the danged job, and I was ready to go back."

At 9 a.m., the original time of the interview, someone did come by. The interview went well.

"I never saw any facilities," he said. "I never saw anything."

Back in Louisiana, he got a call from Athletic Director Vaughn Mancha. The job was his.

He was told he could bring in only one new assistant. The choice was Ken Meyer.

"Well, I had not seen the facilities," he said. "They were terrible. When it rained, it rained inside that locker room.

"There was no office space, and what we had was cramped underneath the stadium. Hardly any space. Everything leaked, and there would be water all around.

"I went to a boosters' meeting that first night in town, and I said something had to be done. Then I asked if anything *could* be done. The president just shook his head. No.

"And I was really upset. But I had five kids to feed and had to make the best of it."

"Really upset" was a state that many at FSU would come to know well. Soon, Peterson found some office space in Tully Gym. Soon, Gov. Farris Bryant listened to his plea for permanent offices and assisted in a maneuver that had new facilities built by 1964.

The importance of discipline

Meanwhile, in that first year, key players were being lost. Just before Peterson's arrival, Bobby Conrad, a promising quarterback, died in a traffic accident. Then Peterson lost Jack Espenship, a big back and possibly the team's best player.

"They had some girls staying at that lake place they called The Reservation near campus, and he climbed the fence to see one," said Peterson. "And they kicked him out of school. Later, he goes up to Canada, to play pro football at Montreal, and he makes it as a starter the first week."

By September, 11 players of first-string caliber had departed for one reason or another. Some others had been kicked out for disciplinary reasons. A couple had quit.

"But, you know, I didn't care," said Peterson. "I figured the only way to build a program was to have people who *wanted* to play for Florida State and were willing to pay the price.

"We put in a disciplined program, and I felt we needed that."

Players who arrived late for the first scheduled meeting found that out. He locked the doors. "We had to show discipline at the start

— we had to establish that, if we were going to get anything done," he said.

Throughout his 11 years, Peterson teams would be praised for their disciplined dress and manner on the road. Flight attendants would remark on their quiet behavior in contrast to other teams.

Among the difficulties Peterson confronted was a continuing turnover at the presidential level. He coached under four — first Strozier, then Gordon Blackwell, John Champion and Stan Marshall.

"They all looked at things a little differently," said Peterson.

He recalled how Strozier looked at one aspect. "I know you have to recruit," Strozier told him, "but I don't believe in it."

Looking over what he had, Peterson regarded recruiting as a high priority.

"About the only thing we had that first year on offense was that little guy named (halfback Bud) Whitehead," said Peterson. "We had no experience at quarterback.

"I decided then we'd put it all on defense. The offense would have to come eventually.

"The coaches set up study halls. We had no tutors, no money to hire them. The assistants did it all themselves.

"I had to drive those coaches. It was the only way."

Recruiting would remain a critical problem for a time.

"We had few resources," said Peterson. "In the spring we hadn't done a very good job of finding out who the prospects were — no money to do that."

But there were pluses.

"Tallahassee itself was one — the people really wanted a team," said Peterson.

"The newness of it all was another. You could tell a prospect, 'Hey, you're going to be the first. The first to go to a big bowl, the first to beat Florida' — that type of thing. They would not be doing things hanging on somebody else's coattails.

"And then the Florida thing was a plus — a great one. They were so far ahead of us. Had so much more money. And we played well against them every year. We got beat, but we never got beat bad.

"The other thing was the stadium. It was so small, and we built it up to 42,000. We did things like that, with a lot of help."

He recalled an active athletic board, led by the two deans, Mode Stone and Coyle Moore.

"Those two, as well as others on that board, were really interested," he said. "But they wanted it all at once — best band, best basketball, best baseball, best football. And I thought that definitely not the right thing to do.

"But they were doing it."

1960: Three squads, three wins

In a day of continued substitution restrictions, and despite a lack of depth, Peterson in his first year utilized a three-team system similar to LSU's national-championship team of 1958. The "Chiefs" operated both ways, the "Renegades" were only on defense, and those in the "War Party" were a special offensive force — mostly sophomores — attuned to goal-line tactics.

All three looked just fine as Richmond went down 28-0 in an opener.

And they looked just fine in the second game — a 3-0 loss to Florida's 12-point favorites. A field goal from 35 yards by Billy Cash — the first ever for the Tallahasseean — was the difference.

Looking good before the game were law-enforcement officials in a quick, well-planned move.

Offered a $4,500 bribe by a New York gambler to help assure Florida wouldn't win by more than 12 points, Jon MacBeth, a Gator fullback, had pretended to go along. In fact, he had reported the initial contact to authorities. As a result, the gambler and his UF student accomplice were jailed prior to the kickoff.

Apparently, the incident had no effect on the game. Florida players were not told of the attempt until later.

After four games, Florida State had yielded just 9 points but owned only two victories. Wake Forest fell 14-6 but The Citadel gained an upset tie, 0-0.

A handful of points separated FSU from a winning season after that tie: a 1-point loss (Houston 7-6), a 2-point loss (Southern Mississippi 15-13) and a 3-point loss (Florida 3-0). The Seminoles would win only once more (against William and Mary, 22-0) in a 3-6-1 season that saw the offense continue to struggle and the defense become overburdened. Bud Whitehead's senior heroics — he led in rushing, pass receiving, kickoff returns, punting and scoring — were hardly enough.

"We simply didn't have enough players," said Peterson. "We used the three-team system, but those 33 players were about all we had. In the last game at Auburn, we were behind by 31-21 in the last quarter, and we gambled and lost big (57-21), but by this game we had plain run out of people."

FSU soon found some people. In recruiting that followed Peterson's first season, the Seminoles landed a quarterback (Steve Tensi) out of Cincinnati and a halfback (Fred Biletnikoff) from Erie, Pa., who would soon become a receiver.

'61: 'Like a death in the family' for Florida

Florida State continued in 1961 to build a defensive foundation. Playing an early schedule that featured Florida, Mississippi and Georgia on successive dates was, said Peterson, "like joining the Army on Monday and fighting a war on Tuesday."

George Washington was beaten 15-7 in a tough home opener. Late in the game, with the Colonials threatening after a fumble, Peterson had shouted: "Give me the Bandits — get the Bandits out there!" It was an allusion to the famed "Chinese Bandits" defensive unit he had known at LSU. Their FSU counterparts, the Renegades, went in and did the job nicely.

Playing Florida for the fourth straight time in Gainesville, the Seminoles exacted a 3-3 tie.

Roy Bickford, defensive back and quarterback, was the great hero — blocking a Florida punt, intercepting two passes, making six tackles. Florida led in first downs (15-5), in yardage (291-108) — and in turnovers (5-1, not counting the blocked punt). John Harlee had given FSU a lead with a first-quarter field goal of 19 yards, and Billy Cash tied it with a second-quarter boot from 18 yards away.

"It was like a death in the family," said Florida coach Ray Graves.

If Florida looked upon the tie as a galling defeat, as Graves indicated, Florida State celebrated it as an exalting victory.

Seminole fans swarmed in to pull down the goalposts on Florida Field, and a fifth quarter of action began. One goalpost had been dismantled into three pieces before Florida supporters moved in, and scuffles broke out. In vain The Marching Chiefs struck up the national anthem, then "Dixie." The fighting continued, much as it did in Tallahassee after a Florida victory in 1982. Florida Field was ill-prepared for the assault, and by some estimates turmoil on that field lasted 30 minutes before it was brought under control.

Back in Tallahassee on Sunday morning, Peterson went to church. Later, he would recall the first hymn: "Blest Be the Tie That Binds."

Mississippi, ranked No. 2 nationally and soon to be No. 1, clobbered FSU in Oxford 33-0, dominating absolutely.

"We tried to put in a lot of new stuff," said Peterson. "That was a mistake."

But another celebration — and another fight — soon came around as Georgia fell 3-0 in Tallahassee on Doug Messer's early 25-yard field goal. Bickford stopped one Georgia thrust with an interception, and the Renegades got a standing ovation from the crowd after holding the Bulldogs after a first down at the FSU 3. Keith Kinderman, a big running back out of Chicago, slammed through Georgia defenders for 101 yards.

"With seconds to go, we had the football," recalled Peterson. "No way to lose as long as we held onto the ball.

"About the time of the last play, some Georgia player made a remark — and all hell broke loose just as the game ended. People came out of the stands to join the fighting.

"I thought I was going to have a heart attack."

There is the story of Don James, coach of FSU defensive backs, about to be pummeled by a big Bulldog player. According to Peterson and others, James shouted: "Don't hit me, don't hit me — I'm a coach!"

But the postgame fight was short. Florida State officials turned on field sprinklers. Wet players, coaches and fans quickly scattered.

Florida State had come up with the sprinkler plan following the goalpost battle at Florida. It was a move that would be emulated by many, but it possibly never again would be as successful as the first time, when everyone was caught by surprise.

The remainder of 1961 was anti-climactic, and disappointing.

Through most of his 11 years, Peterson would find the Virginia Tech teams of Jerry Claiborne notably difficult. One way or another, including tackle-eligible passes that were then legal, Tech often surprised. In 1961 at Blacksburg, the Gobblers won 10-7 on a fluke third-quarter pass that covered 31 yards for the winning touchdown. The ball had bounced off two Florida State defenders before Buddy Weihe pulled it in.

In the final five games, FSU was scoreless in two, got just one touchdown in two others and beat only The Citadel (44-8). FSU finished 4-5-1.

"We did a couple of things, but still had a way to go," said Peterson.

'62: The three-tie season

The following season would be one of Peterson's favorites — a gritty one of more tough defense, a good kicking game, and an offense that was beginning to stir. A season of four victories, three ties and three losses.

It was also a season of just four home games — with Kentucky, Georgia, Miami, Georgia Tech, Auburn and Florida away.

The ties were top-quality ones, all on the road — Kentucky 0-0, Georgia Tech 14-14, Auburn 14-14. Two losses were close ones, to tough foes — Miami 7-6 (the "Now I lay me down to sleep" game) and Houston 7-0. A third loss, to Florida (20-7), was not so close, sandwiched as it was between those ties at Georgia Tech and Auburn, with no open-date respite.

It was a season that had started splendidly. Unbeaten (2-0-1) going into the fourth game at Miami, FSU took an early 3-0 lead on a Messer field goal after a fumble of the opening kickoff. Trailing 7-6 later, FSU lost second-half fumbles at Miami's 19, 15 and 10 — the last one with a minute left. Fullback Gene Roberts, FSU's leading runner for the game, had just banged for 5 yards. The ball would go to him once more.

"I told him just to double up and hang onto the ball, keeping it in position for the field goal," said Peterson. "But he sees a big hole and drives to score — but one of their linebackers (Jim O'Mahoney) hit the ball, and it came out."

A 2-1 Georgia team awaited in Athens, ranked in the nation's top 10 both offensively and defensively.

On the morning of the game, following late developments, Florida State's situation seemed fairly desperate. "Eighteen players had diarrhea," recalled Dr. Bob Johnson, then team physician. "Fortunately, they responded to medication."

In the opening moments, FSU defenders checked Georgia at the 1 following a first down at the 6. Soon, end Y.C. McNease came up with the first of five FSU interceptions — a shovel pass over the middle. Ahead 3-0 at halftime, FSU won 18-0 on a 6-yard scoring pass by Eddie Feely and a 15-yard interception runback by Dave Snyder.

"Feely had a great season for us," said Peterson. "That was a big factor. Another was the punting of Charley Calhoun, who kept people backed up with his punts."

Florida State lost a fourth straight homecoming game — to Houston (7-0) — and Peterson said he would resolve that situation by not scheduling a homecoming encounter the following year.

In Atlanta, Georgia Tech jumped in front 7-0 on an early scoring runback of an interception off Feely. On a third-quarter burst up the middle for 22 yards and a touchdown, Snyder

Jack Shinholser (61) and Dale MacKenzie open holes for Howard Ehler against Virginia Tech in '63.

tied it 7-7. "One of the most determined runs I've ever seen on Grant Field," praised Tech coach Bobby Dodd. On that run, Snyder had run through, over and under defenders.

Soon FSU led 14-7 on a 66-yard pass — one of the early collaborations of a famed combination, Steve Tensi to Fred Biletnikoff. For Biletnikoff, a sophomore who had been hurt earlier in the year, it was his first college touchdown.

"Biletnikoff was a great athlete who could have played any position for us," said Peterson. "After his injury, we could have kept him out and preserved a year of eligibility — but he wanted to play in those late games."

With 6½ minutes left, Tech scored, tying it 14-14. Tight FSU defense choked off a final Tech scoring opportunity.

Peterson called FSU's play the finest effort he had seen on a football field. He would soon see finer, but not at Florida the following week.

'All the Florida rejects'

Sitting in their room at Silver Springs the night before, Florida State players had been riled by a Gainesville television show.

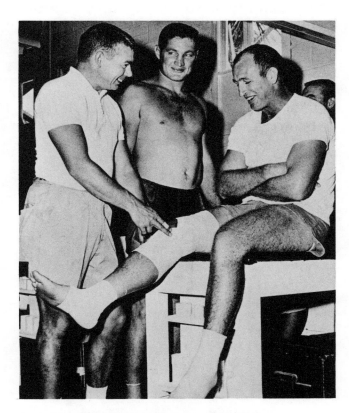

Longtime trainer Don Fauls tends to Y.C. McNease's knee.

Pepper Rodgers, an assistant on the Florida staff then, was interviewing Gator players. One had mentioned he had played in high school with some Seminoles.

And then quarterback Tom Shannon volunteered: "I have no friends there. It seems to me they get all the Florida rejects."

Rodgers winced, apprehensive about words that would arouse FSU, and tried to steer the conversation into safer channels. He asked Shannon what teams Florida State had beaten.

"Furman," retorted sophomore Shannon, with Rodgers quickly adding Georgia and mentioning the Georgia Tech tie.

An angered Florida State team drove quickly to a 7-0 lead. It was 7-6 going into the final half. Suddenly, Hagood Clarke moved, behind superb blocking, to a touchdown on a 63-yard punt return. That broke it open, and Florida went on to win 20-7.

Three times in the first half alone, Biletnikoff had jumped offsides, and Florida defenders were accused of deliberately shouting FSU offensive signals to confuse the Seminoles — an illegal tactic. Graves denied the charge.

In a closing 1962 game, Florida State fell behind Auburn 14-0.

In the third quarter, a Dave Snyder interception paved Feely's 10-yard touchdown pass to Jim Loftin on fourth down. With 6:15 left in the game, Tucker Frederickson fumbled a deep punt, Bruce Darsey recovering for FSU at the Auburn 6. On fourth down, Feely passed 3 yards to John McConnaughay for the tying touchdown.

'63: 'Surprising and shocking'

Sometimes it seemed the Seminoles were taking one step forward and two steps back. A 4-3-3 season was followed by a strange 4-5-1 run in 1963.

At the start, hope soared with a 24-0 conquest of Miami — a shocking outcome, and the first in a series of Peterson victories over the Hurricanes in the Orange Bowl. Florida State had agreed to play there every year in quest of bigger crowds and financial reward.

This was supposed to be a Miami "dream team" — so labeled by Luther Evans, the able Miami Herald writer.

"I'm scared to death of Florida State," said Andy Gustafson prior to the game. In fact, the astute Miami coach was confident. In a conversation a few days earlier, I told him I thought he might get beaten. "I don't think so," retorted Gustafson. "They would have to have a lot better players than they have had."

Florida State had made a start toward better players. Moreover, substitution rules were starting to loosen up, and they would prove to the Seminoles' advantage.

Early in the game Biletnikoff capped a long drive, taking a 23-yard touchdown pass from Tensi. Then it was 14-0 at halftime, after Biletnikoff caught a 17-yard TD throw from Tensi. Miami was having uncommon trouble moving the ball on FSU defenders.

It was 17-0, on a Messer field goal, before Miami got anything going — and then Biletnikoff, operating on defense, scooped up a George Mira pass and ran 99 yards with an interception, scoring his third touchdown.

Slippery quarterback Eddie Feely in 1962.

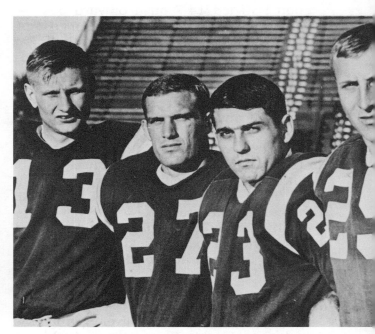

Passing duo of Steve Tensi (13) and Fred Biletnikoff (25) flank Phil Spooner (27) and Wayne Giardino.

"The most surprising and shocking game I've seen in many years," said Gustafson.

In a raging rainstorm at Tallahassee the following week, high hopes were soaked. On an interception that brought a touchdown, and two field goals, Texas Christian University won 13-0. "Jim Fauver's touchdown interception was listed at 47 yards," typed Lonnie Burt in The St. Petersburg Times. "If he had not been a good swimmer he never would have made it."

Tensi threw three touchdown passes as Wake Forest succumbed 35-0. But Southern Mississippi again brought FSU back to reality with a 0-0 tie, and Virginia Tech underscored the point with a 31-23 upset before FSU romped over Furman.

There was dancing in the stands — literally — as Florida State scored its first homecoming victory in five years, 14-0 over firmly favored N.C. State, which had come in with a 7-1 record.

But there were tough losses — Georgia Tech 15-7, Auburn 21-15, Florida 7-0.

The Auburn game — Nov. 23, 1963 — was unforgettable.

On the day before, not long after the Seminoles' arrival for an overnight stay in nearby Columbus, Ga., word had come of the assassination of President John Kennedy. Players and coaches remained in the quiet of their rooms, hearing the somber news on television.

A few college-football games were called off the next day, but most went on as scheduled, FSU-Auburn among them. Rain and overcast

To help cool down locker-room vocabularies, the team started circulating the "cuss can." Here half-back Dave Snyder pays his 5-cent fine. (Top fine was 25 cents, for a real sizzler.)

skies reflected the mood of a nation but seemed to little affect the game itself. Jimmy Sidle accounted for three touchdowns — two passing, one running.

"We were so close, and yet so far," Peterson had said of the Florida game, and he might have said it of the whole season.

But fruits of change had started to ripen.

'64: Filling the air with footballs

Another change — somewhat controversial — seemed to assist the process.

In a move that brought some displeasure on his own staff, Peterson brought in Bill Crutchfield to head his offense. Interestingly, Crutchfield had previously been in charge of Miami's defense.

When Peterson was coach of Mansfield (Ohio) High, Crutchfield had been with him for two years. Later, he served Presbyterian College four years as head coach. When Peterson came to Florida State, he immediately sought to make Crutchfield the one assistant he would hire. Unsuccessful, he hired Ken Meyer instead.

On his own staff, Peterson had difficulty gaining agreement on his inclination to put stronger emphasis on the passing game.

It reflected a widespread view of the time, perhaps best phrased by Darrell Royal. "When you throw, three things can happen," said the Texas coach, "and two of them are bad." Coaches, generally, were fond of pointing to national statistics that showed no passing team had ever won a national title.

"I'm going to throw the football if I have to fire every one of 'em," Peterson said.

He said throwing started growing stronger in his mind when he was at LSU.

"I always felt with great defense, you could make some passing mistakes and overcome them," he said.

"I started going to those pro camps every year. Though it was technically against the law, I used to film games on TV and study them. I had old books and old films stacked to the ceiling at my house.

"My assistants used to say that people lose throwing the football, and they would cite Jack Curtice at Utah, or somebody like that.

"But I had to be boss. And we had to do things differently.

"We were fighting with a short stick, without a big area to attract fans to our games. We had the Gulf of Mexico below us, the Georgia line just above us, and the nearest big city was Jacksonville, 170 miles away. We had not

SEMINOLE CHEERLEADERS—Kneeling are John Sweets, Chattanooga, Tennessee; and David Deutsch, Palatka. Standing with them, left to right, are Dee Weber, West Palm Beach; Toni Beals, Sumpter, South Carolina; Head Cheerleader Kay Lewis, Arcadia; Peggy Thompson, Ormond Beach; and Susan Reinhart, Cocoa Beach.

SONGS AND YELLS

ALMA MATER

High O'er the Towering Pines our voices swell
Praising these Gothic spires we love so well
Here sons and daughters stand, faithful and true
Hailing our Alma Mater—FSU.

FIGHT SONG

We're going to fight, fight, fight, for FSU
We're going to scalp 'em, Seminoles,
We're going to win, win, win, win, win this game
And roll on down and make those goals!
For FSU is on the warpath now,
And at the Battle's end she's great;
So fight, fight, fight, fight for victory
Our Seminoles of Florida State
F-L-O-R-I-D-A S-T-A-T-E!
Florida State! Florida State! Florida State!
—Written by Dr. Thomas Wright,
Associate Professor of Music

FSU CLAP CHEER

(Stomp clap, stomp clap,
stomp clap-clap-clap-clap-clap)
Repeat 3 times, then:
F (clap, stomp clap, stomp clap-clap-clap-clap)
S (clap, stomp clap, stomp clap-clap-clap-clap)
U (clap, stomp clap, stomp clap-clap-clap-clap)
F (clap) S (clap) U (clap-clap-clap-clap)
Go!!

THREE GARNETS

Give me a Garnet, Garnet, Garnet, Garnet, Garnet
Give me a Gold, Gold, Gold Gold Gold
Garnet, Gold
Garnet, Gold
Go Seminoles Go!

GO FLORIDA STATE

G-o-o-o-o-o-o-o-o-o, Florida!
G-o-o-o-o-o-o-o-o-o, State!
Go! Go!
Florida State!

IS EVERYBODY HAPPY!

Is everybody happy?
AUD: Hell, yes!
Is anybody low?
AUD: Hell, no!
Let's railroad Seminoles
And take it slow!
(Spell Seminoles 3 times)
Go, Seminoles!

VICTORY

With a V, With an I,
With a C, T, O, R, Y!
With a V, With an I,
With a C, T, O, R, Y!
With a V I C T O R Y!
VICTORY!!

84

been long at football. We were short on facilities, money and players.

"Crutchfield did play a big role. He was a *concentrator*, and he would simplify things. We were always trying to make it more simple. Don Powell, with the offensive line, played a big part — developing the pass protection we had to have.

"We originated some things. I know the 'hot receiver' started at Florida State. That's when you send a guy vertically or laterally along the line of scrimmage, and when somebody blitzes, you pop that ball off to him. It takes care of those blitzes. We had those hot receivers on every pass route, in case of a blitz.

"I remember lecturing, in Atlantic City, about the hot receiver. This coach jumped me right off. He says we have to talk about this thing. We go to my room, and Vince Lombardi and I went to 2 o'clock in the morning talking about the hot receiver."

Tensi to Biletnikoff

Spring practice in 1964 was marked by a striking sight — Tensi throwing the football to Biletnikoff over and over and over again.

Though this would be a team of significant talent, Crutchfield was very probably the catalyst that brought the greatest dividends. Peterson credits him greatly not only with a big assist on the passing game but with settling Tensi down.

"Tensi's problem was he got mad at himself if he hadn't done things right," said Peterson. "Crutchfield did a great job of keeping him calmed down."

Perhaps because of inconsistency, the 6-foot-5 Tensi had few deep-dyed fans as he entered his senior year.

Vince Gibson had played for Florida State, then coached through five seasons. His blood, indeed, was garnet.

After spring practice, Gibson accepted a job on the Tennessee staff. Before leaving town, he said to me: "This can be a good football team — but talk to that Peterson, and don't let him start Tensi. He can't do it."

Indeed, Peterson was lobbied on this count by several people, including team chaplain C.A. Roberts. Ed Pritchett, a versatile junior quarterback, was the choice of many.

Peterson would listen, and say little.

Whereupon, he started Tensi.

A page from a 1964 football program. Feel free to sing along.

"But it was the fourth game before he really picked it all up," said Crutchfield later. "Then he fully understood what we were trying to do, reading defenses and all."

At about that point, much of the passing game became so easy, it seemed ridiculous. It would be a while before defenses started to catch up.

"It was like stealing," said Peterson.

It started with Miami getting shut out (14-0) for the second straight year on its home field. Two 15-yard passes — Tensi to Biletnikoff — brought the touchdowns, both in the first half. Biletnikoff caught nine passes as he ran his touchdown total against Miami to five in two games.

The Seven Magnificents

But defense was surely the bigger part of the Florida State game at that earlier point. It showed at TCU the following week in a 10-0 victory fired by Bill McDowell's blocked field goal in the fourth quarter, possibly averting a 3-3 tie.

And it showed again in a third successive shutout, 36-0 over New Mexico.

The Seven Magnificents — most famed defensive unit in FSU annals — were shaping up.

A takeoff on the movie "The Magnificent Seven," the Florida State defensive seven — five linemen plus two linebackers — shaved their heads in emulation of Yul Brynner, star of the movie.

The unit, coached primarily by Bob Harbison, had ends George D'Alessandro and Max Wettstein, tackles Frank Pennie and Avery Sumner, middle guard Jack Shinholser and linebackers Dick Hermann and Bill McDowell.

A fine receiver, Wettstein had been switched to defensive end late in 1963 after injuries hit the position. In 1964, he started at defensive end until hurt late in the season, and Terry Garvin became the starter. In 1965, Wettstein went back to offense.

Sumner was credited with the "Magnificents" idea, along with tight end Red Dawson.

The unit received so much acclaim that the members of the defensive secondary would later dub themselves "The Forgotten Four."

Peterson suggested later that the offensive line may really have been the forgotten force of 1964.

"We had a notion we could be exceptional," he said. "We knew we had a good defense. We knew we had a passing game. The offensive line had to come through.

"Del Williams, who then was a sophomore,

Slightly hairier than in the photo at the beginning of this chapter, here are the Seven Magnificents again (George D'Alessandro, Frank Pennie, Dick Hermann, Jack Shinholser, Bill McDowell, Avery Sumner and, replacing Terry Garvin, Max Wettstein). Behind them, with hair intact, are their backfield teammates, the Forgotten Four (Maury Bibent, Jim Massey, Winfred Bailey and Howard Ehler).

had to come through at tackle. So did Dale MacKenzie at the other tackle, and he did. The others called him 'Lucille' there at first, but Lucille did it. We moved Joe Avezzano from defense to guard, and he did the job, too.

"Jack Edwards did a great job at center. He taught the others Spanish, and he called signals in Spanish."

Maybe the biggest win of all

Oct. 10, 1964, may have brought not only Florida State's happiest homecoming ever, but even its happiest, most notable football victory ever.

There are many, surely, who hold that game — Florida State 48, Kentucky 6 — as the biggest.

It made an unbelievable statement, one that no one thought possible.

Perhaps only those who were there can fully appreciate it.

Kentucky came in unbeaten, ranked No. 5 nationally after victories over No. 1 Mississippi and Auburn. Such players as Rick Norton,

Larry Seiple, Rodger Bird and Rick Kester were all viewed as All-America sorts with big pro futures.

Dick Dunkel would call the outcome a "hallmark" game, as well as one of the biggest upsets in the history of his Dunkel Index rating service.

Announcers, disclosing the score on national TV and radio, entered disclaimers. "Surely, this must be a mistake, with the score reversed," said one.

"They kicked our teeth in," said Kentucky coach Charley Bradshaw.

This was the pivotal point for Tensi that Crutchfield talked about. The time of his arrival as a quarterback who had the situation well in hand, who now fully understood the pass-game objectives and had the great tools to achieve them.

It was 21-0 after a quarter, Tensi throwing for the first two touchdowns. But there had been a sticky early moment.

With the game scoreless, a Florida State drive stalled, and it was fourth down at the 2.

"Well, we had worked on the Statue of Liberty play all week," said Peterson. "And it had got us down there. We'd got 'em down there.

"So I turned my back and said, 'Tensi, you call it!'"

Tensi did. Pass to the fullback over the middle — and Lee Narramore grabbed the short pass for a 7-0 lead.

At halftime it was 27-0. In the late going, reserves pushed it to 48-0.

Kentucky scored in the waning moments after Florida State fumbled away a punt near its goal.

If the campus and city were delirious, there was no joy in one sector of the FSU dressing room. Some members of the Seven Magnificents cried, because after four games they had finally yielded a touchdown, and never mind whether it was a cheap one.

Peterson, surely, was all smiles. "This was a tremendous opportunity for us," he said, "and we took it."

Dodging a Bulldog

In Athens the next week, Georgia similarly viewed a tremendous opportunity — and almost took it.

With the notable help of two McDowell fumble recoveries, Florida State took a 10-0 lead. Georgia rallied for a 14-10 lead early in the final quarter. But Tensi-to-Biletnikoff brought the Seminoles back. One fourth-down shot to Biletnikoff kept the drive going, and a payoff came when Biletnikoff grabbed a pass between two defenders and scored on a 20-yard play. Final score: Florida State 17-14.

"They showed what they were made of on that drive," praised Georgia's Vince Dooley.

On a black day for the Seminoles in Blacksburg, always-tough Virginia Tech showed what it was made of.

"We took that ball right down and scored, then took it right down again — and gave the ball away," said Peterson. "We should have been up 14-0."

FSU had settled for a field goal on the first foray but soon trailed 7-3. Tech had moved from an interception to a touchdown on a tackle-eligible pass from Bob Schweickert, who later would run for two more touchdowns.

Tensi completed a school-record 21 passes and Biletnikoff caught a school-record 11. But 423 yards of offense, compared with Tech's 191, got FSU nothing.

Tech scored twice more in the fourth quarter, for 20-3. Only then did FSU score a touchdown. With the clock running down, Biletni-koff caught a 4-yard touchdown pass from Tensi, then grabbed a 2-point toss from Pritchett for a 20-11 final score.

Whereupon, the frustrated Biletnikoff threw the football into the end-zone stands, where jeers turned into boos.

Florida State took it out on Southern Mississippi 34-0, then got checked at Houston in a 13-13 tie.

Before the game, some Florida writers accused Peterson of concealing the fact that Biletnikoff, nursing a charley horse, would not play. Peterson humphed and hawed, debated a bit, and finally told them Biletnikoff would start.

He did.

After one play, Peterson took him out, never to return that afternoon.

With a quarter to go, FSU led 13-0. Houston cut it to 13-7, then got a tying touchdown following an interception. A point-after kick hit an upright, preserving the tie for FSU. Soon after, the Seminoles drove to the Houston 7, but in the final minute a Les Murdock field-goal attempt sailed wide.

Biletnikoff was back, catching two touchdown passes, as FSU sailed past N.C. State 28-6.

A 10-game regular season that started in Miami on Sept. 19 concluded in the shortest possible time, in Tallahassee against Florida on Nov. 21. There had been no open dates.

Oddsmakers rated the game virtually even.

Florida, however, had an open date the prior week. The Gators had one of their better teams — one that led the nation in pass defense, one that many thought quite superior to its 5-2 record of the moment, one that Graves two weeks earlier had called his best ever.

Florida seemed ready, in every way, for its first Tallahassee engagement.

First time — Gators in Tallahassee

Inscriptions on Gator practice helmets had read: "Never, FSU, Never!"

Inscriptions on Gator game jerseys read "Go For Seven" — an allusion to seven straight, following six consecutive Gainesville games without a loss to the Seminoles.

Florida State players, coaches and fans were already riled aplenty.

The pregame atmosphere was electric.

"Don't let them know there is a Gator fan in the stadium!," Peterson had said to FSU's student body during the week. Earlier in the year he had written "7152" on a blackboard — the number of hours before the kickoff of the Florida game, and there had been a daily countdown. Shortly before 2 p.m. on Nov. 21 the number "1" was erased from the board as the team swarmed toward the field.

Peterson recalled one controversy prior to the game.

"The rumor got around that somebody was going to pay $5,000 to whatever Gator got Tensi out of the game," said Peterson. "Well, we talked about that, and the importance of protecting the passer.

"And one of our guards, Joe Avezzano, got up and said, 'Coach, Steve can wear a tuxedo if he wants — nobody is going to touch him.'"

Nobody did.

A Saturday headline of the Tallahassee Democrat — in bold garnet color — read: "THIS IS THE ONE!" Fans came early to a stadium that, in short order, had its capacity roughly doubled, to 43,000. As students jeered Florida's first appearance on the field, Coach Ray Graves smiled and said to a companion: "I think FSU is overemphasizing football."

Florida cheerleaders demonstrated a little emphasis of their own with a yell: "What color is FSU?" Its section responded by waving hundreds of yellow sheets.

On the field, defense was again what FSU would emphasize. The game's biggest play was surely a defensive one.

There was a key offensive wrinkle that saw a tight end in FSU's backfield alignment.

"Crutchfield had that idea," said Peterson. "It was designed to take advantage of the way the defense compensated — it helped our receivers get position on them.

"Florida used a 'monster' on defense, and shaded him over to the side where Biletnikoff would line up, trying to double up on him. What we did was move the tight end away from the monster. For a while, we really had them going, and they didn't know how to react. Another thing, it gave us an extra blocker on one side and better."

In the early going, Florida State lost a fumble at its 19, and quickly Florida had a first down at the 8. Two runs by Larry Dupree, and it was third-and-goal at the 1.

Tom Shannon was quarterbacking — the one who on a TV show two years prior had hung a "rejects" label on the Seminoles.

"It was one of those days you knew you were going to be hot," said Shannon many years later. "Everything was going right."

But suddenly everything was not.

Jack Shinholser, a spectacular middle guard of that '64 season, slammed into center

Bill Carr (later Florida's athletic director) as he snapped the football to Shannon.

The snapped ball eluded Shannon's groping hands, and end George D'Alessandro recovered for FSU at the 2.

"Hit my thigh pad, and went behind me," said Shannon. "It never touched my hands."

Graves had decided to go with the senior Shannon over the less experienced sophomore Steve Spurrier.

"It was the key play," said Graves of the fumble.

"In my estimation, if we had scored then, it would have been a different game," said Shannon.

It was a play that some rank as FSU's most memorable defensive one of all time.

Backed up near its goal after that fumble recovery, Florida State had difficulty digging out of that early hole. Then, a second-quarter Florida fumble gave the Seminoles position at the Seminole 45.

As Tensi immediately faded on first down behind superb protection, a Jacksonville writer screamed: "There he is!" And, indeed, Biletnikoff was there, free behind two defenders. He gathered in the deep pass and, on a 55-yard play, scored untouched, leaping and dancing in end-zone celebration.

It was 7-0 at halftime, and it became 13-0 in the fourth quarter after two Murdock field goals. With 9:30 to play, it became 13-7 on a Jack Harper touchdown from 6 yards out following good Spurrier passing. Whereupon FSU moved, following Florida's futile onside kick, to a rather decisive lead on Murdock's third field goal, and the 16-7 score was final.

Shouts of "FSU one time" and "FSU all the damn time" rang out, and on through the night.

Florida State led in every statistical category except turnovers — Florida had lost the ball six times, FSU three.

Now all that was left was to accept a bowl bid — but even that was steeped in controversy.

What constitutes a rout?

Peterson had been in Jacksonville the Monday before the Florida game, speaking to the Quarterback Club there, and had negotiated with the Gator Bowl's selection-committee chairman.

"What happened was the committee, which always met on Monday, had earlier that day decided it would invite Florida State if it won," said George Olsen, longtime executive director of the Gator Bowl. "If it lost or tied, it would have to re-evaluate the situation.

"I picked Pete up at the airport, and he was unhappy with that. He felt he should have the bid — win, lose or draw. Personally, I agreed with him because I was anxious to land the attraction of Tensi and Biletnikoff. After the Quarterback Club dinner that night, the chairman of our selection committee went up to Pete's hotel room."

It was agreed that the bowl would take Florida State, as long as the game was not a rout. Then a discussion started over what constituted a rout. Finally, Peterson tossed out the number 17. And it was agreed that Florida State had the bid if it won, or got beaten by fewer than 17. There were handshakes.

On the Friday before the game — after bowl committeemen arrived in Tallahassee — Peterson learned that the agreement had been voided, that Florida State must win to be certain of a Gator Bowl bid.

The coach was furious.

What had happened was the bowl's board of directors had overruled the selection-committee chairman. It is true that those directors included, as they almost always have, a strong corps of University of Florida supporters. And Florida State supporters perceived, as they often do, devious maneuvers of rival forces.

After Florida State won the game, stories circulated of Gator Bowl representatives impatiently cooling their heels before Peterson granted them an audience.

"I don't recall the wait being all that long," said Olsen. "I do recall Pete chomping on that cigar of his and saying that the bid was appreciated, and then adding, 'But that does not mean we are accepting.' And our people were a little flabbergasted."

Thumping Oklahoma in the Gator Bowl

Florida State did in fact accept that bid, its first major-bowl date, against Oklahoma. Florida State was 8-1-1, ranked No. 10 in The Associated Press poll. Biletnikoff had become the Seminoles' first bona fide All-American, not only a first-teamer but a consensus selection.

Oklahoma, 6-3-1, went into the Jan. 2 game crippled. Four players — notably future pros Lance Rentzel and Ralph Neely — were ruled ineligible because of premature signing of pro contracts.

Florida State, too, was at less than full strength. Lee Narramore, a tough fullback, was ruled out on an academic count, and Florida State decided not to utilize hot placekicker/kickoff man Murdock because of uncertainty over his eligibility.

At a time when he was desperate for an adequate kickoff man, Peterson had issued an appeal to the student body for help. Murdock had stepped forward and quickly become one of the best FSU would know.

Strangely, his absence at the Gator Bowl may have helped precipitate a rout of Oklahoma — not really as close as the final 36-19

Calming down after getting upset over the nature of the Gator Bowl bid in 1964, Peterson smilingly accepts an invitation to the Jacksonville game after FSU's first victory over Florida. Standing is Ash Verlander, president of the bowl. Next to Peterson are Vaughn Mancha, athletic director; George Olsen, general manager of the bowl; and C.J. Gunter, chairman of the bowl's selection committee.

score reflected. Though FSU kickoffs were on occasion pathetic, the Seminoles passed for touchdowns on fourth down when they otherwise would have attempted field goals.

Tensi was phenomenal — 23 completions of 36 passes for 303 yards and five touchdowns.

Biletnikoff was phenomenal — 13 receptions for 191 yards and four touchdowns.

"We gave them a show, didn't we?" said Peterson. It was the greatest passing show in the history of not only the Gator Bowl but any bowl up to that point.

Biletnikoff signed a pro contract with the Oakland Raiders, under Gator Bowl goalposts, immediately after the game.

Not so long after, Biletnikoff would be wed under Campbell Stadium goalposts. The marriage did not last, and years later Biletnikoff, recalling those vows under the goalposts, said: "I wish the damn things had fallen down."

Serving as receivers coach that year, Bobby Bowden coached Biletnikoff. He remembered Biletnikoff catching Crutchfield's attention right away.

"For some reason in the year before we did not get the ball to him that much," said Bowden. "But Crutchfield's thought was we had to get the ball to this guy.

"That 1964 season was one when Florida State had great defense. When people talk about it, they mention Tensi and Biletnikoff and tend not to remember that great defense.

"Crutchfield played a mighty big role. He understood Coach Pete better than anybody.

"I thought Pete beat everybody to the passing game. Only ones he didn't was John Bridgers when he coached at Baylor, and that guy at Tulsa (Bobby Dobbs). Sending out five receivers on a pass pattern was something unheard of back then, but Pete did it."

'65: The FBI comes to town

Florida State opened in 1965 with a 7-0 loss at TCU. Still a team that had a good defensive nucleus, FSU was minus its stars of offense.

Establishing a polished attack was always a laborious process. "You can teach offense," Peterson once said, "only as fast as your dumbest player can fathom it."

Peterson remembered increased difficulty, following the 1964 season, getting good football players past the registrar.

"We had Dean Moore always on our back

Fred Biletnikoff during pregame ceremonies and in 1965, during his wedding ceremonies — right beneath the goalposts.

about academics," said Peterson. "It was tough — real tough. But I think the fact that we had some pretty good students among our players helped in the long run.

"In 1965 we could only get 18 recruits into school — but, boy, they were special. Still, it really hurt us — not being able to fully capitalize, in recruiting, on the good year we had."

Florida State squeezed by Baylor in Tallahassee 9-7 as rumors of "fix" swirled around town.

John Bridgers, then coach of Baylor (later athletic director at FSU), received more than one phone call from Texans saying that "something funny was going on," that the game had been taken off the boards — bookies would accept no more bets — and that officials would be involved.

The night before the game, Bridgers huddled with FSU officials, including Peterson. Officials of both the Southwest and Southeastern conferences — a split crew worked the game — were notified.

On the game's third play, Baylor's fine quarterback, Terry Southall, left the field with a broken ankle. Looking at films later, Bridgers thought the pass rush that got Southall might have arrived a little late — but the flag that fell was on Baylor for holding.

"Never in my life did a team of mine draw so many holding penalties as that game," said Bridgers. Baylor was assessed 106 penalty yards, FSU 35. On a Florida State pass for the winning touchdown, covering 59 yards, it seemed to Baylor coaches and fans that a Southwest Conference official had screened out a Baylor defensive back who could have made a saving tackle.

False rumor? Coincidental happenings?

Whatever, the FBI investigated, contacting this writer, among others.

Nothing came of it.

A new defense had helped Florida State contain Baylor's passing game.

"We used a two-deep alignment of the defensive backs, and as far as I know it had never been used before in college," said Peterson. "On a visit to California, I got the idea from John McKay, and he had got it from Bear Bryant — but at that time, neither had used it. Later, everybody would use it."

The irony of that was Alabama and Bear Bryant, three games later, would spring that new defense on Florida State.

"And we didn't know what the hell to do with it," said Peterson.

Better knowing what to do after his Kentucky team had been blown out in Tallahassee

48-6 the year before, Coach Charley Bradshaw chafed for vengeance on his own field.

"I don't know when I've ever wanted anything more in my life," said the coach as the Seminoles moved into Lexington.

He got it.

It was 14-14 at halftime, with two Daytona Beach pals collaborating on a 100-yard return of a Kentucky kickoff seconds before the end of the first quarter.

Bill Moreman took the kickoff in the end zone, lateraled to T.K. Wetherell at the 13 — and the swift flanker took it the rest of the way.

Wetherell had been the more coveted prospect, and Moreman had come in a kind of package deal because Wetherell wanted his friend along. Moreman became one of the outstanding runners of the Peterson era. Wetherell, later a state legislator, also contributed impressively.

Ahead 24-20 with less than 6 minutes left, Florida State lost 26-24 as Kentucky struck for a touchdown behind Norton's splendid 16-for-28 passing. "A great display of forward passing," praised Peterson, who had witnessed a few such.

Before 40,112 Campbell Stadium fans, Florida State cast another spell on Georgia. The Bulldogs came in unbeaten (4-0) and ranked No. 5 nationally.

Georgia led 3-0 going into the last half, but its hot-running back, Bob Taylor, soon left the field with a broken leg. On a remarkable 20-yard Moreman run through several defenders on the first play of the final quarter, FSU took a 7-3 lead. Later, a John Hosack punt backed the Bulldogs to their 4. A Pat Hodgson fumble after a reception paved a field goal at the gun that made it a final 10-3.

Georgia's Dooley would remember the uncommon din created by Florida State fans stomping their feet in Campbell Stadium's steel stands, perhaps also a banner in those stands that had proclaimed at the start: "Georgia — Say Goodbye to the Top Ten."

At Alabama, Florida State said goodbye to its delirium.

"Humiliating," said Peterson after Bear Bryant's team prevailed 21-0. "They did the same doggone thing against us with that two-deep defense that we did to Baylor."

Instead of the customary what-happened column in the Tallahassee Democrat the following day, I ran a single small-type line followed by blank space. That line read: "TUSCALOOSA, Ala., Oct. 23 — Aw, forget it...."

(It would hardly rank, however, as my favorite non-column. That one was written by a dear, departed colleague at the Daytona Beach News-Journal. One summer day, below Benny Kahn's column head, a single line read: "Benny Kahn has gone fishing." The following day, my favorite non-column evolved, with a line reading: "Benny Kahn has gone fishing again, since he didn't catch anything yesterday.")

The brief career of Robert Urich

That Alabama game of 1965 was perhaps the most memorable Robert Urich would know. It was his last.

As the second half opened, he streaked downfield to block on the kickoff return. As he threw the block, an Alabama knee caught him in the head.

And more than 20 years later he still had headaches.

Late the following week, on the way to practice, he collapsed. Hospitalized, he got a diagnosis of a midbrain injury — a mild clot. No more football, Urich was told, and look to the probability of headaches the rest of your life.

"He was going to be an outstanding player, I guarantee you," said Peterson. "We had

Bill Moreman (shown above right, in '66 action) and pal T.K. Wetherell (left): They came together, and starred together.

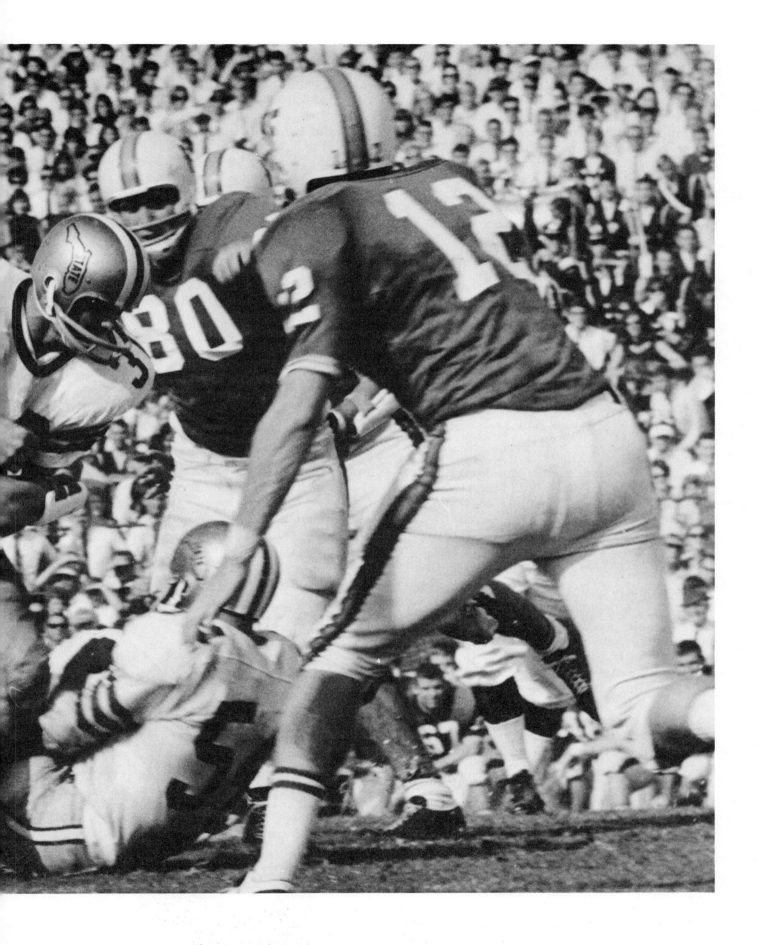

planned to start him at center the following week."

Urich continued, as a team manager, until graduation following the 1967 season. Additionally, Peterson had Urich assist him in production of his TV show, and sometimes the player would be up until 2 a.m. selecting film and putting together an outline. Always interested in theater, Urich moved on after FSU to Michigan State for a master's in broadcasting. Employed later with a Chicago radio station, he was also involved in an actors' workshop.

"Then I met Burt Reynolds, and we had a couple of things in common," said Urich. "Don Fauls had wrapped both our ankles — right?"

With an assist from Reynolds, Urich moved on to stardom as an actor.

In fact, Urich had several things in common with Reynolds. Each had been more promising than the average player. Each was propelled by adversity toward Hollywood.

The son of a steelworking dad, Urich hailed from Peterson's hometown — Toronto, Ohio. Out of high school, he had been sought by many.

Miami flew him down for a visit.

"It was the first time I consumed an alcoholic beverage," Urich later recalled. "Joe Mira (brother of quarterback George) took me out on the town.

"When I got back, somebody had broken into my room and stole my clothes. Then they got me into a poker game and took all my money.

"So I didn't wanta go to Miami."

Like Reynolds, Urich would remain an avid Florida State fan, with occasional returns to campus.

He thought his continuing headaches might not be due to that old football injury. "It could be sinus, it could be the pressure — it could be a lot of stuff," he said.

He was asked what he did when the headaches come.

"I drop back 10 yards and punt," said a smiling Urich.

'One of those years'

Dropping back and punting was a frequent happening in a game that followed Alabama in 1965. Jerry Claiborne's line on Florida State, before his pesky Virginia Tech (5-1) came to Tallahassee, was: "The best team in the country with a 2-3 record."

The record became 3-3 as FSU won 7-6 despite its four turnovers to Tech's none. And then it was 4-3 as Wake Forest tumbled 35-0.

But the Seminoles would win no more.

N.C. State won 3-0 at its homecoming with a hard-rushing pass defense and a 41-yard field goal.

Florida State managed a 16-16 tie with a talented Houston team, fresh from upsets of Ole Miss and Kentucky, and featuring the startling Warren McVea. On a kickoff return, the elusive McVea — one of the first blacks to play in the Southwest Conference — scored on a 92-yarder.

Phil Spooner showed some notable moves himself, scoring on an 80-yard run from scrimmage. Houston tied it 13-13, but FSU went up at halftime 16-13 on a 41-yard Pete Roberts field goal. It was tied again, and for good, on a third-quarter Houston field goal.

Sugar Bowl-bound Florida was a 9-point favorite as Florida State returned to Gainesville for the seventh time in the eight years of the series.

"You can't trust nobody in football no more," said Gene Ellenson, Florida's shrewd defensive coordinator. He had reasoned that Florida State would try to run right at small linebacker Jack Card, as Miami had with telling effectiveness.

Instead, Florida State, notably in the last half, startled UF defenders with short delay passes that came close to achieving an upset.

In the third quarter Florida State trailed 16-3, but rallied, and with 2:10 left it took a 17-16 lead on Ed Pritchett's fourth-down pass to Jerry Jones.

But with 1:19 to go, Steve Spurrier threw

his third touchdown strike, a 25-yarder to Charley Casey that capped a quick 71-yard movement. On the touchdown pass, Spurrier had rolled wide, then waved Casey deeper — into the end zone — before throwing.

"What made the play go," said Spurrier years later, "was an FSU lineman jumped offsides and I saw the referee's flag.

"I knew we had a free play. That's why I waved Casey into the end zone. Even if FSU intercepted, we'd still have the ball."

The Gators got icing on it all when Allen Trammell sped 46 yards with a Pritchett interception to boost the score to 30-17.

Pritchett completed 18 passes — the kind of day that many had projected. But his career was hindered by knee problems. Three times he underwent surgery.

In an innovative move, Florida State utilized five defensive backs — a "nickel" defense well ahead of its time. The Seminoles had also used a traditional, if questionable,

prevent alignment that prevented nothing as Spurrier picked it to pieces on his great drive.

"It was one of those games, and one of those years," said Peterson, and it was.

'66: The arrival of Sellers

It would be one of those games — only more so — the next time against Florida, and it looked a little like one of those years, too, as the Seminoles in 1966 dropped two of their first three.

Houston collared a defense-depleted Florida State team 21-13 in a Tallahassee opener, getting long touchdowns on an 80-yard pass to the gifted McVea and an 82-yard Mike Spratt punt return. FSU quarterback Kim Hammond threw two touchdown passes, but it was not enough.

One of the bright spots of this year, though, would be Ron Sellers.

Sellers came in 1965, the year after Biletnikoff's departure, but in a day when freshmen were ineligible for varsity play. He would compete in 1966, 1967 and 1968, and his career yardage on receptions (3,598) would still stand as a national-collegiate record 20 years later.

But as a stringbean 6-foot-4 and 190, in contrast to Biletnikoff's 6-1 and 180, Sellers was a player nobody much wanted — perhaps Florida State least of all.

It was only because it desperately wanted a quarterback — Peterson always desperately wanted quarterbacks and usually got them — that Florida State indirectly acquired Sellers.

Gary Pajcic was a big quarterback out of Jacksonville's Paxon High, a Sellers teammate. The two had played together not only in football but on a state-championship basketball team as well.

Harbison was recruiting Pajcic. Hard.

"I believe if you take this guy Sellers, you can get Pajcic," John Griner, an FSU running back of the Nugent era, told Harbison.

To Harbison, the skinny Sellers didn't look like much of a football player.

"What he looks like to me is Abe Lincoln," said Harbison.

Harbison checked with Peterson. "Can't play, too fragile," Peterson recalled telling Harbison.

Later, Peterson recalled Harbison calling again, and saying if he didn't sign Sellers, the Seminoles would get nobody they wanted — Pajcic included — in Jacksonville.

"So I told him to sign him," said Peterson. "But there was something about there not

Robert Urich posing for the camera — in 1965 as a Seminole, left, and about 20 years later as a television star.

being a scholarship over there for him to sign. And I said 'Go mimeograph one.'

"You gotta be flexible in this business."

In the second game of the '66 season, the Pajcic-Sellers tandem clicked.

With the Seminoles down 7-0 at Miami, Pajcic came off the bench to throw a 27-yard scoring pass to fellow sophomore Sellers. Miami, with a team that included great end Ted Hendricks, went back up 14-7, but on the kickoff return Moreman and Wetherell worked their palship thing, with Wetherell streaking 82 yards to a touchdown following a lateral. Florida State won 23-20 on Pajcic's 23-yard pass to Thurston Taylor — and recovery of a Miami fumble at the Seminole 4 following a Dale Braggins-led defensive stand.

It was in the Miami game that "The Meeces" were born.

Charley Tate, the Miami coach, observed that smallish Florida State defenders scampered around like field mice. Promptly, that crew dubbed itself "The Meeces," after a cat-and-mice cartoon show of the time. Jinx, the cat, was fond of saying: "I hate them meeces to pieces."

Lane Fenner enters history

No undersized meece, Lane Fenner was a 6-foot-5 junior wide receiver of free spirit out of Evansville, Ind., whose football legacy would be one non-touchdown.

Florida led FSU in Campbell Stadium 22-19 with 28 seconds left, the Seminoles stand-

ing second-and-10 at the Gator 45. Sellers had been shaken up on the previous long pattern, and a fresh Fenner came in. It was not only Fenner's first play of the game, but his first of the season as well.

The play was a post pattern that Pajcic told Fenner to turn outside.

Pajcic rolled right, threw long and perhaps perfectly — roughly 55 yards in the air. A remarkable throw. Fenner had raced downfield, then veered toward the end-zone flag.

Fenner caught the ball, over his left shoulder, one step over the goal line. As defender

Ron Sellers receives an honor and receives a visitor — fellow Seminole Burt Reynolds.

Larry Rentz caught up and tackled him, Fenner was rolled over and well out of bounds.

The primary defender, Bobby Downs, was outrun on the play. Rentz, playing free safety, had come over to help, and he recalled tipping the ball as he and Fenner leaped.

"Fenner made a great catch," said Rentz.

Doug Moseley, the field judge trailing the play, raced into the end zone and started waving his arms in front of his face — no catch, no touchdown! He indicated Fenner was out of bounds.

Spectators packed along the sidelines rushed Moseley. Fenner later recalled his own screaming and cursing.

"It was a touchdown," reaffirmed Fenner 20 years later.

Moseley, 20 years later, still insisted his call was correct.

"I saw the films, both FSU's and Florida's," he said. "I looked at them frame by frame. And there is one frame that showed definite daylight between the ball and Fenner's hands as he's touching out of bounds.

"I have never reconsidered because I made the right call."

The controversial Lane Fenner catch, in the '66 game against Florida. The referee said Fenner did not have possession of the ball before going out of bounds. Fenner and FSU fans strongly disagreed.

Fenner recalled leaving the official in his running wake. "He was tired," said the receiver.

As Florida State fans left the stadium, there was no great furor. Few had been in position to see the play well. Writers in the pressbox, high on the other side of the field, had no quarrel with Moseley's call.

Most of the outrage started surfacing a few hours later. Photographers produced prints showing Fenner catching the ball, apparently firmly in hand, a good yard in bounds.

"A damned tragedy," said Peterson after the game, slamming his keys to the locker-room floor. "I don't know. I just don't know."

Fenner thought he knew. "I'm sure I was in bounds," he said. "I didn't juggle the ball. I didn't believe it when he said I was out."

Moseley, who soon was hung in effigy on campus, seemed to many to be out of position for a proper call. Game films indicated that. Those films also showed FSU fans crowded in too closely on the sidelines, possibly obscuring his vision. Florida State took measures to assure that fans never again would be packed into such areas.

The debate over Moseley's call rolled on as days turned into weeks and into years. Pictures of Fenner's catch became prized items among some Seminole fans. Two decades later the Tallahassee Democrat still received occasional requests for prints.

Raging Seminoles sometimes had salt rubbed into their wounded pride. In his early book "Let No Man Put Asunder," on the history of the series, Julian Clarkson quotes UF graduate Lawton Chiles, later a U.S. senator, grinning as he replied to a Florida State fan: "You're right, he was in and we stole it from you. That makes it even sweeter."

Twenty years after the fact, Ray Graves reflected on the call.

"My impression," said the Florida coach, "was that maybe we got a break."

Florida left town after the "Lane Fenner Game" with a 4-0 record, Spurrier moving toward a Heisman Trophy. Sports Illustrated would say at season's end that he won it on Moseley's call that day in Tallahassee — suggesting that the Gators otherwise would not have had the record to earn Heisman consideration for a player.

Dear Sun Bowl . . .

At Texas Tech, the Seminoles put on an offensive show and won 42-33. In the pressbox during the fourth quarter, one Texas Tech official muttered to another: "Pay those guys, and get them the hell out of town."

Moving through an up-and-down season, Florida State stood 5-4 when it got a surprising bowl bid — with a home game against Maryland still remaining.

On a Sunday afternoon following the ninth game, Lonnie Burt, sports-information director of FSU, and I were talking.

Both of us had fond remembrances of the 1954 Sun Bowl in El Paso and had talked of going back one day. I suggested sending a telegram, telling the Sun Bowl folks of FSU's merit. There was a question of the proper person to receive the telegram, and I drove home and found a Sun Bowl program of the previous year.

Then the two of us composed the glowing telegram and dispatched it to Harrison Kohl, the bowl's executive director. The two of us knew Kohl slightly. Maryland, in the final game, would be no problem, the telegram suggested.

By the following evening, startled Florida State had received and accepted a Sun Bowl bid.

Getting a bowl game with an $8 telegram would soon be beyond the realm of the possible. At the time, the Sun Bowl was a little desperate and was intrigued by the opportunity of landing a team that had been so dazzling two years prior in the Gator Bowl.

A football game on Christmas Eve

Fortunately, Maryland indeed proved to be no problem in the last game as FSU romped 45-21, finished 6-4, and prepared to play 9-1 Wyoming at El Paso on Christmas Eve.

It was a season in which Florida State played many later pro greats — Larry Csonka and Floyd Little of Syracuse, Miami's Ted Hendricks, by way of example — and in the Sun Bowl it would tangle with another.

Jim Kiick's running — and Florida State's lack of same (minus-21 rushing) — were notable factors as the Seminoles fell 28-20.

But Kim Hammond had bolstered expectations for 1967 with three touchdown passes in the bowl.

In a Friday-night opener at Houston, with Pajcic at quarterback, Florida State was slammed 33-13 by a tough opponent. Peterson called it the worst game a team of his ever played. It was also the Seminoles' first-ever venture on artificial turf, as well as their first in the Astrodome.

Sellers didn't like the place at all. "I missed two passes — went right through my hands —

because I couldn't judge the ball," he said. "You can't see in there. The background is terrible."

Peterson had another thought. "When our little boys saw the inside of that *Astronomical* Dome, their eyes got as big as *sausages*," he said on his TV show.

On the following day — a Saturday — the Seminoles' eyes perhaps narrowed a bit as they found themselves practicing, in full pads, back in Tallahassee.

Alabama awaited in Birmingham — unbeaten in 21 straight games, a three-touchdown favorite. ABC would film portions of a documentary on Bear Bryant during the course of the game.

The game was an all-timer, a classic — a stunning 37-37 tie that rocked the football world. And that ABC documentary would show a startled Bear Bryant bellowing on the sidelines just after Walt Sumner returned a punt for a Florida State touchdown: "What's going on out there — what the hell is going on out there!"

In one game Alabama gave up as many points as it had during all of the previous season.

Peterson is inclined to feel that this, in fact, was the most memorable game of his 11 seasons.

"We had so much adversity going into the game," he said. "We had just been blown out at Houston.

"We changed quarterbacks, and we changed centers.

"Ken Hart had started the Houston game at center — a great athlete, but there was some trouble with the snap, and we moved him to guard.

"We put Ted Mosley in there at center, and he came up with a 103-degree fever. We put him in ice to keep it down. And he played a simply great game."

Hammond and Sellers played fantastic

This newspaper photo of an altered billboard appeared in 1967, after FSU tied the Tide.

games as FSU cut out an early 14-0 lead. "He picked us with his passes like you would pick a chicken," said Bryant of Hammond. "We were lucky we weren't beaten." Alabama stayed close only because of the heroics of Ken Stabler at quarterback.

Tough running by halfback Larry Green kept Alabama's defense honest — a key part of the game plan — but FSU heroes were abundant.

For Hammond, it was the start of a swell of popularity that would last a long time.

The next week, bumper stickers read: "Hammond for President — Sellers for Governor."

Hammond, a senior, had served a long apprenticeship on the bench. He had grown impatient waiting for opportunity.

"Hammond told me, 'Coach, I'm wasting my time here,'" recalled Peterson.

"And I told him he could do one of two things — he could quit, or he could be ready.

"He was ready."

Sellers said the team went to Birmingham thinking it could win with a couple of breaks. "We got the breaks," he said, "and we should have beat them."

The Alabama tie was celebrated like few victories in FSU history. "Unless we forget about Alabama, and quickly, we stand to get beat on our own field," warned Peterson.

It happened. N.C. State won 20-10, leaving the Seminoles winless in their first three games.

Florida State lost no more.

Revenge for the Fenner game

On a rainy night in College Station, FSU fell behind 9-0 to a Texas A&M team that would eventually win the Southwest Conference title. In the last half, the rain let up and FSU opened up with rallying passes. A Dale McCullers tackle brought a late Aggies fumble, and Moreman sped 27 yards — "like a streaking comet," described Peterson — for the late touchdown that won it by a point, 19-18.

Rather handily, FSU won five more. One was 38-15 over old nemesis Virginia Tech, on a night when Peterson remained home with a leg problem. Bob Harbison, then in his 20th year as an assistant, was placed in charge.

"It was the only time in my life I was ever a head coach," said Harbison. "We won like we did, and I felt pretty good about that."

High drama remained a hallmark of the Florida-FSU game in a Nov. 25 finale at Gainesville. Never had Florida State won on Florida Field. FSU partisans, the Fenner play of the year before on their minds, wore buttons that read: "Forget, hell!"

A 9-yard Hammond pass to Moreman provided an early 7-3 lead, and the Seminoles never trailed.

On a sneak for a touchdown, Hammond made it 14-3. But in the middle of the second quarter he left the field — unconscious — after a face-mask tackle by linebacker Tom Abdelnour.

"He was just laying there on that field," said Peterson. "I looked out there and thought he was dead."

At halftime, Hammond was out of it — conscious, but not sure where he was. "All I remembered was somebody grabbing my face mask and jerking my head," said Hammond. "Then the lights went out. At halftime I couldn't even recognize our players.

"At one point they asked me to go to the blackboard and diagram one of our plays. I didn't do too well.

"When I went back in late, all of a sudden I could see clearly again."

Particularly enraged that no penalty was called on the play, some FSU fans would attempt to make the Abdelnour matter equivalent to the Fenner matter. Pictures of the play, clearly showing the face-mask tackle, were around for a while. But, unlike Fenner, the Abdelnour matter sort of faded.

In the third quarter, Florida closed to within 14-9. Florida was knocking at FSU's 13 as the last quarter started, but Mike Bugar — who years later would be a Gator coach under Charley Pell — threw a Florida runner for a loss, then moments later recovered a fumble at the 7.

FSU was still in trouble. A run got 1 yard.

Then in came Hammond, for the first time since his injury.

On the first play he threw 51 yards to Sellers at the Florida 41. On the second he handed to Green for 3 yards. And on the third he threw long again, to Sellers.

"I thought it was a duck," said Hammond. Wobbly or not, the ball got to Sellers in the end zone for a touchdown that made it 21-9.

"It was really lucky to catch the ball," recalled Sellers. "It was in the sun."

Following drama had Florida scoring, then threatening again with ample time left, but Hammond's heroics were decisive.

Florida Staters would have to nurture the

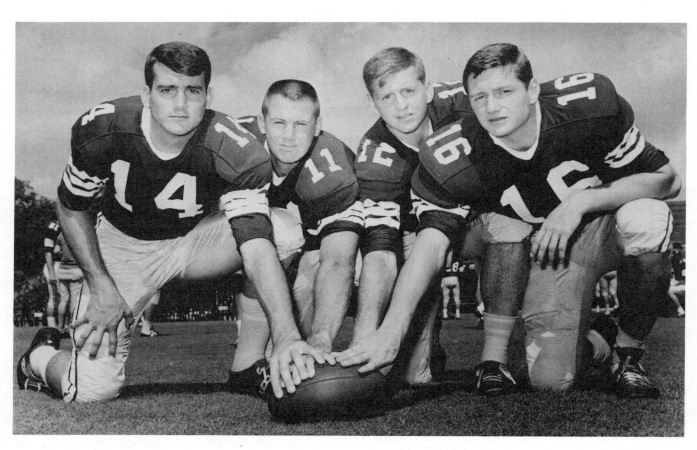

Four quarterbacks: Bill Cappleman, Kim Hammond, Bill Burkhardt, Gary Pajcic.

100

memory of that game a long while. Ten years would elapse before FSU again beat Florida.

The game was starting to change — and in more than accent on passing. Two days before Christmas of 1967, FSU signed its first black player ever — but halfback Ernest Cook never enrolled, opting instead to go to Minnesota, where he did well.

In an improbable Gator Bowl game, the Seminoles did well enough.

"I believe Florida State is the best passing team I've ever seen," said Joe Paterno, the young coach of Penn State days before his team's Gator Bowl date with the Seminoles. Peterson said Penn State had some of the best linemen he had ever seen.

Penn State jumped ahead 17-0.

Early in the second half, after stopping FSU at its 1, Penn State, still ahead 17-0, came up fourth-and-short at its 15. Paterno made the surprising decision to go for it.

Penn State did not make it. Moments later, Sellers cuddled a touchdown pass from Hammond. A fumble provided another opportunity that FSU quickly cashed. With less than 30 seconds left, looking at fourth down on the 8, Florida State tied the game 17-17 on a Grant Guthrie field goal.

"I blew it," said Paterno.

Sports Illustrated, in a postseason appraisal, reckoned 7-2-2 Florida State No. 4 nationally, behind Southern Cal, Oklahoma and Purdue.

In other personnel areas FSU sometimes came up short — but never in quarterbacks, it seemed, during Peterson's time.

'68: Five-touchdown game for Sellers

Hammond was gone, but Bill Cappleman was around, along with Tommy Warren, as FSU looked to a vintage year in 1968. Peterson saw his personnel as probably "the best nucleus" he had known at FSU.

But the start was demanding — Maryland, Florida, Texas A&M on successive weekends.

Maryland fell 24-14. But Florida was — well — Florida.

In a column on the Friday before the game, I suggested that if each team played its game, if there were no peculiar bounces, then "there ain't no way, Florida."

Both sides attempted to turn the phrase into a positive force. Florida State fans chanted "there ain't no way" as Florida players came onto the field. Meanwhile, Florida made sure every player got a copy of the column the morning of the game.

Any qualifying references were quickly forgotten as Florida dominated defensively in a tough game — shutting down Sellers perhaps as he never before had been, and never again would be. Later, Graves said that the Gators had gone in more than willing to risk holding penalties to stop Sellers. Defensive back Steve Tannen was on Sellers like a glove.

"We stopped today an offense that has few peers in college football," said the coach, "and a receiver that has none."

The score was 9-3, accurately reflecting Florida superiority on this day.

"Big thing was Florida stopped a team that wasn't stopped any other time all year," said Peterson.

"We tightened up. It was like we had an 8-foot putt — and we tightened up!"

But Peterson, with his passing game, had forced others to tighten up — most definitely including Florida — and Graves several years later doffed his cap to him.

"No two ways about it, Pete revolutionized football in the South," said Graves. "He influenced us all with the pro-type passing game."

Graves recalled running game film back and forth, trying to fathom Florida State's passing success against his Gators.

"Their pass routes were so new at the time, no way you could stop 'em," he said. "So we put a lot of it in ourselves, and that was about the time Spurrier came along. It was so simple. Defensive coaches at the time just didn't have the answer.

"I remember one night at Baton Rouge when we didn't have over maybe three players who could line up and physically handle the man across from him. But we picked LSU apart, just like Tensi and Biletnikoff had picked us."

In 1968 others were indeed starting to catch on, but Florida State, in the regular season, would lose only once again — to Virginia Tech, the familiar thorn, 40-22. Jerry Claiborne's Gobblers always seemed to defend against FSU passes better than any other foe, and on this occasion six interceptions were more than somewhat helpful.

Peterson had his players in an uproar as they met a good N.C. State team in Raleigh. In the dressing room, he challenged them — told them they were scared.

Dale McCullers, a senior linebacker enjoying an uncommonly good season, challenged the coach, saying that he wasn't scared. Peterson retorted that McCullers hadn't done a thing all year.

If Peterson's idea was to rile his players, he

surely succeeded. N.C. State never knew what hit it. Final score: 48-7.

"We had been an up-and-down team," said Peterson. "If we were going to a bowl game, we had to beat N.C. State.

"I tried in that dressing room to get that whole group mad — challenging them. McCullers' response to that challenge was exactly what I wanted. Fitting the plan perfectly.

"McCullers was one helluva football player."

Endlessly, Peterson sought means — sometimes extreme — to motivate his players.

"We had to come up with something," he said. "So often, we were fighting with a short stick. But what I came up with sure didn't always work.

"I remember one time at Virginia Tech I bragged 'em all up. Told 'em how good they were. It all backfired on me.

"One fullback I bragged on so went out there and just fumbled it away."

The surehanded Sellers made his last home game one to remember — five touchdown catches among his 14 receptions as Wake Forest bowed 42-24. Seven times during his three years Sellers caught 13 or more passes in a game. Tops was 16 against South Carolina in 1968.

The dirty-jerseys game

In the final regular-season game of 1968, Florida State registered what some think was its best effort of all time — whipping vastly favored Houston 40-20 in Jacksonville.

During that era, Houston annually ranked among the nation's top five offensive teams. The Cougars had just blown out Tulsa 100-6, accumulating 762 yards. Stars included Elmo Wright, possibly the game's fastest receiver, and Paul Gipson, viewed by some as the game's best runner.

Florida State had never beaten Houston. This was the celebrated dirty-jerseys game.

Once again seeking to motivate his team, Peterson brought out dirty jerseys from the game before. The tactic again seemed successful.

The coach indicated there would be no clean jerseys. For the game, only dirty ones from the week before would be available.

"In the game before, we had been behind Wake Forest 24-14 in the last half," said Peterson. "Then we cut loose in that last half — maybe the best last half we ever played — with 28 points and won 42-24.

"Somebody said to me we ought to hang on to those old dirty jerseys and wear 'em against

Houston. Not knowing for sure what I would do, I just told Tillman Dixon (equipment manager) not to wash them — just hang 'em up somewhere.

"Well, we took those dirty jerseys — filthy, stinking, I mean — over there to Jacksonville. And I told the squad we were going to pick up where we left off with Wake Forest — wearing those dirty jerseys.

"Boy, those players were mad. Literally steaming!"

While the team warmed up, Peterson had Dixon place clean jerseys in each locker.

"Then I gave them the option to change into clean ones if they wanted," said the coach. "But, at the same time, I discouraged them from changing."

Almost all opted for the dirty jerseys.

Cappleman had a spectacular passing game. Sellers caught 14. And defensive back Walt Sumner, later a pro with the Cleveland Browns for several years, did a number on Wright. It was 25-0 at halftime, with FSU fans chanting "We want a hundred."

FSU's game plan had been simple, involving calculated risk. "We tried to take away three of the four things they did with the option, while hoping they didn't kill us with the fourth," said Peterson. FSU brought up the linebackers and one cornerback — utilizing, in effect, an eight-man line — and dared Houston to throw.

In a season that had seen Sellers break a national record for career pass yardage, his former Paxon mate, Pajcic, faded in the manner of so very many — a series of injuries that had started in his freshman year.

Meanwhile, Cappleman in his junior year had the best statistical year of any FSU quarterback of history — 162 completions of 287 passes for 2,410 yards and 25 touchdowns.

Umbrellas and overcoats were more relevant than statistics to viewers at Atlanta's first annual Peach Bowl on Dec. 30.

LSU won 31-27 on this miserable evening as FSU finished 8-3.

Peterson put Florida State in four bowls over a five-season span, but 1968 would be the last.

Take your pick — Biletnikoff or Sellers

The debate among Seminoles has raged for years: Who was better, Sellers or Biletnikoff?

Peterson would decline to single out Sellers as the most memorable player of his time.

"There were so many," he said. "There was Kim Hammond and Bill Moreman and Dick Hermann and Phil Spooner and Del Williams and Dale McCullers and Jack Edwards and Fred Biletnikoff and James Thomas and. . . .

"Be sure and say they were all memorable to me — important to me.

"Sellers was surely one of the ones. I remember in his first spring practice, every time he got hit I would cringe. One time, though, I saw him catch a hook and three guys hit him, and he came up laughing. And I said, 'Boy, is he going to be a great football player.'"

When the extroverted Sellers caught a pass, he sometimes looked ungainly, as taller folks frequently do. He had phenomenal hands. Some say he never dropped one in a Florida State game — and if he did, surely such times were few. He had deceptive speed, with that long stride, and got open with ease.

The introverted Biletnikoff had such grace in his moves and catches. He worked at those moves and catches far more than most — surely far more than Sellers — and had fine quickness, if not great foot speed.

Biletnikoff catching a short pass often seemed a work of art, and it was. Sellers catching a long one often looked ridiculously easy, and it was.

Both had strong basketball backgrounds and fine ability in that sport. Sellers actually went out for the Florida State team, but that came to an end at 4 a.m. one day when a perturbed Peterson phoned Hugh Durham with a strong suggestion that this situation end immediately, and preferably sooner. Durham gracefully granted his point.

Biletnikoff had the far greater pro career. No comparison there. And what Biletnikoff did in his relatively short, injury-hindered time was very probably more dramatic, from the viewpoint of FSU fans, than what Sellers did in his.

But if you're talking college receivers, the vote here is Sellers. I'm not sure there has ever been a better one at the college level.

In one season, Sellers would come within one of catching as many passes as Biletnikoff did his entire FSU time — and for more yardage and touchdowns. Biletnikoff's career total: 87 for 1,463 yards and 11 touchdowns. Sellers' last-year (1968) total: 86 for 1,496 yards and 12 touchdowns.

Twenty years later, he still had the college numbers: 212 receptions for 3,598 yards — an average of 119.9 receiving yards for every game he played in.

'69: The 27-fumble game

If the weather was ridiculous for the last game of 1968, it hardly approached that of the first game of 1969.

As college football celebrated its 100th anniversary, Wichita State and Florida State showed the game something it never before had seen.

That Campbell Stadium opener spawned a national-record 27 fumbles, plus a national-record 17 fumbles lost, and a national-record 10 fumbles lost by one team. Wichita State got dunked 24-0 as continuous heavy rain made a swamp of the field. FSU lost seven of its 10 fumbles, Wichita 10 of its 17.

One way or another, Florida State would beat Miami, and this time 16-14 on Grant Guthrie's 31-yard field goal with 1:55 left.

And one way or another Florida would continue to beat the Seminoles, and this time 21-7 on three John Reaves touchdown passes, including two to the greatly gifted Carlos Alvarez.

After three victories, FSU managed a 10-10 tie on a blustery day at Virginia Tech on a remarkable 51-yard Guthrie field goal in the final quarter.

(With time to kill prior to the Blacksburg game, Bob Harbison had been walking off some of his nervous energy. He strayed from the stadium, walking to a nearby baseball field. Idly, he picked up a piece of paper blowing across the field. The paper reflected part of Tech's game plan.

("It was relevant, from a defensive standpoint," said Harbison. "It showed their formations, and how they were listed. If you knew how to decipher it, you knew where they would be running the ball. It helped our defense.")

The season tapered downward as Memphis State won 28-26 in Tallahassee, and Houston exacted a measure of Astrodome redemption 31-27. A 6-3-1 record earned no bowl bid.

"Cappleman had a great season for us the year before," said Peterson. "I thought he was the best in the country. But for some reason, his senior year wasn't quite as good. Maybe people were laying for him by then."

And the graduation of the spectacular Sellers surely had something to do with it.

The first black Seminoles to play

Peterson looked to a year of developing young talent, to a sophomore team in 1970. "We said, 'Hey, we're going to win some and lose some, and build for the next year.'"

But the young talent was surely better than he then suspected.

It would include the first blacks to play for

Three of the first black Seminoles to play: (clockwise) James Thomas, Eddie McMillan and Charlie Hunt.

the Seminoles — James "J.T." Thomas, Eddie McMillan, Charlie Hunt. In a Sept. 12 opener against Louisville, Thomas — a starter from the start — would become the first black to see varsity action for the Seminoles.

It was an era when Southern schools were moving gingerly into integrated athletics. Florida State had signed its first black player in December of 1967 — Daytona Beach's Ernest Cook, who failed to enroll. A little later, Calvin Patterson, a running back out of Miami, signed but never played.

Academically ineligible throughout his time at FSU, Patterson committed suicide in the summer prior to the last year he might have played — after Peterson's departure, during the coaching time of Larry Jones.

"Calvin had a lot of problems," said Peterson. "He had ability. I got alarmed when an English teacher sent to me a term paper that indicated suicidal tendencies. I talked to a psychology professor, and he said one thing I could do was try to get him to talk. And he did talk. He talked to me about the problems he had back home. Calvin was very troubled."

Thomas came to Florida State from Macon, Ga., and quickly became the first black to make an impact.

The fleet McMillan was a little slower developing, but soon he and Thomas would constitute what many considered the best set of cornerbacks in the nation. Hunt became a fine defensive end.

All three would play in the NFL later, Thomas an outstanding cornerback for several years with a Pittsburgh team that won three Super Bowls.

Almost, Florida State overlooked Thomas. It had passed on him when Harley Bowers, veteran sports editor of the Macon-Telegraph, called Peterson and made a strong recommendation. Peterson sent that area's recruiter back with instructions to sign Thomas.

One trait of Peterson was that he would not only listen hard to expressed opinions of people but actively seek those opinions. He would ask the thoughts of politicians, administrators, fans, a bellhop — anybody.

To a surprising degree, he often acted on these opinions. Sometimes things worked out extremely well. Sometimes not.

Few coaches ever sought the views of others in the profession more than Peterson, and he was constantly on the phone with many. Among these was Bear Bryant, who once told Peterson he was considering buying a pro team and, if he did, he wanted Peterson to coach it.

Bernie Sliger, in 1987 president of Florida

State for 10 years, was a Peterson friend of more than 30 years. For five years, when both were at Louisiana State, they were next-door neighbors.

"I have never known anyone that worked harder at preparing himself for his chosen field," said Sliger. "He has a brilliant offensive mind."

'70: 'Huff the magic dragon'

While brilliant offense took a while to surface in 1970, the squad's youthfulness showed up immediately.

Opening at home, FSU was fortunate to escape a Louisville team coached by Lee Corso, an outstanding Seminole of the Nugent era. Thanks to Thomas, FSU won it 9-7.

With 24 seconds left, Louisville stood poised for a winning field goal at the FSU 17, fourth down.

Thomas, who had blocked a second-quarter field-goal try, ripped through to block this one — but FSU was offsides, and Louisville got another, close chance.

And Thomas blocked that one, too.

FSU stood 2-1 going into the fourth game against Florida.

In Doug Dickey's first coaching year, Florida fell behind 7-0 but led 38-7 with seven minutes left as, in desperation, the Seminoles went to their No. 3 quarterback.

During those final seven minutes, the No. 3 quarterback — sophomore Gary Huff — passed for three touchdowns that wrought a face-saving final score of 38-27.

One newspaper heralded "Huff the Magic

It was "Huff the Magic Dragon" as quarterback Gary Huff set all-time FSU records for passing and total offense.

Dragon," but the magic would be a while evolving again.

As Huff got his first starting call, McMillan scored on an 80-yard kickoff return, but Memphis State got a touchdown at the gun — following a pass-interference call that had Peterson raging — and won 16-12.

Peterson changed quarterbacks again, going with senior Tommy Warren, a fine and versatile athlete — a heady one who read defenses well.

With the young talent coming along, Warren quarterbacked FSU to five straight victories — the last four romps: Miami 27-3, Clemson 38-13 (at a time when Hootie Ingram, later the FSU athletic director, coached the Tigers), Virginia Tech 34-8, Kansas State 33-7.

Kansas State came to Tallahassee with one of its best teams ever — a team quarterbacked by Lynn Dickey, a team that narrowly missed the Big Eight title, a team with five former Seminoles on the coaching staff (head coach Vince Gibson plus Gene McDowell, Y.C. McNease, Don Powell, Bobby Jackson).

But Kansas State was no match for Warren, Thomas — who intercepted Dickey three times — and mates.

Everything was coming up roses for the Seminoles.

A collapse, and a farewell

And then came a devastating Thanksgiving night at Tampa as FSU closed with Houston in a nationally televised game.

It was a night that changed much, including the destiny of more than one individual. The roses changed to thorns, delight to depression.

At halftime FSU led 21-12, the game seemingly in hand. But Warren had injured his shoulder in that first half, and it had tightened up on him during intermission. The decision to continue to play in the last half was one that did not work out at all. Clearly unable to throw normally, Warren — who rarely suffered interceptions — had three. Houston scored on six straight possessions and won 53-21.

When the score was 39-21, Houston's Nick Hohn, returning a punt along the sidelines, had been tripped by a Seminole standing on those sidelines. Dan Whitehurst, a sophomore linebacker who was a big part of the young talent corps, had impulsively extended a foot in the frustration of the moment.

Shown again and again on national TV, the

School spirit circa 1967, below, at the Gator Bowl. Above, a sign of a happy football town. And right, a Seminole crowd bakes in the 1968 sun.

act drew critical letters and comment that did nothing to alleviate a melancholy situation.

Soon Peterson himself would commit a somewhat impulsive act.

He had, during his 11 seasons, received a number of head-coaching offers. Beyond much question, he could have been head coach of the San Francisco 49ers (who came after him hard following the 1967 season), the Buffalo Bills and perhaps the Miami Dolphins. Clemson was among the colleges seeking him, and former coach Frank Howard thought he had a definite understanding with Peterson that he would come.

On a Sunday afternoon, Peterson made a sudden decision to accept Rice's offer as head coach and athletic director — a role that paid about $25,000 more than his approximate $30,000 base salary as Florida State's coach.

Peterson's attachment to Florida State and its people was strong, but he had coveted the athletic-director role at Florida State, had wanted some other improvements in his position and had been freshly discouraged by prospects of realizing those goals. The athletic director's role was denied him, and so was his request for more resources.

That Rice decision was one he tried to reverse early the following morning, but too late: Reporters and TV cameras had already swarmed to his home the day prior, and the word was all over the nation.

It was all over the nation, too, that during Peterson's last five years, Florida State threw the football better — more consistently, more effectively — than any other team in the land. An NCAA statistical study for the period showed the Seminoles averaging 260.4 yards per game passing while posting a record of 34-15-2. They had also ranked among the nation's 25 winningest teams for the period.

His stay at Rice would be brief. After a beginning that had excited fans, he finally accepted an NFL job — with the talent-poor Houston Oilers. His stay there was brief, too.

Peterson would later return to Florida, to a fund-raising role with FSU and a period of doing football color on radio, as well as serving as athletic director at the University of Central Florida.

Always a man of exceptional energy, Peterson summed up rather well one day:

"A rolling *pin* gathers no moss."

The Jones Years

A gentlemanly coach rides an early tide but gets submerged by a winless season

No coach in Florida State history — not Bobby Bowden nor Bill Peterson nor Tom Nugent nor Don Veller — stood taller than Larry Jones after his first season.

An honest man, a gentle man, Jones had been called by FSU President Stan Marshall "the forerunner of a new breed of coaches." He was, it was said, a coach who related to his players, rather than insisting upon the players relating to him. He spoke of love for his players, and there was sincerity in his word and manner.

Clearly, everybody — including the school's administrators and faculty — identified with him after that first season. A general view seemed to be that there stood no finer man in coaching than this smiling, considerate Arkansas native.

There was a memorable spring night in 1972 when Bob Hope came to town. He put on a show at Tully Gym, and the turnout of campus folks was considerable. When Jones was introduced in the audience, he drew louder, more prolonged applause than the featured star — a fact that did not escape Hope's attention, and he kidded the audience about it.

Less than two years later it had all turned to ashes. Jones became the first football coach Florida State fired.

Much of the "why" of this dramatic turn-around is perhaps woven in the fabric of turbulent times. Campus unrest continued after the sizzling Sixties and there was a growing, if

15 wins, 19 losses

Larry Jones in 1972.

uneasy, perception that the nation's youth must be better served — particularly with more careful attention to what young people had to say. To some, Jones seemed a man for the moment, and one well ahead of his peers in relating to young people.

Part of the turnaround was hard times.

Part of it, surely, was ill luck. Injuries and ailments would play an unusually large role during his three Florida State years.

Part of it, as Jones himself indicated, was failure to sign and retain enough good players to supplement the strong corps of juniors and seniors he inherited. Among those juniors and seniors were eight who would sign pro contracts — including some, such as cornerback J.T. Thomas and quarterback Gary Huff, who would be in the NFL for several years.

"I found a real good team, a very tough team," said Jones several years after the fact. "It was very competitive — the kind of players that really got after you!

"It was an outstanding junior-senior group. But the bad thing was the sophomore-freshman group — well, there was not much there. . . .

"I just know one thing: All those things piled up — the whole situation. It was not fair to Florida State, and it was not fair to me."

Trying to fill Peterson's shoes

Bill Peterson had departed for Rice in December. It remained for Jones and his staff — new, save for holdovers Bob Harbison and Bill Parcells — to round up the bulk of freshman recruits who enrolled in September of 1971.

The early portion of Coach Larry Jones' reign saw many good days. FSU President Stan Marshall, center, was happy; players were happy; fans were happy; Jones was happy.

109

"We did not realize the gap that had to be filled," said Jones. "We should have gone the junior-college route in a hurry. I think people used the fact that Coach Pete was leaving against FSU in recruiting even before he left."

Indeed, rumors of Peterson's impending departure had been around for several years — stemming from the overtures he had received from San Francisco, Miami and Buffalo.

"Whoever came in after Coach Pete left was going to have some problems," said Jones, "and I did not realize that for a while."

But, in Jones' view, the biggest negative, by far, was a lack of resources.

"You had an inadequate dressing-room situation," said Jones. "There was no weight room. I couldn't believe there was no training table, no player dormitory.

"With the progress FSU had made on the field, I couldn't see how they accomplished it with what they had."

Throughout his time, Peterson had fought for improvements — acquiring some, but not nearly as many as he felt were needed. With his teams winning, possibly people reasoned he did not really need anything more.

"The administration wanted to give us the things we needed, but the money simply was not there," said Jones. "I had not realized they had not put the money they made from football into improvements — because they needed that money to operate on.

"It was a time when the university was hurting financially, and the state was hurting, too.

"We kept losing coaches, because we couldn't pay them enough."

Another thing that hurt his program, in Jones' view, was the constant changing of the guard.

"Every time I turned around, there was a new athletic director," he said. "There were three in my three years."

He came to Florida State at a time Vaughn Mancha served. Soon, Clay Stapleton came in. About four months prior to Jones' last season, John Bridgers succeeded Stapleton.

'71: a good start

Larry Jones, like Peterson, had been primarily a product of LSU. During Peterson's coaching time there under Paul Dietzel, Jones had been a player. Later, he coached under Dietzel — at LSU, at Army, at South Carolina. When Florida State hired him, he had gained a reputation, under Bill Battle at Tennessee, as an exceptional defensive coach.

In 1971 — when a half-gallon of ice cream was 49 cents, 12 hot-dog buns 29 cents, Florida State's best football ticket $7 — Larry Bruce Jones drew a starting salary of $27,500 as FSU's sixth head football coach. And the below-the-waist crackback block became illegal.

"We had a good thing going at Tennessee, and I was getting a lot more credit than I deserved," said Jones. "I had never been around that many good players!"

Florida State clearly had a good thing going in 1971 as it opened with a 24-9 victory over tough Southern Mississippi in Mobile. Jones got a happy ride off the field on the shoulders of his players.

Miami fell 20-17 in the extraordinary heat of the Orange Bowl. Scheduled in early afternoon to accommodate regional TV, the game saw temperatures rise to 112 degrees on the artificial turf that then covered the field.

On the opening kickoff, the Seminoles' Eddie McMillan scored on an 80-yard touchdown return.

That helped — and so too, perhaps, the enterprising work of a graduate assistant.

This would be the first game under Fran Curci's coaching, and surely Miami would have something new. Several days earlier, Miami scheduled a tight-security scrimmage in the Orange Bowl. No one would be admitted.

According to a story whispered years later, the graduate assistant, wearing a Miami T-shirt, obtained entry into the stadium several hours before that scrimmage began. He climbed atop a concession stand that gave him a vantage point of the field and lay patiently there, flat on his stomach, for hours. He saw all of the scrimmage and is said to have gained a fair idea of some new things Miami would attempt.

One cannot vouch for the authenticity of the story, but one can say it was the only time a rumor of such activity circulated.

In that game, though, it surely didn't seem Florida State knew anything helpful. Down 7-0, Miami rallied to lead at the half 17-7. Behind Gary Huff passes, the Seminoles tied it, then won it late on the second of two Frank Fontes field goals.

Kansas, Virginia Tech and Mississippi State tumbled without undue difficulty.

And suddenly Florida State was 5-0 with 0-5 Florida ahead in Gainesville. Playing one of its more demanding schedules, Florida had been walloped 48-7 by LSU in its last game. The Seminoles were favored by 10 points.

"Huff had hurt his arm and had not thrown all week," said Jones. "We thought we could run on them.

"Sure enough, we could. But we fumbled it."

Art Munroe, the Seminoles' most dangerous runner, was hurting, too. Playing with an injured shoulder and fractured wrist, he fumbled three times.

Florida State was trailing early 6-0 when Munroe's first fumble was plucked out of the air by Jimmy Barr, who scored easily on a 26-yard romp. A 2-point pass jumped it to 14-0. It stayed that way until the final quarter, when a Florida field goal offset two Huff-spurred touchdowns and a 2-point pass that narrowed it, finally, to a 17-15 Florida State loss.

In the 5-0 vs. 0-5 confrontation, one other 5-0 statistic was compelling. Turnovers: Florida State 5, Florida 0.

Like most always, this Florida-FSU game was not without controversy. A late pass to Rhett Dawson that would have put FSU into position for a winning field goal had been ruled invalid, and FSU partisans thought the call more than questionable.

"No one will ever know how much this game cost Florida State University," said FSU President Stan Marshall that evening.

A heck of a Fiesta Bowl

South Carolina bowed 49-18, but Houston intercepted three passes at or near its goal and won 14-7.

At Georgia Tech, Huff had severe diarrhea, a problem that evolved in midweek.

"He'll play, if he has to play with his pants down," said Steve Sloan, the morning of the game.

Sloan, the former All-American quarterback at Alabama, carried the title of "first assistant and head of the offense." He would serve only that single year at Florida State, but with his outgoing personality and lively sense of humor, he became one of the more memorable and popular FSU assistants.

It was said of Sloan that his real role was simply "the Gary Huff coach." Certainly, he

had much to do with Huff's spectacular season.

Huff had apparently recovered from his disorder by kickoff, but he remained weakened. Still, he might well have led an upset, but for the fact receivers had an uncommonly tough time hanging onto passes. Some of that, as FSU lost 12-6, was simply hard-hitting defense.

Tulsa and Pittsburgh were easy conquests. (After the latter game, in a tunnel going to dressing rooms at Pitt's stadium, a young boy sought Huff's autograph. A few years later, the boy — Monk Bonasorte — would become one of the more valuable performers on Bobby Bowden's best FSU defensive units.)

Huff checked in No. 1 nationally in three categories — total offense (2,653 yards), passing yardage (2,736), touchdown passes (23) — and Florida State accepted an invitation to play in Phoenix's Fiesta Bowl.

It would be the second bowl in three years that Florida State would help inaugurate — coming on the heels of Atlanta's first Peach after the 1968 season.

The bowl would be played in Arizona

Steve Sloan, top photo, was the man Jones put in charge of developing his star quarterback, Gary Huff.

Profile of a pass rush. The Seminoles were going great guns at this point, in early '72. By the way, No. 59 is Larry Strickland, who — in a pileup against Kansas — had bitten an opposing player. In the rump.

State's home stadium — and Arizona State, 10-1 and ranked No. 6 nationally, would be the opponent. FSU spent Christmas in hospitable Phoenix, flying there two days before the holiday for a bowl that would be two days after.

"This was the most memorable game of my time," said Jones. "It was what FSU football was all about.

"Just a great game. Nobody could stop the other. We knew we would score. But they scored, too."

In what surely was one of the most exciting, watchable games of Florida State history, Arizona State won 45-38 on a touchdown with 37 seconds remaining.

After a spectacular duel with Danny White — who later would quarterback the Dallas Cowboys — Huff had completed 25 of 46 passes for 347 yards and two touchdowns, winning acclaim as the game's outstanding back. Huff did it despite acute pressure applied throughout by tackle Junior Ah You, tough native of Samoa.

Arizona State had tied it 21-21 with 47 seconds left in the half, but Huff had put FSU back up 28-21 before intermission after a lightning four-play drive. It was that kind of game.

"We played our guts out," said Huff, and that was so.

Arizona State was better, with more great players at the skill positions, in Jones' view.

"Huff was just superhuman that day," said Jones. "He was throwing with people all over him. Junior Ah You, I believe, was offsides on every play coming after Huff."

Huff would be the most memorable player of Jones' time.

"Though there were so many others, it has to be him — he was the one who made the thing go," said Jones. "He was such an intense competitor.

"I turned him over to Sloan, and we told him he was the quarterback. Didn't care if he had 10 straight interceptions, he was still it.

"That was a great marriage of Sloan and Huff. Sloan was exactly what he needed.

"I wish that they had red-shirted him in his sophomore year (1970, when Tommy Warren quarterbacked most of the way). We could have gotten by on him for three years, no question."

'72: So much promise

Like Cappleman before him, Huff, for whatever reason, was not quite the quarterback as a senior that he had been as a junior.

Many adverse things would happen to Huff and this team. But none was apparent on that blue-sky horizon in the spring of 1972, when Bob Hope came to campus. So many good players were returning from a team that in its previous run had come so very close to being as good as any — including Arizona State on its home field.

Some, like Playboy magazine, talked of an unbeaten team. Most saw nothing worse than 9-2. Huff looked like a big bet for the Heisman, and Barry Smith — with more speed than either Biletnikoff or Sellers — might be the nation's most dangerous receiver.

A rules change made freshmen eligible for varsity action. That made things look even better, as far as helping that enduring Florida State depth problem. Six junior-college recruits were seen as immediate bolstering. Moreover, two newly eligible transfers — Hodges Mitchell (TCU) and Mack Brown (who as a sophomore had led Vanderbilt in rushing) — figured to help the running game.

And the Seminoles started in 1972 just like 1971. Gangbusters!

Like bowling pins, Pitt went down 19-7, Miami 37-14, Virginia Tech 27-15 and Kansas 44-22.

At Kansas, Huff threw four touchdown passes — all in the first half — as the Seminoles led 28-7 at intermission. The Heisman looked quite within his reach. It seemed, possibly, an easy reach.

Some saw Barry Smith as the nation's most dangerous receiver in 1972. At FSU he caught more touchdown passes — 25 — than any other Seminole of the first 40 years.

An odd, memorable incident at Kansas came after a pileup of players. Suddenly, a Kansas player came shooting out of the pile as though rocket-propelled.

He had, it turned out, been bitten. In the rear. The protagonist was Larry Strickland, an exceptionally aggressive and talented linebacker. Though he would have his own problems in life, Strickland on a football field was strictly a problem to the opponent.

If the Kansas player firing out from the pile was a lighter side, the game proved markedly a downer for the Seminoles.

In fact, Florida State may have left its season on that injury-inducing artificial turf at Kansas. It was a far tougher game than 28-7 at halftime suggests.

The chartered plane flying the Seminoles home looked like a hospital emergency room.

Busted legs, busted shoulders, busted ankles. Perhaps never has a Florida State team been so damaged in a single game. The defensive unit, particularly the tackle corps, was hardest hit.

But Florida lay ahead, and no one talks injuries before such a match. Besides, Florida State was 4-0, Florida 1-1.

A season full of injuries

It began to seem the Gators lived and died on Florida State mistakes — 10 turnovers this time (six fumbles, four interceptions). The Seminoles had turned it over on their first three possessions. Soon, a weakened defense was far overburdened.

Florida had one turnover.

The procession of mishaps started as the Seminoles ran out onto the field for the first time, with one among them (Mike Glass) falling down.

Nobody paid attention, but Jones had said before the game his Seminoles would have to score a whole lot of points to win.

How very right he was! Final score: 42-13, Florida.

"All the days can't be beautiful," philosophized Hodges Mitchell.

For Larry Jones, precious few good days remained at Florida State.

One of those few came a week later, when FSU slipped by Mississippi State in Jackson 25-21.

"Nobody would think about this being a great game, but it was for us," said Jones. "They were running the option, and we had a lot of trouble stopping it."

Rocky Felker, who later became Mississippi State's head coach, was quarterbacking that option attack.

FSU was now 5-1, but injuries had mounted — cornerback Thomas among them — and before the Mississippi State game was over a total of 10 ailing starters were on the sidelines.

FSU beat Colorado State (37-0) and Tulsa (23-21), but lost to Auburn (27-14) and Houston (31-27), before moving to South Carolina for a final game — fully expecting to whip the Gamecocks for the seventh straight time and finish 8-3.

But by now, the injury toll was unbelievable. In the previous game, against Tulsa, a scout-squad defensive back — Sam Cowart — had been called from the stands at halftime to dress out. Cowart never played, but the reflection of the circumstances was more ominous than anyone dreamed.

After Tulsa, the Seminoles would not again win through 20 straight games — not from Nov. 11, 1972, in Tallahassee until Nov. 8, 1973, in Miami.

At South Carolina, a Peach Bowl bid seemed nailed down. A win or a tie would do it.

Florida State took a 14-0 lead on Huff touchdown passes to Smith, but soon the Seminoles virtually ran out of linebackers, as earlier they had become barren of tackles and defensive backs. An assortment of players, offensively as well as defensively, were playing half-hurt.

South Carolina rallied and won 24-21 on a 38-yard field goal with 1:21 to go. Seven FSU turnovers, including three in a 6-minute stretch of the last quarter, contributed.

It was a season of 38 turnovers, including 22 interceptions.

"Those terrible injuries we had — to me, a lot of it was due to the fact we didn't have a good weight program," said Jones. "People never realized how critical it was. I was never around a program that got hit like that.

"People also did not realize how critical the rain had been in preseason. We had less practice than any time. The weather surely hurt our conditioning."

Eleven straight games, without an open date that might have tempered injuries, had not helped either.

One school of thought holds that the program's trouble was inevitable because Jones was more lenient than his predecessor — not the disciplinarian, not as demanding in any way.

This school says that initially the players loved the new style but that, in the second year, the motivation faded; players started taking advantage of him, with a breakdown of team discipline. There were those in the second year who felt they saw that breakdown as it happened, and forecast bad times ahead.

On the night before the next-to-last game of the second year, at South Carolina, I sat with Parcells until 4 a.m. discussing the look of the program. It was a mutual view that Jones was losing his grip on his players, and both saw acute problems for the following year.

Parcells said, because of what he thought he saw coming, he would be leaving as soon as he could. He did. And 13 years later he would coach the New York Giants through their biggest season, on to a Super Bowl victory and world championship.

'The chicken-wire scandal'

As that second season wound down, Jones seemed to embark on endeavors to toughen his program, to instill stronger discipline.

One move was to inaugurate a more intense off-season program. These programs during Peterson's time surely had been plenty tough, but they had become less so after Jones' arrival.

Several players rebelled under Jones' newly demanding off-season program. Approximately two dozen quit.

In June, months after the conclusion of that off-season program, The St. Petersburg Times ran a three-part series extremely critical of the program. It suggested brutal treatment of players. The word "dehumanizing" was frequently employed. So was "chicken wire."

The series received national exposure and became generally known as "the chicken-wire scandal." Other newspapers dispatched reporters. Sports Illustrated moved a writer in for more than a week. In its story the magazine made light of much, concluding that FSU's program was not only not unique but also not as demanding as some.

Florida State had used chicken wire as a covering, 4 feet high over a floor area where a wrestling mat was spread. The idea was to help players stay low when wrestling — as linemen are taught to stay low.

Chicken wire is designed, literally, not to harm a chicken, and certainly would not damage players. But, in media reflection, chicken wire seemed to take on a damaging, dangerous, denigrating connotation. Many apparently associated it with barbed wire, which can surely damage.

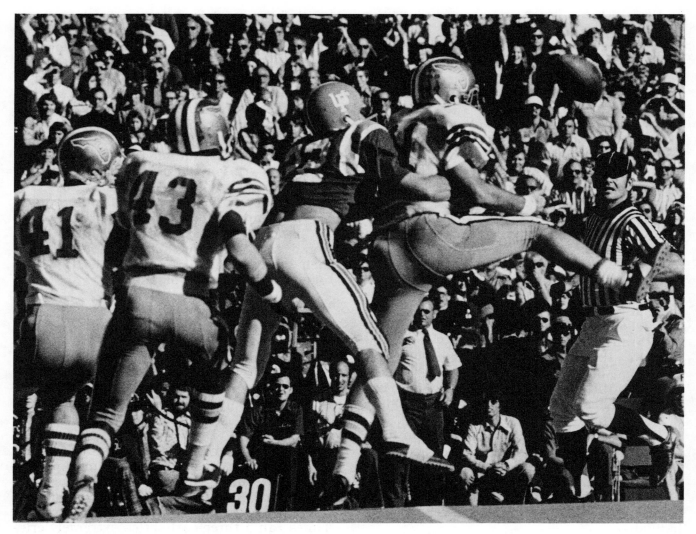

Action from the '72 Florida game. The injury-riddled Seminoles lost this game. How's this for an omen: As the Seminoles ran out onto the field before the game, one of them fell down.

Jones was devastated by the Times suggestions that he had been part of something morally unacceptable. He had considered Fred Girard, the writer of the series, a friend who thought highly of him.

Interestingly, Girard suggested in the last sentence of his series that Florida State had probably done no more in its off-season program than dozens — perhaps hundreds — of other schools.

No dozens, no hundreds had been previously cited in the stories. Only one.

And only Florida State was investigated by the NCAA — which finally extended, in effect, a slap on the wrist. One year's probation, with no sanctions. The NCAA investigation appeared not to indict the Florida State off-season program on the rather sensational charges involving chicken wire, and possible brutality or dehumanization — but rather on a count of it not really being voluntary. Under

NCAA rules, participation of players in off-season programs had to be on a voluntary basis.

The off-season programs would continue, all over, much as they had been. But at Florida State, there would be one exception. No more chicken wire, no matter how harmless.

Florida State asked LeRoy Collins, the respected former governor, to conduct an independent investigation of all the charges. In a lengthy report released in October, Collins concluded that The Times had presented an "inaccurate picture" and denied the charges of dehumanization.

During the remainder of his time — through preseason drills and the season itself — Jones would be unable to get the scandal far from his mind. Those who knew him well felt, beyond question, it hurt his concentration on his work.

"Here we were in a tough position in the

116

first place," said Jones. "Short on facilities, short on money. . . . We were having to fight for our lives in the first place, and particularly in relation to the University of Florida — the big dog.

"And then the newspapers come in and start hitting at people who were already down. I never understood it all."

Stapleton toughens the schedules

Meanwhile, prohibitive schedules were being arranged.

In 1971, Clay Stapleton had moved in as athletic director. A former coach, firm and decisive, Stapleton sometimes kidded about his role.

"Larry Jones and I had been invited, along with our wives, over to the dog track at Monticello," said Stapleton. "Steve Andris, one of our supporters and the president of the track, wanted us to present a trophy. That was the night I learned where the athletic director rated around here.

"Larry made the presentation, and I had to kiss the dog."

In fact, Stapleton played an exceptionally strong role. He felt President Stan Marshall had given him a mandate to improve the schedule. Quickly, Stapleton moved. He scheduled almost 20 games against heavyweight opposition — all on the road, for none of those top teams could be persuaded to come to Tallahassee.

Stapleton's scheduling included five unanswered games at LSU, four unanswered ones at Nebraska, two at Ohio State. For 1981, he arranged a schedule that included consecutive games at Nebraska, Ohio State, Notre Dame, Pittsburgh and LSU.

When word got around that Stapleton might be overscheduling the Seminoles, he apparently was told to desist.

"From now on," Stapleton told an associate, "I'm scheduling only pussy cats."

But he had little time to balance things out. Early in 1973, Stapleton accepted the job as Vanderbilt's athletic director.

Stapleton's extreme scheduling tactics would turn out to be an attention-getting plus for the Seminoles in the time of Bobby Bowden, but for a long time many felt Stapleton had scheduled FSU into football oblivion.

"A university, like its football team, must call its signals on the basis of teamwork and strategies," said President Marshall in 1973, "and yet be unafraid to try a new approach when — or even before — an old one fails."

In football, the Seminoles were closer than anyone suspected to a new approach.

'73: not a single win

"I felt, before that last year, we would win three games," said Jones. "And, probably, if we won no more than three, we could hold on — and wait on the good, young players."

There is little question that had Jones won as many as three, he could have held on. Such was his previous popularity, he might well have survived had he won only one.

But the Seminoles of 1973 won none, and the last five games were a somber procession of blowouts.

"No team can win consistently without a sound offense," said Jones.

And no team could win at all, perhaps, without either a sound defense or a sound offense. Florida State had neither in 1973, but was surely worse offensively than defensively.

The Seminoles had run out of quarterbacks tried and tested in the old system. With Huff, the last in Peterson's string of great quarterback recruits was gone. Another heralded Peterson recruit — Fred Geisler — had transferred, following Peterson to Rice.

FSU started 1973 without a quarterback of any varsity experience.

"I felt Coach Pete would have been able to do better than we did," said Jones more than a dozen years later, "because he would have been able, somehow, to find a quarterback."

The season started with six Florida State turnovers and a 9-7 loss at Wake Forest.

There was a fine no-turnovers effort at Miami. But it was also, for the Seminoles, something of a no-offense game — only 132 total yards. Miami won 14-10.

Florida State played Baylor well (a 21-14 loss), Memphis State well (a 13-10 loss), but that was about it.

Bad got worse, and the Seminoles' last three opponents each ran for more than 340 yards.

One last-game play seemed symbolic of the whole season.

At the start against Florida, the Seminoles — underdogs by 26 points — opened with an onside kick. Florida recovered and quickly gained a 7-0 lead that mushroomed to a final 49-0.

Florida State had gone with a freshman quarterback, Billy Prescott. It was his first start. Because of Florida's insistence, regular quarterback Billy Sexton did not play.

Sexton's neutralization was the reflection

Billy Sexton (16) whoops it up as the Seminoles score one of their rare touchdowns in 1973.

of an old, controversial agreement Florida had insisted upon as a condition of playing both Florida State and Miami. Bob Woodruff, during his time as coach and athletic director of the Gators, had started it.

The stipulation was that the two schools could not play a Southeastern Conference transfer against the Gators. Any other schools could, and did, but not in-state rivals Florida State and Miami — not for a very long time.

Sexton, out of Tallahassee Leon, had been one of the nation's more coveted passers. He had gone to Alabama, where his father had played before him, but because Alabama then favored a wishbone offense, Sexton's style did not fit the system. Bear Bryant, after a period of time, said precisely that, noted that it was unfair to Sexton, and released him to Florida State.

After an idle year as a transfer, Sexton became eligible in 1971 and was confronted with another unfair situation for him — one of FSU's worst teams of history.

A few years later, John Bridgers, who had followed Stapleton as athletic director, would quietly and successfully negotiate a contract that eliminated previous stipulations that no other opponent had insisted upon as a condition of playing FSU.

Some of the potential for controversy between the two rivals was thereby alleviated. But many would long recall that for the first six years, every game of the series was played on Florida's home field, and that for approximately 20 years Florida had forced upon the Seminoles — as a condition of play — rules totally peculiar to SEC members in relation to one another.

Farewell to Jones

As demands arose for firing Jones on the heels of an 0-11 season, Bridgers stood firmly behind the coach who had been notably responsible for his being chosen athletic director. Jones had been impressed with Bridgers when the two served on South Carolina's staff, and Jones had strongly recommended him to FSU when Stapleton departed.

Jones fought hard for another go at it, but four days before Christmas he bowed to the inevitable. He turned in his resignation. In fact, he had been relieved of his job, and was paid in full for the two remaining years on his contract.

Jerry Greene, then a sports columnist for Cocoa Today, had described Jones as "a player's perfect coach," and had suggested he was proof that "nice guys do not have to finish last."

Prior to 1973, such had been a widespread view.

Practicality dictated that Jones not have the additional opportunity he sought.

Florida State was staring at its most binding football circumstances ever. The program in 1973 had run a large deficit, and President Marshall spoke to supporters of the possibility of no more football.

For Jones, perhaps Fran Tarkenton, the old NFL quarterback, said it well: "It's a lonesome walk to the sidelines, especially when thousands of people are cheering your replacement."

Thousands of Florida State fans, however quietly, were cheering for a change in the depressing circumstances — if not for any particular replacement.

A nice guy took the lonesome walk.

But for a while those fans would be quite lonesome, too, not sure of who that replacement would be.

Or whether football would survive.

The Mudra Years

A veteran coach imports a football style that doesn't quite fit, then quickly exits

Place Eddie Robinson, and his 336 victories in 44 seasons at Grambling, on a pedestal somewhere.

Now go to the remaining list, at the beginning of the 1987 season, of college football's active coaches. After Robinson, in total victories, came Michigan's Bo Schembechler with 207 victories, then Penn State's Joe Paterno (199).

And, in fourth place, with 190 victories after 25 head-coaching years, was Darrell Mudra. With 77 losses, 4 ties, Mudra had a .708 winning percentage that ranks with the best. Indeed, it stood as the best — with the notable exception of Robinson's .740 — of any who had been head coaches as long as 25 years.

Consider that 18 of Mudra's 77 losses came in just two seasons at Florida State.

From Adams State to North Dakota to the Montreal Alouettes to the University of Arizona to Western Illinois, before he came to Florida State, Mudra had invariably turned losing programs into winning ones. After he left Florida State, he would continue, at the Division 1-AA level, to produce winning teams.

But Florida State was something else.

Was two years not long enough, as some think?

"I think one thing that happened was the program had developed so fast under Bill Peterson, the university had not kept pace with

4 wins, 18 losses

Darrell Mudra at FSU.

facilities," said Mudra a dozen years after his departure, echoing the views of predecessor Larry Jones. "There were a lot of immediate needs, in terms of facilities.

"We built the weight room while I was there, getting 30 pieces of Nautilus equipment. And we moved the players out of Cash Hall, a place not conducive to producing a good football team, and put them into an apartment complex. Among other things, that cut down on the total cost.

"You could have the best players in the world, you know, and if you didn't have the conditions to train 'em under, you are not going to be successful."

Florida State did not have the facilities, nor did it have the players, suggested Mudra, and nothing was going to come overnight.

"I'll tell you, what Peterson did was a remarkable accomplishment," said Mudra. "Probably no one really knew what an extraordinary job he had done under the conditions."

Mudra also discovered the program's financial problems were far more serious than he had thought.

Challenged by President Stanley Marshall, the school's football supporters moved swiftly to raise money to offset a $300,000 deficit.

Many helped, among them noted alumnus Burt Reynolds. In late 1974, the movie actor pledged $50,000 to the program. Athletic Director Bridgers had traveled to Reidsville, Ga., where Reynolds was filming "The Longest Yard," and sought his assistance.

The name of FSU's support group was changed, in 1974, from National Seminole Club to Seminole Boosters Inc. During his

Reaching — the Seminoles did a lot of it in Coach Mudra's time. History does not tell us whether FSU's Andy Stockton (24) successfully defended against this pass, but it does tell us Mudra was successful in ending a 20-game losing streak in his first season.

time as athletic director, Stapleton had suggested that the word "boosters" had a high-schoolish connotation, and he had changed the name.

Regrouping after the winless season

As Mudra took over a team that had lost 12 straight games, including all 11 the season prior, immediate concern was of quality among the names that would form his squad.

Where Larry Jones had lamented the lack of freshmen and sophomores when he came, Mudra thought his far bigger liability was the absence of juniors and seniors.

"We had a huge sophomore class, but it was obviously a group put together after the athletes were picked over," said Mudra. "Only one or two, I think, were of the quality the University of Florida would have accepted.

"My first year, you see, we were limited to 30 recruits, so I could not go out and get the numbers Jones did."

Indeed, Jones had recruited unusually high numbers in a logical endeavor to stock up before new NCAA limitations on recruiting numbers went into effect. Indeed, there had been some theory that the large number of players — more than could play — contributed to team discontent.

Mudra recruited surprisingly well under the circumstances.

Among those first-year recruits was Larry Key, a small back from Inverness who would evolve into one of FSU's stars.

Overlooked because of his size by all state colleges, except the University of Tampa, Key came to Florida State because Gene McDowell — then on Vince Gibson's staff at Kansas State — had been eager to return to his alma mater and sought a position with Mudra.

Kansas State had also recruited Key. McDowell asked Gibson to release Key to Florida State, and the head coach agreed.

In preseason drills, Florida State for the third straight year was heavily hindered by rain. For a time, Mudra took his players to Norman Park, Ga., drilling them there.

The Seminoles would also be heavily hindered by a schedule that included six bowl teams, among them Alabama, Auburn and, in a Campbell Stadium opener, Pitt.

After consultation with Mudra, Bridgers decided to play all home games at night.

Historically, Florida State had played almost all home games at night, sometimes shifting to afternoon kickoffs for very late-season games, or homecoming games. Addition-

In 1974 — when a new Camaro was $3,649, a pack of 24 Crayolas 44 cents, Florida State's best football ticket $7 — Darrell Eugene Mudra drew a salary of $30,000 as FSU's seventh football coach. And a new rule stipulated a successful field goal must be between the uprights, not over them as previously scored.

ally, the five Campbell Stadium games with Florida had each been in the afternoon.

But Stapleton felt that afternoon was the really appropriate time to play college football. In the all-losing season of 1973, as well as 1972, FSU had played all home games in the afternoon.

Bridgers felt that the majority of Florida State fans favored night games, that a switch would enhance attendance — and possibly also the home-field advantage.

Far more attuned to day games, the University of Florida — faced with playing the Seminoles for the first time at night — immediately protested the decision. So did some newspapers, concerned about their deadlines.

Bridgers, and Florida State, stood firm. And the decision remained firm — with 7:30 p.m. kickoffs — through the remainder of FSU's first 40 years at the game, with isolated exceptions for TV and a single homecoming.

'74: Playing tough, but losing

It surely seemed, as a powerful Tony Dorsett-led Pitt team came to town, that night games might well maximize the home advantage.

Heavy weather — hot, humid — perhaps also contributed. It was an oppressive, draining atmosphere of the type that has run more than a few good Northern teams aground on Southern rocks.

After Florida State drove from the opening kickoff to a 6-0 lead, Pitt tied it in the second quarter 6-6 on a short Dorsett run, then won it 9-6 on a third-quarter field goal.

Bound for the Heisman Trophy, Dorsett had gained more than 1,500 yards running the previous year, but FSU limited him to 81 in 25 carries. In his first action, Key got 63 in 16.

With the exception of a 40-9 blowout loss at Kansas in the first road game, Florida State played its first six opponents exceptionally tough — losing 14-7 to Colorado State, 21-17 to Baylor, 8-7 to Alabama, 24-14 to Florida.

Against Baylor — before a Campbell Stadium crowd that included Burt Reynolds plus pals Lee Majors and Larry Csonka — FSU moved to a stunning 17-0 halftime lead, but the Bears rallied as the Seminoles fumbled.

Surely, the 8-7 loss on Alabama's field was one of the more remarkable games ever for Florida State. With one of the big upsets of college history apparently in hand, FSU lost it on a last-minute field goal that followed a deliberate safety.

"I think an unbalanced line was the biggest thing that helped us," said Mudra. "It was a little bit of a surprise to them, and it enabled us to control the ball enough that we did not put great pressure on our defense."

The unbalanced line was primarily the idea of Bob Harbison, reinstated after Jones had dismissed him following the 1972 season. Mudra had also hired Dan Henning, who had served as an assistant under Peterson and would later be head coach of the Atlanta Falcons.

Later, Henning would employ elements of that unbalanced line as an assistant under Don Shula with the Miami Dolphins, and continue to employ it at other NFL stops.

"Henning commented that I was the one who started him into it," said Harbison. "He kind of adapted it to modern things."

Throughout the first half, the unbalanced line kept Alabama defenders off balance. FSU not only led 7-0 but had notched twice as many first downs and twice as many yards. When it was all done, Key had run for 123 yards, Rudy Thomas for 95. Overall, FSU outgained Alabama, 345 yards to 229.

Bear Bryant said that he had never seen a team so much better coached than his, that he had badly underestimated FSU.

A 44-yard field goal by Bucky Berrey, following a Florida State fumble at its 31, had cut Florida State's lead to 7-3 in the third quarter. FSU promptly drove to the Tide 2, and missed a chip-shot field goal.

Poor kicking games contributed more than a little to a losing streak stretching through 20 endeavors.

Still ahead 7-3 with time running out, Florida State came up with fourth down at its 5. Coaches decided to take a safety that would narrow the score to 7-5 but present an opportunity to get off a free kick from the 20 — a

Few schools recruited Larry Key, but he became a star at FSU.

better kick, they hoped, than Florida State otherwise would get. Mudra said the deciding factor, in favor of a safety, was that Alabama had come close to blocking a couple of punts.

But the free kick, from the 20, was short — 28 yards to the FSU 48. Alabama drove within range for a 36-yard Berrey kick that won it 8-7 with half a minute left.

"No question, this was the most memorable game of my time at Florida State," said Mudra.

"Besides the unbalanced line, one key was using Aaron Carter — he was a freshman then — as a kind of rover on defense. And our defense did an exceptional job of stopping their triple-option game.

"We let Carter go wherever the ball went."

The 5-foot-8, 185-pound Carter would play as a defensive back, linebacker and end. He utilized great quickness in a tough, compact body.

Mudra would also identify Carter as perhaps his most memorable player.

"Gosh, I think the ones you remember are the ones who made the biggest contributions — and the biggest I can recall was that of Carter," said Mudra. "He was too small to play, but he played so hard.

Mudra called Aaron Carter — a defensive back/
linebacker who was Florida State's leading tackler
of the first 40 years — one of his most memorable
players.

"Of course, Larry Key came along and
played real well for us, too. And Jeff Gardner,
who played offensive guard, contributed perhaps as much as anyone with his play and
leadership."

Victory at last

Against Florida, the Seminoles played well
indeed until the final quarter. Down 10-7 after
three, FSU found quarterback Don Gaffney a
little too hot to handle late, and the Gators
took a 24-7 lead before having it trimmed to a
final 24-14.

Florida players praised FSU, Gaffney de-
claring the Seminoles just a year from the top.
It would take a little more time than that, and
only one of the last five games was
encouraging.

A 5-2 Miami team awaited in the ninth
game — a homecoming Friday night in the
Orange Bowl, where the Seminoles had won
seven straight.

And it seemed Florida State *owned* that
Orange Bowl as it made it eight straight —
WINNING by a startling 21-14.

Ahead 14-0 going into the last quarter,
Florida State survived dazzling Miami bombs.
One long scoring pass cut it to 14-7. After FSU
made it 21-7, Miami immediately struck back
with a second bomb, for 21-14. But FSU defenders held the rest of the way.

Jeff Leggett became an overnight hero
when he scored the third — and winning —
touchdown from the 1. Left off the traveling
squad, Leggett had been flown down on a private plane the day of the game when coaches
became apprehensive over mounting injuries.
Leggett proved vital, with his tough running
after Key left early in the game with an ankle
injury.

And once again — with a 20-game losing
run buried — the cry "FSU All the Damn
Time" was heard in the land.

Run over the following week by wishbone-
powered Virginia Tech at a Campbell Stadium
homecoming 56-21, Mudra said it was obvious his coaches and players had not learned
how to handle a victory. "We kind of went to
pieces," he said.

Florida State in 1974 was short on many
things, but it hardly lacked willingness. Mudra would come to resent the notion his teams
lacked *esprit de corps.*

"In my two years, it was an injustice to talk
about the Seminoles not having fine morale,"
said Mudra.

"When I arrived, morale was not bad —
because the players were ready for a change.
In 1974, we were a much inferior team, physically, but we played Pitt 9-6, Alabama 8-7 and
Baylor 21-17.

"Hell, all we had was morale."

'75: A year of improvement

There would be a bit more in 1975 — including Don Fauls' return as trainer following
a three-year absence. The popular "Rooster"
had started as trainer in 1954 but left for a
business venture in early 1972. He would remain with Florida State until his retirement
in 1986.

Mudra had inherited a team that the year
prior to his arrival had given up 4,896 yards
and 331 points, while gaining just 2,864
yards and scoring 99 points.

The first year he had a team that gave up
4,468 yards and 289 points, while gaining
3,472 and scoring 130 points.

Going 3-8 his second year, Mudra would
have a team whose continued improvement
was reflected in defense. The second-year to-

The face that says "spirit" to Florida State fans: Chief Osceola, who rides the mascot Renegade.

Different faces of the FSU Seminole over the years. On the facing page, a fierce warrior from a 1980s poster. At left is Sammy Seminole, a somewhat younger warrior who folded his tent and faded away in the early '70s. And below is the depiction that appeared on the program cover for the '58 Florida-FSU game.

Quarterbacks Jimmy Jordan and Wally Woodham talk with Coach Bowden, who called them two of his most memorable players all wrapped up into one. At right, Jordan in action against Mississippi State in '78.

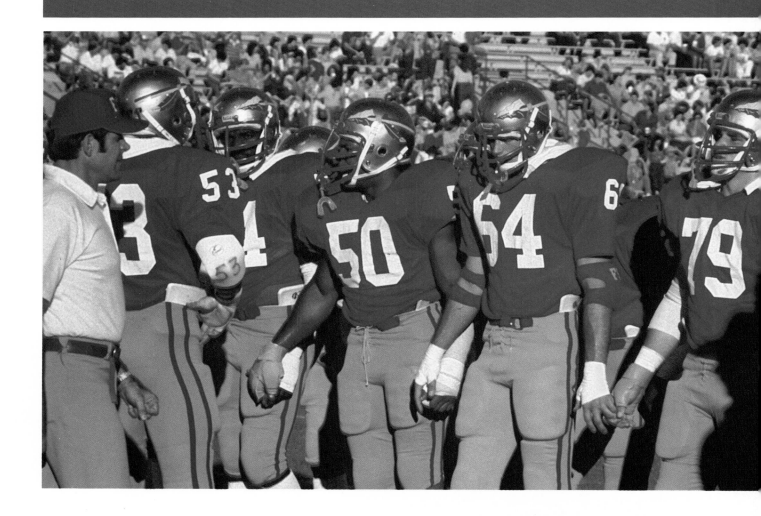

Opposite page: Coach Bowden's other most memorable player — nose tackle Ron Simmons. Above he's pictured in '79 with, from left, Coach Jim Gladden, Paul Piurowski (53), Arthur Scott (54), Jarvis Coursey (64) and Garry Futch (79).

On the following page: Defensive action from the '79 Florida game. From left are Scott McLean (60), Ron Simmons (50), Walter Carter (76), Scott Warren (80) and Reggie Herring (39).

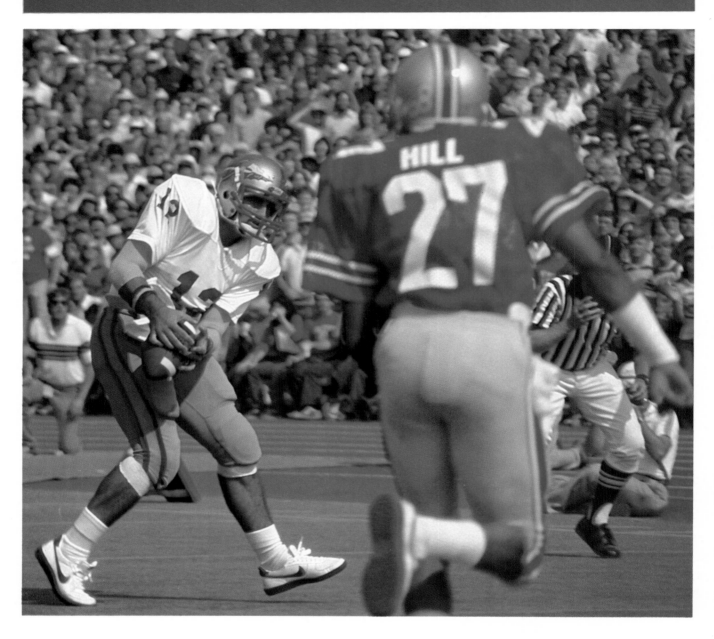

Above, quarterback Kelly Lowrey catches a pass vs. Ohio State in '82 — making him the only player ever to grand-slam the Buckeyes with a touchdown run, a touchdown pass and a touchdown reception. At right, FSU's second coach, Don Veller, wears the jacket of his alma mater — Indiana. That university supplied a number of early FSU players and coaches. On the facing page, Rohn Stark cranks up the leg that set all kinds of punting records at FSU.

The '81 season saw the arrival of explosive No. 26, Greg Allen, who captured the hearts
of Seminole fans. The facing
photo matches two future
National Football League players: FSU's Alphonso Carreker
and Pittsburgh's Bill Fralic.

During Bobby Bowden's time, blocking kicks became a specialty. Here Ken Roe blocks one against South Carolina in '83, with Eric Riley also charging in. Think how much easier blocking would be with eight arms — such as those featured in the tricky photo above. On the following page: Talk about spirited settings. Behold the balloons, in a typical pregame scene from Campbell Stadium.

Opposite page: Cletis Jones sloshes in the rain during the '83 Florida game. Above, Weegie Thompson scores a touchdown during the '83 Peach Bowl. FSU beat North Carolina, 28-3.

Opposite page: Joe Wessel, one of FSU's
best blockers of kicks and punts.
Wessel was the kind of player
who made No. 1 fan Sol Carrol's eyes light up.
Sol, shown above in a homecoming parade,
died in the line of garnet-and-gold duty: on
the way to the '83 Peach Bowl.

You never know which celebrities you'll meet at a bowl game. Jamie Dukes met this long-eared friend before the Citrus Bowl of '84. That's action from the Citrus Bowl at right. FSU tied Georgia, 17-17.

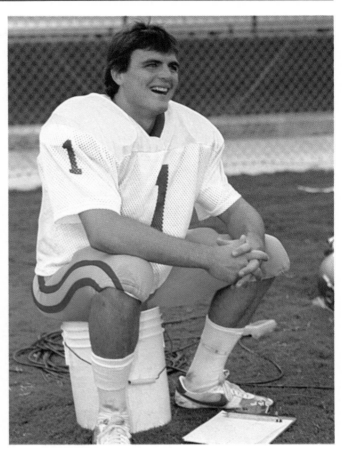

Quarterback Eric Thomas had his share of heroics — and injuries — at FSU.

When the Seminoles went to Nebraska in '85, they came away with a 17-13 win. On the right is center David Schrenker (56), in the middle is tackle John Ionata and at left is quarterback Danny McManus — who had an outstanding game, but also suffered a concussion in the fourth quarter. Speaking of hard hits: That's Paul McGowan at right, making a solo tackle against Memphis State the following week.

The colors of college football show up everywhere. On scalps (this one belonging to Fred "The Head" Miller), on feathers, at practice (featuring strong safety Stan Shiver).

The end zone can be a tranquil place — as it is at right, getting its regular bath of alphabet paint. And it can be a violent place — as it is above, in goal-line action vs. Kansas in '85. On the following page: Fumble recovery against North Carolina in '86. From left are outside linebacker Felton Hayes (46), tackle Gerald Nichols (79), free safety John Parks (19) and cornerback Martin Mayhew (32).

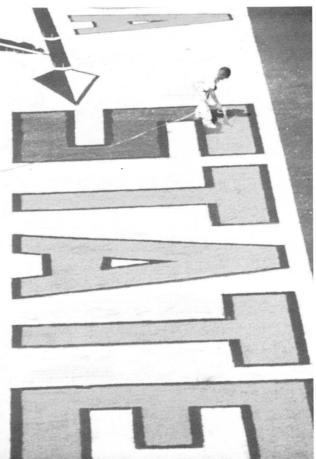

Three strong performers from '86: running backs Victor Floyd (27) vs. Michigan and Sammie Smith (33) vs. Tulane, and kicker Louis Berry in practice. Facing page: Bobby Bowden at work in his office. On the following page: The sight that quickens the pulse of FSU fans and television networks — Renegade rearing before a game.

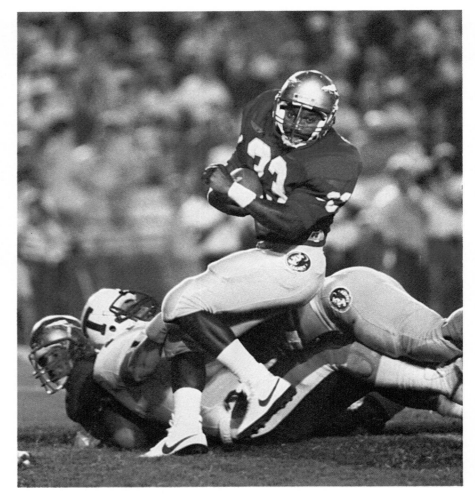

Clyde Walker fit well as quarterback of the winged-T offense of 1975.

tals: 3,453 yards and 213 points yielded, 3,688 yards and 187 points gained.

Second-year improvement possibly would have been greater except for offensive change. The Seminoles switched from a veer offense to the winged-T in that second year as Henning departed the coaching staff and Gary Grouwinkel, who had been with Mudra at Arizona, came in as offensive coordinator. Another new coach in 1975 was Eddie Wilson. Formerly with the Kansas City Chiefs, Wilson would coach quarterbacks.

"I thought one of the really outstanding coaching achievements was Wilson's development of Clyde Walker that second year," said Mudra.

A red-shirt sophomore, Walker in 1975 completed 117 of 203 passes for 1,619 yards and 10 touchdowns as the trigger man of the winged-T.

What might have been had Florida State stuck with its veer for another year, or if it had stuck with the winged-T for more than a year, is the stuff of conjecture.

Henning had not been on the same wavelength as Mudra, to say the least, and his departure was involuntary.

Whatever Henning's merit, it often requires more than a year for a coaching staff to mesh, and more than a year for a new offense to mesh. Beyond much question, Mudra would have been better off not to have hired

Henning as offensive coordinator at all — if he were going to make a change after one year.

Florida State three years running had used a different offense. Soon, the style would change for the fourth straight year.

Mudra had forecast for 1975 "a team that would be able to play with most people."

The assessment was essentially correct.

But Florida State won only one of its first seven — Utah State 17-8.

In the two games following Utah State, the Seminoles managed just 6 points, losing to Iowa State 10-6 and Georgia Tech 30-0. Then in its next two, FSU got just two touchdowns, falling at Virginia Tech 13-10 and to Florida in Gainesville 34-8.

Florida State would play its last five opponents exceedingly well — losing to Auburn and Memphis State by identical scores (17-14), but between those two demolishing Clemson on its home field by a shocking 43-7, then falling to Miami 24-22 despite a 16-point rally in the last quarter, and closing with a surprising 33-22 conquest of Houston in the Astrodome.

But elements of Mudra's personal style had begun to disturb some Florida State people well before the last game.

The coach's image

Mudra talked often of democratic principles in the operation of a football team — of more involvement and responsibility for assistant coaches and players. He seemed little associated with the traditional discipline guidelines of his peers, and reflected no concern about length of hair or dress codes.

In few ways was Mudra traditional, in many ways very different.

At games, he sat in the pressbox.

Accustomed to coaches appearing to lead their teams on the sidelines, Florida State fans generally seemed uncomfortable with the fact. They were perhaps less comfortable when word spread that Mudra was little involved in the pressbox, furthering the impression that his assistants did in fact run the team. Mudra had said as much but was not taken so seriously.

The image of a head coach who was not serious enough about his role was enhanced by reports Mudra occasionally went fishing on the day of a game, sometimes left practice early or came late and maybe now and then not at all.

An outdoorsman, and a good one, Mudra often did go fishing. He was a man, clearly, who felt there was far more in life than foot-

ball. He was also a man good with his hands, who would build his own home near Tallahassee with used bricks. And he was a learned man, with a doctorate, who frequently wrote scholarly articles.

Once Mudra, at a booster luncheon, strongly criticized a player for an infraction he had committed during the game. Immediately, he got a clear message from fans who did not approve of his criticizing a player publicly. They seemed to feel the player indeed should be chastised privately, but never publicly. Mudra quickly acknowledged he had gotten their message.

The incident, though relatively small, seemed indicative of a lack of identity with the Mudra style. Some spoke of their fondness for Mudra — a smiling, thinking, articulate man — but not his football style. It was often as though he and Florida State supporters did not speak the same language.

Mudra had sought a stronger waiver of admission standards for football players than Florida State was accustomed to granting. There were those who felt he was seeking to move too far in a direction that would seriously damage the university's reputation.

So it was that despite his team's definitely improved play in late 1975, Mudra entered the last game at Houston uncertain of his future.

However, President Marshall had decided that Mudra should have another year. On the morning of that game in the Astrodome, he told a few people he would make the announcement when he spoke on the Seminole Radio Network at halftime.

In the end, the ghost of Gen. George "Blood and Guts" Patton may have shot Mudra down.

The Patton factor

Mudra had invited Marshall, and me, to listen as he spoke to his team following the Saturday-afternoon pregame meal.

On the evening prior, the team had seen the movie "Patton." The demanding, authoritative Patton symbolized a philosophy diametrically opposed to Mudra's.

Marshall and I heard Mudra sharply criticize Patton and his authoritarian way. My recollection is that he likened Patton's style to Adolf Hitler's.

Perhaps 20 minutes after the meeting broke up, I saw Marshall in a hallway.

The president said that regardless of how a person feels about Patton — and he mentioned that the general has many critics — a coach should not show a movie to his team from a positive standpoint, and then shortly before the kickoff address that movie from a negative standpoint.

It seemed clear to me that, regardless of the outcome of that night's game, Mudra would not be back.

Marshall went on radio at halftime, as scheduled. But he did not announce Mudra would have another year.

When Florida State beat Houston, 33-22, the outcome perhaps delayed the inevitable. Possibly Marshall was giving the matter further consideration.

But soon a private drive had started to obtain pledges to buy up Mudra's remaining contract. Coincidence or otherwise, at about the time the pledge goal was in sight, a change was made.

Florida State's decision to fire him apparently came as an absolute surprise to Mudra, despite all the indications.

On the Saturday before the Sunday announcement, Mudra expressed strong confidence that he would return in 1976. The Orlando Sentinel, quoting Mudra, ran a top sports-page story saying he would be retained.

"I never even thought for a second that, as much of a struggle as we had financially, changing coaches halfway through my contract was a real possibility," said Mudra, "and it really came as a shock."

Looking back in 1986, he said, "We had a fun experience. It was intense and it was tough." But he also said: "I was not really distraught about leaving, because it was such a hard job."

Reflecting more, he concluded: "If I had a real fault, it was being naive."

But, surely, Mudra was not naive about talent. He left behind more good players than almost anyone suspected.

Almost anyone except Bobby Bowden.

Right away, he got a little excited.

The Bowden Years

A coach who speaks FSU's language gains eight bowls in first 11 seasons

"He is a Southern Cracker, to the manner born — perfectly adaptable to us Southern Crackers and rednecks of Northern Florida.

"He speaks our language, adheres to our religious faith, and fits our needs just like a glove."

This word picture of Bobby Bowden, fitting so like a glove, was drawn by a man who had been around Florida State and the South forever.

Coyle Moore was at the school long before it became Florida State University, and proudly cited the heritage of high standards set by the Florida State College for Women. For many years dean of FSU's College of Social Welfare, he was also dean, one might say, of a concerted effort to establish a strong athletic program.

Challenging and pushing, Moore often barked at students, athletes, coaches, administrators, politicians and fans. But it was a smiling, benevolent bark.

Few had his long-range perspective. He had seen most of the games, known all the coaches and had a role in hiring most. He had fought for stronger academics with stronger athletics. Along with a fellow dean, Mode Stone of the School of Education, he had offered a strong guiding hand through all the changes of the guard that saw school presidents come and go along with coaches.

"Hell, I've seen it all," he said, and that was so.

Jamie Dukes lifts Eric Williams in celebration during the Kansas game of '85. An outstanding leader and player, All-American guard Dukes started a school-record 48 straight games for FSU.

90 wins, 36 losses, 3 ties

Bobby Bowden in the 1980s.

From that considerable perspective, following Bowden's fourth season, Moore offered his vivid description of a coach who suited the Seminoles and their following like none other he had known.

In that fourth season of Bowden, the Seminoles had become the first major-college team in Florida ever to post an unbeaten regular season.

Interestingly, Bowden had been extended, there in that 1976 beginning, a four-year contract.

"At Florida State that means two years," cracked Bowden. "I'll have to hurry."

And what he thought, deep inside, was it would not take two years to put this team on a winning road.

"I took a look at those players and my impression was, 'Boy, is this a good-looking group!'" he said.

"And I'm thinking how many games we are going to win that first year. I'm thinking we are going to win about eight."

This was his first sight of those players, inside a meeting room, where Athletic Director John Bridgers had just introduced the new coach.

Right away, Bowden asked Bridgers to leave. He wanted to be absolutely alone with his players as he spoke to them.

"What I told them was what I thought we had to do to win," he said. "And one thing they had to do was do it my way.

"I'm sure there was some inward snickering. Their lifestyle and habits had been a little bit different from what I would ask."

His way meant some adjustment, rather inevitable with any coaching change.

"Now, I think there is more than one way to skin a cat, and had Darrell Mudra stayed and coached 'em, he would have won, too," said Bowden.

Spring practice came and went.

"I still thought we would win," said Bowden. "There had been some raggedness, but I found out we had a good group willing to listen.

"But for some, it was too late."

That first team, in 1976, lost its first three, and five of its first seven.

"When I thought we would win eight, I left out one important factor — attitude," said Bowden. "Not that it was bad.

"It was just that we were not on the same page. And some had lost so many games, they felt they could not win. That had to be changed."

A return to the Deep South

Florida State supporters had hardly been on the same page in quest of a successor to Mudra.

Twice previously — when Bill Peterson left, then when Larry Jones departed — Bowden had been interested, but Florida State apparently not so much.

This time, just off a fine season at West Virginia, Bowden had little interest. And Florida State again seemed to be moving in another direction.

Bridgers was primarily responsible for making Bowden the surprise choice.

"John contacted me in Tampa, where I was coaching an all-star game following the season," said Bowden. "Then he flew down, along with President Marshall.

"They did not offer me the job, but sounded like they might. They wanted me to come to Tallahassee for an interview.

"I talked it over with my wife, Ann. I was interested — but not enough to leave West Virginia with four kids in school there. Right now, we were thinking, just is not the right time.

"But we decided, after that Tampa game, to go to Tallahassee and take a look. Bridgers met me at the airport at 8 a.m., and I met the athletic board and we talked for an hour.

"Then I flew back to West Virginia. And by the time we got there, both Ann and I had about decided we wanted to come back. It was an accumulation of little things, including our wanting to get back in the Deep South. If it had been, say, Georgia Tech, Southern Missis-

sippi or Miami, we probably would have gone there, too."

An Alabama product all the way, Bowden had been a quarterback first at Alabama, then at Howard (now Samford) in hometown Birmingham, where he earned Little All-America recognition. He had been head coach at South Georgia Junior College, at Howard, but his first major-college job had been on Bill Peterson's Florida State staff.

His roots were indeed deep in the Deep South.

Bowden suggested he had slipped on the ice once too often in West Virginia.

"We got out of the car up there last night," he said at a Tallahassee press conference just after getting the FSU job. "I was standing upright when my feet slipped out from under me on that ice, and laying there I hollered at my wife, 'I'll take it, I'll take it!'"

Actually, Bowden had already made up his mind, and had called Bridgers from a pay phone at the West Virginia airport to tell him.

"But when I slipped on that ice, there was no doubt I made the right decision," he said.

A man who liked people

Florida State had hired a coach who saw humor in most things, and good in most things.

Little things — or big things — seemed not to bother Bowden for long. Soon he's laughing. He laughs a lot.

There are few people who, like Will Rogers, never met a man they didn't like. But Bowden, over a long period of Florida State time, seemed to be such a person.

"I think people are good, before I think they are bad," Bowden once said. "Too many people the first time they meet somebody don't like 'em right away. My first reaction is always to like 'em.

"I don't know of a person in this world I detest."

Deeply religious, Bowden was also deeply tolerant.

"I really think God loves the sinners as much as he does the upright," he said. "If you take nearly all the apostles Jesus had, they were sorry at times.

"Ain't nobody perfect."

When he was young, a number of people suggested to Bowden that he should be a minister.

"But I never felt like I was called," said Bowden. "It was more like I was called to coaching."

A Baptist, Bowden frequently has spoken from the pulpit to religious groups of many faiths.

He is an ardent golfer. Sometimes he chews on an unlit cigar — just chewing, never lighting. He has never drunk alcohol.

For Bowden the best of times is on the beach with his family.

"Sometimes when I'm just sitting there in a chair out on the beach with my feet in that water, I can't imagine anything better," he once said.

But the zest for the quest of football is never far away.

"I want to win every game and have the best team in the United States," he said.

"Some nights I go home and I just can't wait for sleep to be over. Just so I can go out and begin the next day."

From the beginning, Bowden spoke a language that Florida State fans not only understood but also seemed to agree with — strongly.

Bell-ringing words at that first press conference included:

• "I definitely believe in discipline. But if you hold a bird in your hand too tight, you squeeze him to death. And if you hold that bird too loose, he gets away."

• "My philosophy on offense is to take what they give you on defense. I want the ability to run or pass equally well. But don't misquote me — I didn't say 50 percent of one or the other."

• "Everything I do is optimistic. I'm an optimistic person."

• "There is going to be a common cause: those folks down yonder, down in Gainesville. Florida — that's the game we've got to win. I know it's tough.

• "I know a lot of you look at me and ask if this is a big-time coach. I don't know what a big-time coach is. But I know if I beat Florida, I'll be a big-time coach."

• "I believe in a three-team system. Offense, defense — and academics. I don't say that to be funny. When a boy comes to school and doesn't want academics, you're in trouble."

• "I'm going to lose some games, and they're going to get on me bad. If they didn't get on me, there'd be something wrong."

. . . And a man who could win games

After his first 11 Florida State seasons, Bowden had indeed lost some games, and fans had indeed got on him bad.

But the grand total of losses was 36 — of which six came the first year.

The victory total stood at 90.

He had inherited a team that had gone 4-29 in its three previous seasons, turned it into one that was 90-36-3 in its next 11.

Astonishing success away from home gained Bowden acclaim as "King of the Road." Entering his 12th season, the record included 4-1 for games played in LSU's stadium, 2-2 at Nebraska, 2-0 at Arizona State, 2-0 at Ohio State, 1-0 at Notre Dame, 1-0 at Syracuse, 1-0 at North Carolina, 1-0 at Oklahoma State, 1-0 at Boston College.

His Florida State record also showed eight bowl games in those 11 seasons, including two successive Orange Bowl appearances and five straight bowls without a loss.

Bowden's overall 21-year record of 163-68-3, including 32-6 at Samford and 42-26 at West Virginia, had earned him No. 4 rank among active Division 1-A coaches in total victories (163), and No. 11 rank in terms of percentage (.703).

At a coaches-writers seminar in 1987, Bowden was described in an NCAA presentation as "the No. 1 good ol' boy in college football, the savior of Florida State football, an inspirational lay preacher and quintessential family man," also as "a one-liner artist who never met a TV minicam he didn't like," and as a fellow who might well have been "a golf pro, or a comedian, or a salesman, or a public-relations man, or a politician, or a minister."

A sampling of the Bowden wit

The flow of Bowden quips and one-liners is constant.

• "When I was at Alabama, all I heard was 'Beat Auburn.' When I was at West Virginia, all I heard was 'Beat Pitt.' When I got to Florida State, their bumper stickers read 'Beat *Anybody!*'"

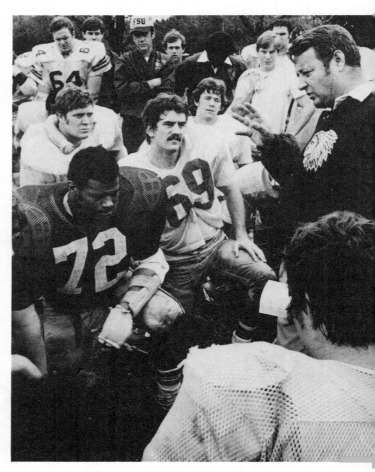

Three looks at Coach Bowden: Left, pausing during spring practice in '84; top, pretending to punch out Miami coach Howard Schnellenberger before the '83 game; and lecturing his team in '77.

• On filmed segments with Burt Reynolds for his TV show: "They'd be pretty good if I could teach the guy to act."

• At boosters' luncheon following loss: "OK, who wants to throw out the first barb?"

• On knee injury of North Carolina coach Dick Crum in sideline mishap: "That just scares me to death. I mess up my knee like that, and it means my backswing is shot."

• "The good news is our defense is giving up only one touchdown per game. The bad news is our offense is, too."

• Replying to Oklahoma's Barry Switzer, who spoke glowingly prior to Orange Bowl of fine coaching by Florida State staff: "I'll swap my coaches for your players."

• Of wife Ann and their six children: "When our first one was born I said, 'This is our cheerleader.' As our sons came after that I would say, 'This is our quarterback,' or 'This is the center,' and so on. When the sixth child came, Ann said to me, 'This is the end.'"

• On distaste for moral victories: "They're like a 6-foot man drowning in 3 feet of water. He's still dead."

• After an upset loss to Tulane when quarterback Jon English, an ineligible architect of the defeat, obtained a court ruling that permitted him to play: "What we've got to do is learn to defense the injunctions."

• On more than discipline being required in football: "I've always said that if short hair and perfect manners won football games, Army and Navy would play every year for the national championship."

• On his relationship with Michigan's Bo Schembechler: "It's kind of a mutual friendship. I like him, and he can't wait to play me."

• On a substitution at fullback after a fumble: "We were just one play too late with that one, weren't we?"

• On the frustration of losing to Florida: "I'm telling you, if I can't find a way to beat them, I think enough of Florida State to say maybe they ought to find someone better — right now, though, I can't think of anybody."

• Following a game in which his Seminoles were blown away: "We out-slopped the world."

• On his identity with food: "I've got no prejudices — I'll eat anything."

Bowden seems to have no prejudices either toward the media and their persistent pursuit of stories.

"We are in the selling business, and we need the press," Bowden said. "I don't agree with everything writers write, but when one walks into my office I nearly feel like I owe him a story. He does not owe me."

Media people find Bowden's uncommon candor more than refreshing. His accessibility, his readiness to comment on virtually any subject, make their assignments easier. Many think Bowden may be the Florida media's all-time favorite coach of any sport.

Sample Bowden candor: "When I came to Florida State, I didn't really think I'd stay. I figured I'd do good and move on — or get bombed out."

For a time there, following an 0-3 start in 1976, it looked as though Bowden would be bombed out.

'76: A slow start

It was a schedule that began with three straight on the road. But Bowden figured his Seminoles would take the opener at Memphis State, even though the Tigers had upset Mississippi 21-16 the week prior.

Spurred by quarterback Lloyd Patterson, Memphis State turned a 7-3 halftime lead into a quick 21-3 advantage in the third quarter. FSU got a touchdown and a safety to cut it to a final 21-12.

"Now, I thought we were going to win that game," said Bowden. "But with Miami ahead in the next game, I was *sure* we would win.

"Oh, yeah — definitely! After all, Florida State had beaten Miami the year before. And they had to be about as bad as us."

If Miami was as bad, it was not so immediately apparent.

"We were in it — right up until the opening kickoff," said Bowden. "That was when we fumbled, on the first play."

With Ottis Anderson spurring a running charge, Miami led 17-0 after a quarter, 31-0 after a half. When it was over, Florida State had experienced the second-worst loss in its history — the 47-0 score exceeded only by 49-0, Florida, three years prior.

"It's gonna take longer than I thought," said Bowden.

"We had been beaten 47-0, and it could have been 100-0. Carl Selmer (Miami coach) tried to hold the score down.

"I remember exactly what I was thinking after that thing was over — we might not win a game!"

Bring in the freshmen

At this early point, Florida State made a big decision that followed a classic pattern.

"If we were going to get beat, let's get the young guys ready," said Bowden, spelling out that decision.

The question was if Miami had won 47-0, what would Oklahoma — on its home field in Norman — elect to make the score?

And Bowden had decided to start six freshmen.

"I remember the six names like yesterday," said Bowden a dozen years later.

"Kurt Unglaub and Jackie Flowers at the wideouts, Scott Warren at defensive end, Mike Good at guard, Mark Lyles at fullback, Walter Carter at defensive tackle.

"And if you count Dave Cappelen, our kicker, that made it seven freshman starters."

On Oklahoma's first play from scrimmage, Kenny King dashed 50 yards before getting wrestled down at about the 30.

"They run three plays, don't make a first down, and settle for a field goal," said Bowden.

"Then we drive 80 yards and go up 6-3."

Larry Key, after leading the drive, scored from the 5.

Oklahoma scored and led 10-6. Florida State grabbed a fumble, drove to the 1 — where Key fumbled after being hit hard, the ball rolling through the end zone for a touchback. The Sooners moved to a second touchdown and a 17-6 halftime lead.

Moving behind an unbalanced line in the second half, Florida State had two drives nullified by turnovers, then got one of its own and a Cappelen field goal that cut it to 17-9. With 7:15 left, Oklahoma got the touchdown that made it a final 24-9.

A game in which Florida State seemed to have no chance was one it might have won. Reiterating his distaste for moral victories, Bowden added: "These things are forgotten."

But this one would not be. The effort at Oklahoma — the day those six freshmen started — is remembered as a significant Bowden turning point.

Jimmy Black, settling in at quarterback in his senior year, had run for 86 yards against Oklahoma, and Key had netted 89.

Down 10-0 at halftime to Kansas State in Bowden's first Campbell Stadium game, the Seminoles rallied behind a turnover-grabbing defense and won 20-10 as Black threw for two touchdowns.

Wind, rain and a highly favored foe awaited Florida State at Boston College, but the Seminoles had gained some familiarity with wet weather back home during the practice week, and were also gaining some familiarity with highly favored foes.

Boston College led 6-0 but FSU moved ahead 7-6 at the half, 14-9 after three quar-

ters, and won 28-9 behind Black, Key and the defense.

Had Bowden turned this team around after just five games?

"It ain't turned around," said the coach, "until we beat the Gators."

A close one against the Gators

Playing for the second time under Campbell Stadium lights, Florida jumped ahead 10-0 before FSU rallied for a brief 17-13 lead shortly before halftime. It seesawed, before Florida took a 33-23 lead in the fourth quarter.

Black, after 12 straight pass completions, left the game with seven minutes remaining.

In came Jimmy Jordan, the popular and strong-armed Tallahassee freshman. Quickly, he passed FSU downfield, and a Cappelen field goal cut it to 33-26 with five minutes left. With 1:08 left, Jordan and pals had a final chance, starting at their 24. As Unglaub caught two, FSU swiftly knocked off 54 yards to the Florida 22. With time running out, and under heavy pressure, Jordan missed two open receivers on following plays, and it stayed 33-26.

"I don't think you can ask for any better effort," said Bowden.

At Auburn, facing a team that included fullback William Andrews, Florida State led 7-0, then 13-7 but trailed at halftime 14-13. But quarterback Phil Gargis would score four touchdowns to lead a 31-19 Auburn victory.

FSU led Clemson at the half 9-0. Then the Tigers brought on Steve Fuller at quarterback to lead a surprising rally that downed FSU 15-12. Bowden's first-year record, following this somewhat galling loss, dropped to 2-6.

Once again, with three straight losses, Florida State had its back in a familiar position. Up against the wall.

But, ah, the final three games — Southern Mississippi, North Texas State, Virginia Tech — produced one of the most exciting and incredible stretches in the history of college football.

One 90-yard play after another

November 1976 surely ranks with this viewer as the most memorable Florida State football month of them all.

One gridiron miracle followed another.

Consider the "Miracle of the 90-yard Plays."

In those three games, the Seminoles had

four scoring plays from scrimmage exceeding 90 yards.

Consider that in the first 30 years of Florida State football, there were *no* other scoring plays from scrimmage of 90 yards or more.

Moreover, in the 10 Florida State seasons following, there were none.

"Do you realize how rare the 90-yard scoring play from scrimmage is?" asked Jim Van Valkenberg, veteran statistician of the NCAA. "What Florida State did in that three-game stretch is just amazing.

"Though we do not keep records on all scoring plays from scrimmage over 90 yards, I'd feel free to say that what Florida State did in those three games was something no one had done before."

Many schools playing the game much longer than Florida State show no such plays.

Auburn, Georgia Tech and Miami are among those with only one. Alabama has two. Georgia and Notre Dame have only four — same as Florida State.

Florida State's four plays, in order:

1. Jimmy Black's 95-yard screen pass to Rudy Thomas (Southern Mississippi).

2. Black's 91-yard pass to Kurt Unglaub (in the snow at North Texas State).

3. Larry Key's 97-yard run (Virginia Tech).

4. Jimmy Jordan's 96-yard pass to Unglaub (also Virginia Tech).

20 points, just like that

It all started with homecoming on Nov. 6 in Campbell Stadium with the "Rudy Thomas Miracle."

With less than 12 minutes remaining, Southern led 27-10.

Disappointed, disgusted fans were moving out of the stadium. One of those who left, at the start of that last quarter, was Ann Bowden, the coach's wife.

"I think she just packed it in," said Bowden years later. "Oh, she might have said she left early to get ready for entertaining prospects, or something.

"But she has left a lot, when things are not going like she likes. Because she can't stand to watch, she'll go off somewhere.

"Heck, that night she might have *led* that crowd of folks out of the stadium early!"

Then it happened.

In a startling span of 7 minutes and 23 seconds on the field clock, Florida State rocketed in front to stay 30-27.

Rudy Thomas, a senior back from Quincy, scored all three touchdowns.

It was Thomas on a determined run from the 10, for a touchdown that cut it to 27-17 with 11:28 to go.

With 6:53 to go, Thomas scored on a 4-yarder, and the score was 27-23 after a futile 2-point pass.

And then, on third down, Florida State was backed to its 5 for what perhaps was a last-chance play.

Behind the line of scrimmage, Thomas took a screen pass from Black and rambled 95 yards for the touchdown that won it.

"That game was definitely the beginning of something big for us," said Bowden.

"From that point on, through the next three years, we might not have lost but four or five games."

In fact, Florida State lost five over the next two regular seasons, then none in the third.

Let's play snowball

After the Southern Mississippi breakthrough came the "Make-the-World-Go-Away Miracle."

On the evening prior to their date at North Texas State, the Seminoles went about a normal motel routine, including early to bed. They awoke the next morning to what for most was an eye-popping sight. Snow blanketed everything.

In the lobby of the motel, President Bernie Sliger looked outside and hummed a melancholy country tune, "Make the World Go Away."

The snow did not go away. Five inches covered the field. Sideline markers and yard stripes were obscured.

In that snow, North Texas had only one turnover.

The Seminoles had six — including five fumbles — and a whole lot of fun.

That snow seems to have been a motivational plus for the Seminoles, most of whom had never seen snow — much less played in it.

"We turned it into something like a street game — really wild, laughing and sliding around, having fun," said Black.

Unglaub loped away with the 91-yard scoring pass from Black in the third quarter.

"That pass was kinda funny," recalled Unglaub. "I had run down the field, and actually stopped in front of the defensive back.

"Then I started up again — and the defensive back fell down, allowing me to get open. I bobbled the ball several times.

"It was hard to tell where you were out there, and I just told myself I was going to run

Quarterback Jimmy Black goes back to pass during the snowy game against North Texas State in '76. Was it cold? Ask trainer Don Fauls, right.

further than where the goalposts actually were."

Unglaub thought game conditions favored a slower receiver because of the slippery footing.

"None of the players thought we were really going to play that day," said Unglaub. "It was snowing. I mean, when we went out on the field, and it never let up.

"Then the coaches said 'Get dressed.' And we still didn't think we would play under the conditions. When we warmed up, we were relaxed, horsing around, throwing snowballs.

"Then all of a sudden, we found ourselves lining up for a kickoff, and we needed to get serious. The snow was coming down in sheets, like rain. The wind was blowing.

"It was tremendously cold, very windy and that field was terribly slick. I remember the biggest thing I tried to do was stay warm."

Florida State was ill-equipped for a game in the snow. Frank DeBord, the veteran equipment manager, had rushed out that morning in a quest for gloves.

"What he bought from a hardware store were gloves — well, they must have been garden gloves," said Unglaub. "Gloves like that kind of stay wet."

Players had trouble lining up properly, because yard lines were obscured.

"Both teams often lined up offsides," said Unglaub.

"One humorous thing was Coach Bowden asking officials for a fourth-down measurement, and they told him there was no way to get a measurement out there."

Moving into the game's final minutes, FSU trailed 20-13.

A 10-play drive was capped by Jeff Leggett's 1-yard TD run with 2:13 to go, leaving it 20-19. Going for 2 and a 21-20 victory, FSU got it on Key's surprise pass to Unglaub.

"After we won, there was this big hill we had to go up to get to the dressing room," said Unglaub. "On that hill, we were tackling each other, rubbing each other's face in the snow, having a good time out there.

"Probably 70 percent of us had never seen snow."

Players dressed and boarded buses for the long ride from Denton to the Dallas-Fort Worth airport.

"Here we were on those buses, looking out at the snow on the way, and singing Christmas carols — coaches, players, everybody," said Unglaub.

"It was unique. A happy feeling."

Bowden agreed.

"I believe the most *fun* game I've ever been associated with was that one," he said years later.

"The only thing I could think to tell 'em beforehand was 'Go out there and have fun.'

"It was the only thing to put it all in perspective. How could you dare tell 'em before that game to 'Get serious'? Not when most of those guys had never *seen* snow!"

Unglaub grabs another one

Perhaps the biggest fun play — if not game — for Key came a week later.

But his school-record 97-yard scoring run from scrimmage was missed by many because of threatening weather.

Following an all-day rain, Florida State had well over 5,000 no-shows for a closing encounter with Virginia Tech.

Trailing 6-0 early, Florida State soon after was backed to its 3 following a mishandled punt.

As he hit off the left side, Key seemed stopped cold — but suddenly pulled away from tacklers and went the route. Throughout his time, Key characteristically broke tackles with his uncommon strength built through persistent weightlifting.

Ahead 14-6 at the half, FSU fell behind 21-14. It became 21-20 as Jimmy Jordan hit Jackie Flowers with a TD pass, but a 2-point try went awry.

Tech seemed about to salt it away when Scott Warren forced a fumble that teammate Walter Carter claimed at the FSU 4. Promptly, Jordan faded in the end zone and found Unglaub with a strong-armed throw at midfield, and the receiver eluded defenders the rest of the way on a 96-yard play that won it 28-21.

"This was basically the same kind of pass I had caught at North Texas State in the snow," said Unglaub. "I just kind of jumped between two defenders, and when I came down with the ball both were on the ground. Funny thing, a cornerback came from the other side of the field and had run me down about the 12, but instead of just tackling me, he dived and missed."

Looking back on the two 90-yard passes years later, Unglaub shook his head.

"I couldn't believe it," he said. "They happened so fast. And here the quarterbacks were back deep in their end zones, and they're going to throw a bomb to a slow receiver."

Bobby Bowden was beginning to believe.

"I think," said the coach as his first FSU team finished 5-6, "the excitement is back in Florida State football."

Unglaub thought Bowden had lit a fire.

"All of a sudden, late in the year, we had a good mix — seniors trying to go out on a good note, and young players coming along," he said.

"(Black) was brilliant — a good student who was so respected. He could make things happen, in a tremendous fashion, more than any quarterback I was ever around.

"He was not as poised, nor was he quite the leader that Wally (Woodham) was, and he did not have the fire potential of Jimmy (Jordan).

"But he could make it happen. And as soon as that ball was snapped, you knew it."

A feeling grew that Bowden was about to make things happen.

'77: The arrival of Ron Simmons

Early in 1977, Bernie Sliger was named president after a period of carrying the title "acting president." Bowden sent the popular Sliger a telegram that read: "You won the big one!"

Sliger replied with a telegram that read: "Luke 10:37."

That biblical text admonishes: "Go forth and do likewise."

Bowden did.

The Seminoles were on the verge of what the coach would call his most satisfying football year.

"Over my coaching time anywhere, it surely was," said Bowden 10 years later.

"In 1977, Florida State got back to where it was supposed to be.

"We won 10 games, and that was a school record.

"We returned to the top 20. We won a bowl game.

"And we beat Florida 37-9.

Maybe bigger than anything, it was the year Ron Simmons came to Florida State football.

A prep All-American out of Warner Robins, Ga., Simmons was listed at 225 pounds. He ran the 40-yard dash in a spectacular 4.6 seconds. His strength was extraordinary. At first, he was listed at 6-foot-2. Later, that would be adjusted to 6-1. Later still, word would get around that Simmons was actually a fraction short of 6 feet.

It scarcely mattered.

Every Florida State fan came to know that Simmons stood 7 feet tall. At least.

Tom McEwen, the Tampa Tribune sports editor, provided perhaps the best description:

"Simmons was not born. He was chiseled of brown Georgia granite, had the wings of

Mercury attached to his ankles, and had life breathed into him by whatever saint is assigned to Bobby Bowden. He . . . can bench-press 525 pounds, and could tomorrow win a position as stand-in for the Incredible Hulk."

With a spectacularly muscled body that indeed resembled that of television's giant Hulk, Simmons throughout his Florida State time drew as much attention off the field as on it. On that field, he often would be double-teamed, sometimes triple-teamed.

And introducing Wally Jim Jordham

A starter from the beginning, Simmons brought Florida State its first touchdown of the season — blocking a Southern Mississippi punt, teammate Scott Warren running it in from the 2.

"The play of the game," proclaimed Bowden on the heels of a 35-6 victory considerably more difficult than the score hints. Ahead by a bare 7-6 at halftime, limited to 77 yards of offense, Florida State had been "set afire" by

The year 1977 brought three players who would become stars: noseguard Ron Simmons and two quarterbacks — Jimmy Jordan (left) and Wally Woodham (above) — known collectively as Wally Jim Jordham.

Simmons' blocked kick a minute before the half.

That Sept. 10, 1977, date in Hattiesburg, Miss., also saw the debut of the most sensational quarterback in Florida State annals — the one a Sports Illustrated writer would later christen Wally Jim Jordham.

Wally Woodham and Jimmy Jordan had each played under Gene Cox at Tallahassee's Leon High, one following the other by a year.

When Woodham was a Leon senior, in 1974, he set a national high-school passing record with 3,560 yards. Succeeding him as a Leon starter the following year, Jordan broke that national record with 4,098 yards.

Woodham had enrolled at Florida State in 1975 but played only junior-varsity ball. When Jordan enrolled in 1976, he had played as a freshman while Woodham was redshirted.

The two entered 1977, then, as sophomores — each with three years of eligibility.

Jordan started that game in Hattiesburg and threw for two last-half touchdowns. Woodham came in late and threw for one.

139

Exultation from two gifted Seminole receivers:
Mike Shumann (opposite page) and Kurt Unglaub.

Soon a pattern would evolve. For three seasons running, one would rescue the other — and the team — from trouble. Bowden would start one or the other, usually according to a simple formula — which one he felt held the hottest hand. Sometimes Jordan might start three or four games in a row, sometimes Woodham.

Listed at 6-1 and 185, Jordan was about 2 inches taller and 5 pounds heavier than Woodham.

Jordan had the phenomenally strong and accurate arm, and it was generally felt he threw the long pass better. Woodham was usually seen as a splendid all-round quarterback, a better runner, an unusual leader who could surely pass well enough.

In 1977, the two had more than casual acquaintance with moves of two of the gifted receivers — senior Mike Shumann and sophomore Kurt Unglaub, also Leon High products.

Shumann would later play for several years in the NFL. Unglaub, seen by some as "another Biletnikoff," had his potential blunted by continuing injury.

A big date at Oklahoma State

After running its 2-year winning streak to five games with an 18-10 triumph at Kansas State, the 1977 team had its potential blunted by Miami in Tallahassee.

In each of the previous five games, the Seminoles had come from behind to win. Against Miami, the Seminoles trailed 10-0 after a quarter, but rallied to lead 17-10 in the early minutes of the last half

This time, however, it was Coach Lou Saban's Miami players who did the decisive rallying. Thirteen last-quarter points toppled the Seminoles 23-17.

Apparently, however, Florida State's steadily improving defense became even stronger in the Miami game, with the first-time deployment of Louie Richardson as a starting tackle. Defensive coordinator Jack Stanton called his performance unbelievable.

Florida State comeback tactics returned to winning form with a striking upset of Oklahoma State's defending Big Eight Conference champions in Stillwater. The favored Cowboys were spurred by hard-running Terry Miller, a Heisman Trophy hopeful.

In a game that saw Miller churn for 156 yards on 26 carries, FSU fell behind 17-3 early in the final quarter before Woodham, in relief of Jordan, ignited a 22-point explosion that won it 25-17.

Larry Key did some igniting, too — running for 127 yards on a school-record 32 carries, catching three passes for 72 yards, returning kickoffs for 60 more.

In the last quarter, FSU defenders granted Miller and friends little, including not one first down.

For Bowden, Oklahoma State at Stillwater was in a sense as pivotal as Oklahoma at Norman had been a year prior. The Oklahoma State upset signaled a coming-together of offense and a defense often led by the freshman Simmons and the junior end Willie Jones.

Jingle those keys

Cincinnati showed Florida State something about playing defense in a sticky Tallahassee encounter that the Seminoles won 14-0. What Florida State showed Cincinnati, in addition to some defense, was an unlikely receiver.

Roger Overby, a senior who had thought of

quitting the game as recently as spring practice, caught nine of Woodham's 16 completions. If it was just about the first many fans had heard of Overby, it wouldn't be the last.

In '77, FSU beat Auburn for the first time. Is that why Larry Key (44) is doing a headstand?

What Auburn showed Florida State in Tallahassee was three future NFL backfield stars — William Andrews, Joe Cribbs, James Brooks.

It was not nearly enough.

Florida State beat Auburn for the first time in 11 tries, 24-3, and a Southeastern Conference opponent for the first time since 1972.

Brooks had played on the same Warner Robins team as Simmons. While Simmons had quite a game — 10 tackles and nine assists, including three tackles for losses — neither Brooks nor Andrews nor Cribbs did anything much worth writing home about. Of the three, Cribbs came out best with 52 yards on 12 runs.

On this evening, Key alone outdid the three — his school-record 170 yards, on 25 carries, topping their 134 yards on 38 endeavors.

Campbell Stadium fans outdid themselves at homecoming the following week as North Texas State came in out of the cold with a 7-1 record and ranked 16th in the nation. Final score: Florida State 35, North Texas State 14.

Whenever Key ran, fans jingled their keys — a tribute to the senior, and the inauguration of a tradition that would continue through the remainder of a sparkling season. Key responded with 94 yards on 21 carries.

Meanwhile, Simmons jangled quarterbacks. Five times he registered sacks — including four in the fourth quarter alone — for losses totaling 52 yards, as he again had 10 tackles and nine assists. The Associated Press saluted him as lineman of the week, and Sports Illustrated proclaimed him defensive player of the week.

"When I was at West Virginia, I watched Tony Dorsett turn the Pittsburgh program around," said Bowden after the game. "Simmons is doing the same thing here."

Unveiling the reverse

At Blacksburg, the Seminoles almost got themselves turned around by Virginia Tech's one-time winners. Always, Tech could be counted on to shuffle the deck in quest of a new trick.

This time it seemed a big tight end playing fullback — one Mickey Fitzgerald — might be just the card.

But Tech perhaps overplayed its hand. In a game that saw Fitzgerald run 25 times for 112 yards, Tech took a 14-3 lead. Then it tried an onsides kick that FSU covered and quickly converted into a touchdown.

Bowden played a surprise card that would become most familiar to fans — a reverse that, over so many following years, became something of a trademark.

On this occasion, FSU utilized the reverse three times, with Shumann stacking up 99 yards. Shumann also caught three passes for 80.

But there at the end it was Dave Cappelen kicking his third field goal of the game — a 29-yarder with 4:57 remaining — to win it 23-21. However, it was a reverse — and a 39-yard Shumann pass off of it — that paved the winning field goal.

"I felt like we dodged a bullet," said Bowden. So often that seemed so when FSU escaped the clutches of the Gobblers.

In a final home game, FSU shot down Memphis State 30-9.

Now the team stood 8-1, ranked No. 13 in both wire-service polls — and was 13 ever an unlucky number!

At San Diego State, the Aztecs led 14-0 early, 38-10 at the half — and 41-16 at the finish. FSU was never in it.

"We were victimized by going out there in the first place, by seeing Sea World when we got there and all that," said Bowden. "Plus, San Diego State had a fine football team.

"They played a super ball game."

Jilted by the Gator Bowl prior to the game, Florida State fans and players were in a disappointed and — as developments indicated — dangerous mood.

Third and 30 and . . . unbelievable!

Florida awaited in Gainesville, and FSU had not beaten the Gators in the previous nine games — not since 1967 and 21-16.

In contrast to FSU's 8-2, Florida stood 6-3-1.

Florida had several players who soon would be NFL draft choices, but one — the great receiver Wes Chandler — was freshly sidelined with injury. Similarly, the Seminoles had newly lost Bill Duley, gritty and capable punter. Steve Dykes, a replacement who never before had punted in varsity play, would average 27.5 on four boots.

Single, dramatic plays sometimes shatter close, dramatic games — changing their form, making the rest suddenly easier.

Let us set the scene:

Florida State had taken an early 7-0 lead on Woodham's 37-yard pass to Unglaub, but soon Bowden would turn to the hotter hand of the day — that of Jordan, who soon hit Overby with a 4-yard scoring strike. Cappelen contributed a field goal.

Florida fought back and on three Berj Ye-premian field goals — all in the second quarter — stood within 17-9 range at intermission.

And that's how it stood early in the third quarter, with Florida defenders backing Florida State to its 12, assisted by a holding penalty and a sack of Jordan.

Third down, 30 yards to go — and sticky!

And Key runs 38 yards to the 50 on a draw.

"He changed directions about once," recalled Bowden. "Larry just broke it — got clear, and sprinted for that first down.

"It was one of those games, one of those situations where everybody in the stands knew you had to throw. Only you didn't."

Among all the plays of all the years — all the touchdown passes, all the blocked punts, all the 100-yard kickoff returns, all the scoring runbacks of interceptions — this one is a personal favorite.

Perhaps there were bigger plays, but surely not too many.

This was the one!

Third and 30 at your own 12 — and a draw play that gets the priceless first down. Unbelievable!

Ah, but there was so much unbelievable on this most golden of Gainesville afternoons!

• Roger Overby scoring three touchdowns, in the end zone after the third one waving the ball on high, and Jordan pitching to him for all three — 4 yards once, 20 yards twice.

• Key running 20 times for 143 yards to become the first Seminole to gain more than 1,000 in a single season, and Jordan completing 13 of 19 passes for 240.

• FSU defenders in the third quarter, led by Jimmy Heggins, turning back Florida on fourth down at the 1, then Jordan launching a killer 99-yard scoring drive.

• Florida State beating Florida for the first time in 10 years, and for only the third time in 20 — and doing it by four touchdowns, a 28-point margin.

• The Seminoles winning nine games in a regular season for the first time in history.

• And two anonymous, opportunistic entrepreneurs hustling to a trailer in the parking lot to print garnet-lettered stickers reading "37-9" and selling them for a buck apiece like so many hotcakes to hungry Seminoles screaming "FSU all the damn time" as they left Florida Field.

• More than 5,000 fans, back in Tallahassee, turning out for a Campbell Stadium welcome of the Seminoles after they bused home, and President Sliger proclaiming: "This is more than a victory — it brings home the importance of a successful football program!"

FLORIDA 9 F S U
2 TIME OUTS LEFT 2 37-0
DOWN TO GO BALL ON QTR 4

10:00

37 9
SEMINOLE TERRITORY

Larry Key in his last game, against Texas Tech in the '77 Tangerine Bowl.

• The Tallahassee Democrat on the following day selling more than 4,000 additional Sunday papers.

If more than 20,000 Florida State fans flocking to the Tangerine Bowl in Orlando further underscored their feelings about the magnitude of such a victory over Florida, it would be a while before Bowden himself became fully aware of its meaning to them.

Looking back on that 1977 Florida game 10 years later, Bowden acknowledged it.

"I did not realize the importance of the Florida game then," he said. "Now I realize it.

"The last six games I've realized it."

After a 1986 loss to Florida, the Seminoles had experienced six straight setbacks.

"I've had to get beat those six straight times," said Bowden candidly, "to really know just how important it is."

A farewell to Key

Two days before Christmas, few things seemed more important to success-starved FSU fans than the Tangerine Bowl, and they swarmed into Orlando for a happy celebration of what had been and what would be.

What an unbelievable afternoon in Gainesville. The scoreboard — as well as the bumper sticker, one of hundreds printed in a trailer in the parking lot right after the game — tells the score of this '77 Florida game.

Texas Tech, coached by former FSU aide Steve Sloan, quickly found itself overmatched. Scoring in every quarter, FSU won 40-17 as Key — hearing the keys jingle for the last time — ran 21 times for 83 yards, caught six passes for 100 more, and returned three kickoffs for 131.

"Larry Key was a relatively short, compact, strong and very durable player," recalled Bowden 10 years later.

"His work during his senior year I still cite as an example to our players. That year his practice habits improved like from daylight to dark.

"I don't know that we've ever had a back work as hard as he did that senior year."

Key's practice habits had not always been exemplary.

"The first year, I remember calling him under an oak tree out there on the practice field and asking him if he wanted to go home," said Bowden. "He wasn't into it. Wasn't hustling. I don't know what it was. That happens sometimes when you change coaches.

"He changed, but not like overnight. By golly, it was like a light came on in his head.

"And I don't think we have ever had a back that made the one-season impact that Larry Key did in 1977."

As the Seminoles finished 10-2, on the heels of their first bowl game in seven years, Bowden had received a new five-year contract, and a pattern evolved of annual automatic renewal for five more years.

'78: Renegade gallops in

Evolving patterns with his football team in 1978 were sometimes difficult to discern.

"We started eight sophomores on defense," recalled Bowden, "and they were gonna have to sink or swim."

They started swimmingly.

In an opener at Syracuse, end Scott Warren and linebacker Reggie Herring sandwiched Bill Hurley between them early. The touted Syracuse quarterback left the game with three busted ribs.

Homes Johnson, a sophomore tailback starting for the first time, ran through the Orangemen for 135 yards in 17 efforts. With the persistent threat of Johnson, FSU broke open a close game with 21 last-quarter points and won 28-0.

FSU swam on to 3-0 as Oklahoma State tumbled 38-20 and Miami 31-21.

Possibly the most memorable aspect of the Oklahoma State game was the introduction of Renegade.

With rider Jim Kidder, dressed in Seminole Indian attire, astride the horse Renegade, a colorful, attention-attracting tradition was born on Sept. 16, 1978, in Campbell Stadium.

At all home games thereafter, and for occasional road games where permission was granted, Renegade and a rider who would come to be called Chief Osceola, after the heroic Seminole chief, would lead the Seminoles upon the field shortly before kickoff. Soon, Renegade would move to the center of the field, and Osceola would stab a flaming spear into the ground as the home crowd went wild and opposition players glared.

It was an idea that initially came to Bill Durham, a Tallahassee businessman, when he was a Florida State student in 1962. "We couldn't get the university to sponsor the idea," he recalled.

For a number of years prior to Bowden's coaching time, Florida State had a popular early mascot in "Sammy Seminole" — a student dressed as an Indian brave who cavorted and cartwheeled on the playing field prior to games and on the sidelines. But these gifted acrobats came primarily from Florida State's nationally acclaimed gymnastics team, which went 42-4-1 in dual meets — before FSU dropped intercollegiate competition in gymnastics in 1960.

In the early 1970s, FSU dropped the "Sammy Seminole" logo, and the imagery of a scowling Indian lad, no more than 8 years old, brandishing a tomahawk.

"I was sitting around talking with Coach Bowden one day," recalled Durham, "and he recalled how West Virginia had a traditional mascot, and he mentioned the tradition here of Sammy Seminole and his back flips when he had been an assistant."

Durham mentioned his horse-and-rider idea to Bowden, who liked it. But it was still a tough sell to the administration. Athletic Director John Bridgers expressed apprehension about Florida State "getting into the horse business." Boosters, too, were initially opposed.

"We knew we were going to have trouble opening doors," said Durham.

Ann Bowden, wife of the coach, volunteered to help.

"She opened the doors," said Durham.

Later, Bridgers would enthusiastically endorse the idea, and the boosters would assist financially in maintaining a tradition. Some individual boosters would donate food and veterinary service.

"We visited with Howard Tommy, chief of the Seminoles at the time we started the tradition," said Durham. "He confirmed that his tribe, in fact, once rode horses but said Andrew Jackson stole all of them.

"The Creeks — most Seminoles were Creeks — had a heritage of great horsemanship."

Chief Tommy said women of the tribe would sew the colorful costume for the Florida State riders. They did, but the costume arrived late. For the debut, there was improvisation. The bathrobe of fan Kathy Chenoweth — a splendid garment of turquoise, red, blue and yellow stripes — was borrowed for the first game.

Renegade is invariably an appaloosa, perhaps the most colorful of all horses. "The Nez Perce tribe, out in Arizona, bred appaloosas," said Durham. "They like colorful things, and these horses are bred strictly for color."

Appaloosas, often stubborn, tend to have high rumps and strong legs — characteristics that some coaches associate with good players.

Only rarely do Renegade and rider go on the road — because only rarely will an opposing team grant permission.

One year, at Tallahassee, when Osceola flew the flaming spear into the ground prior to kickoff, Southern Mississippi partisans moved in with a fire extinguisher. "Now, we have a security group watching for that, and more," said Durham.

But if opposing teams do not, television networks adore Renegade and Osceola, and call prior to bowl games to make sure they are going to be there.

"The first inkling we had that Florida State was going to get an Orange Bowl bid following the 1979 season came when the network called from New York," said Durham. "They wanted to know about the horse."

Two consecutive nail-biters

Florida State's sink-or-swim sophomores next took on Houston in Tallahassee. Scoring the first four times it got the football, Houston led 27-0 as it controlled the line of scrimmage.

Woodham came off the bench to spark a rally that cut it to 27-21 in the third quarter. A holding call late in the final quarter canceled what might have been Florida State's biggest comeback in history as Woodham collaborated with Jackie Flowers on a 36-yard play. It stayed 27-21.

One of the great winning plays of Seminole history came against Cincinnati in the following game.

This time it was Jordan off the bench, leading a fourth-quarter charge. Cincinnati led 21-14.

Jordan directed a 91-yard scoring drive, but it stayed 21-20 when a 2-point attempt failed.

With less than 2 minutes left, Florida State came to fourth down, 22 yards to go at its 46.

In quest of the first down, Jordan threw about 23 yards over the middle to Sam Platt, who retreated a bit for running room. Had he been tackled, he would have missed the first down.

But the swift Platt found the room he sought, and tore away on a scoring play of 54 yards. The scoreboard showed 1:29 and Florida State a 26-21 winner.

"My stomach won't take much of this," said Bowden.

A loss to Pitt — but an encouraging one

The real stomach-turner for a young team now beginning to hurt a little from mounting injuries came at Mississippi State's homecoming on a windy afternoon.

Down 14-0 early, FSU rallied behind Jordan for a 21-14 halftime lead. Whereupon the Bulldogs exploded for three touchdowns in each of the last two quarters and romped 55-27.

"We just got the heck beat out of us," said Bowden, alarmed over a defense that had given up 596 yards, including 378 passing.

Next week, at Pitt's homecoming, the offense had its problems, failing to score a touchdown for the first time in 28 games as the Seminoles fell 7-3. One play that had the brief appearance of being a touchdown — Jordan to Platt for 89 yards — was erased by a ruling that Platt had been out of bounds before catching the ball. An NCAA rule, new that year, said that if a receiver was forced out of bounds by a defender, he could make a valid catch. FSU felt Platt had been forced out.

But it was a strong Pitt team, and if ever there was a turning point for a group of Florida State players, this game was it.

Highly encouraged by the defensive endeavor, Bowden again and again over coming years would point to the Pitt loss as one of the most significant of all games.

Playing a prominent role (seven tackles, 11 assists) in a near upset was defensive back Monk Bonasorte, a native Pittsburgher and one-time FSU walk-on.

"Pitt had a great team on defense," said Bowden. "But the big thing in this game was our own defense had come to life."

In a third straight road game, Woodham — making just his second start of the season — threw four touchdown passes and Southern Mississippi fell 38-16. "Let's hope this is the beginning of something good," said Bowden. It was.

Two last-quarter touchdowns provided something good to quell forever-tough Virginia Tech 24-14.

In Florida State's first and only encounter of the first 40 years with a service-academy opponent, Navy became a 38-6 homecoming victim on a warm November afternoon as Jordan threw four last-half touchdown passes — three to Platt.

But on this Nov. 18 afternoon of official bowl invitations, Florida State found itself surprisingly left out. Many had written off the Seminoles following a 4-3 beginning that included the blowout at Mississippi State. Some were apprehensive about the 7-3 Seminoles' remaining game with Florida.

"I think our getting left out of the picture was due a whole lot to our not knowing how to handle bowls," said Bowden. "That was especially so as far as I was concerned.

"But a big thing had been our 4-3 start, and our not being very attractive until late."

At the time, Bowden expressed hope the bowl snub would make his Seminoles "more ornery" for Florida.

Three of the keys to FSU's strong defensive teams of the late '70s: Bobby Butler and Monk Bonasorte (also shown above, teaming up in the Orange Bowl game following the '80 season), and Willie Jones, as he looked after joining the Oakland Raiders.

Florida State was ornery at the start. Simmons forced a fumble on the Gators' first scrimmage play, and soon FSU had jumped in front 21-0. In a dramatic turnabout, Florida tied it 21-21 in the second.

As Willie Jones, the big and fast defensive end, held Florida's offense at bay, FSU moved behind Woodham to two touchdowns and a field goal that won it 38-21.

"He was a fifth player in our backfield," said Doug Dickey of Jones, who five times threw Gators for losses.

A senior, the popular Jones moved on following that 8-3 finish to become the Senior Bowl's most valuable player, and to a promising career with the Oakland Raiders that ended all too soon because of problems off the field.

Few contributed more to turning a program around than Willie Jones, who later returned to Florida State to pursue his degree.

For Dickey, it was a final game as Florida coach. Among other things, he had lost two in a row to Florida State, and there were Gators who considered such a cardinal sin.

Dickey, of course, was the first Florida coach to lose two straight to the Seminoles. His successor, Charley Pell, would also lose his first two to FSU. Under circumstances generally considered extenuating, Pell survived.

'79: The unbeaten regular season

Florida State's striking ability to stop opponents in the vital second half would soon become a celebrated fact.

But Bowden had a problem at the start. George Haffner, his heralded offensive coordinator, left for Texas A&M. (Soon, he would move from there to Georgia.)

In a move that raised eyebrows, Bowden made his defensive-line coach, George Henshaw, offensive coordinator. Henshaw's background had been exclusively defense. It was a move mildly reminiscent of a controversial one Bill Peterson had made in the mid-'60s, naming Bill Crutchfield offensive coordinator though his background had been a defensive one at his previous stop (Miami).

Like the questioned Peterson move, Bowden's worked out quite well.

"A good coach," said Bowden of Henshaw's switch from defense, "is a good coach."

The offense knitted despite the loss of two keys. Unglaub fractured a foot two days before the first game, and eventually was redshirted. Homes Johnson, one of the more gifted runners FSU had known, quit — because of a troubling calcium deposit on his ankle, he said.

But Florida State had enough as it reached for — and got — the most coveted prize of all: an unbeaten season.

Enough included a superb kicking game, with sophomore punter Rohn Stark and junior placekicker Bill Capece evolving into two of the country's best.

A surprising recruiting plum, Stark had been plucked off film by the venerable Bob Harbison. A strikingly handsome and gifted athlete from faraway Fifty Lakes, Minn., the 6-foot-3 Stark would become not only a Florida State record-buster but a strong NFL performer with the Indianapolis Colts.

John Crowe, a standout former FSU defensive back who had gone into the Air Force, had sent film from the Air Force Academy prep school, calling players other than Stark to FSU's attention.

"I was looking at these other guys on films," recalled Harbison. "But I kept seeing this kicker whomping the ball, and I say, 'What the hell — is that thin air out in Colorado responsible, or what!'

"I tell Crowe to send me more film. We get it. And then we go after Stark."

A case of stage fright

The unlikely Stark would greatly assist Florida State in getting past an unlikely major obstacle in that 11-0 run — Southern Mississippi at the very start.

His eight punts averaged 46 yards in that Campbell Stadium opener.

FSU had billed this home season as "Saturday Night Fever," and fans were getting pretty hot as the last quarter rolled around with their Seminoles trailing 14-3.

Whereupon, they got feverish contributions from two defensive backs, unlikely types themselves.

First, Bonasorte, the former walk-on, blocked a punt to present an opportunity at the foe 15. On fourth down, Jordan found Flowers with an 8-yard scoring pass.

Soon after, Southern Mississippi punted again.

Gary Henry, a defensive back in a punt-return role, had drawn boos for fair-catch calls on six previous punts.

But he fielded this one at his 35 and moved toward the sidelines.

Pausing for a couple of blockers to do their work, Henry moved laterally, then sprung away — untouched — on a 65-yard scoring return with 6:28 left that won it 17-14.

Two superb kickers at practice: Rohn Stark (above) and Bill Capece.

"Thank goodness!" said Bowden. "And thank goodness our defense played like world champions!

"Our offense had the worst case of stage fright I think I've ever seen. I don't think there was a receiver who didn't drop a pass, or a back who didn't run the wrong way."

Some thought Florida State had gone the wrong way when, responding to agitation from Tampa fans, it moved a home game with strong Arizona State to Tampa.

On a memorably rainy night, Ron Simmons went the right way time after time after time. Florida State dominated the Sun Devils' high-powered offensive unit and won by a stunning 31-3.

Arizona State, netting just 123 yards all night, found itself down 24-0 at halftime. Bonasorte, with two early interceptions, had given Simmons quite an assist in blunting that attack.

"Awesome — unbelievable!" Frank Kush, tough coach of Arizona State, said of Simmons.

"We tried everything. Double-teaming, running away from him, axing, holding — you name it!

"That No. 50 ate our lunch. He may be the best noseguard I've ever seen."

Wins over Miami, Virginia Tech . . .

Florida State ate Miami's lunch — and for the first time ever in Tallahassee: 40-23. "I knew we were coming into a hornets' nest," said Coach Howard Schnellenberger. "Florida State is a good team that could become a great team."

Looking something less than great in Blacksburg, the Seminoles struggled and rode defense to a 17-10 decision over Virginia Tech.

"She wasn't pretty, but she was a win," said Bowden. "A lot of it on offense has to do with the play calling, and I'm responsible for a lot of that junk we called."

At Louisville, the home team managed a mere 93 yards, with FSU moving to 5-0 after 27-0 success.

Mississippi State saw more of the same — the wishbone-running Bulldogs did not complete a pass until the last quarter — as FSU prevailed 17-6. On one of the more memorable defensive plays of Campbell Stadium history, FSU defensive back Keith Jones averted a

150

touchdown with a shattering fumble-inducing tackle of James Otis Doss as the big back bore down on the FSU goal line. The ball rolled into the end zone, and FSU's Edenbur Richardson covered it for a touchback.

Into Baton Rouge the Seminoles rolled for the beginning of former athletic director Clay Stapleton's commitment to five straight games with LSU there.

In a mild surprise, Bowden started Jordan for the first time at quarterback in 1979. He had, however, played about equally with Woodham.

"LSU's coverage was predictable," said Bowden. "It was perfect for Jimmy's rifle arm — his fast ball. He could shred 'em."

Jordan responded with one of his great games, throwing mostly deep as he completed 14 of 31 for 312 yards, including three for touchdowns.

Down 13-7 shortly before halftime, FSU seemed in deep trouble as LSU moved to midfield. But tackle Mark Macek forced a fumble, and one play later Jordan hit freshman Hardis Johnson with a 53-yard bomb to put FSU up 14-13. On a 35-yarder to Flowers, FSU stretched it to 21-13, and a Cappelen field goal pushed things to 24-13 before LSU countered with a late TD that made it a final 24-19.

Wally saves the day

But Simmons was hurting and so were the Seminoles as they moved into Cincinnati. With the star noseguard sidelined with an injury, FSU took a 7-0 lead and seemed to relax after Cincinnati failed to gain a first down in the opening quarter.

Suddenly, Bowden looked at the scoreboard and found his unbeaten team behind 21-7. Tony Kapetanis, a Florida kid out of Coral Springs, produced sensational quarterbacking results — passing for one touchdown, running the ball in for two others.

At the start of the second half, the ailing Simmons went into the game for the first time — and school was out. "Our defense," said Bowden, "was different with him in there."

Calmly, Woodham guided the Seminoles to 19 last-quarter points that won it.

Repeatedly, he called the number of Mark Lyles, who earlier had twice fumbled, and the big fullback ran for 142 yards on 29 carries, caught seven passes for 92 more. On a drive that saw two fourth-down plays succeed, FSU got a touchdown on a determined 10-yard Lyles run with just 10:57 to play.

Soon a 5-yard pass to Flowers narrowed it to 21-19.

With 1:38 left, FSU won it on Mike Whiting's 8-yard run — paved by Lyles' 31-yard gain with a swing pass right on the heels of Gary Henry's big 40-yard punt return.

"I had a good alibi ready," said Bowden. "Then those crazy guys go out and win the game."

Many years later, Bowden remarked: "This was a game Wally came in and did the great job — as great as Jordan had the week before."

Ray Staub, the Cincinnati coach, just shook his head. One year before, FSU had whipped his Bearcats on a 4th-and-29 play with 1:29 left. This time it had moved like lightning to the winning TD with 1:38 to go.

"They set up a wall on Henry's punt return," he said, "and I would have to say that did it."

Florida State tried to set up a wall to retain Bowden as coach. With rumors that Louisiana State wanted him as a successor to Charley McClendon, FSU offered a new contract that would guarantee Bowden about $125,090 a year in total income. With homecoming ahead, everybody seemed happy indeed as he signed.

Still unbeaten, even after Florida

George Rogers, headed for the Heisman Trophy, led one of South Carolina's better teams into town. On a swift and overpowering run of 80 yards, Rogers got a second-quarter touchdown.

That was it.

Playing perhaps its best of the season, Florida State won 27-7 as Dave Cappelen kicked four field goals. Lyles whammed in from the 1 for one touchdown, and Sam Childers got another on a short Jordan pass.

And, suddenly, Orange Bowl talk was everywhere.

One hour before the Nov. 17 home game with Memphis State, formal announcement came of an Orange Bowl bid for Bowden's 9-0 team.

Whereupon, Memphis State became a reluctant victim in a 66-17 celebration.

"I thought we might get beat," said Bowden later. "I mean it. I think we had our minds on other things in the first quarter.

"But, as hot as we were, we could have gotten more points."

For a time, it seemed the Seminoles had their minds on other things as they confronted Charley Pell's first Florida team in Gainesville — the Gators 0-9-1, FSU 10-0.

In an incredibly long game — 3 hours, 12

minutes — televised nationally on a Thanksgiving Friday, the Seminoles struggled against aroused Florida.

Not until Mark Lyles scored from the 3 with 1:20 left did Florida State nail down its 27-16 victory.

An errant officiating call helped. With less than 5 minutes remaining, FSU ahead 17-10, the Seminoles' Walter Carter intercepted a desperate Larry Ochab pass at the Florida 10. Four plays later, a Bill Capece field goal padded FSU's lead to 20-10.

TV replay clearly showed the ball hitting the ground before Carter was credited with an interception. "Six officials — and none of 'em saw it!" snorted Pell after the game.

Florida scrambled to a touchdown, with 2:26 left, that made it 20-16. On the following onsides kick, a Florida player caught the ball in the air. But FSU's Rick Stockstill — then playing on specialty teams — had alertly signaled for a fair catch, and had not been given an opportunity to catch it, as rules say he must. Awarded the ball, FSU moved swiftly from that point to its clinching touchdown.

"Keith Kennedy was behind me, and when I signaled for a fair catch he hollered, 'I got it, I got it,'" recalled Stockstill. "And then he thought I was going to take it. I was backpedaling to get to the ball when I was interfered with.

"Then the ball hit the ground and everybody was trying to come up with it."

Ochab, a walk-on quarterback, completed 22 of 54 passes for 270 yards, though intercepted five times.

FSU had gone up 10-0 early, but Florida tied it 10-10 with the help of two interceptions off Jordan. Early in the final quarter, Woodham had guided an 80-yard march capped by Lyles' 20-yard scoring burst.

Among the many keys was cornerback Bobby Butler's spectacular coverage of Florida's tall-and-talented Cris Collinsworth, who caught five but without significant damage.

Bridgers says bye

With 11-and-0 now a reality, Florida State would go to Miami for its Orange Bowl date with Oklahoma ranked No. 4 nationally in the polls of both AP and UPI.

At this high point, John Bridgers tendered his resignation as athletic director.

In his seven years, the Seminoles had gone from 0-11 to 11-0.

He had arrived, literally, at the worst of times — in the late spring of 1973 as the off-season scandal broke, swiftly followed by a winless season.

A wise and gentle man, an Alabama native and Auburn graduate, low-key in approach, Bridgers had been considerably responsible for rebuilding an athletic program encompassing much more than football.

While some among us had lobbied for other coaches following the 1975 season, Bridgers had quietly and swiftly moved to hire Bowden — an eminently correct decision.

Persistent and stubborn, Bridgers had played a significant role in fund-raising and in successful planning for a building program that would soon be a fact.

Perhaps the most popular athletic director of all time with both men and women coaches at Florida State, Bridgers was not so popular with supporters. Some became impatient with his careful style.

He accepted the athletic directorship at New Mexico, a school that had at least as many athletic difficulties as Florida State upon his arrival. One attraction was the presence in Albuquerque of his twin brother, Frank.

After accepting the New Mexico job, Bridgers declined an invitation to go to the Orange Bowl with the Seminoles anyhow.

Phil Fordyce, a Florida State vice president, served well as interim athletic director. About a year after Bridgers left, FSU hired Cecil "Hootie" Ingram, another well-backgrounded son of Alabama, as athletic director. Soon Ingram would, among other things, steer football toward improved, more reasonable schedules.

Orange Bowl: The victory string ends

Talk about steering!

Few ever steered a football team better than Julius Caesar Watts, the adroit quarterback of Oklahoma's wishbone attack.

On a cool Jan. 1 evening in the Orange Bowl, he ran 61 yards for one touchdown, brilliantly faked and pitched out to Billy Sims for a second touchdown on a 34-yard run, then faked outside before handing off to Stanley Wilson inside for a 5-yard touchdown run.

The favored Sooners won 24-7 in a game that Florida State seemed to have a chance to win.

FSU went in front 7-0 as Jordan quarterbacked an 80-yard movement, Whiting scoring from the 1. Suddenly, the Seminoles had opportunity to double the score as Butler blocked a punt at the Sooner 17. FSU got to the 2 before a procedure penalty set it back. A

Clowning around the week before the Orange Bowl following the '79 season are Simmons, Jordan and Woodham.

bobbled snap on a field-goal try saw the Seminoles emerge with nothing.

And soon Watts, Sims & Friends were off and running.

"Florida State always had somebody out there on Billy for the pitch," said Watts later. "That left me plenty of room to cut upfield for yardage.

"Early in that second quarter we had a third down and 15 at our 39 — an obvious passing down. But from the sidelines they called in an option play. I couldn't believe it, but appreciated the confidence in me."

Watts moved out to the corner, and with FSU defenders focusing on Sims, suddenly took off. The play brought a 64-yard touchdown run.

But cornerback Bobby Butler, said Watts, gave him fits throughout.

"He really played me tough," said Watts. "He'd fake like he was going for the pitch man, usually Sims, and then make an incredible move back to tackle me. That was going on all night, and I kept saying, 'Boy, I'm gonna stop him from sucking eggs.'"

In the fourth quarter, a tackle of Watts by a

tiring Butler was not enough to forestall a pitch to Sims, who scored easily.

Possibly, the outcome would have been different had Florida State capitalized on an early opportunity.

"That is the thing I remember most — our getting down there around the 5 and getting nothing," said Bowden years later. "It was a game we might have won had we got that second touchdown.

"But, no doubt about it, we were out-personneled in this one."

On the sidelines, Bowden wore a microphone that permitted NBC-TV to air his words to millions. Oklahoma's Barry Switzer had declined a similar NBC invitation.

"We are still in the selling business at Florida State," said Bowden later. "We are a young school, and we have had to fight more for what we've got. I felt it would be a plus."

But Bowden became concerned about language he might employ at a tense moment. As his defenders closed in for a tackle, the coach remembered screaming into the microphone: "Kill 'em!"

While millions might think he really meant

Rick Stockstill takes a break during practice in '81.

it, those who knew him well, Bowden suggested, knew he did not. "Not kill 'em dead, anyhow," said Bowden.

But, thinking of what he might say and the millions who did not know him well, the coach decided not to wear a TV microphone on the sidelines again.

A year later in an Orange Bowl rematch, Bowden would feel his personnel equal to

Oklahoma. J.C. Watts, however, had the capacity to turn an equal struggle into an unequal one.

Wally Jim Jordham, who often also made unequal struggles out of equal ones, would not be around.

Here's to you, Wally Jim Jordham

"Probably the most unique thing about our 11-0 football team in 1979 was Jimmy and Wally," said Bowden.

"So many times one would come and rescue the other.

"So many times one or the other would get us out of the hole."

When asked, in 1987, his most memorable player, Bowden paused.

"Gosh, I think three," he said.

"Simmons, Jordan and Woodham.

"But, if I could take two as one, that would be it — Jimmy and Wally."

Which seems a clear enough Bowden vote for Wally Jim Jordham.

Throughout their time at Florida State, Woodham and Jordan were pals who occasionally hunted together while engaging in intense competition for the starting role.

"Gosh, I've thought a hundred thousand times of how it might have been had just Wally or just me been the quarterback," said Jordan. "And I still can't give an honest answer on how it really would have been.

"I know I wish I could have stayed in sometimes when I came out, and would have liked that chance to dig myself out of the hole."

But Jordan recalled the hole the team was in during the first half of that 1979 game at Cincinnati, with Woodham coming on to spur the rally that enabled that team to finish unbeaten. "The whole thing just shifted," said Jordan.

The two of them, suggested Jordan, both wanted something bigger than their own ego satisfaction.

"At the time, we — the team — were so hungry to win after all the bad times earlier," said Jordan. "It didn't matter, not so much our starting, just so we won. And I know that sounds crazy, but that was the way it was.

"When I was in there Wally was pulling for me, and when he was in there I was pulling for him."

Looking back as Jordan had, Woodham recalled, interestingly enough, a game with Cincinnati, too — the one in 1978, when Jordan's memorable 4th-and-long pass to Sam Platt had lifted the Seminoles to a late victory.

"And I'll never forget the 1977 game with Florida either," said Woodham. "I started, and we were leading 10-3. Then Jimmy came on, and the fireworks really started.

"What it was between us was good hard competition, with the intensity of that toned down a bit because we both knew we were going to play."

And what it was for Florida State fans, as the two played, was perhaps the very best years of the first 40.

'80: Enter Rick Stockstill

Waiting his turn with apparent patience for three years, including one redshirt season, Rick Stockstill was ready enough for a quarterbacking role that had previously been handled by two.

Over the next two seasons, he would lead the Seminoles to some of their most remarkable victories of all time.

In an opener at LSU, Bowden proceeded cautiously with his new quarterback — favoring a running game, relying on defense, letting Stark punt (seven times for 46.3 average), throwing only 11 passes (six completions). It was a classic by-the-book game, with Florida State making no turnovers and winning 16-0.

LSU's storied "Death Valley" was becoming "Pleasant Valley" for the Seminoles as they won their second straight there.

"Amazing," said Bowden of Stockstill's first-game effort.

In Tallahassee, Louisville tumbled 52-0 and East Carolina 63-7.

But in the latter game, on successive plays, Florida State lost its top two centers, John Madden and Bob Merson, to ankle injuries.

At Miami, in the fourth game, Florida State desperately moved Redus Coggin, a guard who had broken his hand in the spring, to the position. Playing on his nose was Jim Burt. One of college football's toughest noseguards, Burt later would distinguish himself with the New York Giants' Super Bowl champions of the 1986 season.

Result: an uncertain exchange with the quarterback, several faulty snaps that helped to precipitate seven fumbles, two of which Florida State lost.

With the help of a 49-yard penalty for pass interference that placed the ball on FSU's 1 — Jim Kelly's pass was far overthrown — Miami took a 7-0 lead just before halftime. It became 10-3 in the late going.

On the interference call, receiver Larry Brodsky said he had banged into FSU defender Gary Henry. "I was as surprised as everybody else when there was a flag," he said.

Stockstill directed a march that narrowed it to 10-9, passing 11 yards to Sam Childers for the touchdown.

With 39 seconds left, Stockstill passed in a quest for 2 points that would have won the game, and receiver Phil Williams was open in the end zone.

But Burt got in the way, the ball hitting his helmet.

"I just went flying on that play," said Burt. "I shed the center and looked for the guard, who had been coming after me all day, jumped over him, went up the middle, and I was just lucky to get to the ball."

"Phil was open — we had it!" said Bowden. "Then that noseguard got in the way."

Miami's victory terminated FSU's 18-game regular-season winning streak.

But there followed one of Florida State's most remarkable victories of all time — one at Nebraska that Bowden called his most memorable and "the greatest one."

And one of the most remarkable player contributions in Florida State history was a key.

In comes the unknown hero

Still looking for a center, the Seminoles turned in desperation to a non-scholarship player, a sophomore walk-on who never before had played a varsity down. "Until we get that problem solved, we are not going to beat anybody," Bowden said that week.

Coaches had observed that Jerry Coleman snapped the ball very well. He and Stockstill had worked together the previous season on the scout squad. There was a question about his blocking as well as his lack of experience. He seemed, however, the best bet — the one chance — with Madden and Merson still unable to play.

The decision was made. Florida State would start an untested walk-on against one of the nation's best teams, and on its field.

"So, I sent his mother some flowers, and a card of sympathy," kidded Bowden later.

A few months before Bowden had sat with Coleman in his office, and gently tried to talk him out of his request to be redshirted, trying to get across the message that he had little future in football, stressing what a good student he was and that for him football might be a waste of time.

"I thought I had him convinced," recalled Bowden. "Then, just before he got up to go, I asked why did he want to be redshirted. And with tears in his eyes, nearly, he told me he thought he could never play for Florida State unless he was redshirted." Impressed, Bowden immediately told Coleman: "Buddy, we're going to redshirt you!"

The season of 1980 was to have been his redshirt year. Bowden's decision to allow that was perhaps the only reason Coleman was still around.

With the decision made to start him against Nebraska, Coleman kept quiet about an injury he had received in a junior-varsity game the week prior. He had sprained the index finger and thumb on his snapping hand. "None of 'em knew," said Coleman of the coaches. "I didn't say anything to anybody."

On the second series against Nebraska, he bruised his side and received a painful hip-pointer. "My teammates all around me were playing hurt — pulled muscles, pinched nerves, sprained ankles," recalled Coleman. "We sucked it up. We kept going."

Playing every down, Coleman snapped the ball flawlessly. There was not one faulty exchange. Not one turnover.

In one of college football's great human-interest stories, Coleman emerged a consider-

Paul Piurowski (53) and Reggie Herring bring down a Miami player in '80.

156

able Seminole hero among many that day. He would play little the rest of his time, but he had earned a battlefield commission — a scholarship that Bowden awarded him on the strength of that game, and as soon as permissible under NCAA guidelines.

"My high-school coach always said good things happen to good people," said Coleman. "And this football team is good people."

A red-letter day at Nebraska

On a glorious day in Lincoln, with its traditional "sea of red" that constitutes the 78,152 fans filling Memorial Stadium, Florida State came away an 18-14 winner over a team with an eye on the national championship, with a Heisman Trophy nominee in tailback Jarvis Redwine.

A Sports Illustrated writer had come to Lincoln to feature Redwine and that national-title bid. Instead, he wrote of Florida State — focusing on the kicking game.

With the final score on the board, Redwine, tackled at FSU's 29, left the game after a jarring tackle by linebacker Reggie Herring. He limped off after 145 yards in 25 carries.

But Nebraska drove on — to a first down at the Florida State 3 with 21 seconds remaining.

On second down, following a pass that missed, quarterback Jeff Quinn rolled left, and linebacker Paul Piurowski — ignoring his assignment on the play — chased him, got him, forced a fumble that teammate Garry Futch covered.

"We were in man-to-man coverage, and I was supposed to be covering the fullback on the play," said Piurowski. "I hadn't been playing man-to-man too well."

Bowden quickly forgave him.

"That darling Piurowski — that sweet Futch!" enthused Bowden in the dressing room.

There were a number of FSU "darlings."

Perhaps never was a Florida State kicking game more effective. On seven punts, Stark averaged an incredible 48.4 yards. Capece accounted for 12 of FSU's 18 points — four field goals of 32, 27, 40 and 41 range.

It was a game in which Florida State trailed 14-3 at halftime, a game that saw Simmons struggling with a bum ankle, a game in which Nebraska outgained FSU by 202 yards (368 to 166), a game in which Nebraska also led in turnovers (4 to 1). Two Nebraska fumbles, two FSU interceptions each came in the critical last half.

"They hit us harder in the last half," said

Quinn, who also praised Simmons. "A lot of guys are mouthy, but he had a lot of class — their whole team did."

"Class" would be a word Florida State would employ again and again in reference to Nebraska itself in a series of four games — all in Lincoln — that concluded in 1986.

The Seminoles found astonishing the tribute of Nebraska fans following that 1980 triumph. Those fans applauded them as they moved victoriously toward their dressing room, and some waited around for words of personal praise after they had dressed.

Bowden later wrote a letter to a Lincoln newspaper in salute to the Cornhuskers' fans.

A week later, a win over Pitt

As impressive as the Nebraska victory was, purists might argue that the following week's 36-22 Tallahassee victory over Pittsburgh was more impressive.

Surely, those back-to-back triumphs over Nebraska and Pitt constituted the most laudable Florida State accomplishment in successive games of all time.

"That Pitt team, I believe, was the most talented I've ever lined up against anywhere and any time in my 34 years of coaching,"

George Henshaw, the FSU offensive coordinator who came up with the "mirror offense" against Pitt.

Bowden said in 1987. "Why, 17 of their players went into the pros the following year!"

And some, like quarterback Dan Marino, would go into the pros a couple of years later.

Florida State was freshly minus Piurowski, who required an emergency appendectomy, and Homes Johnson, the gifted runner who had earlier quit but returned for another try. He quit for the second and last time — saying he wasn't playing enough — the week of the Pitt game.

But John Madden — later to marry Bowden's daughter Ginger — was well enough to again start at center.

Studying Pitt's great defense, offensive coordinator George Henshaw observed overloading tactics: that is, the Panthers stacked their alignment to an unusual degree to the side they felt the play was most likely to go.

Henshaw suggested a "mirror offense" — plays designed to go to either side. Stockstill, looking over the defense, would then note if Pitt was cheating to the strong side. If so, he would "check off," with vocal signals that would send the play to the other side.

After the game, Bowden estimated Stockstill checked off more than 50 percent of the time. Thereby, FSU was able to run against Pitt better than it ever figured to do. Platt alone ran for 123 yards in 26 carries.

"Henshaw and his offensive staff just felt like Pitt had too much on defense, and that it was just impossible to block that overloaded side," said Bowden. "He felt the 'mirror offense' was our one chance."

Before the game, Bowden had suggested that fans would not need to know Pitt's great end Hugh Green wore number 99. "He's the one with his jersey white in back, and dirty in front," said Bowden.

On the game's first scrimmage play, Green identified himself — sacking Stockstill on the FSU 2.

Pitt took an early 7-0 lead, but Florida State got two touchdowns and three field goals to lead 23-7 at halftime.

Florida State flashed a few identifying characteristics, too.

Capece and Stark outdid themselves. In an overall performance that exceeded the fantastic Nebraska effort, Capece kicked five field goals — 24, 43, 50, 30, 44 yards — and Stark averaged 48.1 on seven punts. Bud Wilkinson, the great Oklahoma coach turned ABC commentator, called it possibly the most brilliant example of the kicking game on any field.

Florida State got three touchdown passes from Stockstill and another performance strikingly free from binding error. FSU had no turnovers, Pitt had seven.

"We had just come off that Nebraska game, you know, and I thought — we thought — we could do anything in the world," said Stockstill.

"Actually, I think we used that mirror offense about 80 percent of the time. Whichever way their noseguard and tackle shaded, we went the other way."

For that great Pitt team, it was the season's only loss, and an 11-1 finish earned Jackie Sherrill's Panthers final No. 2 rank, behind Georgia.

Beating the Gators again

Rolling now, the Seminoles whipped Boston College 41-7 as Capece booted four more field goals, Memphis State 24-3 as Platt ran for 188 yards in 29 efforts, Tulsa 45-2 and Virginia Tech 31-7.

That last game was Nov. 8. Now 9-1, and with a second consecutive Orange Bowl bid in hand, Florida State did not play again for a month — the Florida finale shifted to Dec. 6 to accommodate network television.

Florida surprised with a running game, featuring two tight ends. After an early 3-0 lead on a field goal, the Seminoles found themselves trailing 13-3 at intermission.

All season long, no opponent had scored a touchdown on Jack Stanton's defense in the last half — save Pitt, which got two.

The pattern held.

Hard running by tailback Ricky Williams at the start of the last half forced Florida defenders to respect FSU's ground game. Williams had replaced Platt, sidelined early with a separated shoulder.

Florida State moved 82 yards, behind Williams and timely passing, to a touchdown that came on Stockstill's 19-yarder to Hardis Johnson.

The Seminoles won it, 17-13, in the fourth quarter with Stockstill's second scoring pass to Johnson, a 20-yarder.

It was the fourth straight Bowden victory over Florida — and Simmons' last regular-season game. The Seminoles had made good on Simmons' boast that they would never lose to Florida in his time.

"We should come and cheer at FSU graduation ceremonies," commented Charley Pell, well aware the Seminoles would lose several fine players in addition to Simmons.

The words were noteworthy. Florida would become stronger, Florida State weaker. And

Two Orange Bowl coaches: Barry Switzer and Bobby Bowden.

through 1986, the Gators would win six straight over their rival.

A crack at No. 1

Ranked No. 2 nationally in both polls, behind Georgia, Florida State headed for an Orange Bowl date against No. 4 Oklahoma with a chance for the national championship.

But Julius Caesar Watts was still quarterbacking the Sooners.

Forty-nine seconds before halftime, Florida State took a 7-0 lead on a Ricky Williams scoring run from 10 yards out. But Oklahoma had time to get in position for a 53-yard Michael Keeling field goal that made it 7-3.

"That dadgummed field goal may come back to haunt us," an upset Bowden said on the way to the dressing room. Oklahoma had been out of field-goal range, but on the next-to-last play had gained 15 yards on a rolling fumble that it recovered. Still, the Sooners seemed too far away. "Their kicker didn't have that kind of range," said Bowden. "But he comes in there and kicks the ball a mile."

On the last half's opening series, Oklahoma drove 88 yards to a 10-7 lead. FSU tied it 10-10 not long after on a 19-yard Capece field goal, after the Seminoles had gained a first down at the 1.

FSU went up 17-10 in the fourth quarter, when a helmet-high snap sailed over punter Keeling's head, rolling into the end zone. With Herring muscling Keeling aside, Bobby Butler jumped on the ball for a Florida State touchdown.

But Watts took Oklahoma on an 88-yard drive to a touchdown and 2 points that won it 18-17. On third-and-9 at his 23, Watts connected with Steve Rhodes for 42 yards.

"It was a gutsy play for Steve," said Watts. "He had a pulled hamstring, and had not been in the game."

AT FSU's 21, Watts, pressured by noseguard James Gilbert, threw hastily and Garry Futch seemed to have an interception. He dropped the ball.

"We ran a screen, and as I was going down I saw our halfback and figured I'd dump it off to him," said Watts. "But this big tackle (Futch) read what I was doing, and I threw the ball right to him.

"Thank goodness tackles can't catch. He had it right in his hands — kept fumbling it around while I was in agony, and finally let it fall to the ground. I was never so relieved in my life."

On the following play, Watts ran to the 11. Jarvis Coursey got his hands on Watts' next pass, but couldn't hang on. One more play saw Watts throw to Rhodes for the touchdown. Whereupon, tight end Forrest Valera caught a Watts pass for the winning 2-pointer.

"We had it — we lost it!" said Bowden.

Florida State had confounded Oklahoma with a surprise defensive maneuver — shifting defensive end Coursey to the middle, where he moved with the flow of the Sooners' wishbone.

"Florida State had great defense that night," said Barry Switzer months later. "They came up with something there we were not prepared for, and it really worked for them. It wouldn't be very good if you had prepared for it, but we hadn't.

"We had never seen anybody do that. By going with that end in the middle, Florida State had an extra defender to either side."

Surely, that defense would have worked even better had Simmons been in there. Hurt in the first half, the All-American noseguard ended his wondrous Florida State time on the bench — unable to play the final 30 minutes.

"He had that big-play capability — because of his strength, and sheer ability that so many did not have," said Bowden years later.

"He became, I think, a man other teams tried to solve before they did anything else in preparing for us.

"Now, with Simmons we had a lot of good

Offensive tackle Ken Lanier (left) and defensive back Keith Jones were among the top players of 1980.

players. But he had the great speed and quickness, the great strength. And he was hungry all the time."

'One of the best teams ever'

So many good players, indeed. Seniors departing along with Simmons included:

— Capece, who set a single-season NCAA record for points by a kicker (104).

— The three outstanding defensive backs — Bobby Butler (soon to be an Atlanta Falcons starter), Monk Bonasorte (interceptor of more passes than any other Seminole ever), and the hard-hitting Keith Jones.

— Two whom many would rate the best set of linebackers in FSU annals, Reggie Herring and Paul Piurowski.

— Offensive tackle Ken Lanier, soon to be a Denver Broncos starter.

Little wonder that Charley Pell proposed a graduation celebration among all Gators.

So close they came in 1980 ... a season when a pair of 1-point losses separated Florida State from a 12-0 finish and a probable national championship.

Among those caught up in the excitement of that season was Brent Musburger, the CBS sportscaster who early in the year had suggested on the "NFL Today" show the Semi-

noles were college football's No. 1 team, continuing that suggestion in the weeks that followed. Speaking at FSU's team banquet after the season, Musburger said: "I gotta thank these guys. It was the greatest fun I had all year — to live vicariously with this team."

Bowden reckoned it could have been lots more fun.

"I thought we were better than Oklahoma that time around," he said years later. "It was just one of the most disappointing games I've known.

"But I think you have to say this was definitely one of the best teams ever for Florida State.

"They blocked punts, intercepted passes — did what they had to do to win. Stockstill was the good leader, playing better than I thought he could."

Bowden received a notable personal tribute when, in February, he received the Bobby Dodd Coach of the Year Award. Those named before him were Georgia's Vince Dooley, Michigan's Bo Schembechler, Nebraska's Tom Osborne and Brigham Young's LaVell Edwards. Bowden was described as "an honest man who wins in an honest manner."

According to the NCAA's toughest-schedule calculations, that 1980 FSU schedule was No.

1. But the one ahead, by universal calculation, was tougher.

And according to accountants, the Orange Bowl check for $1,517,062 was the largest FSU football payday ever.

There would be no bowl payday of any kind the following season.

'81: A trip down Murderer's Row

With only three Orange Bowl starters returning on defense, only three returning on offense, Florida State awaited the long-talked-about "Murderer's Row" lined up by prior Athletic Director Clay Stapleton.

On successive dates, FSU would play *at* Nebraska, *at* Ohio State, *at* Notre Dame, *at* Pittsburgh, *at* Louisiana State.

Bud Wilkinson proclaimed that the most difficult run in the history of college football. One national magazine compared it to the Bataan Death March.

At the time, Bowden kept much of his thinking about the schedule to himself.

Years later, he spoke of how, deep inside, he had viewed that obstacle course.

"When I first knew about it, I had considered, really, whether I should stay or leave," he said. "To myself I said, 'Bobby Bowden, you better be gone by then!'"

But Bowden publicly spoke of that schedule with some degree of hope.

"Schools like Oklahoma don't rebuild — they *reload!*" he said. "This year we'll find out if *we* can reload."

For an unbelievable while, it seemed Florida State could. Then it ran out of ammunition.

A shaky start

An indication of the youth of this team came in an opener. Freshmen accounted for every point as FSU struggled past Louisville 17-0 on a Mike Rendina field goal, Jessie Hester's 11-yard touchdown catch and Billy Allen's 50-yard run.

Somewhat similarly, the Seminoles got past Memphis State 10-5.

But Nebraska in Lincoln turned loose Roger Craig for 234 running yards — most ever against FSU by an individual — and won 34-14. Still, FSU trailed only 10-7 at halftime. Swiftly, in the third quarter Nebraska spun away on a long Irving Fryar punt return and a fumble at FSU's 13 that Tony Felici plucked out of the air for an easy touchdown.

Unbeaten, seventh-ranked Ohio State awaited in Columbus. An open date helped the battered Seminoles.

A 52-yard Rendina field goal and linebacker Ron Hester's 35-yard scoring scamper with the punt he blocked gave FSU a surprising 10-7 lead. A third unlikely FSU score came on a fake field-goal attempt from the 9, holder Kelly Lowrey rearing up, rolling out, then tucking the football for a run into the end zone.

A 14-yard scoring pass to Tony Johnson had FSU ahead 23-21 at halftime. Ohio State had moved to two swift touchdowns on Art Schlichter passes.

It became 30-21 quickly in the third quarter as Stockstill topped an 88-yard drive with a 7-yard strike to Sam Childers. Promptly, Schlichter took the Buckeyes to a first down at FSU's 2, where defenders checked three plays and on the fourth one a wide-open receiver dropped a pass in the end zone.

From inside the 1-yard line, Stockstill quarterbacked a clinching 99-yard drive, Ricky Williams scoring from the 3.

In a 36-27 victory, Stockstill passed for 299 yards. Schlichter, however, had passed for 458 yards, while Nebraska the week before had run for 472 — each a record total on a Florida State team.

"We got 'em guessing," joked Bowden when someone cited the successive sums by differing means.

Pilgrimage to Notre Dame

Bowden had particularly looked forward to the next game — Notre Dame in South Bend. He had not relished the prohibitive total schedule, but had wanted a chance to "shake down the thunder" on the Fighting Irish. It was the stuff of personal dreams.

Stopped early by Notre Dame, unable to get much going, Florida State gambled. Once Stark, back to punt on fourth down, ran successfully for the needed yardage. Finally, FSU got close enough for a Rendina field goal that tied it 3-3 before halftime.

Soon behind 6-3, Florida State drove from its 8 following a penalty. FSU moved on the running of Williams to a touchdown that came on Stockstill's short pass to Michael Whiting. Another Rendina field goal provided a 13-6 lead.

On the first play of the final quarter, a Greg Bell touchdown brought a 13-13 tie. A James Harris interception provided FSU an opportunity at the Notre Dame 30, and Stockstill cashed it in on a 5-yard pass to Whiting.

In a game that FSU dominated statistically, with Williams running for 135 yards in 16 carries, the Seminoles prevailed 19-13. They

This is a running style that FSU opponents became familiar with in 1981 — when Greg Allen arrived.

became just the second team ever to beat Notre Dame in South Bend on its first trip there.

"To me personally, it was the biggest win I'll ever have," said Bowden in the glow of the moment.

The glow faded quickly at Pittsburgh. Dan Marino picked FSU's defense to pieces and the Panthers romped 42-14.

"You can't just keep playing these big games back to back to back," said Bowden.

202 yards for Greg Allen

One big one remained in the killer series of five — a homecoming game at LSU.

And once again Bowden surprised Coach Jerry Stovall with a running game, this time spurred by the promising Milton freshman Greg Allen.

Seldom have LSU's whooping followers been silenced so swiftly. On the Seminoles' first play, Allen whammed through a gaping off-tackle hole and sped 66 yards to the Tiger 9. A Rendina field goal brought a 3-0 lead, which soon became 17-0. Following more Allen running, a fake culminated in a Stockstill pass to Dennis McKinnon for 22 yards and a touchdown. Warren Hanna's blocked punt brought a quick Allen TD, and LSU was down 17 points in the first quarter.

Running 31 times, Allen gained 202 yards — highest single-game total ever for a Seminole to that point.

Ahead 24-7 at the half, FSU won in Baton Rouge for the third straight year, this time 38-14.

The killer run that Bowden had referred to as "Oktoberfest" — four of the five straight big road games came in October — was over. Florida State had won three of the five, and stood 5-2. "I was afraid we would be destroyed," acknowledged Bowden, "but it didn't happen."

That feared destruction, for a now-depleted team, was not far away.

Another record-setting day for Allen

Homecoming against West Carolina saw Allen score early on a 95-yard kickoff return, but FSU led only 13-7 at halftime.

Allen, however, stacked up 322 yards running from scrimmage — an NCAA-record sum for a freshman. With the addition of receiving and return totals, he had 417 all-purpose yards — another NCAA record — as FSU pulled away and won 56-31.

Allen became only the second freshman in NCAA history to accomplish back-to-back

games in excess of 200 yards. The other: Georgia's celebrated Herschel Walker.

Twice again during his FSU time Allen would have 200-yard running games — 201 against LSU in 1983, 223 against Arizona State in 1984. In the Seminoles' first 40 seasons, only three others would top 200 — Victor Floyd with 212 against South Carolina in 1985, Tony Smith with 201 in the 1985 Gator Bowl and Sammie Smith with 205 in the 1986 All-American Bowl.

Allen would become Florida State's top runner of the first 40 seasons, a total of 3,769 yards on 624 carries for an incredible 6.0 average. He would also become the school's leading scorer of those years — 278 points on 46 touchdowns and a run for two extra points.

"If we get it down inside their 5, Greg's going to get it in," said receiver Jessie Hester.

Running out of gas

After Allen's big night in 1981 against Western Carolina, FSU's record was an astonishing 6-2.

Then came a more astonishing three straight losses — the first two on network television.

Ahead 13-10 at halftime over a Miami team recently stung by announcement of its NCAA probation, Florida State fell 27-19 on Danny Miller's stunning 57-yard field goal and Jim Kelly's passing.

About this time Stockstill spoke of his enjoyment of the season, but added: "It's been a long, hard year for us. Everybody is physically and mentally tired."

Stockstill himself was playing on a bum knee. It had been something of a problem since he first hurt it in the Orange Bowl.

With the gifted, lightning-like Reggie Collier quarterbacking, 10th-ranked Southern Mississippi came to Tallahassee unbeaten, its 7-0-1 record blemished only by a tie with Alabama.

Scoring on its first seven possessions, the Golden Eagles won 58-14 after leading 30-0 at halftime in what surely must have been Florida State's most surprising losing outcome of all time. Collier ran for 150 yards and passed for two touchdowns, completing seven of the eight passes he threw.

Closing action at Florida saw the Gators, ahead 13-3 at intermission, win 35-3 for the first triumph over the Seminoles in five games.

"We just flat ran out of gas there in the last three games," said Bowden. "There were just too many physical and emotional highs.

Things looked good against Pitt in '82 — until the rain came.

"I myself have never been so tired."

Years later, Bowden spoke of how the season had been.

"It was a year," he said, "that saw us load everything for those five big games — our reverses, our personnel planning, our total strategy. Everything.

"Miami had a great team there at the end. And though we led at the half, we were beat-up so bad we could not hold.

"And then we got killed in our last two games.

"If we had somehow been able to finish well, the whole thing might have gotten Florida State more recognition than anything ever."

Some more recognition, at least, was not far away.

'82: Another rough schedule

If Florida State fans reckoned the 1981 schedule the nation's toughest, the NCAA calculated the one ahead would be the toughest of them all.

That 1982 season started much as 1981 had ended. FSU struggled.

In an opener, Cincinnati once again played far better than most thought it could, taking an early 14-0 lead. FSU rallied for a 28-21 halftime lead. Ahead 38-31 in the late going,

Florida State won by that score after Manny Carbello, a reserve fullback, made a possibly game-saving tackle of Antonio Gibson, a swift defensive back who seemed headed for a touchdown with an interception.

For No. 1 Pittsburgh, in Tallahassee the following week, Florida State had a secret — perhaps almost as dramatic as the "mirror offense" that had been instrumental in the 1980 upset of a similarly talented Pitt team.

Something dramatic seemed in order for FSU to have a chance against Dan Marino and his passing. Ample opportunity was provided by an open date following Cincinnati.

FSU's secret was an option attack quarterbacked by Kelly Lowrey, who would come on as a replacement for starter Blair Williams. A key part of the game plan was the anticipated heat and humidity of that Sept. 18 date.

"We had put that option in during the spring, but we had not used it up to this point," said Bowden. "We saved it for Pitt because of the type defense they had — our thinking that particular defense would not hold up against the option."

Things started well on a hot evening, FSU

Opposite page: Jessie Hester leaps high against East Carolina in '82.

taking a 10-0 lead behind Williams' quarterbacking. Swiftly Marino & Co. countered, and FSU found itself in arrears 17-10.

At this point, FSU switched to Lowrey. Running the option, mixing in timely passes, he took the Seminoles 75 yards to a touchdown that tied it 17-17 at halftime. Pitt seemed baffled by the option, and maybe the heat was wearing its big linemen down a bit.

"It was obvious they were having a hard time with that option," said Bowden.

Things changed swiftly. Rain swept Campbell Stadium on the skirts of an unseasonable drop in temperature. Water was 6 inches deep on the sidelines. Temperatures dropped as thunder and lightning came with the downpour that continued in the last half.

In those conditions, Pitt won 37-17, behind Marino's impressive quarterbacking.

"He was a great quarterback — a lot like Joe Namath," recalled Bowden later. "We had tried to recruit him. Because we threw, he and his parents had expressed interest in us. But it didn't work out."

Still, Bowden thought on this night Florida State could have won had the weather stayed as hot as it was in the first half.

"Our not being able to effectively run the option under those conditions did not hurt as much as the actual rain itself," he said.

"What the rain did was drop the temperature way down, making it possible for all those big guys Pitt had to go better under cooler conditions. Big people play better in the mud than little people — it's a great advantage for them.

"But heat and humidity wears down big people and that was what we had hoped for. That was the way it started.

"Remember when Pitt came to Tallahassee for an opening game when Darrell Mudra was coaching in 1974? Well, Pitt liked to have died in that heat. That may have been the worst game Tony Dorsett ever had in college."

A winning streak begins

With the option now in, Florida State used it effectively as long as Lowrey was around and healthy.

"This was a year we were not supposed to have anything," Bowden later recalled. "But it was not a bad one for us."

Indeed.

Florida State won its next seven, and stood 8-1 with two games remaining. Lowrey in a starting role was a notable key.

The streak started at Southern Mississippi, with Florida State determined — whatever

else — to stop the dangerous Collier. Setting defenses to stop the quarterback's running, Florida State "gave" Southern the middle. And Southern took advantage, with tailback Sam Dejarnette slashing — mainly up the middle — for 304 yards on 43 carries. Over the first 40 years, Dejarnette's total carries and total yardage were easily more than those of any other opposing runner.

In the middle of the last quarter, the score deadlocked 17-17, Florida State came to fourth down at the Southern 2-yard line, where Greg Allen had twice run for naught.

Placekicker Phil Hall lined up for an apparent field-goal attempt. But Lowrey, in to hold after the snap, suddenly tucked the ball under his arm, and whipped up the middle for a surprising touchdown that won it 24-17.

Bowden had reasoned that the way Dejarnette was running, a field goal would not be sufficient; therefore, the fake.

Florida State had beaten essentially the same team that embarrassed it so much in 1981 — and on Southern's own field.

Tempting Fate at Ohio State

But twice in a row over Ohio State on *its* home field is a rare accomplishment indeed — and that's what Florida State did, following the 36-27 success of 1981 with a 34-17 stinger in 1982 on an unusually hot Columbus afternoon.

"Our hard work paid off," Bowden said. "We were ready for that heat."

Hot — and rare — accomplishment, too, was Lowrey's feat — after *catching* a pass for the first touchdown — of becoming the first quarterback ever to run, pass and catch for touchdowns against the Buckeyes. He had run for one the prior year, on a field-goal fake. The second time around, he completed the unusual triple.

Trailing 7-0, FSU was at Ohio State's 11 when Lowrey dealt the ball to Cedric Jones, who then passed to the quarterback — uncovered as a receiver in Ohio State's man-to-man defense — for a tying touchdown.

Lowrey passed to tight end Zeke Mowatt for the next touchdown as Florida State moved on to a 21-10 lead that Ohio State cut to 21-17 just before intermission.

As linebacker Tommy Young twice intercepted Ohio State passes in the third quarter, FSU maneuvered to a 28-17 lead on Blair Williams' 9-yard touchdown pass to Jessie Hester. Williams had come in for an injured Lowrey. Ricky Williams ran for a later touchdown.

Talking four years later of Florida State's

two straight victories over his team, Earle Bruce said it was mainly a matter of the Seminoles playing so well.

"The first year, they took a lot of chances," he said. "The second year, they just came in and beat the hell out of us."

Bruce was discussing with writers the perception of games.

"What is the big game?" he asked. "Well, the big game is the one you lose."

Two years running, Florida State was at least one of the Buckeyes' big games.

Bowden liked the way Williams had moved the team as Lowrey's replacement in that last Ohio State game.

"I remember several times Blair came in there in that 1982 season and helped us out," said Bowden later, looking back. "We nearly had a dual-quarterback system."

Battle with Miami

Returning to Tallahassee, the Seminoles romped over Southern Illinois 59-8 on a homecoming evening, and East Carolina 56-17.

With an open date prior to Miami, Bowden made an unusual move. At the request of Howard Schnellenberger, he flew to Miami to help promote the game. In 1983, the popular Miami coach returned the favor by catching a plane to Tallahassee to help hype the game.

FSU took a 10-0 lead and a Young-led goal-line stand kept it that way at halftime. Miami had a first down at the 4, but it came to fourth down at the 1.

Anticipating that Miami, in those circumstances, would send big fullback Mark Rush diving over the middle, as it had so often before, FSU had worked extensively on defense against the play.

"Rush came on that dive for what looked like a sure touchdown," said Bowden. "Except here came Tommy Young on a counter-dive. And they *kissed* in midair. One of 'em had to fall backwards. Rush fell backwards."

Miami cut it to 10-7 in the third quarter.

On a memorable fourth-down play — the first of the final period — at the Miami 24, Lowrey passed over the middle to huge sophomore tight end Orson Mobley, who bowled over tackles and powered into the end zone for the touchdown.

"This was a play we called 'Gator Pass,' because we had first used it against Florida," said Bowden. "It was one of those passes you might go two years without using. It is a play where the tight end hides — drops back — as you send the fullback out for what looks like a

screen pass. When the defense reads that screen, and moves over to get that fullback, you send the tight end down the middle.

"Orson had a head of steam, and he ran over about three guys.

"Never had the play worked better. It broke the game open."

It was a play that never would have been called except for a Miami timeout just before the snap. Florida State had called for a true screen pass.

But during the timeout, word came down from an assistant in the pressbox that Miami's defense was set for the screen. Huddling anew, Florida State called for "Gator Pass," and Mobley made it work spectacularly as the Hurricanes again lined up in anticipation of a screen.

"Divine intervention," smiled Bowden.

Soon, Mobley would become academically ineligible, but he would find his way to Salem College in West Virginia and thence to the Denver Broncos. His 1986 rookie season would help propel the team to the Super Bowl against the New York Giants, whose lineup would include Zeke Mowatt, the starting FSU tight end of 1982.

The attraction at Salem was Bowden's son Terry, head coach there then. Two other Bowden sons also became coaches, and 1987 found son Tommy an assistant at Alabama, while son Jeffrey and son-in-law Jack Hines were at Samford as assistants to Terry, who by then was head coach at his dad's old Birmingham alma mater. A fourth Bowden son, Steve, was at the same time with Samford as a professor of religion.

In the Miami game that Mobley helped break open, Greg Allen's second touchdown of the afternoon wrapped it up for Florida State, 24-7.

Building up an 8-1 record

The sophomore scored four more on runs the following week against South Carolina in a dazzling display of ability that led to his topping the nation in touchdowns (21) and scoring (126 points) for 1982.

"Greg had some great games his four years with us," said Bowden after the tailback's departure. "He was injured some, but he was just a great back, and particularly near the goal.

"He was very aggressive, a slasher — not one of those deliberate pickers. He was an explosive type who could run by you, over you or through you."

In a 56-26 game, Florida State led 28-12 at

halftime, broke it open with three third-quarter touchdowns that made it 49-12.

The record became 8-1 with a 49-14 crunching of Louisville as Allen scored thrice more.

And now Louisiana State, in the Seminoles' fourth straight game at Baton Rouge, stood between Florida State and its third Orange Bowl bid in four seasons.

Mindful of those three straight FSU losses, LSU — notably Coach Jerry Stovall — declined, after some debate, to move the game from Tiger Stadium's traditional nighttime kickoff to an afternoon kickoff that would have assured a network-TV date. It was a decision that cost an irate FSU $550,000.

With its devastating 55-21 victory, LSU itself got the Orange Bowl date — a startling development that assuredly cost Florida State more than $1 million more.

It all seemed to turn with the final 40 seconds of the first half, when Stovall's team shattered a 14-14 tie.

Twice FSU had come from behind for that 14-14 tie, but LSU, brilliantly quarterbacked by Alan Risher on this evening, took a 21-14 lead on freshman Dalton Hilliard's short run in the final minute of the half. When FSU's Tony Smith fumbled away the following kickoff, LSU struck quickly on a 34-yard Risher pass to Eric Martin.

Two more third-quarter touchdowns made it 42-14 as river fog blanketed the stadium, and Florida State was out of it. Oranges flew onto the field from the hands of delirious Tiger fans — hitting an official and Bowden himself, among others.

The fact the game had not been moved for TV mattered little, suggested Bowden. "They could have beaten us at high noon or 3 o'clock in the morning," he said. "They played better than any team we've played in a long time."

Receiving considerable credit for the upset was Mack Brown, new LSU offensive coordinator — a one-time Florida State running back who soon would become Oklahoma's offensive coordinator, and later head coach of Tulane.

Under a bowl agreement struck prior to the Nov. 20 game, the loser received a bid to the Gator while the winner went to the Orange.

"We're glad," said Bowden after the game. "It could have been, you know, the Orange Bowl or nothing.

Three '82 Gator Bowl quarterbacks take a stroll: Kelly Lowrey of FSU, Jeff Hostetler of West Virginia and Blair Williams of FSU.

"We've got to put on a show for the Gator Bowl."

Florida State did.

But before that bright side loomed a familiar dark shadow — the Gators.

The Gators chomp down

With the defense blunting three early Florida thrusts, FSU took a 10-0 lead in Campbell Stadium.

"We had 'em," recalled Bowden. "Wayne Peace at that point was 0-for-8 with his passing."

Florida switched quarterbacks — Bob Hewko in for Peace. But, with FSU anticipating the pass, Florida turned loose Lorenzo Hampton on runs of 34 and 18 yards. On a keeper from the 5, Hewko scored, cutting it to 10-7.

Hampton and Neal Anderson, both destined for NFL careers, each ran for more than 100 yards.

With a Wilber Marshall-led defense dominating, Florida checked FSU, controlled the ball in the last half. With rain falling, UF drove in the early minutes of the third quarter to a field goal. One Florida State penetration to the UF 9 saw Phillip Hall fail on a short field goal. A walk-on, Hall had entered the game 6-for-6 on field goals. His only previous miss of the season had been a lone extra point.

In the fourth quarter Florida won it 13-10 on Jim Gainey's second field goal, a 22-yarder.

"That's one Florida game we should have won," said Bowden. "We go down and miss a chip-shot field goal. They go down and kick one, and the game is over."

Not a bad year at all

A blanket of gloom seemed to wrap FSU fans and players as a Gator Bowl date with West Virginia approached. The mood was hardly helped by Bowden's announcement that two potentially formidable players — defensive end Allen Dale Campbell and tailback Tony Smith — had been dismissed from the squad for failure to attend class.

No coach, no player, no trainer, no manager, no equipment man radiated optimism in an atmosphere of preparation that bordered on grim. Even the normally even-mannered Bowden seemed more tight-lipped.

For 10th-ranked West Virginia, the Gator Bowl weather — rain, cold, mud — seemed ideal.

With Blair Williams operating at quarterback, Florida State surprised with passes from the shotgun formation. Bowden had the team work on the shotgun primarily for its novelty value to morale. The players liked it, and Williams seemed made for it.

But defense and Billy Allen's 95-yard scoring kickoff return were early keys. At halftime FSU led 17-6 after a 27-yard scoring pass by Williams to a somersaulting Dennis McKinnon.

Greg Allen scored on a 29-yard run, and a 65-yard McKinnon reverse paved another Allen TD as Florida State won 31-12.

Given the circumstances, it was a stunning outcome as FSU finished 9-3.

"It was a year we were not supposed to have anything much," said Bowden. "It could have been a great year. It wasn't a bad one."

Ahead was a year that looked bright.

"We could be as good as anybody," said Bowden. "But how Kelly Lowrey goes, so goes our offense."

'83: Something wild

But 1983 was a season in the tradition of a game played with an oblong ball. It was a might-have-been season, with a continuing question of defense and Lowrey's health.

Coming off a preseason shoulder injury, Lowrey played phenomenally in a phenomenally wild game — a Tallahassee opener that saw East Carolina fall 47-46.

Hitting 28 of 35 passes for 322 yards, Lowrey brought FSU back from a 46-41 deficit in the last 5 minutes. Eric Riley provided opportunity with an interception. Tom Wheeler hauled in a 5-yard Lowrey pass for the winning points. Moments later, Riley recovered a John McLean-forced fumble to assure victory.

"I've never seen anything like this one — never!" said a relieved Bowden.

Almost, he saw that game's clone the following week in Baton Rouge — the Seminoles' fifth straight season in Tiger Stadium!

In a game that saw Florida State score 31 unanswered points for a 33-14 lead, the Seminoles found themselves hanging on at the end to win 40-35.

LSU moved ahead 14-0, but on two short Lowrey keepers Florida State tied it 14-14 by halftime. In the third quarter Lowrey passed for two — 16 yards to Hassan Jones, 20 to Jessie Hester. A 28-yard Greg Allen touchdown run brought a 19-point lead early in the fourth quarter.

Lowrey scored again on a short run for what proved to be the winning margin as LSU exploded for three touchdowns — including two in the final minute.

"Football is a game of momentum," said Bowden later, remarking on FSU's 31 points in a row. "Last year they scored a big touchdown right before the half, and though the game was still close they blew us out. Our touchdown this time did the same thing for us just before the half."

And despite prohibitive matchmaking that placed his Seminoles in Tiger Stadium five years running, Bowden had blown away all odds and won four out of those five.

You name it — it went wrong

Call FSU's Sept. 17 date against Tulane in the New Orleans Superdome the "Murphy's Law Game."

Everything that could go wrong did go wrong.

A police escort due to meet the Seminoles' charter at the New Orleans airport got mixed up, met Central Florida instead and whizzed the Knights to the same downtown hotel where FSU stayed. Meanwhile, FSU buses got blocked by an 18-wheeler that flip-flopped in expressway traffic.

"Don't believe in omens," said Bowden, continuing to read a newspaper as he waited — and waited — for traffic to clear.

Pretty soon his beliefs would be tested.

At the hotel, a computer breakdown confused room assignments. More delay, with players assigned to rooms — including honeymoon suites — that compounded distraction. The computer problem precipitated other difficulties in the crowded hotel. Conventioneers, confused about meeting rooms, wandered in and out during team meals and strategy sessions.

"It was not just the traffic problem before we got to the hotel, but the traffic problem *after*," said Bowden.

"It was a kind of clumsy weekend all the way around — and we played that way, too!"

Tulane played the game with an ineligible quarterback — Jon English, son of the coach, Wally English. Challenging NCAA rules regarding his status as a transfer, the quarterback had obtained a court injunction permitting him to play.

At the start, Florida State drove to the Tulane 7, as though it were nothing. But when Lowrey — playing with the flu and running a slight temperature — threw across field, Treg Songy stepped in front of the pass and sped 99 yards with the interception to a touchdown.

It was Lowrey trying to run Songy down.

"He had to chase that guy about 80 yards — and he was dead!" said Bowden.

From that moment, Tulane had the bit in its teeth. What figured to be a mismatch became a war — a war in which English was heavy artillery. He completed 16 of 29 passes for 210 yards.

Ahead 21-14 at halftime, Florida State struggled throughout the last half. Greg Allen was sidelined with a knee injury in the third quarter.

Tulane won 34-28.

"What can you say?" sighed Bowden after the game. "They kept making big play after big play after big play on us."

In the dressing room, Bowden lost a valued ring, given to him by Palatka fans. An exhaustive search was futile.

"I guess that ring was the prettiest thing I ever had — gold, with garnet stones reading 'FSU,'" said Bowden.

Months later, the NCAA instructed Tulane to forfeit the game to Florida State because of the ineligibility of English. Forfeits in football, well after the fact, are rather meaningless.

"Naw, nothing — not one thing!" said Bowden when asked if the forfeit meant anything at all.

Tough defeats

At Auburn, following an open date, the Seminoles were plagued anew by ill fortune.

At halftime, Florida State trailed 20-10. Auburn had scored a touchdown on the closing play of that half — an unlikely screen pass to fullback Tommy Agee, who somehow maneuvered and stumbled through would-be tacklers.

Meanwhile, Rosie Snipes' 87-yard scoring run had been called back to the Auburn 47 — where he had stepped out of bounds.

On two Lowrey touchdowns from close in, Florida State rallied, led 24-20 with 6:46 to go.

Randy Campbell quarterbacked Auburn downfield, to fourth-and-8 at the FSU 15.

On a short screen pass, Lionel James loped into the end zone for the touchdown that won it 27-24.

"We knew the play they were going to run, because of their tendencies," said Bowden.

"On the play, they came down and blocked on a forward pass — you can't do that! If we had been lucky, that infraction would have been called.

"Earlier, on a fourth-down play they did not have enough men on the line of scrimmage. You have to have seven. They had six."

A third straight tough defeat followed at Pittsburgh, 17-16.

Ahead 13-7 at halftime, FSU trailed 17-16 with 8:29 showing on the clock.

The Seminoles never got the ball back as Pitt drove the ball steadily, magnificently behind the blocking of giant lineman Bill Fralic.

"We never gave our offense much of a chance," said Bowden. "We couldn't get the ball back. Here was a case of our not being good enough."

Florida State was good enough to slam Cincinnati 43-17 as Allen and Snipes each ran for more than 100 yards. And good enough to quell Louisville 51-7 as Allen ran for 145 yards and three touchdowns.

Bob Davis and 'The Drive'

The Seminoles seemed not good enough to beat Arizona State in Tempe, but they were — and in unbelievable style!

Ahead 14-10, Florida State lost Lowrey — severe knee injury — early in the final quarter.

In came backup quarterback Bob Davis. A pass to Snipes resulted in a 38-yard touchdown play, but Florida State found itself behind 26-22 and the ball in foe hands inside FSU territory with 2:38 to play. FSU defenders allowed nothing, forcing a punt.

From the FSU 18, Davis quarterbacked one of the Seminoles' more memorable drives — an 82-yard movement that became celebrated as simply "The Drive."

It included a fourth-and-5 pass for 16 to Tom Wheeler at the FSU 23. With less than 30 seconds remaining, Wheeler took an over-the-middle pass 20 yards to the Arizona State 10. Then Jessie Hester, on a square-out pattern, fooled a defender and grabbed the touchdown pass in the end zone that won it 28-26. The clock showed 6 seconds.

"Florida State's offense was the best I've ever coached against," said Darryl Rogers, the losing coach. "*Ever!*"

With Lowrey still sidelined the next week, Florida State trailed 24-17 in the early moments of the last half, then erupted for touchdowns on each of their first three third-quarter possessions and bagged a 45-30 victory over South Carolina.

In the closest of encounters, Miami maintained a chance at a national championship it would eventually win, slipping past the Seminoles in Campbell Stadium 17-16.

A 19-yard Jeff Davis field goal on the game's last play did it.

With 5:23 to go, ahead 16-14, Florida State

had the football but could not keep it. A 17-yard Eddie Brown punt return put Miami in position at midfield. Quarterback Bernie Kosar steadily guided the Hurricanes to the 2-yard line with 3 seconds left. After a timeout, Davis booted true.

Impressed with Florida State's effort, the Peach Bowl extended a bid.

"We played hard," said Bowden. "This was the fourth game we lost like this."

Tulane 34-28, Auburn 27-24, Pitt 17-16 and Miami 17-16. So close.

There was no agonizing over a close loss at Florida.

Capitalizing on a half-dozen FSU turnovers, Florida won with incredible ease. It was 10-0 after a quarter, 23-6 at halftime, 43-6 after three quarters, and 53-14 at the end.

"I hope we've learned one thing — you can't turn the ball over against a team like Florida on your own side of the field," said Bowden. "We had six turnovers, and they scored after every one."

The passing of the No. 1 fan

Soon the Seminoles lost more than a game. They lost Sol Carrol.

One of the more colorful fans Florida State ever knew, he died of a heart attack on a bus carrying fans from Tallahassee to Atlanta for the Peach Bowl early on the morning of the game. He was 77, and he had been an old man when he adopted the Seminoles as his own.

He had come, uninvited and unknown, at the worst of times — several months before the all-losing season of 1973. Camping with his wife, Jean, near Tallahassee, he struck up an acquaintance with some track athletes and came to FSU to see a meet. "When he saw the university, he didn't want to go anywhere else," his wife later recalled. He never did.

Shaking his tambourine, cheering, joking in his raspy voice, Sol Carrol was everywhere garnet and gold colors were. He went to swimming meets, softball games, volleyball games, basketball games, tennis matches — whatever was out there involving Florida State athletes.

Proclaiming himself, at a rather early stage, as Florida State's No. 1 fan, he and his persistent style brought some resentment.

But Sol kept coming. He passed out candy and doughnuts to favorites, as well as to charity groups. He sold Seminole souvenirs for the boosters. He drove a car adorned with the colors of Florida State, and wore those colors everywhere. Coming early to luncheons and other gatherings of FSU supporters, he would deck the halls with ivy, so to speak — garnet-and-gold decorations. When a coach arrived, Sol would be first to spot him, first to herald him with the "FSU Fight Song" that sprung, like magic, from the little music box he always carried. He wangled trips to out-of-town FSU sporting events, for he had little money of his own.

And if he could not go, he stayed home, listened on the radio or watched on TV — then met the team on its return, shaking that tambourine and cheering. There is memory of the football team arriving at the airport at 3 a.m. on a rainy night, and no one there to welcome the players — except Sol, grinning and shaking that tambourine.

As the worst of times turned into the best of times, he kept coming. Unchanged.

He never stopped. Win or lose, made no difference. If some thought this old man a bit of a pushy pest, that made no difference either. Sol was always there.

"It seemed to me his entire existence was built around enhancing the Seminoles," said Gene McDowell, assistant coach and former FSU linebacker. "He wanted to make sure FSU was on the map — showing those FSU colors always.

"I don't think there was ever a more avid fan than Sol Carrol."

He was, said Bowden, like the school logo. "Everybody recognized Sol as a symbol of FSU athletics," said the coach.

Indeed, he had been nationally recognized, in a color spread in Esquire magazine, as one of college football's more lively Super Fans.

"It is probably the way he would have wanted to have left," said FSU President Bernie Sliger. "Going to a game."

And the Seminoles left Atlanta as they would have wanted, as Sol would have wanted. Victorious.

Looking for change

With third-year sophomore Eric Thomas making his first quarterbacking start, FSU scored the first two times it got the football, sped on to a 21-0 halftime lead and a 28-3 triumph over surprised North Carolina.

"We just went to it," said Bowden. "Nothing fancy.

"The story of the game was that both offense and defense played well."

But Thomas looked fancy enough, passing for two touchdowns and running the option well on a frigid Atlanta evening.

Officially, the season ended 8-4, by NCAA decree that stipulated Tulane's forfeiture of its

34-28 victory. To Bowden, though, the record was still 7-5, and he was unhappy with it.

"You sure can't go very long saying 'We almost beat them' and 'Look how close we came,' " he said.

He talked of fundamentals, and he talked of change — notably on defense. "I want a defense so simple even I can understand it," he said as Jack Stanton departed as defensive coordinator and Mickey Andrews succeeded him.

In 1980 Stanton's unit gave up fewer points (85) than any other team in the land, but a rebuilding process had been slow. Only Florida State's 0-11 team of 1973 had given up more points (331) than the 1983 Seminoles (312).

'84: A rousing start

With Thomas at quarterback, Florida State opened brightly in 1984.

East Carolina tumbled in a Tallahassee opener 48-17 as the Seminoles ran for a surprising 327 yards. And, as Joe Wessel sacked a punter before he could boot the ball and blocked a later punt, FSU swept by Kansas 42-16.

In an eyebrow-raising Orange Bowl struggle, Florida State sacked Bernie Kosar and Miami's defending national champions 38-3.

In Andrews' first season as defensive coordinator, Florida State had been able to disguise, in its first two games, the pass coverages it planned for Miami.

"Getting ready for Kansas, we had practiced all those goodies we were saving for Miami," said Bowden. "At the same time, Kansas was a good passing team and that helped us, too, in getting ready for Miami."

Derek Schmidt kicked three first-half field goals, and Jessie Hester swept 77 yards on a reverse for a touchdown. Snipes ran for two more touchdowns.

Bigger, Seminole defenders sacked Kosar six times, for minus-75 yards.

Temple tumbled 44-27 as Wessel blocked a punt and a field goal.

And Florida State headed for Tennessee and a date with Memphis State expecting to come home 5-0.

But it proved a game FSU was lucky to tie 17-17. Behind 10-0 in the opening quarter, trailing 17-14 at the half, FSU tied it on the game's last play — a 42-yard Schmidt field goal in the rain.

An astonishing Campbell Stadium struggle saw Auburn score a last-minute touchdown that tipped the Seminoles 42-41.

Thomas completed 18 of 29 passes for 357 yards, but it wasn't enough. Trailing 29-17 in the early moments of the last half, Florida State rallied to lead 36-29, but that wasn't enough either. Auburn drove 66 yards at the end to a Brent Fullwood touchdown from the 4.

A wild game that saw FSU lead in yardage 592 to 372 and in first downs 32 to 20 saw only two turnovers — a fumble by each.

"Thing I remember most about that game was their quarterback (Pat Washington) had not been an effective passer anytime before," said Bowden. "But he was against us. On the first play he threw that ball way downfield, and we had perfect position, but Freddy Weygand took the ball away from our guy (Eric Riley) at the 3.

"I had felt we would beat Auburn in Tallahassee."

Block that kick

Opposing kickers surely were taking a beating.

With the momentum of two blocked punts — by Jesse Solomon and Lenny Chavers — the Seminoles sailed past Tulane 27-6.

The assault on punters continued as Florida State won 52-44 at Arizona State, completing a three-game sweep of the Sun Devils that started with a game at Tampa in 1979.

Chavers blocked one punt, and the trailing Wessel ran it in for a touchdown. Later, Chavers blocked another and ran that one in, too.

In a script that followed the previous year, FSU's starting quarterback left the game with an injury and his replacement played heroically. This time it was Kirk Coker — in for Thomas (painful hip-pointer) — completing eight of 11 passes for 203 yards and two touchdowns.

Ironically, the passing performance of the losers' Jeff VanRaaphorst — 38 completions of 59 throws for 532 yards — set four FSU records for an opponent. In addition to the most passing yardage, VanRaaphorst also accounted for the most total-offense yardage, as well as the most passes and the most completions.

Again, a big victory at Arizona State was costly. Thomas would not be effective in the three remaining games. Nor would Greg Allen, who left with a knee injury after gaining 223 yards on 22 runs.

Slip-sliding in South Carolina

In another Murphy's Law sort of game,

Florida State bowed 38-26 to unbeaten South Carolina.

Down 17-7 at the half, Florida State compounded circumstances with *nine* second-half turnovers (seven interceptions, two fumbles).

The Gamecocks' Bryant Gilliard intercepted four passes — most ever by an individual against FSU. Raymond Brown ran the second-half kickoff back 99 yards for a touchdown.

"His knee hit the ground at the 4, and the ball should have been dead right there," recalled Bowden. "Television showed that replay over and over. No question about it. The guy picks up the ball and takes off. Instead of being at their 4 — a tough place for any team to start — they got a touchdown."

There was a reason for all the interceptions. Intended FSU receivers were *falling down.* Often.

"It was a peculiar thing — the playing surface up there," said Bowden. "Slick as a billiard table.

"What happened was they had removed the artificial turf from the field earlier, and regular grass had not had enough time to grow good.

"You could not cut, unless you really knew what you were doing. Our quarterbacks would throw the ball on target, but nobody would be there — they had fallen down — and somebody would come up to intercept.

"We knew about this, and had phoned people to inquire about it. We had seen opponents falling down in the film. We had taken different kinds of shoes up there. Nothing worked. It was kind of like somebody being used to playing in the rain, I think, and somebody else was not.

"Now, I won't say this was the reason we lost the game — South Carolina played great. But I will say it was the nightmare I remember about that game."

Back in Campbell Stadium for homecoming, FSU ran up 454 rushing yards and thumped Tennessee-Chattanooga 37-0.

But once more Florida was a Gator of another color. In the first game of the series Galen Hall coached, Florida won a game played in the rain more decisively than the 27-17 score suggests.

The talent Pell had assembled would be a factor long after his firing early that 1984 season for dozens of NCAA violations that brought two years of probation. For the third straight game, Snipes ran for more than 100 yards, but Florida led 17-3 at halftime as Kerwin Bell threw touchdown passes of 38 and 5 yards to Frankie Neal and John L. Williams.

"I thought we had a chance," said Bowden, looking back. "But there in the rain, we didn't. Our fumbling hurt.

"But, boy, they had a good football team! We would have had to play perfect ball, and get hot."

Injured-quarterback syndrome again

Surely, the highest-scoring team of Florida State's first 40 years would have been somewhat more devastating except for late quarterback problems once again.

For five of six seasons, beginning with 1981, and excepting 1982, starting quarterbacks were hindered by injury.

It began with Stockstill and a knee injury in the Orange Bowl game of Jan. 1, 1981. The knee bothered him through the 1981 campaign, but most notably toward the end.

It continued with Kelly Lowrey severely damaging a knee in the eighth game at Arizona State. In the remaining four games, including the Peach Bowl, Lowrey was not a factor.

History repeated. Eric Thomas, in the eighth game of 1984 at Arizona State, received a hip-pointer. Nor was he a real factor in the last four games, including the Citrus Bowl.

In 1985 it would be Thomas, after two shoulder operations, hurt again in early practice. Then starter Danny McManus, after leading a 4-0 start, would be out for the season in the fifth game at Auburn, with dizzy spells following a concussion.

And in 1986, it would be McManus sidelined with a thumb injury on his throwing hand in the eighth game at Miami.

"It did all start with Stockstill, and the funny thing is I never had it happen before," said Bowden. "Jimmy Black had never missed a game that first year. Neither had Wally (Woodham) and Jimmy (Jordan).

"We have been very unfortunate with our quarterbacks since 1980, and I don't know why."

A good season, and yet . . .

A 1984 team that started 4-0 and finished the regular season 7-3-1 scored more points (389) and averaged more (35.3) than any other of the first 40 years.

In the Citrus Bowl that followed, Florida State rallied to tie Georgia 17-17 after trailing 14-0 at intermission.

With 3:58 remaining, behind 17-9, Florida State forged a chance as Chavers ripped in to block his third punt of the season. Wessel scooped it up and rambled 14 yards for the touchdown. On a reverse, Darrin Holloman got the 2 points that tied it.

It was a season that saw the alert Wessel block five kicks, and score four touchdowns off blocked kicks.

And it was a team that blocked more punts (eight) and scored more touchdowns off blocked kicks (six) than any other of the first 40 years.

"Blocking kicks is something we have always worked on during my time at Florida State," said Bowden. "In 1984 Wessel got hot, and Chavers got hot to combine for our biggest year at blocking kicks.

"I think a lot of it was due to Wessel. He was a walk-on who didn't have great speed. I remember I had not been worried whether he would come back for his senior year, because I figured he couldn't start.

"But he might have been as valuable that year as anybody we had. He had a great knack — a great desire. And I think he was a person who just wanted to be good in some football area; he didn't care where. He had that pride.

"And he would get a great jump on the ball. He would get penalties for being offside, and we would look at film and see he wasn't really offside at all. He just got off faster than anybody else.

"I remember in the Arizona State game we had a punt return on, but Joe not only blocked it, but ran it in for a touchdown."

Bowden recalled that Bobby Butler and Warren Hanna had earlier filled notable kick-blocking roles for the Seminoles.

But despite those blocked kicks, the 1984 season surely was not what it might have been.

"We were beat at Memphis State, and we tied it," mused Bowden, pondering a strange run. "Against Georgia in that Citrus Bowl, we were beat — and we tied it again."

'85: McManus debuts

In 1985, the Seminoles started 4-0 for the second straight season — and for the second straight season Auburn dealt a crushing first defeat.

Opening in New Orleans on Aug. 31 — its earliest game ever — FSU skipped past Tulane 38-12 behind an exciting new quarterback — the sophomore Danny McManus.

Defensive lineman Anthony Williams battles his way through tires in practice, to simulate pass-rush blocking.

Quarterback Kirk Coker came to the rescue more than once.

In the Memphis State game of '85, as in the Nebraska game a week earlier, quarterback Danny McManus took a hard shot.

"He was better than I thought he was," said Tulane coach Mack Brown, shaking his head later.

Touchdown passes by McManus to Phillip Bryant and Darrin Holloman precipitated a 14-12 halftime lead. Cletis Jones, on a 14-yard scoring run, bolstered the lead on an opening drive of the third quarter. In the fourth quarter, McManus on short sneaks twice scored.

Two touchdowns passing, 14 completions of 19 passes, two touchdowns running — not a bad start for the sophomore.

A hot time in Lincoln

At Nebraska, an unbelievable heat wave brought astonishing discomfort to fans and players.

Early on the morning of the game, over coffee, Bowden casually discussed with Frank DeBord, equipment manager, the possibility of buying sun visors for players to ward off the heat a bit.

Then, characteristically, Bowden turned somewhat less than serious as he grabbed a nearby newspaper.

"Remember when we were kids?" he said. "Let's see, you fold it this way, that way — now, how did we used to do that?"

Suggesting hats made of newspapers for his players, Bowden suddenly had all around him laughing as he placed one atop his head.

"Lord, have mercy!" said team chaplain Ken Smith, shaking his head.

But Bowden had his team loose for the game, and convinced that the heat was to Seminole advantage. Surely, Florida State was more accustomed to such.

Whereupon, Florida State moved behind McManus to one of its great victories, the 17-13 final score strikingly similar to the 18-14 upset wrought over Nebraska in 1980.

Nebraska led 7-0 after fullback Tom Rathman's 60-yard scoring burst. FSU tied it 7-7 on a 4-yard McManus pass to Darrin Holloman. After a Schmidt field goal from 20-yard range, Nebraska regained the lead, 13-10, on Doug DuBose's 1-yard sweep.

With 5:23 to play in the half, end Garth Jax sacked Nebraska punter Dan Wingard at his 7, and two plays later Cletis Jones scored from the 2 for 17-13.

"They're in our briar patch now," said Bowden into a national-TV microphone as he trotted off the field at halftime.

One of FSU's hottest receivers, Hassan Jones, in '85.

The temperature on the artificial turf had soared to 130 degrees Fahrenheit. Soon concession stands ran dry after more than 80,000 pounds of ice was used up, more than 75,000 soft drinks sold. Later, the Red Cross would disclose that more than 100 people were treated at the stadium for heat exhaustion.

"I never dreamed it could get that hot up there," said Bowden. "It gave us a physical advantage over them — if we could avoid getting crushed early. The fourth quarter should be ours.

"Well, we shut 'em out in that second half — one of our all-time great defensive games — and that doesn't happen too often to Nebraska at home."

Unable to pass — only three completions all day — Nebraska found itself checked by a defense led by linebacker Paul McGowan. On offense, McManus mixed passing with strong ball-control running by two Smiths, freshman Sammie and senior Tony, each of whom gained 46 last-half yards.

But in the fourth quarter, McManus suffered a concussion that would prove costly. In came Kirk Coker.

"Kirk did a great job for us," said Bowden. "Among other things, he maneuvered a nice drive that ate up a whole lot of time."

Aboard a chartered plane on the Lincoln runway waiting to take off, Bowden was impatient over some delay. "Let's crank this thing up — let's *scratch*, baby!" he said.

Back in Tallahassee, there was dancing in the streets, and assorted celebrations that precipitated a roadblock of a main street running by campus. But there were those who recalled an even bigger Tallahassee celebration following the 1980 triumph at Nebraska.

Minutes after the FSU plane finally took off, a weary Bowden was sound asleep in his seat. And perched on his happy head was a trophy of sorts — a bright red cap, with white lettering that read, approximately:

"Nebraska — 100% butt-kicking football."

Playing catch-up

It seemed for a time, back in Tallahassee the following game, that the celebration had lasted too long.

Memphis State jumped on the Seminoles 10-0. In the second quarter, a blind-side tackle left McManus unconscious for the second straight game.

On successive 51-yard Schmidt field goals, FSU trimmed the score to 10-6 by halftime.

After a third-quarter touchdown pass, Coker to Darrin Holloman for 13 yards, Schmidt kicked last-period field goals of 42 and 24 yards.

And with the considerable assistance of Schmidt's four field goals, Florida State won 19-10.

With McManus sidelined, the Seminoles found themselves trailing Kansas 20-10 in the last quarter as the Jayhawks moved on the extraordinary passing of Mike Norseth.

With 13:53 remaining, Bowden ushered freshman Chip Ferguson into action. On his second play, Ferguson hit a streaking Phillip Bryant with a bomb on a 67-yard scoring play.

Soon a Martin Mayhew interception brought more Ferguson opportunity at FSU's 38.

In four plays — the big one a 32-yard run by freshman Victor Floyd — a winning touchdown was on the board. Floyd got it on a 6-yard run that made it a final 24-20.

As Norseth hit 28 of 44 passes for 308 yards, he was slowed by three last-half interceptions and two sacks that kept the Jayhawks away from the goal line.

Burned by Auburn

But in the next game it took Auburn only five plays to cross FSU's goal. It sprung Bo Jackson on the game's fifth play for 53 yards and a 7-0 lead.

McManus, back in action, quickly brought FSU back, an 80-yard drive climaxed by Holloman's 5-yard run on the reverse for a touchdown that tied it 7-7.

Soon, McManus had the Seminoles threatening again — but, experiencing dizziness, he left the game.

McManus would not play again all season long.

Soon after the McManus departure, Schmidt missed a 29-yard field-goal attempt.

But Eric Williams' 17-yard dash with an interception off Pat Washington put FSU up 14-7.

By halftime it had become a 17-17 tie. A Brent Fullwood scoring smash from the 1 was swiftly followed in the last half by a 35-yard Jackson touchdown sprint that made it 31-17.

FSU countered with a Thomas-engineered drive and a Tony Smith touchdown from the 2.

With 6:21 left in the game, a 47-yard Schmidt field goal narrowed Auburn's lead to 31-27.

But as FSU gambled defensively trying to get the ball back, Tommy Agee sprung away on a 68-yard run that was followed by Freddy Weygand's 13-yard touchdown on a reverse.

An interception followed by a fumble opened the floodgates.

In that final 6:21, Auburn scored four touchdowns that made it a final 59-27.

These two freshmen brightened the '85 season: Keith Ross (20) and Victor Floyd.

"It was anybody's football game for about 55 minutes despite the loss of McManus," said Bowden. "And then, it wasn't."

Returning home, Florida State demolished Tulsa 76-14, scoring a school-record 11 touchdowns as well as a school-record 76 points. Among the 11 touchdowns was a 100-yard Deion Sanders return of an interception, another school record.

And Tulsa was hardly an everyday patsy. Winning its last four games, it finished 6-5. In one of those, Wichita State, tailback Gordon Brown ran for 214 yards and quarterback Steve Gage for 206 — first time in NCAA history two backs on the same team each ran for more than 200 yards.

Once more, at North Carolina, the Seminoles found themselves temporarily on the short side of the scoreboard. As FSU turned the ball over five times in the first half, UNC sprinted to a 10-0 lead.

After a Tracy Sanders interception, Schmidt's 23-yard field goal provided FSU with its first points late in the third quarter. Chip Ferguson, who had replaced Thomas in that third quarter, threw to Hassan Jones — for 45 yards, then for a scoring 10 yards — to tie it 10-10 in the last quarter.

Quarterback Chip Ferguson, tough freshman hero of the '85 Gator Bowl.

With 2:17 left, Schmidt's 51-yarder put FSU up 13-10. Martin Mayhew provided a cushion with a 62-yard interception runback for a last-minute touchdown, and with it a final 20-10 score.

Tested by Testaverde

Now 6-1 and dreaming of a New Year's bowl, Florida State tapped Ferguson as a first-time starter as Miami came to Tallahassee.

In a classic struggle, Florida State got 10 second-quarter points to lead 24-10. But a classic passer rallied the Hurricanes to a 35-27 victory.

Vinny Testaverde completed 23 of 43 passes for 339 yards and four touchdowns, including a winning pair in the last quarter.

All this, despite seven sacks — including three by tackle Isaac Williams. "We kept plugging — and they kept plugging!" said Williams.

"They were giving 150 percent all the time to get to me," praised Testaverde.

"Seems like I'd block one guy and another one would show up right behind him," said fullback Alonzo Highsmith. "I couldn't figure out where they were all coming from."

Miami's Jerome Brown, the All-American defensive tackle, said it was the hardest-hitting game he had ever known. "I took a beating," said Brown, who most of the game confronted Pat Tomberlin, a giant freshman playing guard for the Seminoles.

Twice in succession Florida State blocked Miami punts. After the first was nullified by a delay penalty against Miami, John Hadley blocked the second and teammate Brian Davis covered the ball in Miami's end zone for a touchdown.

"We led by 10, and I can't remember our losing before when we had that big a lead," said Bowden. "We played good, but we were not good enough to do it."

Charging FSU defenders, while sacking Testaverde, also checked Miami running. The Hurricanes finished with minus-18 yards, an FSU record.

But Miami's defense had restricted FSU to 3 last-half points. And that, along with the 21 that Testaverde engineered, made a difference.

"I am concerned about a letdown," said Bowden before his Seminoles let South Carolina down 56-14.

Two freshmen — Victor Floyd and Keith Ross — ran for 217 and 163 yards. Running just 15 times, Floyd averaged 14.1.

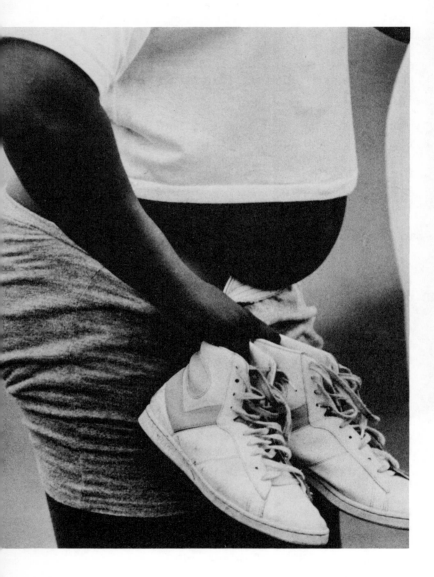

Football is played by young men who are made of muscle — and maybe the occasional ounce of body fat. This belly, whose owner was participating in a Florida State practice, was captured by the camera in 1986.

FSU's Bart Schuchts watches a fumble roll away during the '86 game against North Carolina. FSU had to settle for a tie that game — and UNC coach Dick Crum had to settle for a severely damaged knee when a player came flying into the sideline crowd.

Bobby Bowden is easygoing but occasionally does disagree with a referee.
This is a scene from the '86 Tulane game.

Ross got 103 and senior Tony Smith 114 as Western Carolina went south, 50-10.

But when the Seminoles went east — to Gainesville — it was a familiar story. Kerwin Bell threw for 343 yards and three touchdowns as Florida romped 38-14. Behind 28-0 at halftime, FSU pulled to within 28-14 before Bell again opened up.

Call it the Ferguson Bowl

Dragging an 8-3 record behind it, Florida State headed for the Gator Bowl and a date with Oklahoma State.

His fiery freshman baptism behind him, Ferguson was magnificent.

He broke his collarbone in the first quarter but played on — hitting 20 of 43 passes for 338 yards and two touchdowns.

Out of action were FSU's top three receivers — Hassan Jones, Darrin Holloman, Phillip Bryant — and Oklahoma State reasoned the Seminoles would go with their strong runners. Instead, Ferguson threw on 15 of the first 20 plays. Herb Gainer caught seven passes, for 148 yards and two touchdowns.

"They bit on practically every move," said Gainer.

The threat of Tony Smith was perhaps one reason why. In his last game, the senior tailback rambled for 201 yards on 24 carries. In front 13-0 at halftime, FSU won with ease, 34-23.

Smith reckoned it was the passing game that opened the door for him. "Their linebackers started taking such deep drops, a 5-yard gain was automatic," he said.

'86: Back to Nebraska

A deep breath was what Bowden took as he looked to a 1986 schedule that listed games at Nebraska and Michigan among the first four.

"I felt we had to come out of those first four 3-and-1 if we were to have a great year," he said after the season, "and the worst we could come out to do really well was 2-and-2."

Florida State came out 1-2-1.

Overcoming six turnovers, the Seminoles slipped past Toledo 24-0 in a Tallahassee opener.

At Nebraska, the Seminoles took a 14-10 halftime lead as Sammie Smith, on a fake reverse off a pitchout, outran defenders on a 57-yard touchdown run 33 seconds before intermission.

But Nebraska quarterback Steve Taylor was a little much — passing for two touchdowns, running for two more.

A little much, too, was a Nebraska last-half

defense, led by noseguard Danny Noonan. In those last two quarters, Florida State had minus-2 yards of total offense.

As Ferguson passed for just 97 yards, he got sacked seven times, including four by Noonan. Final score: Nebraska 34, Florida State 17.

"This was a season when a lot of the time we were just not good enough in the fourth quarter," said Bowden.

The death of Pablo Lopez

It was also a season that saw a player die tragically one week after the Nebraska game.

In a parking lot outside a campus dance on that open-date weekend, Pablo Lopez, a senior offensive tackle, was killed by a shotgun blast. One of the team's more popular players, he was also one of the team's best.

"We lost Pablo, and we lost our best offensive lineman, to be honest," said Bowden. "It might have made a big difference, had we not lost Pablo."

A Derek Schmidt kick with 8 seconds left *would* have made a big difference, but the 37-yard field-goal attempt that many Campbell Stadium partisans thought good was ruled invalid by officials. Thereby, North Carolina went home with a 10-10 tie.

And thereby Bowden, who had gone his first 18 coaching seasons without knowing a tie, in his 21st season became acquainted with his third. In 1984, Memphis State and Georgia had given him his first knots.

Behind 7-0, Florida State gained a third-quarter safety when Felton Hayes blocked a punt through the end zone. FSU led 10-7 after a 28-yard touchdown catch, Peter Tom Willis to fellow freshman Ronald Lewis, and a 2-pointer, Willis to Gainer.

The sticky Tar Heels tied it on a 22-yard field goal early in the last quarter.

In a relatively unusual arrangement, only officials from North Carolina's conference — the Atlantic Coast — had worked the game. The season prior, at Chapel Hill, only officials from the Southern Independent Officials Association had been involved.

'It was ridiculous'

If Bowden was not enchanted with the officiating in the North Carolina game, he surely was not at Michigan either.

"Another official warned us about one of their guys before we went to Michigan," Bowden said a few days after the game. "The official who talked with us said he had worked with the particular Big Ten guy before."

Miami quarterback Vinny Testaverde gingerly shakes hands with the injured
Danny McManus after their '86 game.

Referring to calls favoring Michigan he said that official made in the game, Bowden concluded: "It was ridiculous."

Florida State was penalized eight times for 84 yards, Michigan nine for 88. Of course, it is quite possible for a few penalty yards to be far more damaging to a team than many penalty yards for another.

Historically, Florida State coaches have felt — as do coaches of the majority of independents — that officials employed by a conference tend, subconsciously or otherwise, to favor that employer. And league coaches often do have a say-so in the employment of officials.

The historical view of Florida State coaches on this matter definitely was one key to the formation of the Southern Independent Coaches Association.

Prior to that time, Florida State employed Southeastern Conference officials but felt it often was at a decided disadvantage when playing an SEC team.

At Michigan, it was a 10-10 halftime tie, the Wolverines getting their touchdown following a Florida State fumble at its 13.

Clearly, more than one FSU drive in the critical second half was adversely affected by penalties.

Michigan took a 13-10 third-quarter lead that became 20-10 with 8:35 remaining in the game on a splendid 90-yard Michigan drive.

Moving in for Ferguson at quarterback, McManus quickly took Florida State to a touchdown on a 20-yard toss to Gainer. A 2-point toss to Pat Carter narrowed it to 20-18.

That score became final as an onsides kick failed, and Michigan controlled the ball the remainder of the way.

Speaking to a Quarterback Club much later in the season, Bowden said of officials generally: "They mess up, and sometimes it seems we're getting more of it than anybody. But that is because we're looking at it from our side."

Talking to writers following the last game of 1986, Bowden spoke of his distaste for split crews — some officials from one group, some from another. In split-crew circumstances, he suggested, Southern Independent officials sometimes seem timid and are perhaps dominated by the other group. In relation to most other groups, the Southern Independent officials are less experienced at the college level.

Alternately jesting and turning serious in that interview, Bowden said at one point: "I didn't mind if they sent Jesse — but sending Jesse *and* Frank!" One writer, laughing, urged Bowden to keep talking in the same vein. "OK, the Youngers, too!" retorted Bowden.

Then serious, Bowden said:

"I don't know what to do. You don't know where to turn. We sure need to do something."

He compared the problems of officials to the problem of playoffs for the major-college teams.

"Something positive should be done," he said. "But what reasonably can be done?"

The return of McManus — and Testaverde

What Florida State was able to reasonably do, after Michigan in 1986, was regroup against Tulane (54-21), Wichita State (59-3) and Louisville (54-18).

"This was a year we played teams ranked No. 1, No. 2 and No. 3 in the country at one time or another," said Bowden, referring to Nebraska, Michigan and Miami. "And we played two of those early.

"Fortunately, we were able to come back."

In his first start in a year, McManus threw for 171 yards as Florida State erupted for 40 last-half points on Tulane.

One oddity saw 9 FSU points in 7 playing seconds. After John Parks blocked a punt for a safety, Ross ran back the free kick 70 yards for a touchdown.

McManus threw three first-half touchdown passes as FSU took a 38-0 lead over Wichita at intermission.

On the way to becoming the first-ever FSU team to score more than 50 points in three straight games, the Seminoles got 30 against Louisville in the second quarter alone. Again McManus threw three touchdown passes in the first half.

But in the Orange Bowl against unbeaten Miami, injury again sidelined McManus — and just when it seemed Florida State was on its way to a shocking upset.

Trailing 14-7 in the first quarter, Florida State had startled Miami — and a national TV audience — with a 100-yard kickoff return that tied it.

FSU coaches had figured about a 40-percent chance of success on a return that involved a lateral.

Fielding the ball 6 yards deep in the end zone, Ross momentarily bobbled it before moving out to the 15.

"We told Keith to come out of that end zone no matter what happened," said Bowden later. "It works better when the other side thinks you're making a wrong move."

As tacklers converged on him, Ross stopped and whipped the ball across the field to Dexter Carter, who cuddled it on the first bounce at about the 10. The freshman speedster scored, untouched.

Ross said he almost fell as he threw the lateral. Carter had practiced fielding the ball on the bounce.

On two second-quarter Schmidt field goals, FSU led 20-14.

Threatening again, Florida State faked a field goal on fourth down at the Miami 19. Kneeling to hold for the snap, McManus ran instead when he got the ball.

As he got tackled just short of a first down, McManus injured the thumb on his throwing hand.

He was out the remainder of the game.

Miami drove from the second-half kickoff to a touchdown that Testaverde ran in from the 8 and led 21-20. Soon Schmidt put FSU back up 23-21 with his third field goal.

Three minutes into the last quarter Miami regained the lead on a Testaverde touchdown pass. Soon the quick, tall quarterback ran in another and passed for a third in a 20-point burst that won it for Miami 41-23.

Despite five sacks — including noseguard Thomas Harp's three — Testaverde, much like the prior season against FSU, had hit 21 of 35 passes for 315 yards and three touchdowns. Also, he had run for two touchdowns.

"You put a quarterback down like we put him down and he's supposed to stay down," said FSU defensive back Dedrick Dodge. "Vinny didn't.

"Any other quarterback would have stayed out after he had been helped off. Vinny didn't. Any other quarterback would have run out of bounds. Vinny didn't."

On the first play of the second quarter, Testaverde had limped off with strained foot ligaments.

As he often does when an opposing player has played so well, Bowden searched out Testaverde immediately after the game to congratulate him on a great performance.

The day after that Nov. 1 game, Testaverde addressed a letter in longhand to Bowden.

Excerpts:

Sir . . . I just wanted to drop you a line to tell you that I admire and respect you a great deal. I know I would have loved to play under you.

Even though Miami won the ball game Saturday, both teams gained a great deal of respect throughout the country — and both teams are winners off and on the field!

I never wrote a letter to any coach before, but I felt I had to let you know you are a great inspiration to a lot of young men around the country, including myself, and you set great examples to follow.

Keep up the great job and good luck. . . . I'm pulling for you all the way!

Another dose of Gators and rain

The rest of the way started with a return to Columbia and another scare.

Making like Testaverde, freshman quarterback Todd Ellis passed for two early touchdowns and ran for another as South Carolina led 21-6. FSU narrowed it to 21-17 by halftime on Ferguson's 24-yard pass to Floyd and the second of two Schmidt field goals.

Bowden had made an early move. With FSU down 7-3, he replaced Peter Tom Willis, who started at quarterback, with Ferguson.

In a spectacular third quarter, Florida State scored on each of four possessions — on two runs by tailback Floyd, two more by fullback Dayne Williams.

But Ferguson's passing was a clear factor. He struck on 15 of 22 throws for 228 yards. Final score: Florida State 45, South Carolina 28.

A clear factor as Florida State closed at home with a 17-13 loss to Florida was a driving rain and a staggering sum of 15 penalties for 116 yards.

Florida led 7-0 on an 8-yard Octavius Gould run on the heels of an interception at the FSU 40. FSU cut it to 7-3 on Schmidt's 36-yard field goal. It was 10-10 at halftime as Jeff Dawson booted a 19-yard field goal and Sammie Smith countered with a 1-yard touchdown run after a 73-yard drive.

In the third quarter, Smith took a pitchout, slipped away from tacklers, and sped 52 yards to a touchdown.

But a flag had fallen. Late. On a holding penalty, the run was erased, and it stayed 10-10.

With effective passing generally shut down by the rain, FSU struggled to a 13-10 lead on Schmidt's 21-yard field goal with 3:06 left in the quarter.

But Bell — eight-for-27 and a total of 65 yards all evening — surely got off one telling pass. A game winner, it was.

Florida State had maneuvered, with its 3-point lead, to Florida's 29. On fourth and 15, a 46-yard Schmidt field-goal effort in the mud was blocked.

Taking over at their 40, the Gators drove, mainly on the hot running of Wayne Williams. On a third-and-6 play, Bell found Ricky Nattiel open in the end zone for an 18-yard touchdown pass that won it 17-13.

Florida State thought it had the play covered.

"We had a man on it — if he hadn't moved," said Bowden. "Don't know why he moved. It was like he saw something over there fluttering in the bushes, or something."

The clock showed 3:50 to go, but McManus — five-for-18 and 48 yards passing — could not connect in the heavy rain.

In that rain and mud, Florida State got just 248 yards of offense — 116 of it by Smith on 24 runs. Florida managed 201 — with 60 of it on that winning drive.

'We *should* have beat Florida'

With a 6-4-1 record, Bowden found his disappointment difficult to measure.

So many would measure it simply in terms of six straight losses to Florida.

"I thought, to be honest, that maybe 8-3 would be the worst we would do, though we started the year with so much inexperience," he said.

"I really thought we'd beat Florida. We *should* have beat Florida.

"You face the dilemma for 365 days — and you multiply that by six! Then you know the magnitude of this dilemma.

"We've got 365 days to go through this thing. If everybody didn't remind me, it would be different. But they'll remind me. Every day."

Sammie Smith battles the rain and a Gator's grip on the way to a big effort in '86.

It is the way it is.

Another day — tomorrow — is also the way it is in a game that, some say, is so much like life.

And on a Dec. 31 day in Birmingham, a few thousand Seminoles toasted a New Year.

As Indiana fell 27-13 in the All-American Bowl, the freshman who ran for 116 yards in the mud against Florida got 205 more on another bad-weather night.

"All of a sudden, Sammie Smith has become a force," said Bowden.

All of a sudden ...

All of a sudden, Florida State fans might have known where Sammie was coming from.

All of a sudden, in four swift decades that followed an 0-5 start, their Seminoles had become a force.

All of a sudden, they had gone unbeaten in a season.

All of a sudden, they were in a bowl.

All of a sudden, they were playing Florida.

Then all of a sudden, as a pressboxer screamed *"There he is!,"* Biletnikoff was wide open for that Tensi pass and they were *beating* Florida.

All of a sudden, as a dizzy Hammond came

off the bench not knowing where he was but knowing somehow where Sellers was, they were beating Florida again!

All of a sudden, along came Simmons, and they were beating Florida four straight times.

All of a sudden, they had gone unbeaten in a season again.

All of a sudden, they were beating Nebraska and Pittsburgh. Back to back.

All of a sudden, they were in the Orange Bowl. And then again.

All of a sudden, they had plodded through 5 inches of snow at Denton, Texas, and sweated through 130 degrees of heat at Lincoln, Neb., and come home like few others could have — victorious!

Then all of a sudden, they were struggling anew. Backs to the wall, the position they knew so well. Like home. Where it all began, where it all would continue.

All of a sudden, the new/old cycle of tears and laughter, of frowns and cheers, of gloom and joy.

And through it all — yesterday, tomorrow — somebody rising from the pack, all of a sudden, to lead the proud-and-defiant cry of camaraderie and home:

"FSU all the damn time!"

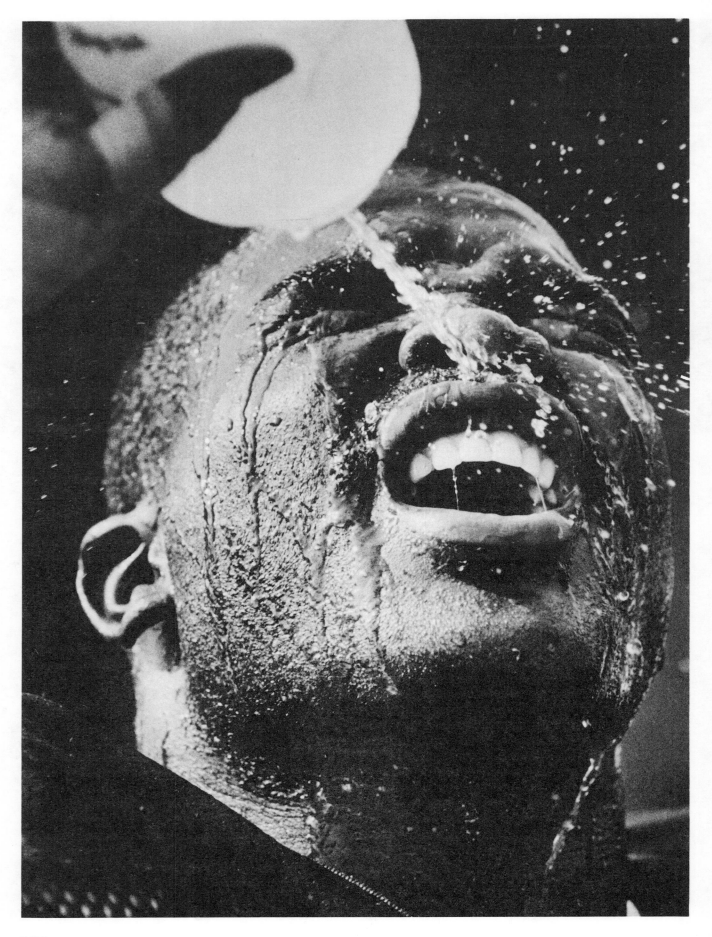

More than a game

College football, peculiarly American, is so pervasive in our society — and perhaps particularly in our Southland, which may have a greater identity with the sport than any other area.

For many of us it is a celebration, a joy, a philosophical way with coveted values, objectives and rewards. It is part of us, and a decidedly important part.

Robert Strozier, a former Florida State president, was on the staff of the University of Chicago when the school was considering the revival of the sport. He observed then that football tended to say something favorable about a university that could be said in no other way.

Yet, during his time at Florida State, he referred to football at least once as a can of worms.

Perhaps he was right on both counts.

Possibly football is indeed a mirror of life itself — sometimes a bowl of cherries, sometimes a can of worms.

But to the forever optimists, which we football fans tend to be, the positives far outweigh the negatives. We live with the game in the best of times, and die with the game in the worst of times, knowing there is always a next time, thinking so often of tomorrow and next year. Each among us knows where Florida coach Ray Graves was coming from when he said, after that stinging 3-3 tie with Florida State in 1961, "It was like a death in the family."

Imagine Abe as wide receiver

We will cite history, chapter and verse, and we will quote American presidents, so many of whom played the game or identified with it.

Woodrow Wilson: "I have always thought that it was an accepted fact football was an educational factor.... To excel personally, and collectively to win, a player must mobilize into action the following mental acts: judgment, persistency, initiative, aggressiveness, fortitude, courage, chivalry and the will to win.

Work and sweat are part of the game, as noseguard Thomas Harp illustrates. Harp, who sacked Miami's Vinny Testaverde three times in 1986, struggled to keep his weight down — also a part of the game.

Repeatedly doing so makes these acts traits of his own character."

Calvin Coolidge: "I have in my Cabinet four football guards. In fact, wherever I turn in Washington I meet with officials who once were famous players. They tell me this characteristic runs all through public life in the state, county and municipal governments."

Dwight Eisenhower: "In the midst of World War II, I was on constant lookout for natural leaders.... I noted with real satisfaction how well ex-football players seemed to have leadership qualifications, and it wasn't sentiment that made it seem so — not with names that turned out to be Bradley, Patton, Keyes, Simpson, Van Fleet, Harmon, Hobbs, Jouett, Patch, and Pritchard. Among many others, they measured up.... I believe that football, more than any other sport, tends to instill in men the feeling that victory comes through hard — almost slavish — work, team play, self-confidence, and enthusiasm that amounts to dedication."

And if this sample is not ample, be assured that enthusiasts out there are still researching possible football-related utterances and logical playing positions of Abe Lincoln and George Washington, not to mention David and, of course, Goliath.

Enthusiasts can nod in agreement to the thoughtful counsel of FSU philosopher and religion professor Leo Sandon: "As we shout and scream, it might be wise to remember that the fortunes of the season are of something less than ultimate importance."

But, as Sandon also says, football in our land has come to represent "the here and the now."

And the here and the now — the agony and the ecstasy, as the TV-network people say — can *seem* ultimate indeed. Ask the Seminoles after four straight victories over Florida; this ecstasy was *never* going to end! Ask the Seminoles, too, after six straight losses to Florida; this agony was *never* going to end!

Indeed, we fans need reminders that the agony and ecstasy are not forever with us.

In college town after college town — in Gainesville and Tuscaloosa and Stillwater and Austin and Tallahassee, not to forget Slippery Rock — football is a continuous and con-

suming tie that binds, as Strozier suggested, like no other. The swimmers and golfers and cross-country runners leave, and when they return it is to the football games — to the one sport that keeps them in touch with their university.

Football is indeed the unifying force that generates more interest — and contributions — from supporters than would otherwise be possible. Perhaps it should not be that way, but it is that way — so much like life.

A matter of priorities

Bobby Bowden has spoken of the reality, and placed it in perspective for himself, and surely millions of others.

"Football figures in a way of life — it is a microcosm of life, full of battles and full of goals," said the coach. "Full of laws, and full of penalties that can get you into trouble if you don't abide by 'em.

"There are a lot of teaching experiences, learning experiences in football that are so valuable. A lot of pressure that makes a young man better able to compete in life."

In Bowden's expressed priorities, God comes first, followed by family, country, then football.

There was an interesting time in Bowden's young life, so steeped in football, when the game was forbidden to him. A high-school tailback in the old single wing, he came down with rheumatic fever. For a full year, he lay flat on his back.

The family doctor told him he could never play football again.

"And that is why," recalled Bowden, "we changed doctors."

Remarkably, he played again.

Once described as a man who always sees the blue in the sky and the green in the grass, Bowden considerably personifies the football optimist, and the dreamers who see a better tomorrow in a good today.

Such is an integral aspect of the bond.

And an integral aspect of the old-school tie, for so many, are the individuals who have provided favorable continuity. Alumni/supporters have seen familiar blue in the sky and green in the grass of Florida State through such men as Don Fauls, trainer for 29 seasons . . . Claude Thigpen, popular tickets manager for more than 25 years . . . Billy Smith, who for 22 years of the first 40 was Mr. Reli-

A game like no other: "Over yonder now they're gathering the balloons — the garnet ones, the gold ones — to let loose into the heavens."

able as the state patrolman in charge of team security . . . Charley Durbin, the splendid jack-of-all-trades through 39 of the first 40 . . . and, of course, Bob Harbison, for 37 years the assistant who served seven head coaches so well.

An extraordinary 40 years

So very high, in an elite football class, stood the Seminoles after four decades.

Among all teams, in an NCAA study, Florida State ranked No. 26 in accomplishment based on won-lost percentage over the past 50 years.

Out of 422 games, the Seminoles had won 240, lost 166, tied 16, a .588 percentage. By comparison, Miami was 30th (293-216-10 — .574) and Florida 33rd (283-216-21 — .564).

Moreover, for all time, Florida State had played in more bowl games (16) and won a higher percentage (7-7-2 for .500) than Florida had in 80 years (7-8 for .467) and Miami in 61 seasons (5-7 for .417).

Such was, and is, the garnet glory of the Seminoles.

"I would not think there is a team in the country with a more colorful football history than Florida State," said Darrell Mudra. He was head coach only two years, but it takes not so much time around the school to know that the first 40 seasons of football were more extraordinary — more vivid and spectacular — than many schools would ever know.

In 1987 Mudra, at Northern Iowa, and Bowden were the only ones among FSU's first eight coaches who were still head coaches. Three were retired: Ed Williamson and Don Veller in Tallahassee, Tom Nugent at Indian Harbour Beach. Bill Peterson was in Orlando working part time for the FSU Foundation, with plans for an early move back to Tallahassee. Perry Moss, with a permanent home in Orlando, was an assistant coach with Central Florida. Larry Jones was an assistant athletic director at Louisiana State.

During the ups and downs of these men, the game — on balance — served Florida State extraordinarily well.

"Intercollegiate football has brought recognition that the university could not have purchased with 30 public-relations employees working around the clock," said FSU President Bernie Sliger after the conclusion of the first 40 years.

"Properly policed and controlled, the game can be a very positive force in the academic enhancement of a university.

"There is ample evidence that it has in-creased our enrollment significantly. It has been important to our private fundraising for academic matters.

"It does bring friends, alumni, faculty, staff and students together in a way nothing else does."

And in a way few things else have, the engrossing history of Florida State football has drawn my attention.

More than 350 games over more than 34 seasons. From San Diego to Boston, from the searing heat of Lincoln, Neb., on a September day to the chilling snow of Denton, Texas, on a November afternoon.

Through victory and defeat — and through defeats that seemed like victories, and victories like defeats. Through ties celebrated as triumphs, and ties that wrought mass depression.

Driving the 140 miles to Gainesville and, so often, the 940 miles back.

The distances are, of course, the same for Florida fans coming to Tallahassee. But the fortunes of football have not provided them with a proportionate number of long drives home.

And after six straight, they tended to feel as Florida State fans did when they started yawning after four straight over the Gators.

Fred Abbott had it right.

"We almost live and die to play Florida State," said the Gator linebacker in 1971.

It is indeed a live-and-die game, as games go. Only when one rival dominates is it less. The familiar shoe on the other foot has the effect of a shoe strategically placed elsewhere. One quickly becomes newly aware.

Such is our nature as the cycle of ecstasy and agony rolls on, sometimes unevenly.

So many stories to tell

Sometimes uneven, too, is the process of putting together a book.

If one counts 422 games over 40 years, surely there were more than 5,000 young men who wore the uniforms on the practice field or playing field. You may be certain there were more than 5,000 stories, most of them good stories. And if there is a wish as these words dwindle down, it is that more stories of more people might have been told, and more logical pictures run.

This is a book that we tried to make better, more readable than most of its sort, with what we hope were insightful and appealing stories of people and circumstances. This is a book that, most probably, never would have seen print without the interest of Carrol Dadisman, publisher of the Tallahassee Democrat, who proposed that the newspaper publish it. This is a book that would not be nearly what it is without the considerable work of two Democrat colleagues — Ron Hartung and Gerald Ensley. Many others gave unstinting assistance.

It is done, and if there is no cause for dancing in the street, there may be sufficient motivation for a step or two — albeit a waltz — in a backroom somewhere. The greater joy of writing a book, clearly, is in having finished it.

But, ah, there's joy now, too, in a deep-down stirring — such a good twinge of anticipation in one's belly — as the excitement and the hope of the new season come.

It is the here and the now.

And one sees anew the swirl of the pompons, the lightning grace of Biletnikoff, the rifle that was Jordan's right arm and the cannon that was Stark's left foot. Listen now, and you can hear the beat of the drums, the rolling thunder of Simmons, the laments of Veller and the laughter of Bowden, plus those infernal tambourines of Sol Carrol (bless you, Sol).

It is the coming of our festival — our parade, our hoedown, our jamboree.

Our here and now.

Oh, it is such a long, long way from January to September, when the festival comes anew, with all its sweetness of honey — and the hibernating bears of football again come alive!

One more time.

The joy of the game

If there are those who do not quite know what the excitement is all about, perhaps we should dispatch missionaries.

Understand, and understand well, that the pleasure of football is considerably derived from the association with a particular team.

The joy of the game is interwoven in the joy of people in their enduring battle against the elements.

Florida State's game has seemed so special to so many because those elements, over 40 years, have often been extreme. And because those who identify with the school — for one reason or another, or no particular reason at all — perceive it as the place of their roots. Of camaraderie, and of home.

A sense of place comes, here and now, from over there beyond the practice field — from among those trees with leaves starting to turn. Such a rumble of excitement — the

warm-up strains of the Marching Chiefs preparing for the new season.

And one hears now the noise of popping pads, the hoarse cry of a coach demanding *on*. And on and on and on.

Over yonder now they're gathering the balloons — the garnet ones, the gold ones — to let loose into the heavens.

It is time, soon, for the team to run out of the tunnel as waves of noise pound from a colorful sea. As Renegades rears and chafes for the battle. As Chief Osceola slams the challenging 10-foot spear there on the 50-yard line. As the crowd is overwhelmed by its own cheering.

It is the advent of garnet glory.

One more time.

Personifying the best in a Florida State football tradition of persistence, Roger Overby (88) played not so much until his senior year. Then he became a surprising star who caught three touchdown passes against Florida in his last regular-season game.

192

Return Trip to Hogtown

In 1969, during the week of the FSU-Florida game in Gainesville, I wrote a Tallahassee Democrat column titled "Origin of the Species."

A kind of rainy-day, tongue-in-cheek narrative, the column stemmed from information in Florida's press guide on the roots of the Gators' nickname.

In later years, the information was deleted from that press guide. And it may have been that not all Florida fans were totally enchanted with the column, or with attention to the historical fact that Gainesville was once Hogtown.

For a number of years, the piece was reprinted in the Democrat during the week of the game between the rivals.

Florida State fans came to call it "The Hogtown Column." Over following years I received far more requests for copies of this column than any other, but maybe not so many from Gainesville.

Listen, my children, and you shall hear . . . of the origin of the reptilian species known as gator — and, yea, more.

There was this little seminary, which is a kind of school, that was first in Ocala and then in Lake City, and it must have been that nobody wanted it.

And finally they moved it to Hogtown, which some say was logical enough. They changed Hogtown's name to Gainesville, and the seminary's name to University of Florida — and, if you doubt that as the gospel, go look it up and you will find I speak not with forked tongue.

Well, before this seminary moved to Hogtown, which was in 1905, it was playing football, or trying to play, but though UF traces its beginning back to Ocala in 1853, it does not trace its football back beyond 1905 when it moved to Hogtown. Not that anyone could really blame 'em for disowning the football part.

But Alabama, Georgia Tech, Georgia and some others trace that football back. They count those games, and so does the Southeastern Conference in its record book. So you have such as their series standings reading one thing in Athens, and another thing in Hogtown.

Way back yonder, when the students got to Hogtown, they were nameless ones, and they even went at that football without a name.

There lived in the village at that time a merchant who purveyed sarsaparilla and cathartics to the students, and often they gathered there. And he, being a benevolent pill-pusher, took their money and smiled upon them.

His name was Phillip Miller, and when it came time to send his own son to a university, to study law, he sent him to the University of Virginia, with the money he had graciously accepted from the students. The son's name was Austin.

There was this time Phillip went to visit his son in Charlottesville, and Austin kindly ask him how things were in Hogtown. He say they were tolerable, if barely, because he is making money selling sarsaparilla and cathartics to students of the ex-seminary, which is still trying to play football.

And Phillip say son, this is a football team that has no name, much less any pennants — which I could sell if we had some. Austin say, old dad, you really ought to have some pennants so you could sell 'em. But whoever heard of a pennant without Bulldogs or Seminoles on it, or something?

And the son say, let us give them a name. Whereupon he did. He gave them the name The Alligators, and old pop went right out, right there in Charlottesville, to this firm that made pennants and got 'em to print up a mess of 'em with The Alligators printed on 'em. They had a heckuva time finding a picture of an alligator to do the artwork by, but finally they found one in the library of the University of Virginia.

And, if you don't think that a true fact, look it up, too. It's right there, page 43, of the 1969 Gator football handbook. . . . Not in such ingenious wording, of course, but it is there.

"I had no idea it would stick, or even be popular with the student body," a prosperous Austin Miller was quoted in 1948.

The first shipment of pennants, he recalled, included blue banners, 3 by 6 feet, showing a large orange alligator.

Those Hogtown boys loved it, and one say, go gator, and the others brightly join in and say, go gator, too.

But that gator don't go nowhere much. It was 1925 before he won as many as eight games, and then only with the help of such well-backgrounded Tallahassee folks as Rainey Cawthon — who is about as good a gator as you will find because it was he who played a big hand in getting the Florida State Seminoles on their way, bulldozing the drive to build Campbell Stadium.

Anyhow, the gator flops along, winning some but losing more, getting into the Southeastern Conference in 1935, debuting 3-7 and following up 4-6, 4-7, 4-6-1 — and not having a winning season in the league until 1944, when it goes 4-3, including 36-6 over Mayport Naval Air Station and 26-20 over Jacksonville Naval Air Station. Following year, he lose to the U.S. Amphibs 12-0.

Meanwhile, the gator say he gotta have a rival, like everybody else, and so he think up Georgia, which Georgia ain't thinking at all. Because Georgia got this thing going with Georgia Tech, not to mention Alabama and Auburn. And besides it is no fun having a rival you beat like 75-0 in 1942, not to mention 51-0 in 1968, and 38-12, 34-0, 33-14 and 34-6 in 1944, 1945, 1946 and 1947.

But everybody gotta have somebody, and the gator say, "Georgia, you it."

Well, about this time, something big is going on over in Tallahassee. Florida State College for Women, right after World War II, has gone coed but not yet the school in Hogtown, which ain't quite up on the birds and the bees.

They change FSCW's name to Tallahassee Branch of the University of Florida, or something like that, and them proud Seminoles out there, as they form their first football team, say we ain't having none of that stuff.

So they make the name Florida State University and, you know something, by 1950 the Seminoles have an unbeaten, untied team, and so what if it was against Troy State, Randolph Macon, Howard, Newberry, Sewanee, Stetson, Mississippi College and Tampa? The gator in the same year is bellowing about beating The Citadel 7-3 in an opener.

But the gator sense something going on in Tallahassee and he say, hmmmm, what's going on over there?

Along about then, he say, "Maybe girls ain't so bad, and maybe them Seminoles know something we don't know about."

So the gator goes coed, too, but only a little at first. The gator, he is so cautious.

But then, suddenly, he starts floundering around like mad, and he win some games, which he oughta been winning all along. But, to this day, he ain't won no Southeastern Conference title or gone unbeaten. He does, however, start getting off his fat haunches.

And now everything the Seminoles do over here, the gator watch. The gator say a lot of time they ain't doing right over here, and he get himself members of the Board of Regents to serve on his athletic boards for several years so they can tell 'em all about them bad old Seminoles and make 'em feel sorry for old gator, poor little rich boy that he is. But some things they see the Seminoles doing they don't bother to go to the athletic-board regents with; they just copy it, and say nothing to nobody.

So now that big gator think he is something — and he is really something. In forthwith recognition thereof, we will spell him with a capital letter, like Gator. It is about time he is something.

It was all a grand plan of the Seminoles starting back about 1947. They knew to play football you have to have a name, so right away they picked out the grand name Seminoles. They know, too, to play football you got to have a big rival. But there wasn't one around. So they had to make one. And they gigged the Gator, gigged him and gigged him, until they made a worthwhile rival out of him.

And, now, what we gonna do with him?

Coach Harbison's All-Time Team

Defense

Linebacker: PAUL PIUROWSKI
Linebacker: DICK HERMANN
Outside linebacker: WILLIE JONES
Outside linebacker: MIKE BLATT
Defensive end: ROBERT McEACHERN
Defensive end: MARK MACEK
Nose tackle: RON SIMMONS
Weak cornerback: BOBBY BUTLER
Strong cornerback: JAMES THOMAS
Strong safety: LEE NELSON
Free safety: WALT SUMNER

Offense

Wide receiver: FRED BILETNIKOFF
Wide receiver: RON SELLERS
Split tackle: KEN LANIER
Split guard: JAMIE DUKES
Center: ALLEN DEES
Strong guard: DEL WILLIAMS
Strong tackle: BILLY RHODES
Tight end: ZEKE MOWATT
Quarterback: KIM HAMMOND
Tailback: LARRY KEY
Fullback: FRED PICKARD — or JACK ESPENSHIP or KEITH KINDERMAN.

Kicking

Punter: ROHN STARK
Place-kicker: DEREK SCHMIDT
Kickoffs: BILL CAPECE

Bob Harbison considered the suggestion that he select an all-time team.

"What are you going to base it on?" he asked, pondering all the changes in the game.

Associated with Florida State football for 37 of its first 40 years, almost exclusively as a line coach (offense and defense), Harbison was a witness to the revolutionary as well as the evolutionary in styles and rules.

Some stars of yesterday would not play in a differing formation, and some stars of today would be ill-equipped for the cockeyed-T and 'for both-ways play.

Harbison decided to pick an all-time team that would line up according to 1987 specifications.

The all-time defense

On defense he would place:

Paul Piurowski and Dick Hermann at linebackers.

Willie Jones and Mike Blatt at outside linebackers.

Robert McEachern and Mark Macek at defensive ends.

Ron Simmons at nose tackle.

Bobby Butler (weak corner), James Thomas (strong corner), Lee Nelson (strong safety) and Walt Sumner (free safety) in the secondary.

"This is a modern defense, where what used to be ends are now outside linebackers, and what used to be tackles are now ends.

"A guy like Mike Blatt, playing to the strong side, could cover a tight end all over the field — just take that tight end out of the game. Plus, he was a fine pass rusher. At the other end, the split side, you got Willie Jones, who can play like a son-of-a-bleep and is going to drive you absolutely nuts over there.

"Now a guy like Macek at tackle — he did it against Oklahoma and people like that. You give people extra points for playing well against the big boys. A lot of 'em can play good against those others.

"McEachern was one of the best pass rushers I ever saw out there. A real quick tackle, he made play after play against Georgia Tech one day.

"You line up Dick Hermann as a split-side linebacker — you want a guy there with a lot of speed, which he had. At the strong side, where the power plays come, a guy like Piurowski is going to do just fine.

"Now at nose tackle, nobody but Simmons. Instrumental in turning the whole damn program around — devastating, you know. So strong, he just ate people up.

"Butler was a smart, quick cornerback who could do whatever you needed him to do. Really good on one-on-one coverage, and he proved himself in the NFL.

"Thomas, like Butler, could just do it all — block kicks, anything. Remember the two field goals he blocked in succession against Louisville in the first game he ever played? Probably saved us from one of the most embarrassing losses ever. He had the size and strength that made him a great tackler. Here's one that could really play with the big boys, as he did with the Steelers on their championship teams.

"Nelson was just exceptionally tough. He never played on a good team at Florida State, never got the recognition. And it surprised everybody that he played so long with the Cardinals in the NFL. He had a whole lot of football knowledge, too.

"Sumner was pretty special — tough, fast enough, and I never will forget how he covered Houston's Elmo Wright one on one in 1968. I won't ever forget the punt return against Alabama for a touchdown either. In all his time, Bear Bryant never had more than three or four punts run back on him for touchdowns, I think, and Sumner got one."

The all-time offense

On offense, Harbison picked:
Fred Biletnikoff and Ron Sellers as wide receivers.
Ken Lanier at split tackle.
Jamie Dukes at split guard.
Allen Dees at center.
Del Williams at strong guard.
Billy Rhodes at strong tackle.
Zeke Mowatt at tight end.
Kim Hammond at quarterback.
Larry Key at tailback.

Bob Harbison

And Fred Pickard — or Jack Espenship or Keith Kinderman — at fullback.

"Biletnikoff — all he could do was catch the ball," said Harbison. "It was like he was built for that position. When you bogged down, he was your first down, and he may have helped drive Hootie Ingram out of coaching when he was in charge of Georgia's secondary. He might have been just about the first receiver that made college coaches see you could win with the passing game.

"He worked hard at it, understood what you were trying to do — and he could do it! But how the hell did he do it? It was hard to tell. It seemed like sometimes he would go up for the ball, and just hang there in the air."

Sellers differed from Biletnikoff.

"He was more of an all-the-way type," said Harbison. "I thought Ron Sellers was simply the best college receiver I ever saw.

"Most of the time, one guy covering him didn't have a chance. His hands were fantastic. If he could touch the ball, he had it. I don't remember him ever dropping a pass."

Harbison recalled that Lanier was a noseguard when he came to Florida State in the same freshman class as Simmons.

"There was no way he was going to beat Simmons out," said Harbison. "But we put him at a spot (split tackle) where we didn't have to worry about it for a long while. He was really an intelligent player — a good athlete who could do the job.

"The big pass rusher comes at that split tackle. For a righthanded passer, it's a blind spot — an area where Lawrence Taylor, and people like that, come at you. Your split tackle better be able to take that kind of thing away. Lanier could. He was very fluid, and he adjusted so naturally to it."

Rhodes, at the other offensive tackle, was of a different breed from most, Harbison suggests.

"Well, they say you can tell in a locker room, how a guy acts, whether he plays offense or defense," said Harbison. "Like defensive players, you know, are supposed to throw things around. But you couldn't tell Rhodes.

"Now he could get nasty out there. His toughness was really unusual. He was one of those who never cared how rough it was. Rhodes loved a good fight. Any time."

Harbison places Dukes, at split guard, alongside Lanier.

"I know Jamie never played split guard, but I don't think he can beat out Del Williams at strong guard," he said.

"Dukes was another highly intelligent player. He could run, pull out and lead plays. And he could play from the start. He started 48 straight games. That was more than anybody we ever had out there.

"Del was awfully strong, awfully good. He proved he could hold his own with the best of the pros. So powerful and such a competitor. He had more raw power, one on one, than any we've had."

Quickness, intelligence and good height were factors in his choice of Dees at center.

"He was probably the quickest center they ever had," said Harbison. "And with that plain quickness, he had enough speed to go out on screens and lead plays. He could do all the things you needed a center to do, and was a lanky type that I always liked at center. The quarterback didn't have to squat down to get the ball."

Harbison views Mowatt as the best-blocking lineman he ever saw at Florida State.

"When we played Pitt, he knocked Hugh Green's butt all over that field," he recalled. "Zeke was just like a tractor, churning right over 'em."

Harbison sees Hammond as the quarterback one would want for a team that had a lot.

"A smart guy who will take full advantage of the whole team, yet talented enough," said Harbison, explaining his quarterback choice. "You're not relying on him to carry the team."

Harbison picks the running backs, too, in a special context — according to whether the choice is a split backfield or one that includes elements of the I-formation.

"But Key is a choice, regardless," he said.

"If you're going with split backs — where the other is, in effect, a tailback, too — I'm going with Pickard.

"But, now if you're going with the I-formation and looking for the big fullback who can block, I'm thinking a big tough guy who can also catch passes, like Jack Espenship or Keith Kinderman."

In his praise of Key, Harbison is not sparing.

"If things were not going good, his ball carrying was an inspiration," he said. "I think he was a lot like that guy (Walter Payton) with the Bears.

"I swear — when Key did his thing, other guys on the team would say, 'Well, hell, we oughta help him out a little bit.' And they would.

"And the best run I ever saw in football was on the goal line in one of our practices. Key ran, I swear, over everybody — twice! It was a run that sure looked like he did.

"When he bounced off a guy, going now in another direction, he would kind of ricochet off. Such great balance. And that's why they called him 'Ricochet Rabbit.'

"Key was one you weren't going to tackle with no fingernail."

Pickard was lots like Key — relatively short, durable, great balance.

"He would seem to hit a pile of guys," said Harbison, "and it was like he would go over the top of 'em, run down the other side, and keep going.

"Espenship and Kinderman — they were about halfway mean. Big people, they were going to go in there and knock somebody down. Neither was afraid of any kind of contact. Now, everybody likes to carry the ball, and they could carry it a lot better than most. But here were two, I think, that had just as soon block as run. Blocking sure wasn't going to bother them at all, you know?"

In addition to giving points for playing well against the big boys, Harbison also measured character. "You're talking about some class people," he said, allowing for a possible exception here and maybe there.

The all-time kicking team

Harbison's kickers were:
Rohn Stark (punts).
Derek Schmidt (place kicks).
Bill Capece (kickoffs).

At the start of the 1987 season, Schmidt, with his 277 points, had a chance to check in as college football's leading scorer of all time. His 277 points were 91 short of the four-year record of former Arizona State kicker Luis Zendejas.

"It sticks in my mind, that game at Miami when we blew 'em out 38-3," said Harbison. "Well, at halftime we were struggling, and nobody has anything — except Schmidt, who has kicked three field goals, including one from 54 yards, to put us ahead 9-0.

"Kickers can make a big difference. He put us in position to do it like we did."

Harbison suggests that Stark may have been the college game's best punter ever.

"I never saw Ray Guy when he was at Southern Mississippi, but I don't know if anyone else would even be a rival," said Harbison.

"I don't know how anyone could beat Stark. He was just amazing. With him around, your defense never started in a bad position."

They Called Him Charley Driver

Charley Durbin, in many ways, typifies the football enthusiast, the believer.

And so especially the Florida State football believers, many of whom never attended the school, or perhaps played the game little or not at all.

Reared around the tobacco fields not far from Tallahassee, he never went to college — but he went to the infantry, and once said that after working in tobacco, he had no problem at all with the infantry.

Filling a varied Florida State role as cinematographer, equipment supervisor and bus driver, he saw more football games of those first 40 years — virtually all except the first-year ones of 1947 — than any other person.

He drove FSU buses nearly 2 million miles, drove them hard, and for all of that received only two speeding tickets — "both of which came in the great state of Georgia."

He would drive the football team to Gainesville, and never see a minute of the game — staying beside his bus, guarding it, making sure of no flat tires or no sand in the gas tanks when those players got ready to go home.

Charley Durbin

The coaches were always the authority, but still he never tattled on players for smoking or the like.

Durbin had his way, though.

Once, after the last game of a basketball season during the early days of Coach Bud Kennedy, he detected players taking beer on the bus. "Coach Kennedy wouldn't want you to do that," said Durbin. That was all he said. But on the return trip from Macon, Ga., when those players came up and whispered to him for a rest stop, Durbin was silent — and drove on.

On another occasion, athletes were moving around on the rolling bus, and Durbin advised them that could be dangerous. When there was no positive response, Durbin a few minutes later abruptly hit his brakes. As the players struggled off the floor, Durbin said: "Excuse me!"

A man for all coaches

Coaches made many requests of him, and he always obliged. "Never turned one down," he said, matter-of-factly. "No way I would do that."

He never knew any hours. Four times, in the old days, he drove buses to Omaha and back for the College World Series.

"Some people think this is an eight-hours-a-day business, but in athletics there ain't no such thing," said Durbin. "Never has been. Never will be.

"But if you enjoy what you are doing, you are pretty well OK."

Bill Peterson used to ask him to go to his home, at odd hours and on Sundays, to film San Diego Chargers games off TV.

"He'd even give me a Coca-Cola every now and then," cracked Durbin, laughing.

"Coach Pete filmed everything, except sometimes we would fake it. On occasion, he used to climb to the top of that tower where I was and tell me to just pretend I was filming it — said the players went at it harder if they thought it was being filmed."

Getting by with little

Durbin's heavy involvement in films started in Peterson's first year.

In a move that seems typical of innovative Florida State moves with limited resources,

Athletic Director Vaughn Mancha bought normally expensive equipment to process films. "He got it for near-about nothing from the government's war-surplus stuff," recalled Durbin in 1987, "and we're still using it."

Durbin remembered coaches doing lots with little.

"Coach Pete never had a defensive line really big enough to play, but he did so much with what he had," said Durbin. "I often think about the size some teams had, compared to what we played with back then."

With filming all those practices over the years, Durbin became most knowledgeable about the game.

Once a heralded linebacker enrolled. After a few days, Durbin quietly observed to a friend: "If he's a linebacker, the woods are full of them." Pretty soon, the touted one indeed proved himself not much of a player, and no linebacker at all.

Two linebackers of the early Bowden era, Paul Piurowski and Reggie Herring, were among his favorites.

"I don't think coaches get 'em that way," he said of the two. "I just think they come here that way — ready to play.

"All you had to do was sling those gates open — and they'd go get it. So often, the other team's best just wasn't good enough against people like them — people like Fred Pickard, Scott Warren and Larry Key."

A special person

Durbin echoed Coyle Moore on his assessment of Bobby Bowden as a coach much suited to Florida State people.

"Not to take anything away from any of them, but they don't come no better than Coach Bowden — as far as this community, this area is concerned," he said.

In 1979, Durbin received a letter from Hugh Durham, the Georgia basketball coach who for so long had been at Florida State as a player and coach.

"You are the most loyal, most competent, most honest and hardest worker," Durham wrote in part, "that has been associated with the Florida State athletic department. You are a special person."

Looking at the letter some time later, Durbin said: "Ain't that something!"

Indeed, as Durham indicated, the man some athletes came to call Charley Driver was something — something special. Durbin became much the epitome of the diligent effort and spirit that elevated a school above the pack. And he was among those who assisted greatly in spectacular accomplishment in a remarkably short time.

All-Time Lettermen

A

Abraira, Phillip, 1967, 68, 69
Adams, Hugh, 1949, 50
Adams, Robert, 1978, 80
Allen, Billy, 1981, 82, 83, 84
Allen, Glenn, 1949
Allen, Greg, 1981, 82, 83, 84
Allen, Mike, 1972, 73, 74
Amman, Richard, 1969, 70, 71
Anderson, Bob, 1973
Anderson, Bobby, 1971, 72, 73
Andrews, Paul, 1959, 60, 61
Anthony, Terry, 1986
Arnold, Jim, 1950, 51, 56, 57
Arnold, Phil, 1971, 72, 73
Ashley, Tracy, 1981, 82, 83
Ashmore, Robert, 1969, 70, 71
Askin, Ahmet, 1972, 73
Avezzano, Joe, 1963, 64, 65

B

Baggett, Leo, 1954, 55, 56, 58
Bagnell, Clare (Bud), 1956, 57, 58, 59
Bailey, Tom, 1968, 69, 70
Bailey, Winfred, 1962, 63, 64
Baker, Sam, 1950
Banakas, Chris, 1947, 48, 49
Barber, Bob, 1953, 54
Barco, Barry, 1983, 84, 85
Barnes, Mike, 1976, 77
Barnes, Troy, 1954, 55, 56, 57
Barnes, Wendell, 1947
Barwick, Parrish, 1982, 84, 85, 86
Bass, Theron, 1968, 69, 70
Battaglia, Carmen, 1955, 56, 57, 58
Beckman, Ed, 1973, 74, 75, 76
Bengston, Brian, 1970
Benner, Wayne, 1950, 51
Benson, Joe, 1966, 67, 68
Berry, Louis, 1983, 84, 85, 86
Beville, Steve, 1969
Bibent, Maury, 1963, 64, 65
Bickford, Roy, 1959, 60, 61
Bigbie, Abner, 1958, 59, 60
Biletnikoff, Fred, 1962, 63, 64
Bisbee, Hamilton, 1955, 56, 57
Bishop, William, 1947
Black, Jimmy, 1973, 74, 76
Blankenship, Buddy, 1965
Blatt, Mike, 1965, 66, 67
Blazovich, Mike, 1960, 61, 62
Bloodworth, Steve, 1983
Bonasorte, Monk, 1977, 78, 79, 80
Booth, Charles, Jr., 1951, 52, 53
Boris, Frederick, 1947
Bowden, Jeff, 1981, 82
Boyer, George, 1952, 53, 56, 57
Bradley, Preston, 1950, 51
Braggins, David, 1965, 66
Brannon, Tom, 1979, 80, 81
Bratton, Steve, 1970, 71, 72, 73
Bright, Leon, 1974, 75, 76
Bringger, Harry, 1949, 50, 51, 52
Brinkley, Larry, 1961, 62, 63
Brown, Bill, 1955, 56, 57, 58
Brown, Charlie, 1951, 52
Brown, Mack, 1972, 73
Brown, John, 1986
Brown, Tommy, 1950, 51, 52
Browning, Bob, 1947, 48
Brownlee, Roger, 1981, 82
Bruner, Jerry, 1961, 62, 63
Bryant, Buddy, 1947, 50, 53
Bryant, Phillip, 1985
Bugar, Mike, 1965, 67, 68

Burkhardt, Bill, 1966
Burnett, Ken, 1980, 81, 82
Burt, Bobby, 1968
Burton, Clint, 1966, 67, 68
Butler, Bobby, 1977, 78, 79, 80

C

Cahoon, Phil, 1973, 74
Calhoun, Charles, 1961, 62, 63
Campbell, Allen Dale, 1981, 82
Campbell, Bill, 1965, 66
Campbell, Curt, 1950, 51, 52
Camps, Joe, 1974, 75, 76
Capece, Bill, 1977, 78, 79, 80
Cappelen, Davy, 1976, 77, 78, 79
Cappleman, Bill, 1968, 69
Carnes, George, 1952
Carballo, Manny, 1982
Carolla, Phil, 1986
Carreker, Alphonso, 1980, 81, 82, 83
Carrell, Duane, 1969, 70, 71
Carter, Aaron, 1974, 75, 76, 77
Carter, Dexter, 1986
Carter, Keith, 1986
Carter, Pat, 1984, 85, 86
Carter, Walter, 1976, 77, 78, 79
Carter, Wes, 1947
Causey, Jim, 1962, 63
Caven, Jay, 1976, 77
Chaudron, Ralph, 1947, 48, 49
Chavers, Lenny, 1981, 83, 84, 85
Cherry, Gator, 1976, 77
Cheshire, Bill, 1967, 68
Childers, Sam, 1978, 79, 80, 81
Cicalese, Pat, 1984
Clark, Ed, 1985
Clayton, Harvey, 1980, 81, 82
Coffield, Randy, 1973, 74, 75
Coggin, Redus, 1980, 81, 82
Coker, Kirk, 1984, 85
Coleman, Jerry, 1981, 82
Coleman, Jug, 1948
Collier, Danny, 1980
Cone, Ken, 1959, 60
Conrad, Harold, 1947
Conway, Pat, 1964, 65, 66
Cooper, Burt, 1972, 73, 74
Coppess, Ron, 1974
Corcoran, Dan, 1976
Corral, Kent, 1970, 71
Corso, Lee, 1953, 54, 55, 56
Costello, Jim, 1947
Coursey, Jarvis, 1978, 79, 80, 81
Cox, Billy, 1966, 67, 68
Cox, Gene, 1955
Craig, John, 1954, 55, 57, 58
Crenshaw, Bob, 1952, 53, 54, 55
Crona, Joe, 1947, 48
Crowe, John, 1966, 67, 68
Cullom, Bill, 1954
Curchin, Jeff, 1968, 69

D

D'Alessandro, George, 1963, 64, 65
Daly, Bill, 1961, 62, 63
Dane, Doug, 1975, 76, 77
Daniel, Jim, 1959, 60, 61
Daniels, Dan, 1971
Darsey, Bruce, 1960, 61, 62
Davis, Bo, 1958
Davis, Bob, 1983
Davis, Brian, 1985, 86
Davis, Darish, 1981, 82
Davis, Ed, 1971, 72, 73
Davis, George, 1969
Davis, Lemuel, 1947

Davison, Mike, 1972, 73, 74
Dawkins, Bill, 1948, 49, 50, 51
Dawson, Bill, 1962, 63, 64
Dawson, Rhett, 1969, 70, 71
DeCosmo, James, 1947
Dees, Allen, 1970, 71, 72
DeFrancesco, Frank, 1960, 61
DeMaria, John, Jr., 1970, 71, 72, 73
Dennis, Wendell, 1950
Denson, Dwayne, 1984
Dilsaver, Ed, 1947
Dimare, Scott, 1986
Dobosz, Stan, 1952, 53, 56, 57
Dodge, Dedrick, 1986
Donatelli, Donald, 1959, 60, 61
Dowell, J.D. 1983, 84
Downey, Joe, 1972, 73, 74
Driver, Bill, 1950, 51, 52
Duckworth, Bob, 1949
Dukes, Jamie, 1982, 83, 84, 85
Duley, Bill, 1975, 76, 77

E

Eaford, John, 1984, 86
Eagerton, Terry, 1967, 68
Eason, Chuck, 1966, 67, 68
Edwards, Jack, 1962, 63, 64
Ehler, Howard, 1963, 64, 65
Elam, Bobby, 1972, 73
Elliot, Chuck, 1966, 67, 68
Elliot, Robert, 1955, 56
Espenship, Jack, 1958, 59
Eubanks, Norman, 1948, 49, 50
Everett, Jimmy, 1972, 73, 74, 75

F

Falvo, Tony, 1974, 75
Feamster, Tom, 1954, 55
Feely, Eddie, 1960, 61, 62
Fenner, Lane, 1966, 67
Fenwick, Jack, 1966, 67, 68
Fergers, Bob, 1947
Ferguson, Charles, 1978
Ferguson, Chip, 1985, 86
Fick, Happy, 1960
Filchock, John, 1948
Fiore, Dano, 1971
Fiveash, Bobby, 1951, 52, 53
Flasher, Tim, 1984
Flowers, Jackie, 1976, 77, 78, 79
Floyd, Don, 1962, 63, 64
Floyd, Victor, 1985, 86
Fontes, Frank, 1970, 71
Fotjik, Brad, 1982, 83
Fountain, Bob, 1956, 57, 58
Fox, Ed, 1948
Foy, Walter, 1948, 49
Fucarino, Dan, 1975
Futch, Garry, 1979, 80, 81
Futch, Greg, 1977, 78, 79 80

G

Gabbard, Steve, 1985, 86
Gainer, Herb, 1984, 85, 86
Gardner, Jeff, 1973, 74, 75
Garvin, Terry, 1964, 65
Gavin, Stan, 1982
Gaydos, Kent, 1969, 70, 71
Giardino, Wayne, 1964, 65, 66
Gibbs, Shane, 1970, 71, 72
Gibson, Vince, 1954, 55
Gilberg, Leonard, 1947
Gilbert, James, 1978, 79, 80, 81
Gildea, Steve, 1968, 69, 70
Gilman, Brent, 1968, 69
Gladden, Don, 1950
Glass, Chip, 1966, 67, 68

Glass, Mike, 1970, 71, 72
Glisson, Guy, 1969, 70, 71
Glosson, Doug, 1973
Goldsmith, Joe, 1972, 73, 74
Good, Mike, 1976, 77, 78, 79
Graganella, Jim, 1983
Graham, Billy, 1953, 54
Graham, Jerry, 1956, 57, 58
Grant, Donald, 1947, 48
Grant, Kevin, 1986
Gray, Darryl, 1982, 84, 85
Gray, Hector, 1978, 79
Gray, Eddie, 1950
Gray, Mike, 1968
Green, Carl, 1953, 54
Green, Larry, 1965, 66, 67
Gridley, Buddy, 1969, 70, 71
Griffin, Chris, 1973, 74, 75
Griffis, Kevin, 1983
Griggley, Terry, 1984
Grimes, Fred, 1959, 60, 61
Griner, John, 1952, 55
Grossman, Rin, 1949
Gunter, Bill, 1967, 68
Gunter, Cliff, 1961, 62, 64
Gurr, Doug, 1966, 67, 68
Guthrie, Grant, 1967, 68, 69

H

Hadley, John, 1985, 86
Haggins, Odell, 1986
Hall, Phillip, 1982, 83
Hall, Randy, 1968, 69
Hammond, Kim, 1966, 67
Hanks, David, 1977
Hanna, Warren, 1981, 82
Hardy, Jack, 1958, 59, 60
Harlee, John, 1961, 62
Harlow, Brian, 1982
Harmeling, John, 1973, 76
Harp, Herbert, 1982, 83
Harp, Thomas, 1986
Harris, James, 1979, 80, 81
Harris, Larry, 1980, 81, 82
Harris, Wes, 1986
Harrison, Bruce, 1974, 75, 76
Hart, Ken, 1966, 67, 68
Haskin, Jack, 1947
Hayes, Eric, 1986
Hayes, Felton, 1985, 86
Hebron, Tim, 1985, 86
Heggie, Bruce, 1983, 84, 85, 86
Heggins, Jimmy, 1974, 75, 76, 77
Henderson, Gerald, 1955, 56, 57
Henderson, Nat, 1977, 78
Hendley, Jim, 1984, 85, 86
Henry, Ferrell, 1961, 62, 63
Henry, Gary, 1978, 79, 80, 82
Henson, Bill, 1970, 71
Hermann, Dick, 1962, 63, 64
Herring, Reggie, 1978, 79, 80
Hester, Jessie, 1981, 82, 83, 84
Hester, Ron, 1980, 81
Hewitt, Ted, 1948, 49, 50
Hiatt, Phil, 1968
Hillabrand, Tom, 1960, 61, 62
Hinson, Ron, 1959
Holloman, Darrin, 1984, 85, 86
Holloman, Tanner, 1985, 86
Holt, Joe, 1953, 54, 55, 56
Holton, Steve, 1957, 58
Hood, Larry, 1960, 61
Hooks, Jim, 1957, 58, 59
Hosack, John, 1965, 66
Houston, Rick, 1980
Howell, Bobby, 1970

Huey, Mac, 1950, 51, 52
Huff, Gary, 1970, 71, 72
Huggett, Ernie, 1950, 51
Hughes, Bill, 1968
Hughey, Harry, 1947
Humes, Earl, 1973, 74
Hunt, Charlie, 1970, 71, 72
Hunter, Ivory Joe, 1977, 78, 79
Hurst, John, 1966

I

Ionata, John, 1982, 83, 84, 85
Ionata, Joe, 1986
Italiano, Nelson, 1950, 51, 52

J

Jackson, Bobby, 1974, 75, 76, 77
Jackson, Lenx, 1983
Jacobi, Howard, 1971, 72
Jacobs, Charlie, 1956
Jacobs, Greg, 1984
Jacobs, Jerry, 1952, 53, 54, 55
Jarrett, James, 1969, 70, 71
Jax, Garth, 1982, 83, 84, 85
Johns, John, 1947, 48, 49
Johnson, Bob, 1939
Johnson, Eddie, 1955, 56, 57
Johnson, Greg, 1973, 74, 75
Johnson, Hardis, 1979, 80
Johnson, Homes, 1979
Johnson, Tony, 1981, 82, 83
Johnson, Wade, 1974, 75, 76
Johnson, Wayne, 1967, 68, 69
Johnston, Duke, 1967, 68, 69
Jones, Bob, 1972, 73, 74
Jones, Cedric, 1981, 82, 83, 84
Jones, Cletis, 1983, 84, 85
Jones, Donovan, 1967
Jones, Fred, 1983, 84, 85, 86
Jones, Hassan, 1982, 83, 84, 85
Jones, Jerry, 1965, 66, 67
Jones, Keith, 1978, 79, 80
Jones, Larry, 1973
Jones, Phil, 1973, 74, 75
Jones, Willie, 1975, 76, 77, 78
Jordan, Jimmy, 1976, 77, 78, 79

K

Kaiser, Randy, 1973, 74
Kalenich, Steve, 1950, 51, 52, 53
Kalfas, Chris, 1947, 48
Karlowicz, John, 1951
Kendell, Dick, 1948
Kendrick, Dub, 1948, 49, 50
Kestner, Ken, 1968, 69, 70
Key, Larry, 1974, 75, 76, 77
Keyes, Robert, 1976
Kimber, Bill, 1957, 58
Kincaid, Mike, 1975, 76, 77, 78
Kinderman, Keith, 1961, 62
King, Grady, 1978, 79, 80
King, Ronnie, 1953, 54
Kinnaman, Joe, 1966, 67
Kinnan, Joe, 1966, 67
Kinsey, Rocky, 1982, 83, 84
Kissam, Larry, 1965, 66
Kissner, Mike, 1974, 75, 76
Klesius, Steve, 1959, 60, 61
Kolbus, Marty, 1966
Kratzert, Bill, 1947
Kuipers, Jason, 1986

L

Lamb, Ray, 1958, 59, 60
Lanahan, John, 1969, 70, 71
Lanier, Ken, 1977, 78, 79, 80
Lazzaro, Greg, 1976, 77
Leggett, Jeff, 1974, 75, 76

Leonard, Bud, 1953, 54, 55, 56
Levings, John, 1960, 61, 62
Lewis, Buzzy, 1971, 72, 73
Lewis, Ronnie, 1986
Lockard, Ed, 1950
Loftin, Jim, 1962
Logan, Randy, 1968, 69
Lohse, Bill, 1968, 69, 70
Lombardi, Carmine, 1950
Loner, Frank, 1966, 67, 68
Lopez, Pablo, 1984, 85
Loucks, Garry, 1972
Lowe, Ron, 1969
Lowrey, Kelly, 1981, 82, 83
Lurie, Howard, 1964, 65
Lyles, Mark, 1976, 77, 78, 79

Mc
McClure, Don, 1947
McConnaughhay, John, 1960, 61, 62
McCormick, Gene, 1958, 59
McCormick, Tom, 1981, 82, 83
McCoy, Jerome, 1984
McCrary, Brian, 1982, 83, 84
McCullers, Dale, 1966, 67, 68
McDougal, Tom, 1973
McDowell, Bill, 1963, 64, 65
McDowell, Gene, 1960, 61, 62
McDuffie, Wayne, 1965, 66, 67, 68
McEachern, Robert, 1968, 69, 70
McGee, Joe, 1957, 58
McGowan, Mike, 1972
McKinnie, J.W., 1969, 70, 71
McKinnon, Bobby, 1973, 74, 75
McKinnon, Dennis, 1980, 81, 82
McLean, John, 1980, 81, 82, 83
McLean, Richard, 1964, 66, 67
McLean, Scott, 1979, 80, 81
McManus, Danny, 1985, 86
McMillan, Charles, 1947
McMillan, Eddie, 1970, 71, 72, 73
McMillan, Jack, 1947
McNease, Y.C., 1961, 62
McPhillips, Billy, 1973, 74, 75, 76

M
Macek, Mark, 1977, 78, 79, 80
Mack, Kim, 1982, 83, 84
MacLean, Ken, 1947, 48, 49
MacKenzie, Dale, 1962, 63, 64
Madden, John, 1978, 79, 80, 81
Magalski, Paul, 1969, 70, 71
Majors, Joe, 1957, 58, 59
Makowiecki, Al, 1953, 54
Maloy, Rudy, 1973, 74, 75, 76
Maltby, Duke, 1949, 50
Mangan, Bob, 1964, 65, 66
Mankins, Jim, 1965, 66
Mann, Ed, 1952
Manuel, Bo, 1947, 48, 49
Marcus, Frank, 1948
Marcus, Joe, 1948, 49
Massey, Harry, 1953, 54
Massey, Jim, 1963, 64, 65
Mathieson, Steve, 1974, 75, 76
Matt, Prince, 1982, 83
Matthews, Jay Mac, 1965, 66
May, Monte, 1948, 49, 50
Mayhew, Martin, 1984, 85, 86
Mead, Addison, Jr., 1947
Melton, Leonard, 1947, 48, 49
Menendez, Bob, 1966, 67
Merson, Bob, 1980, 81, 82
Merson, Scott, 1982
Meseroll, Mark, 1976, 77
Meseroll, Scott, 1973, 74

Messer, Doug, 1961, 62, 63
Messinese, Jimmy, 1952, 53, 54
Metts, Buck, 1953, 54, 55, 56
Meyer, Carl, 1959, 60
Middlebrooks, D.L., 1947
Miles, David, 1971, 72
Miller, Fred, 1973, 74, 75
Mindlin, Jeremy, 1978, 79
Minor, Roger, 1970, 71
Mitchell, Doug, 1969
Mitchell, Hodges, 1972, 73
Mobley, Orson, 1982
Montgomery, George, 1969
Montgomery, Hal, 1966, 67, 68
Montgomery, Howell, 1966, 67, 68
Montgomery, John, 1969, 70, 71
Moore, Ron, 1958, 59
Moore, Ron, 1983
Moran, Terry, 1958
Moreman, Bill, 1965, 66, 67
Morrical, Jerry, 1949
Morris, Dan, 1983, 84
Mosley, Ted, 1967, 68
Mowatt, Zeke, 1980, 81, 82
Munroe, Art, 1969, 70
Murdock, Les, 1963, 64
Murphy, John, 1972, 73, 74
Musselman, Bill, 1954, 55, 56, 57
Mustain, Don, 1959

N
Narramore, Lee, 1964
Newell, Greg, 1984, 85, 86
Nichols, Gerald, 1982, 84, 85, 86
Nicklaus, Steve, 1983
Nellums, Bob, 1956, 57
Nelson, Lee, 1974, 75
Norris, Brent, 1971

O
Odom, Billy, 1954, 55, 56
Oglesby, Paul, 1972
Olsen, Jim, 1953
O'Malley, Tom, 1985, 86
O'Neal, Earl, 1950, 51, 52
Oreair, Rick, 1970, 71, 72
Orlando, Mark, 1973
Osha, Dwight, 1949, 50
Osteen, Billy, 1947
Overby, Roger, 1974, 75, 77

P
Pacifico, Al, 1953, 54, 55, 56
Page, Mike, 1967
Paige, Lee, 1982
Pajcic, Gary, 1966, 67, 68
Palermo, John, 1972, 73
Palmer, David, 1984, 85, 86
Panton, Pete, 1983, 84, 85
Parishcq, Red, 1947, 48, 49
Parker, Clint, 1970, 71
Parks, John, 1985, 86
Parris, Gary, 1970, 71, 72
Parrish, Joe, 1963, 64, 65
Passwaters, Earl, 1972, 73
Pederson, Don, 1968, 69, 70
Pell, John, 1968, 69
Pendleton, Larry, 1966, 67, 68
Pennie, Charles, 1965, 66
Pennie, Frank, 1963, 64, 65
Peterson, Dick, 1948, 59
Petko, Joe, 1963, 64, 65
Philpcq, Gerald, 1956, 57
Pickard, Fred, 1958, 59
Pickens, Chuck, 1967
Pittman, John, 1967, 68
Pitts, David, 1964
Piurowski, Paul, 1977, 78, 79, 80

Platt, Sam, 1978, 79, 80
Polak, Nat, 1951, 52
Pope, Edwin, 1965, 66
Pope, Melvin Jr., 1957
Ponder, David, 1980, 81, 82, 83
Porter, Dave, 1974, 75, 76
Pounds, Greg, 1972, 73
Powell, Cliff, 1950
Powell, Don, 1952, 53, 54, 55
Prescott, Billy, 1976
Prestwood, Tom, 1972
Pritchett, Ed, 1963, 64, 65
Prior, Brad, 1976
Prinzi, Vic, 1954, 55, 56, 58
Proctor, C.N., 1947
Proctor, William Lee, 1955

Q
Quigley, Bill, 1947, 48
Quitley, Ed, 1947
Quinn, John, 1949

R
Ragins, Smokey, 1973, 74, 75
Rainey, Reese, 1971
Ramsey, Greg, 1977, 78, 79
Ratliff, Floyd, 1967
Ratliff, Ron, 1970, 71, 72, 73
Reddick, Ernie, 1948, 49
Render, Ricky, 1981, 82, 83
Rendina, Mike, 1981, 82
Renn, Bobby, 1956, 57, 58
Restivo, Sam, 1981, 82, 83
Reynolds, Burt, 1954
Reynolds, Detroit, 1973, 74, 75, 76
Rhodes, Bill, 1966, 67, 68
Rice, Barry, 1968, 69, 70
Rice, Beryl, 1968, 69, 70
Richardson, Bill, 1985
Richardson, Ed, 1977, 78, 79
Ridings, Jeff, 1974, 75, 76
Riggs, Marty, 1985, 86
Riley, Eric, 1981, 83, 84
Rimby, Bill, 1969, 70, 71
Riopelle, Jerry, 1983, 84
Riser, Butch, 1966
Risk, Alan, 1975, 76
Rivas, Vic, 1974, 75, 76
Robertson, Ulysses, 1983, 84
Roberts, Gene, 1961, 62
Roberts, Marion, 1961, 62, 63
Roberts, Oscar, 1971, 72
Roberts, Pete, 1965, 66, 67
Robinson, Chuck, 1961, 62, 63
Robinson, Terry, 1985
Rodrigue, Ted, 1955, 56, 57
Roe, Ken, 1981, 82, 83
Rogers, Ramon, 1958, 59
Romeo, Tony, 1958, 59, 60
Ross, Keith, 1985, 86
Rountree, Phil, 1947
Rushing, Tom, 1975, 76, 77
Russom, Kenneth, 1960, 61, 62
Rust, Benny, 1969, 70
Ryan, Eric, 1980, 81, 82

S
Salva, Mark, 1984, 85, 86
Sammons, Mike, 1969, 70
Sanders, Deion, 1985, 86
Sanders, Tracy, 1985, 86
Sanders, Terry, 1976, 77, 78, 79
Sawyer, Bill, 1974, 75, 76
Schmelz, Bob, 1948, 49, 50, 51
Schmidt, Brian, 1975, 76, 77, 78
Schmidt, Derek, 1984, 85, 86
Schomburger, Ron, 1954, 55, 56, 57
Schrenker, Dave, 1985, 86

Schuchts, Bart, 1986
Scott, Arthur, 1977, 78, 79, 80
Scott, Carlton, 1984
Scott, Stanley, 1983, 84, 85
Sellers, Don, 1960
Sellers, Mike, 1950, 51
Sellers, Ron, 1966, 67, 68
Sexton, Billy, 1973
Shaw, Bill, 1969, 70, 71, 72
Sheppard, John, 1956, 57, 58
Shinholser, Jack, 1963, 64, 65
Shively, Randy, 1972
Shiver, Stanley, 1985, 86
Shumann, Mike, 1974, 75, 77
Simmons, Ron, 1977, 78, 79, 80
Sims, Jim, 1960, 61, 62
Singletary, J. Keith, 1975, 76
Slay, Steve, 1962
Slicker, Tom, 1960, 61, 62
Smiley, Anthony, 1983, 84
Smith, Abe, 1976, 77
Smith, Barry, 1970, 71, 72
Smith, Mike, 1978, 79, 80
Smith, Sammie, 1986
Smith, Tony, 1982, 83, 84, 85
Snell, David, 1970, 71, 72
Snipes, Roosevelt, 1983, 84
Snyder, Dave, 1961, 62, 63
Solomon, Jesse, 1984, 85
Southwood, Keith, 1984, 85
Sowers, Craig, 1970
Sparkman, Don, 1971, 72, 73
Spivey, John, 1957, 58, 59
Spooner, Phil, 1963, 64, 65
Staab, Ray, 1954
Stark, Rohn, 1978, 79, 80, 81
Stephens, John, 1964, 65, 66
Stewart, Mike, 1976, 77
Stiehl, Eric, 1984, 85, 86
Strickland, Larry, 1970, 71, 72
Strickler, Joe, 1969, 70, 71
Stockton, Andy, 1974, 75
Stockstill, Rick, 1979, 80, 81
Stokes, Jay, 1969, 70, 71
Strauss, Buddy, 1948, 49
Stroud, Todd, 1983, 84, 85
Sumner, Avery, 1962, 63, 64
Sumner, Walter, 1966, 67, 68
Sutton, Lenny, 1986
Swantic, Len, 1953, 54, 55, 56
Swoszowski, Bob, 1958, 59, 60
Sytsma, Henry, 1962
Szczepanik, Vic, 1949, 50, 51, 52

T
Tanks, Michael, 1986
Taylor, Henry, 1981, 82, 83, 84
Taylor, Jimmy Lee, 1951, 52, 53, 54
Taylor, Rick, 1983
Taylor, Thurston, 1965, 66, 67
Tensi, Steve, 1962, 63, 64
Terry, Nat, 1976, 77
Thames, Jon, 1973, 74, 75, 76
Tharpe, Al, 1947
Thomas, Curtis, 1985, 86
Thomas, Danny, 1968, 69
Thomas, Eric, 1983, 84, 85
Thomas, James, 1970, 71, 72
Thomas, Rudy, 1974, 75, 76
Thompson, Jim, 1982, 83, 84
Thompson, Roy, 1951
Thompson, Shelton, 1986
Thompson, Weegie, 1981, 82, 83
Tillman, George, 1960
Tomberlin, Pat, 1985, 86
Trado, Jim, 1954

Trancygier, Ed, 1960, 61
Tully, Jack, 1947, 48
Turk, Richard, 1950, 51, 52
Tuten, Rick, 1986
Tyre, Bill, 1961, 62
Tyson, Jim, 1968, 69, 70

U
Ulmer, Al, 1957, 58, 59
Unglaub, Kurt, 1976, 77, 78, 79
Urich, Bob, 1963, 64
Urquhart, Whitney, 1948, 49

V
Verbinski, Joe, 1959, 60, 61
Versprille, Pat, 1955, 56
Vohun, Frank, 1967, 68, 69
Voltipetti, Barry, 1980, 81

W
Wachtel, John, 1961, 62, 63, 64
Walker, Clyde, 1975, 76, 77
Walker, Stan, 1967, 68, 69
Wallace, Lou, 1957
Wallace, Ron, 1968, 69, 70
Wallace, Wade, 1978, 79
Waller, H.T., 1966
Warren, Scott, 1976, 77, 78, 79
Warren, Terry, 1984, 85, 86
Warren, Tommy, 1968, 69, 70
Watson, John, 1947
Weaver, Billy, 1955, 56, 57
Wells, Chuck, 1985
Wesley, Gil, 1977, 78, 79
West, Tom, 1962, 63, 64
Wessel, Joe, 1982, 83, 84
Wetherell, T.K. 1965, 66, 67
Wettstein, Max, 1963, 64, 65
Wheeler, Tom, 1982, 83
Whigham, Frank, 1970, 71
White, Gaylon, 1984, 85, 86
White, Randy, 1985, 86
White, Tom, 1969, 70
Whitehead, Bud, 1958, 59, 60
Whitehead, Willie, 1960
Whitmer, Bob, 1951
Whiting, Mike, 1978, 79, 80, 81
Widner, Terry, 1982, 83
Williams, Alphonso, 1985, 86
Williams, Anthony, 1986
Williams, Blair, 1981, 82
Williams, Brian, 1981, 82, 83, 84
Williams, Dayne, 1986
Williams, Del, 1964, 65, 66
Williams, Dick, 1947
Williams, Eric, 1984, 85, 86
Williams, Isaac, 1982, 83, 84, 85
Williams, Phil, 1978, 79, 80, 81
Williams, Ricky, 1979, 80, 81, 82
Williams, Waldo, 1975, 76
Williamson, Larry, 1965, 66
Willis, Peter Tom, 1986
Wilmot, Horace, 1947
Woodrich, Bob, 1950, 51, 52
Woodham, Wally, 1977, 78, 79
Woolford, Gary, 1975, 76
Wooten, Jerry, 1963

Y
Yeldell, Bill, 1968
Yeomans, Tony, 1986
Young, Tommy, 1981, 82

Z
Zaffran, Ted, 1969, 70
Zion, Harvey, 1966, 67, 68

Year-by-Year Record

1947 (0-5)
	FSU	FOE
Stetson (H)	6	14
Cumberland (A)	0	6
Tennessee Tech (H)	6	27
Troy State (H)	6	36
Jacksonville State (H)	0	7
	18	90

1948 (7-1)
	FSU	FOE
Cumberland (H)	30	0
Erskine (A)	6	14
Millsaps (A)	7	6
Stetson (A)	18	7
Mississippi College (H)	26	6
Livingston State (H)	12	6
Troy State (A)	20	13
Tampa (H)**	33	12
	152	64

1949 (9-1)
	FSU	FOE
Whiting Field (H)	74	0
Mississippi College (A)	33	12
Erskine (H)	26	7
Sewanee (A)	6	0
Stetson (H)	33	14
Livingston State (A)	6	13
Millsaps (H)**	40	0
Tampa (A)	34	7
Troy State (H)	20	0
CIGAR BOWL		
Wofford (N)	19	6
	291	59

1950 (8-0)
	FSU	FOE
Troy State (A)	26	7
Randolph Macon (H)	40	7
Howard (H)	20	6
Newberry (A)	24	0
Sewanee (H)**	14	8
Stetson (A)	27	7
Mississippi College (H)	33	0
Tampa (H)	35	19
	219	54

1951 (6-2)
	FSU	FOE
Troy State (H)	40	0
Miami (Fla.) (A)	13	35
Delta State (H)	34	0
Sul Ross State (H)	35	13
Stetson (H)**	13	10
Jacksonville Navy (A)	39	0
Wofford (H)	14	0
Tampa (H)	6	14
	194	72

1952 (1-8-1)
	FSU	FOE
Louisiana Tech (H)	13	32
Louisville (H)	14	41
VMI (H)	7	28
N. Carolina State (A)	7	13
Stetson (N)	6	6
Mississippi So. (H)	21	50
Furman (H)**	0	9
Georgia Tech (A)	0	30
Wofford (A)	27	13
Tampa (H)	6	39
	101	261

1953 (5-5)
	FSU	FOE
Miami (Fla.) (A)	0	27
Louisville (H)	59	0
Abilene Christian (H)	7	20
Louisiana Tech (A)	21	32
VMI (H)	12	7
Mississippi So. (A)	0	21
Furman (H)	7	14
Stetson (H)**	13	6
N. Carolina State (H)	23	13
Tampa (A)	41	6
	183	146

1954 (8-4)
	FSU	FOE
Georgia (H)	0	14
Abilene Christian (H)	0	13
Louisville (A)	47	6
Villanova (H)	52	13
N. Carolina State (A)	13	7
Auburn (A)	0	33
VMI (H)	33	19
Furman (H)**	33	14
Stetson (A)	47	6
Mississippi So. (H)	19	18
Tampa (A)	13	0
SUN BOWL		
Texas Western (A)	20	47
	277	190

1955 (5-5)
	FSU	FOE
N. Carolina State (H)	7	0
Miami (Fla.) (A)	0	34
Virginia Tech (H)	20	24
Georgia (H)	14	47
Georgia Tech (A)	0	34
Villanova (H)	16	13
Furman (H)	19	6
The Citadel (H)**	39	0
Mississippi So. (A)	6	21
Tampa (A)	26	7
	147	186

1956 (5-4-1)
	FSU	FOE
Ohio University (H)	47	7
Georgia (A)	0	3
Virginia Tech (H)	7	20
N. Carolina State (A)	14	0
Wake Forest (H)**	14	14
Villanova (A)	20	13
Miami (Fla.) (A)	7	20
Furman (H)	42	7
Mississippi So. (H)	20	19
Auburn (A)	7	13
	178	116

1957 (4-6)
	FSU	FOE
Furman (H)	27	7
Boston College (A)	7	20
Villanova (A)	7	21
N. Carolina State (H)	0	7
Abilene Christian (H)	34	7
Virginia Tech (H)**	20	7
Miami (Fla.) (H)	13	40
Mississippi So. (A)	0	20
Auburn (H)	7	29
Tampa (A)	21	7
	136	165

1958 (7-4)
	FSU	FOE
Tennessee Tech (H)	22	7
Furman (H)	42	6
Georgia Tech (A)	3	17
Wake Forest (H)	27	24
Georgia (N)	13	28
Virginia Tech (H)	28	0
Tennessee (A)	10	0
Tampa (H)**	43	0
Miami (Fla.) (A)	17	6
Florida (A)	7	21
BLUEGRASS BOWL		
Oklahoma State (N)	6	15
	218	124

1959 (4-6)
	FSU	FOE
Wake Forest (H)	20	22
The Citadel (H)	47	6
Miami (Fla.) (H)	6	7
Virginia Tech (A)	7	6
Memphis State (A)	6	16
Richmond (A)	22	6
Georgia (A)	0	42
William & Mary (H)**	0	9
Florida (A)	8	18
Tampa (H)	33	0
	149	132

1960 (3-6-1)
	FSU	FOE
Richmond (H)	28	0
Florida (A)	0	3
Wake Forest (H)	14	6
The Citadel (H)	0	0
Mississippi So. (A)	13	15
William & Mary (H)	22	0
Kentucky (H)**	0	23
Miami (Fla.) (A)	7	25
Houston (H)	6	7
Auburn (A)	21	57
	111	136

1961 (4-5-1)
	FSU	FOE
George Washington (H)	15	7
Florida (A)	3	3
Mississippi (A)	0	33
Georgia (H)	3	0
Richmond (H)	13	7
Virginia Tech (A)	7	10
Kentucky (A)	0	20
The Citadel (H)	44	8
Mississippi So. (H)**	0	12
Houston (A)	8	28
	93	128

1962 (4-3-3)
	FSU	FOE
The Citadel (H)	49	0
Kentucky (A)	0	0
Furman (H)	42	0
Miami (Fla.) (A)	6	7
Georgia (A)	18	0
VPI (H)	20	7
Houston (H)**	0	7
Georgia Tech (A)	14	14
Florida (A)	7	20
Auburn (A)	14	14
	170	69

1963 (4-5-1)
	FSU	FOE
Miami (Fla.) (H)	24	0
Texas Christian (H)	0	13
Wake Forest (H)	35	0
So. Mississippi (A)	0	0
Virginia Tech (A)	23	31
Furman (H)	49	6
Georgia Tech (A)	7	15
N. Carolina State (H)**	14	0
Auburn (A)	15	21
Florida (A)	0	7
	167	93

1964 (9-1-1)
	FSU	FOE
Miami (Fla.) (A)	14	0
Texas Christian (A)	10	0
New Mexico State (H)	36	0
Kentucky (H)**	48	6
Georgia (A)	17	14
Virginia Tech (A)	11	20
So. Mississippi (H)	34	0
Houston (A)	13	13
N. Carolina State (H)	28	6
Florida (H)	16	7
GATOR BOWL		
Oklahoma (N)	36	19
	263	85

1965 (4-5-1)
	FSU	FOE
Texas Christian (A)	3	7
Baylor (H)	9	7
Kentucky (A)	24	26
Georgia (H)	10	3
Alabama (A)	0	21
Virginia Tech (H)	7	6
Wake Forest (H)**	35	0
N. Carolina State (A)	0	3
Houston (H)	16	16
Florida (A)	17	30
	121	119

1966 (6-5)
	FSU	FOE
Houston (H)	13	21
Miami (Fla.) (A)	23	20
Florida (H)	19	22
Texas Tech (A)	42	33
Mississippi State (H)	10	0
Virginia Tech (A)	21	23
South Carolina (A)	32	10
Syracuse (A)	21	37
Wake Forest (H)**	28	0
Maryland (H)	45	21
SUN BOWL		
Wyoming (N)	20	28
	274	215

1967 (7-2-2)
	FSU	FOE
Houston (A)	13	33
Alabama (A)	37	37
N. Carolina State (H)	10	20
Texas A&M (A)	19	18
South Carolina (H)	17	0

**Homecoming

(1967)

	FSU	FOE
Texas Tech (H)**	28	12
Mississippi State (H)	24	12
Memphis State (A)	26	7
Virginia Tech (H)	38	15
Florida (A)	21	16
GATOR BOWL		
Penn State (N)	17	17
	250	187

1968 (8-3)

	FSU	FOE
Maryland (A)	24	14
Florida (H)	3	9
Texas A&M (H)	20	14
Memphis State (H)	20	10
South Carolina (A)	35	28
Virginia Tech (H)	22	40
Mississippi State (A)	27	14
N. Carolina State (A)	48	7
Wake Forest (H)**	42	24
Houston (N)	40	20
PEACH BOWL		
LSU (N)	27	31
	308	211

1969 (6-3-1)

	FSU	FOE
Wichita State (H)	24	0
Miami (Fla.) (A)	16	14
Florida (H)	6	21
Tulsa (A)	38	20
Mississippi State (H)	20	17
South Carolina (H)**	34	9
Virginia Tech (A)	10	10
Memphis State (A)	26	28
N. Carolina State (H)	33	22
Houston (A)	27	31
	220	182

1970 (7-4)

	FSU	FOE
Louisville (H)	9	7
Georgia Tech (A)	13	23
Wake Forest (H)	19	14
Florida (H)	27	38
Memphis State (A)	12	16
South Carolina (A)	21	13
Miami (Fla.) (A)	27	3
Clemson (H)	38	13
Virginia Tech (H)**	34	8
Kansas State (H)	33	7
Houston (N)	21	53
	254	195

1971 (8-4)

	FSU	FOE
So. Mississippi (N)	24	9
Miami (Fla.) (A)	20	17
Kansas (H)	30	7
Virginia Tech (A)	17	3
Mississippi State (H)**	27	9
Florida (A)	15	17
South Carolina (H)	49	18
Houston (A)	7	14
Georgia Tech (A)	6	12
Tulsa (H)	45	10
Pittsburgh (H)	31	13
FIESTA BOWL		
Arizona State (A)	38	45
	309	174

1972 (7-4)

	FSU	FOE
Pittsburgh (A)	19	7
Miami (Fla.) (A)	37	14
Virginia Tech (H)	27	15
Kansas (A)	44	22
Florida (H)	13	42
Mississippi State (N)	25	21
Colorado State (H)**	37	0
Auburn (A)	14	27
Houston (H)	27	31
Tulsa (H)	23	21
South Carolina (A)	21	24
	287	224

1973 (0-11)

	FSU	FOE
Wake Forest (A)	7	9
Kansas (H)	0	28
Miami (Fla.) (H)	10	14
Baylor (A)	14	21
Mississippi State (H)	12	37
Memphis State (H)**	10	13
San Diego State (A)	17	38
Houston (A)	3	34
Virginia Tech (A)	13	36
South Carolina (H)	12	52
Florida (A)	0	49
	98	331

1974 (1-10)

	FSU	FOE
Pittsburgh (H)	6	9
Colorado State (H)	7	14
Kansas (A)	9	40
Baylor (H)	17	21
Alabama (A)	7	8
Florida (H)	14	24
Auburn (A)	6	38
Memphis State (A)	14	42
Miami (Fla.) (A)	21	14
Virginia Tech (H)**	21	56
Houston (H)	8	23
	120	289

1975 (3-8)

	FSU	FOE
Texas Tech (A)	20	31
Utah State (H)	17	8
Iowa State (H)	6	10
Georgia Tech (A)	0	30
Virginia Tech (A)	10	13
Florida (A)	8	34
Auburn (H)	14	17
Clemson (A)	43	7
Memphis State (H)	14	17
Miami (Fla.) (H)**	22	24
Houston (A)	33	22
	187	213

1976 (5-6)

	FSU	FOE
Memphis State (A)	12	21
Miami (Fla.) (A)	0	47
Oklahoma (H)	9	24
Kansas State (H)	20	10
Boston College (A)	28	9
Florida (H)	26	33
Auburn (A)	19	31
Clemson (H)	12	15
So. Mississippi (H)**	30	27
N. Texas State (A)	21	20
Virginia Tech (H)	28	21
	205	258

1977 (10-2)

	FSU	FOE
So. Mississippi (A)	35	6
Kansas State (A)	18	10
Miami (Fla.) (H)	17	23
Oklahoma State (A)	25	17
Cincinnati (H)	14	0
Auburn (H)	24	3
N. Texas State (H)**	35	14
Virginia Tech (H)	23	21
Memphis State (H)	30	9
San Diego State (A)	16	41
Florida (A)	37	9
TANGERINE BOWL		
Texas Tech (N)	40	17
	314	170

1978 (8-3)

	FSU	FOE
Syracuse (A)	28	0
Oklahoma State (H)	38	20
Miami (Fla.) (A)	31	21
Houston (H)	21	27
Cincinnati (H)	26	21
Mississippi St. (A)	27	55
Pittsburgh (A)	3	7
So. Mississippi (A)	38	16
Virginia Tech (H)	24	14
Navy (H)**	38	6
Florida (H)	38	21
	312	208

1979 (11-1)

	FSU	FOE
So. Mississippi (H)	17	14
Arizona State (N)	31	3
Miami (Fla.) (H)	40	23
Virginia Tech (A)	17	10
Louisville (A)	27	0
Mississippi State (H)	17	6
Louisiana State (A)	24	19
Cincinnati (A)	26	21
South Carolina (H)**	27	7
Memphis State (H)	66	17
Florida (A)	27	16
ORANGE BOWL		
Oklahoma (N)	7	24
	326	160

1980 (10-2)

	FSU	FOE
Louisiana State (A)	16	0
Louisville (H)	52	0
East Carolina (H)	63	7
Miami (Fla.) (A)	9	10
Nebraska (A)	18	14
Pittsburgh (H)	36	22
Boston College (H)**	41	7
Memphis State (A)	24	3
Tulsa (H)	45	2
Virginia Tech (H)	31	7
Florida (H)	17	13
ORANGE BOWL		
Oklahoma (N)	17	18
	352	85

1981 (6-5)

	FSU	FOE
Louisville (H)	17	0
Memphis State (H)	10	5
Nebraska (A)	14	34
Ohio State (A)	36	27
Notre Dame (A)	19	13
Pittsburgh (A)	14	42
Louisiana State (A)	38	14
Western Carolina (H)**	56	31
Miami (Fla.) (H)	19	27
Southern Mississippi (H)	14	58
Florida (A)	3	35
	240	286

1982 (9-3)

	FSU	FOE
Cincinnati (H)	38	31
Pittsburgh (H)	17	37
Southern Mississippi (A)	24	17
Ohio State (A)	34	17
Southern Illinois (H)**	59	8
East Carolina (H)	56	17
Miami (Fla.) (A)	24	7
South Carolina (A)	56	26
Louisville (H)	49	14
Louisiana State (A)	21	55
Florida (H)	10	13
GATOR BOWL		
West Virginia (N)	31	12
	388	254

1983 (8-4)

	FSU	FOE
East Carolina (H)	47	46
Louisiana State (A)	40	35
*Tulane (A)	28	34
Auburn (A)	24	27
Pittsburgh (A)	16	17
Cincinnati (H)**	43	17
Louisville (H)	51	7
Arizona State (A)	28	26
South Carolina (A)	45	30
Miami (Fla.) (H)	16	17
Florida (A)	14	53
PEACH BOWL		
North Carolina (N)	28	3
	381	312

1984 (7-3-2)

	FSU	FOE
East Carolina (H)	48	17
Kansas (A)	42	16
Miami (Fla.) (A)	38	3
Temple (H)**	44	27
Memphis State (A)	17	17
Auburn (H)	41	42
Tulane (H)	27	6
Arizona State (A)	52	44
South Carolina (A)	26	38
Tennessee-Chattanooga (H)	37	0
Florida (H)	17	27
CITRUS BOWL		
Georgia (N)	17	17
	406	254

1985 (9-3)

	FSU	FOE
Tulane (A)	38	12
Nebraska (A)	17	13
Memphis State (H)	19	10
Kansas (H)	24	20
Auburn (A)	27	59
Tulsa (H)	76	14
North Carolina (A)	20	10
Miami (Fla.) (H)	27	35
South Carolina (H)	56	14
Western Carolina (H)**	50	10
Florida (A)	14	38
GATOR BOWL		
Oklahoma State (N)	34	23
	402	258

1986 (7-4-1)

	FSU	FOE
Toledo (H)	24	0
Nebraska (A)	17	34
North Carolina (H)	10	10
Michigan (A)	18	20
Tulane (H)	54	21
Wichita State (H)	59	3
Louisville (A)	54	18
Miami (Fla.) (A)	23	41
South Carolina (A)	45	28
Southern Mississippi (H)**	49	13
Florida (H)	13	17
ALL-AMERICAN BOWL		
Indiana (N)	27	13
	393	218

*Tulane forfeited on 2/3/86
**Homecoming

Record Against All Opponents

Team	First Meeting	Last Meeting Date	Site	Score	W	L	T
Abilene Christian	1953	1957	H	34-7	1	2	0
Alabama	1965	1974	H	7-8	0	2	1
Arizona State*	1971	1984	A	52-44	3	1	0
Auburn	1954	1985	A	27-59	1	12	1
Baylor	1965	1974	H	17-21	1	2	1
Boston College	1957	1980	H	41-7	2	1	0
Cincinnati	1977	1983	H	43-17	5	0	0
Citadel, The	1955	1962	H	49-0	4	0	1
Clemson	1970	1976	H	12-15	2	1	0
Colorado State	1972	1974	H	7-14	1	1	0
Cumberland	1947	1948	H	30-0	1	1	0
Delta State	1951	1951	H	34-0	1	0	0
East Carolina	1980	1984	H	48-17	4	0	0
Erskine	1948	1949	H	26-7	1	1	0
Florida	1958	1986	H	13-17	6	22	1
Furman	1952	1963	H	49-6	7	2	0
George Washington	1961	1961	H	15-7	1	0	0
Georgia*	1954	1984	N	17-17	4	5	1
Georgia Tech	1952	1975	A	0-30	0	7	1
Houston	1960	1978	H	21-27	2	12	2
Howard	1950	1950	H	20-6	1	0	0
Indiana	1986	1986	N	27-13	1	0	0
Iowa State	1975	1975	H	6-10	0	1	0
Jacksonville Navy	1951	1951	A	39-0	1	0	0
Jacksonville State (Ala.)	1947	1947	H	0-7	0	1	0
Kansas	1971	1985	H	24-20	4	2	0
Kansas State	1970	1977	A	18-10	3	0	0
Kentucky	1960	1965	A	24-26	1	3	1
Livingston State	1948	1949	A	6-13	1	1	0
Louisiana State*	1968	1983	A	40-35	4	2	0
Louisiana Tech	1952	1953	A	21-32	0	2	0
Louisville	1952	1986	A	54-18	9	1	0
Maryland	1966	1968	A	24-14	2	0	0
Memphis State	1959	1985	H	19-10	7	7	1
Miami	1951	1986	A	23-41	13	17	0
Michigan	1986	1986	A	18-20	0	1	0
Millsaps	1948	1949	H	40-0	2	0	0
Mississippi	1961	1961	A	0-33	0	1	0
Mississippi College	1948	1950	H	33-0	3	0	0
Mississippi State	1966	1979	H	17-6	7	2	0
Navy	1978	1978	H	38-6	1	0	0
Nebraska	1980	1986	A	17-34	2	2	0
Newberry	1950	1950	A	24-0	1	0	0
New Mexico State	1964	1964	H	36-0	1	0	0
North Carolina*	1983	1986	H	10-0	2	0	1
North Carolina State	1952	1969	H	33-22	8	4	0
North Texas State	1976	1977	H	35-14	2	0	0
Notre Dame	1981	1981	A	19-13	1	0	0
Ohio	1956	1956	H	47-7	1	0	0
Ohio State	1981	1982	A	34-17	2	0	0
Oklahoma*	1965	1980	N	17-18	1	3	0
Oklahoma State*	1958	1985	N	34-23	3	1	0
Penn State*	1968	1968	N	17-17	0	0	1
Pittsburgh	1971	1983	A	16-17	3	5	0
Randolph Macon	1950	1950	H	40-7	1	0	0
Richmond	1959	1961	H	13-7	3	0	0
San Diego State	1973	1977	A	16-41	0	2	0
Sewanee	1949	1950	H	14-8	2	0	0
South Carolina	1966	1986	A	45-28	11	3	0
Southern Illinois	1982	1982	H	59-8	1	0	0
Southern Mississippi	1952	1986	H	49-13	10	7	1
Stetson	1947	1954	A	47-6	6	1	1
Sul Ross State	1951	1951	H	35-12	1	0	0
Syracuse	1966	1978	A	28-0	1	1	0
Tampa	1948	1959	A	33-0	9	2	0
Temple	1984	1984	H	44-27	1	0	0
Tennessee	1958	1958	A	10-0	1	0	0
Tennessee-Chattanooga	1984	1984	H	37-0	1	0	0
Tennessee Tech	1947	1958	H	22-7	1	1	0
Texas A&M	1967	1968	H	20-14	2	0	0
Texas Christian	1963	1965	A	3-7	1	2	0
Texas Tech	1966	1977	N	40-16	3	1	0
Texas Western*	1954	1954	N	20-47	0	1	0
Toledo	1986	1986	H	24-0	1	0	0
Troy State	1947	1951	H	40-0	4	1	0
Tulane**	1983	1986	H	54-21	4	0	0
Tulsa	1969	1985	H	76-14	5	0	0
Utah State	1975	1975	H	17-8	1	0	0
Villanova	1954	1957	A	7-21	3	1	0
Virginia Military	1952	1954	A	33-19	2	1	0
Virginia Tech	1955	1980	H	31-7	14	10	1
Wake Forest	1956	1973	A	7-9	7	2	1
West Virginia*	1982	1982	N	31-12	1	0	0
Western Carolina	1981	1985	H	50-10	2	0	0
Whiting Field	1949	1949	H	74-0	1	0	0
Wichita State	1969	1986	H	59-3	2	0	0
William & Mary	1959	1960	H	22-0	1	1	0
Wofford*	1949	1952	A	27-13	3	0	0
Wyoming*	1966	1966	N	20-28	0	1	0

*Bowl Games Included   **Forfeit Included

Coaches and Captains

Year	Coach	Captains	W	L	T	FSU Pts.	Opp Pts.
1947	Ed Williamson	Jack McMillan, Phil Rountree	0	5	0	18	90
1948	Don Veller	Game Captains	7	1	0	152	64
1949*	Don Veller	Hugh Adams	9	1	0	291	59
1950	Don Veller	Duke Maltby	8	0	0	219	54
1951	Don Veller	Bill Dawkins	6	2	0	194	72
1952	Don Veller	Curtis Campbell, Vic Szczepanik	1	8	1	101	261
1953	Tom Nugent	Steve Kalenich	5	5	0	183	146
1954*	Tom Nugent	Game Captains	8	4	0	277	190
1955	Tom Nugent	Bob Crenshaw, Don Powell	5	5	0	147	186
1956	Tom Nugent	Joe Holt, Buck Metz	5	4	1	178	116
1957	Tom Nugent	Ron Schomburger	4	6	0	136	165
1958*	Tom Nugent	Vic Prinzi, Bobby Renn	7	4	0	218	124
1959*	Perry Moss	John Spivey, Al Ulmer	4	6	0	149	132
1960	Bill Peterson	Tony Romeo	3	6	1	111	136
1961	Bill Peterson	Steve Klesius	4	5	1	93	128
1962	Bill Peterson	Gene McDowell	4	3	3	170	69
1963	Bill Peterson	Charlie Calhoun, Chuck Robinson	4	5	1	167	93
1964*	Bill Peterson	Bill Dawson, Fred Biletnikoff, George D'Alassandro	9	1	1	263	85
1965	Bill Peterson	Bill McDowell, Max Wettstein	4	5	1	121	119
1966*	Bill Peterson	Game Captains	6	5	0	274	215
1967*	Bill Peterson	Game Captains	7	2	2	250	187
1968*	Bill Peterson	Game Captains	8	3	0	308	211
1969	Bill Peterson	Game Captains	6	3	1	220	182
1970	Bill Peterson	Game Captains	7	4	0	254	195
1971*	Larry Jones	Rhett Dawson, John Lanahan	8	4	0	309	174
1972	Larry Jones	Gary Huff, Larry Strickland	7	4	0	287	224
1973	Larry Jones	Jim Malkiewicz, Don Sparkman	0	11	0	98	331
1974	Darrell Mudra	Joe Goldsmith, Bert Cooper	1	10	0	130	289
1975	Darrell Mudra	Greg Johnson, Jeff Gardner	3	8	0	187	213
1976	Bobby Bowden	Jimmy Black, Jeff Leggett, Joe Camps, Rudy Thomas	5	6	0	205	258
1977*	Bobby Bowden	Aaron Carter, Bill Duley, Larry Key, Tom Rushing, Nat Terry	10	2	0	314	170
1978	Bobby Bowden	Nate Henderson, Willie Jones, Ivory Joe Hunter	8	3	0	312	208
1979*	Bobby Bowden	Mike Good, Ivory Joe Hunter, Scott Warren, Wally Woodham	11	1	0	326	160
1980*	Bobby Bowden	Reggie Herring, Greg Futch, Ron Simmons, Ken Lanier	10	2	0	352	85
1981	Bobby Bowden	James Harris, James Gilbert, Rohn Stark, Michael Whiting, Rick Stockstill	6	5	0	237	251
1982*	Bobby Bowden	Game Captains	9	3	0	419	254
1983*	Bobby Bowden	Game Captains	8	4	0	353	256
1984*	Bobby Bowden	Greg Allen, Joe Wessel, Henry Taylor	7	3	2	389	237
1985*	Bobby Bowden	John Ionata, Todd Stroud, Kirk Coker	9	3	0	402	258
1986*	Bobby Bowden	Fred Jones, Gerald Nichols, Louis Berry, Jim Hendley	7	4	1	366	205
Totals			**240**	**166**	**16**	**9548**	**6852**

*Bowl Game Included

Coaches' Cumulative Records

Name	Tenure	Years	W-L-T	Pct.	FSU Pts.	Opp Pts.
Ed Williamson	1947	1	0-5-0	.000	18	90
Don Veller	1948–52	5	31-12-1	.716	938	504
Tom Nugent	1953–58	6	34-28-1	.548	1123	865
Perry Moss	1959	1	4-6-0	.400	149	132
Bill Peterson	1960–70	11	62-42-11	.587	2234	1602
Larry Jones	1971–73	3	15-19-0	.441	407	505
Darrell Mudra	1974–75	2	4-18-0	.182	317	502
Bobby Bowden	1976–	11	90-36-3	.705	3712	2331

Individual Records

(Bowl games not included) ***NCAA Record **NCAA Freshman Record**

TOTAL OFFENSE

Most Plays
Game—61, Gary Huff vs. Houston, Nov. 4, 1972
Season—429, Gary Huff, 1972
Career—921, Gary Huff, 1970–72

Most Yards Gained
Game—490, Bill Cappleman vs. Memphis State, Nov. 15, 1969
Season—2,770, Gary Huff, 1972
Career—6,086, Gary Huff, 1970–72

Most Touchdowns Responsible For
Game—6, Gary Huff vs. South Carolina, Oct. 23, 1971
Season—26, Gary Huff, 1972; Bill Cappleman, 1968
Career—54, Gary Huff, 1970–72

RUSHING

Most Rushes
Game—33, Greg Allen vs. East Carolina, Sept. 3, 1983
Season—239, Larry Key, 1977
Career—625, Larry Key, 1974–77

Most Yards Gained
**Game—322, Greg Allen vs. Western Carolina, Oct. 31, 1981
Season—1,134, Greg Allen, 1983
Career—3,769, Greg Allen, 1981–84

Most Yards Gained (Season)
By a Freshman—888, Greg Allen, 1981
By a Sophomore—817, Homes Johnson, 1978
By a Junior—1,134, Greg Allen, 1983
By a Senior—1,117, Larry Key, 1977

Most Games Gaining 100 Yards
Season—6, Sam Platt, 1980; Greg Allen, 1984
Career—16, Greg Allen, 1981–84

Consecutive 100-Yard Games
Career—3, Sam Platt, 1980; Greg Allen, 1981 and 1983;
   Roosevelt Snipes, 1984

Most Games Gaining 200 Yards
Season—2, Greg Allen, 1981
Career—4, Greg Allen, 1981–84

Most Games Gaining 300 Yards
Season—1, Greg Allen, 1981
Career—1, Greg Allen, 1981

Highest Average Per Rush
Game (Min. 10 atts.)—14.1, (15-212), Victor Floyd vs. South
   Carolina, Nov. 9, 1985; (Min. 20 atts.)—10.1, (22-223),
   Greg Allen vs. Arizona State, Nov. 4, 1984
Season (Min. 100 atts.)—7.3, (133-971), Greg Allen, 1984
Career (Min. 200 atts.)—6.0, Greg Allen, 1981–84

Most TDs Rushing
Game—4, Greg Allen vs. South Carolina, Nov. 6, 1982; vs.
   Louisville, Nov. 13, 1982
Season—20, Greg Allen, 1982
Career—44, Greg Allen, 1981–84

Longest Rush
Game—97, Larry Key vs. Virginia Tech, Nov. 11, 1976

Most All-Purpose Yardage
*Game—417, Greg Allen vs. Western Carolina, Oct. 31, 1981
Season—1,605, Greg Allen, 1982
Career—4,996, Greg Allen, 1981–84

PASSING

Highest Passing Efficiency Rating
Season (Min. 10 atts./game)—151.8, Blair Williams, 1982
Career (Min. 150 cmp./game)—133.0, Gary Huff, 1970–72

Most Passes Attempted
Game—58, Gary Huff vs. Florida, Oct. 7, 1972
Season—385, Gary Huff, 1972
Career—796, Gary Huff, 1970–72

Most Passes Completed
Game—31, Bill Cappleman vs. Memphis State, Nov. 15, 1969
Season—206, Gary Huff, 1972
Career—436, Gary Huff, 1970–72

Highest Completion Percentage
Game (Min. 15 atts.)—84.0, (21-25), Gary Huff vs. Virginia Tech,
   Oct. 2, 1971
Season (Min. 100 atts.)—61.0, (94-154), Wally Woodham, 1977
Career (Min. 300 atts.)—57.4, (273-476), Wally Woodham, 1975,
   77–79

Most Passes Intercepted
Game—5, Bill Cappleman vs. Virginia Tech, Nov. 2, 1968
Season—23, Gary Huff, 1972
Career—42, Gary Huff, 1970–72

Lowest Interception Percentage
Season (Min. 100 atts.)—1.65, (2-121), Steve Tensi, 1962
Career (Min. 300 atts.)—4.27, (15-351), Kim Hammond, 1965-67

Most Yards Gained
Game—508, Bill Cappleman vs. Memphis State, Nov. 15, 1969
Season—2,893, Gary Huff, 1972
Career—6,378, Gary Huff, 1970–72

Most 200-Yard Games
Season—9, Gary Huff, 1972
Career—15, Gary Huff, 1970–72

Consecutive 200-Yard Games
Career—11, Gary Huff, 1971–72

Most 300-Yard Games
Season—3, Gary Huff, 1971; Kim Hammond, 1967
Career—5, Gary Huff, 1970–72

Consecutive 300-Yard Games
Career—3, Kim Hammond, 1967

Most Yards Per Attempt
Game (Min. 15 atts.)—15.0, (374-25), Gary Huff vs. Virginia Tech,
   Oct. 2, 1971
Season (Min. 100 atts.)—8.6, (1,535-179), Jimmy Black, 1976
Career (Min. 300 atts.)—8.0, (6,378-796), Gary Huff, 1970-72

Most Yards Per Completion
Game (Min. 15 atts.)—23.8, (285-12), Gary Huff vs. Tulsa, Nov. 20, 1971
Season (Min. 100 atts.)—15.6, (1,218-78), Eric Thomas, 1984
Career (Min. 300 atts.)—14.6, (6,378-436), Gary Huff, 1970–72

Most TD Passes
Game—5, Gary Huff vs. South Carolina, Oct. 23, 1971; Bill Cappleman vs. Wake Forest, Nov. 23, 1968
Season—25, Bill Cappleman, 1968; Gary Huff, 1972
Career—52, Gary Huff, 1970–72

Consecutive Games with TD Pass
Career—13, Gary Huff, 1971–72

Longest Pass
Game—96, Kurt Unglaub from Jimmy Jordan vs. Virginia Tech, Nov. 20, 1976

RECEIVING

Most Passes Caught
Game—16, Ron Sellers vs. South Carolina, Oct. 26, 1968
Season—86, Ron Sellers, 1968
Career—212, Ron Sellers, 1966–68

Consecutive Games Catching a Pass
Career—30, Ron Sellers, 1966–68

Most Yards Gained
Game—260, Ron Sellers vs. Wake Forest, Nov. 23, 1968
Season—1,496, Ron Sellers, 1968
*Career—3,598, Ron Sellers, 1966–68

Highest Average Per Reception
Game (Min. 5 rec.)—34.6, (173-5), Ron Sellers vs. Maryland, Sept. 21, 1968
Season (Min. 30 rec.)—21.7, (738-34), Hassan Jones, 1985
Career (Min. 70 rec.)—20.1, (2,392-119), Barry Smith, 1970-72

Most TD Passes Caught
Game—5, Ron Sellers vs. Wake Forest, Nov. 23, 1968
Season—13, Barry Smith, 1972
Career—25, Barry Smith, 1970–72

Yards Gained Per Game
Season—149.6, Ron Sellers, 1968
Career—119.9, Ron Sellers, 1966–68

Most 100-Yard Receiving Games
Season—8, Barry Smith, 1972
Career—18, Ron Sellers, 1966–68

Most 200-Yard Receiving Games
Season—4, Ron Sellers, 1968
Career—5, Ron Sellers, 1966–68

SCORING

Most Points
Game—30, Ron Sellers vs. Wake Forest, Nov. 23, 1968
Season—126, Greg Allen, 1982
Career—278, Greg Allen, 1981–84

Most Touchdowns
Game—5, Ron Sellers vs. Wake Forest, Nov. 23, 1968
Season—21, Greg Allen, 1982
Career—46, Greg Allen, 1981–84

Most PAT Attempted
Game—10, Derek Schmidt vs. Tulsa, Oct. 19, 1985

Season—53, Philip Hall, 1982
Career—128, Derek Schmidt, 1984–86

Most PAT Made
Game—10, Derek Schmidt vs. Tulsa, Oct. 19, 1985
Season—52, Philip Hall, 1982
Career—127, Derek Schmidt, 1984–86

Highest Percentage of PAT Made
Season (Min. 25 att.)—100.0, (38-38), Bill Capece, 1980; Derek Schmidt (42-42), 1984 and (44-44), 1985
Career (Min. 50 att.)—99.2, (127-128), Derek Schmidt, 1984–1986

Consecutive PAT
Career—108, Derek Schmidt, 1984–86

Most Points Kicking
Game—18, Bill Capece vs. Pittsburgh, Oct. 11, 1980
Season—104, Bill Capece, 1980
Career—277, Derek Schmidt, 1984–86

PUNTING

Most Punts
Game—12, Joe Downey vs. Houston, Nov. 3, 1973; Bill Cheshire vs. Florida, Sept. 28, 1968
Season—81, Joe Downey, 1973
Career—244, Rohn Stark, 1978–81

Highest Average
Game (Min. 5 punts)—54.8, (329-6), Rohn Stark vs. Florida, Nov. 28, 1981
Season (Min. 30 punts)—46.0, (2,941-64), Rohn Stark, 1981
Career (Min. 100 punts)—42.7, (10,418-244), Rohn Stark, 1978–81

Most Yards on Punts
Game—465, Joe Downey vs. Houston, Nov. 3, 1973
Season—3,092, Joe Downey, 1973
Career—10,418, Rohn Stark, 1978–81

Longest Punt
Game—84, Tommy Brown vs. Tampa, 1950

PUNT RETURNS

Most Punt Returns
Game—10, David Snell vs. South Carolina, Oct. 24, 1970
Season—40, David Snell, 1970
Career—102, David Snell, 1970–72

Most Yards on Punt Returns
Game—137, Bobby Jackson vs. Virginia Tech, Nov. 16, 1974
Season—363, David Snell, 1970
Career—850, David Snell, 1970–72

Highest Average Per Punt Return
Game (Min. 3)—45.7, (137-3), Bobby Jackson vs. Virginia Tech, Nov. 16, 1974
Season (Min. 10)—20.1, (241-12), Phil Abraira, 1969
Career (Min. 25)—14.0, (377-27), Buddy Blankenship, 1964-65

Most TDs on Punt Returns
Game—2, Joe Wessel vs. Arizona State, Nov. 3, 1984
Season—3, Joe Wessel, 1984
Career—3, Joe Wessel, 1981–84

Longest Punt Return
Game—92, Phil Abraira vs. North Carolina, Nov. 22, 1969

KICKOFF RETURNS

Most Kickoff Returns
Game—6, Larry Key vs. Miami, Sept. 24, 1977 and vs. Miami, Sept. 18, 1976; Joe Goldsmith vs. Mississippi State, Oct. 13, 1973; Billy Allen vs. East Carolina, 1983
Season—29, Joe Goldsmith, 1973
Career—67, Larry Key, 1974–77

Most Yards on Kickoff Returns
Game—184, Leon Bright vs. Virginia Tech, Nov. 16, 1974
Season—583, Keith Ross, 1986
Career—1,348, Larry Key, 1974–77

Highest Average Per Kickoff Return
Game (Min. 3)—46.0, (184-4), Leon Bright vs. Virginia Tech, Nov. 16, 1974
Season (Min. 10)—27.5, (358-13), Bill Odom, 1955
Career (Min. 35)—25.7, (1001-39), Keith Ross, 1985–86

Most TDs on Kickoff Returns
Game—1, 10 players, latest Dexter Carter, Miami, Nov. 1, 1986
Season—1, 10 players, latest Dexter Carter, Miami, Nov. 1, 1986
Career—2, Eddie McMillian, 1970–72; T.K. Wetherell, 1964–66

Longest Kickoff Return
Game—100, Leon Bright vs. Virginia Tech, Nov. 16, 1974; Bill Moreman/T.K. Wetherell vs. Kentucky, Oct. 9, 1965; Keith Ross/Dexter Carter vs. Miami, Nov. 1, 1986

FIELD GOALS

Most Field Goals Attempted
Game—8, Frank Fontes vs. Wake Forest, Sept. 26, 1970
Season—30, Bill Capece, 1980
Career—73, Derek Schmidt, 1984–86

Most Field Goals Made
Game—5, Bill Capece vs. Pittsburgh, Oct. 11, 1980
Season—22, Bill Capece, 1980
Career—50, Derek Schmidt, 1984–86

Highest Percentage of Field Goals Made
Season (Min. 10 atts.)—73.3, (22-30), Bill Capece, 1980
Career (Min. 40 atts.)—68.5, (50–73), Derek Schmidt, 1984–86

Longest Field Goal Made
Game—54, Derek Schmidt vs. Miami, Sept. 22, 1984

BLOCKED KICKS

Most Blocked Kicks
Game—2, Joe Wessel vs. Temple, Sept. 29, 1984; J.T. Thomas vs. Louisville, Sept. 12, 1970
Season—5, Joe Wessel, 1984
Career—7, Bobby Butler, 1977–80

Most Blocked Punts
Game—1, many players, latest John Hadley vs. Miami, Nov. 2, 1985
Season—4, Joe Wessel, 1984
Career—6, Bobby Butler, 1977–80

Most Blocked Field Goals
Game—2, J.T. Thomas vs. Louisville, Sept. 12, 1970
Season—2, J.T. Thomas, 1970
Career—2, Alphonso Carreker, 1980–83; J.T. Thomas, 1969–71

Most TDs Scored Off Blocked Kicks
Game—2, Joe Wessel vs. Arizona State, Nov. 3, 1984
Season—3, Joe Wessel, 1984
Career—3, Joe Wessel, 1981–84

Most TDs Scored Off Blocked Punts
Game—2, Joe Wessel vs. Arizona State, Nov. 3, 1984
Season—3, Joe Wessel, 1984
Career—3, Joe Wessel, 1981–84

Most TDs Scored Off Blocked Field Goals
Game—1, many players, latest Eric Riley vs. Temple, Sept. 29, 1984
Season—1, many players, latest Eric Riley, 1984
Career—1, many players, latest Eric Riley, 1980–84

FUMBLES

Caused Fumbles
Game—2, many players
Season—13, Ron Simmons, 1977
Career—17, Ron Simmons, 1977–80

Fumble Recoveries
Game—3, Ron Wallace vs. Wichita State, Sept. 20, 1969
Season—6, Ron Wallace, 1969
Career—8, Ron Simmons, 1977–80; Willie Jones, 1975–78; Ron Wallace, 1968–70

TACKLES

Total Tackles
Game—29, Dale McCullers vs. Texas A&M, Oct. 5, 1968
Season—181, Aaron Carter, 1977
Career—512, Aaron Carter, 1974–77

Quarterback Sacks
Game—5, Ron Simmons vs. North Texas State, Oct. 29, 1977
Season—12, Ron Simmons, 1977
Career—25, Ron Simmons, 1977–80

Tackles for Loss
Game—4, Isaac Williams vs. Temple, Sept. 29, 1984
Season—17, Ron Simmons, 1979
Career—44, Ron Simmons, 1977–80

INTERCEPTIONS

Most Passes Intercepted
Game — 3, Tommy Brown vs. Stetson, Nov. 10, 1950, and vs. Georgia Tech, Nov. 22, 1952; Bud Whitehead vs. Virginia Tech, Oct. 10, 1959; James Thomas vs. Kansas State, Nov. 21, 1970.
Season — 8, Curt Campbell, 1951; Monk Bonasorte, 1979.
Career—15, Monk Bonasorte, 1978–80

Most Yards on Interceptions
Game—100, Deion Sanders vs. Tulsa, Oct. 19, 1985
Season—111, Willie Whitehead, 1959
Career—197, Harvey Clayton, 1979–82

Most TDs on Interceptions
Game—1, many players, latest Martin Mayhew vs. North Carolina, Oct. 26, 1985
Season—1, many players, latest Martin Mayhew vs. North Carolina, Oct. 26, 1985
Career—1, many players, latest Martin Mayhew vs. North Carolina, Oct. 26, 1985

Longest Interception Return
Game—100, Deion Sanders vs. Tulsa, Oct. 19, 1985

Team Records
Single-Game Offense

TOTAL OFFENSE

Most Plays—100, vs. East Carolina, Sept. 20, 1980
Most Plays, Both Teams—173, vs. San Diego State, Oct. 27, 1973
Most Yards Gained—706, vs. East Carolina, Oct. 16, 1982
Most Yards Gained, Both Teams—1,219, Arizona State, Nov. 3, 1984
Most Touchdowns—9, vs. East Carolina, Sept. 20, 1980; vs. Memphis State, Nov. 17, 1979

RUSHING

Most Rushes—81, vs. East Carolina, Sept. 20, 1980
Most Rushes, Both Teams—120, vs. Oklahoma, Sept. 25, 1976
Most Yards—479, vs. Western Carolina, Oct. 31, 1981
Most Yards, Both Teams—706, vs. Louisville, Nov. 13, 1982
Most Touchdowns—7, vs. East Carolina, Sept. 20, 1980

PASSING

Most Passes Attempted—59, vs. Florida, Oct. 7, 1972
Most Passes Attempted, Both Teams—94, vs. Ohio State, Oct. 3, 1981
Most Passes Completed—31, vs. Memphis State, Nov. 15, 1969
Most Passes Completed, Both Teams—56, vs. Ohio State, Oct. 3, 1981
Highest Percentage Completed (Min. 20 atts.)—84.0, (21-25), vs. Virginia Tech, Oct. 2, 1971
Most Passes Intercepted—7, vs. South Carolina, Nov. 10, 1984
Most Yards Gained—508, vs. Memphis State, Nov. 15, 1969
Most Yards Gained, Both Teams—761, vs. South Carolina, Oct. 25, 1968
Touchdown Passes—5, vs. Wake Forest, Nov. 23, 1968; vs. South Carolina, Oct. 23, 1971; vs. Tulsa, Oct. 19, 1985

SCORING

Most Points—76, vs. Tulsa, Oct. 19, 1985
Most Points, Both Teams—96, vs. Arizona State, Nov. 3, 1984
Greatest Margin of Victory—74, vs. Whiting Field, 1949*; 59, vs. Louisville, 1953
Greatest Margin of Defeat—49, vs. Florida, 1973
Most Touchdowns—10, vs. Tulsa, Oct. 19, 1985
Most Touchdowns, Both Teams—13, vs. East Carolina, Sept. 3, 1983
Most PAT Made—9, vs. East Carolina, Sept. 20, 1980
Most PAT Made, Both Teams—12, vs. Tulsa, Oct. 19, 1985
Most Field Goals Made—5, vs. Pittsburgh, Oct. 11, 1980
Most Field Goals Made, Both Teams—6, vs. Florida, Dec. 3, 1983

*Not recognized by the NCAA

FIRST DOWNS

Most First Downs—36, vs. East Carolina, Sept. 20, 1980
Most First Downs, Both Teams—55, vs. Louisiana St. Sept. 10, 1983; vs. Arizona State, Nov. 3, 1984
Most Rushing First Downs—24, vs. East Carolina, Sept. 20, 1980
Most Rushing First Downs, Both Teams—32, vs. Auburn, Oct. 23, 1976
Most Passing First Downs—21, vs. Memphis State, Nov. 17, 1979
Most Passing First Downs, Both Teams—37, vs. South Carolina, Oct. 26, 1968
Most Penalty First Downs—4, vs. Furman, Sept. 29, 1962; vs. Pittsburgh, Oct. 17, 1981; vs. South Carolina, Nov. 10, 1984; vs. Florida, Dec. 1, 1984; vs. South Carolina, Nov. 9, 1985
Most Penalty First Downs, Both Teams—7, vs. Pittsburgh, Oct. 17, 1981

PUNTING

Most Punts—12, vs. Houston, Nov. 3, 1973; vs. Florida, Sept. 28, 1968
Highest Average (Min. 5)—54.8, (329-6) vs. Florida, Nov. 28, 1981

PUNT RETURNS

Most Punt Returns—10, vs. South Carolina, Oct. 24, 1970
Most Yards Gained—171, vs. Virginia Tech, Nov. 16, 1974
Most Touchdowns—2, vs. Arizona State, Nov. 3, 1984

KICKOFF RETURNS

Most Kickoff Returns—9, vs. Miami, Sept. 18, 1976; vs. Auburn, Nov. 19, 1960
Most Yards Gained—205, vs. Virginia Tech, Nov. 16, 1974
Most Touchdowns—1, nine times, latest vs. Miami, Nov. 1, 1986

FUMBLES

Most Fumbles—10, vs. Wichita State, Sept. 20, 1969
Most Fumbles, Both Teams—27, vs. Wichita State, Sept. 20, 1969
Most Fumbles, Lost—7, vs. Wichita State, Sept. 20, 1969
Most Fumbles, Lost, Both Teams—17, vs. Wichita State, Sept. 20, 1969

PENALTIES

Most Penalties—15, vs. Florida, Nov. 29, 1986
Most Penalties, Both Teams—31, vs. South Carolina, Nov. 9, 1985
Most Yards Penalized—172, vs. Furman, Sept. 21, 1957
Most Yards Penalized, Both Teams—264, vs. South Carolina, Nov. 9, 1985

Single-Game Defense

TOTAL DEFENSE

Fewest Plays—38, vs. Memphis State, Nov. 4, 1967
Fewest Yards—23, vs. Citadel, Sept. 15, 1962
Most Yards—651, vs. Arizona State, Nov. 3, 1984

RUSHING DEFENSE

Fewest Rushes—22, vs. Pittsburgh, Oct. 11, 1980
Fewest Yards— -18, vs. Miami (36 carries), Nov. 2, 1985
Most Yards—466, vs. Houston, Nov. 23, 1974

PASS DEFENSE

Fewest Passes Attempted—4, vs. Georgia Tech, Oct. 4, 1975; vs. Virginia Tech, Oct. 11, 1975; vs. Memphis State, Nov. 4, 1967
Fewest Passes Completed—0, vs. William & Mary, Oct. 22, 1960
Lowest Percentage Completed (Min. 10 atts.)—15.4, (2-13), vs. Kansas State, Oct. 2, 1976; vs. Citadel, Sept. 15, 1962
Fewest Yards—0, vs. William & Mary, Oct. 22, 1960
Most Yards—532, vs. Arizona State, Nov. 3, 1984
Most Passes Intercepted—5, five times, latest vs. Florida, Nov. 23, 1979
Most Yards on Interceptions—134, vs. Tulsa, Oct. 19, 1985
Most TDs on Interceptions—2, vs. Tulsa, Oct. 19, 1985

FIRST DOWNS

Fewest First Downs—2, vs. Citadel, Sept. 15, 1962
Fewest Rushing First Downs—0, vs. Louisville, Sept. 13, 1980
Fewest Passing First Downs—0, seven times, latest vs. East Carolina, Sept. 20, 1980

BLOCKED KICKS

Most Blocked Kicks—2, many times, latest vs. Arizona State, Nov. 3, 1984; vs. Tulane, Oct. 20, 1984; vs. Temple, Sept. 29, 1984
Most Blocked Punts—2, Tulane, Oct. 20, 1984; vs. South Carolina, Nov. 6, 1982; vs. Arizona State, Nov. 3, 1984
Most Blocked Field Goals—2, vs. Louisville, 1970
Most TDs Scored off Blocked Kicks—2, vs. Arizona State, Nov. 3, 1984; vs. Tulane, Oct. 20, 1984
Most TDs Scored off Blocked Punts—2, vs. Tulane, Oct. 20, 1984; vs. Arizona State, Nov. 3, 1984
Most TDs Scored off Blocked Field Goals—1, many times, latest Temple, Sept. 29, 1984

FUMBLES

Most Fumbles Caused—17, vs. Wichita State, Sept. 20, 1969
Most Fumbles Recovered—10, vs. Wichita State, Sept. 20, 1969

TURNOVERS

Most Turnovers—12, (2 int.-10 fum.), vs. Wichita State, Sept. 20, 1969

Single-Season Offense

TOTAL OFFENSE

Most Yards Per Game—465.8, (5, 124-11), 1982
Highest Average Per Play—6.2, (5,124-825), 1982
Most Yards—5,124, 1982
Most Touchdowns—53, 1982

RUSHING

Most Yards—3,021, 1984
Most Yards Per Game—274.6, (3,021-11), 1984
Highest Average Per Play—5.3, (3,021-571), 1984
Most Touchdowns—30, 1982 and 1983

PASSING

Most Passes Attempted—389, 1972
Most Passes Completed—209, 1972
Highest Average Per Attempt—8.3, (2,040-247), 1976
Highest Average Per Completion—16.3, (1,938-119), 1984
Most Yards—2,974, 1972
Most Yards Per Game—284.4, (2,844-10), 1968
Highest Completion Percentage—59.0, (147-249), 1964
Most TD Passes—29, 1968
Highest Passing Efficiency Rating Points—141.5, 1968

SCORING

Most Points—389, 1984
Most Points Per Game—35.3, (389-11), 1984
Consecutive 50-Point Games—3, 1986
Most Touchdowns—53, 1982
Most PAT Made—52, 1982
Most Field Goals Made—22, 1980

FIRST DOWNS

Most First Downs—269, 1983
Most Rushing First Downs—146, 1984
Most Passing First Downs—129, 1972
Most Penalty First Downs—20, 1973 and 1975

PUNTING

Most Punts—81, 1973
Fewest Punts—41, 1964
Highest Average Per Punt—45.2, (2,941-65), 1981

PUNT RETURNS

Most Punt Returns—44, 1970
Fewest Punt Returns—14, 1960
Most Yards—496, 1970
Highest Average Per-Punt Return—13.7, (424-31), 1969
Most Touchdowns—4, 1979

KICKOFF RETURNS

Most Kickoff Returns—56, 1973
Fewest Kickoff Returns—15, 1962 and 1964
Most Yards—998, 1974
Highest Average Per-Kickoff Return—24.5, (412-36), 1965
Most Touchdowns—2, 1970 and 1981

FUMBLES

Most Fumbles—42, 1969
Most Fumbles Lost—27, 1969
Fewest Fumbles—10, 1966
Fewest Fumbles Lost—5, 1965 and 1966

PENALTIES

Most Penalties—89, 1984
Most Yards Penalized—794, 1972
Fewest Penalties—40, 1976
Fewest Yards Penalized—423, 1976

Single-Season Defense

TOTAL DEFENSE

Fewest Yards—1,811, 1964
Fewest Yards Per Game—181.1, (1,811-10), 1964
Lowest Average Per Play—3.3, (3,410-658), 1964
Fewest Touchdowns—8, 1980

RUSHING DEFENSE

Fewest Yards—750, 1964
Fewest Yards Per Game—75.0, (750-10), 1964

Lowest Average Per Play—2.1, (750-355), 1964
Fewest Touchdowns—2, 1980

PASS DEFENSE

Fewest Yards—675, 1958
Fewest Yards Per Game—63.5, (698-11), 1975
Fewest Yards Per Attempt—4.7, (693-148), 1962
Fewest Yards Per Completion—10.3, (693-67), 1962
Lowest Completion Percentage—34.1, (91-267), 1979
Fewest Touchdowns—2, 1956; 1958; 1963; 1964
Most Interceptions—25, 1968
Most Yards on Interceptions—307, 1985
Most TDs on Interceptions—4, 1985

SCORING

Fewest Points—66, 1964
Fewest Points Per Game—6.6, (66-10), 1964

FIRST DOWNS

Fewest First Downs—90, 1962
Fewest Rushing First Downs—45, 1962
Fewest Passing First Downs—28, 1958
Fewest Penalty First Downs—2, 1957

KICKOFF RETURNS

Lowest Average Per-Kickoff Return—15.7, (502-32), 1962

PUNT RETURNS

Lowest Average Per-Punt Return—3.3, (39-12), 1978
Most Punts Returned for Touchdown—4, 1984

BLOCKED KICKS

Most Blocked Kicks—9, 1982 and 1984
Most Blocked Punts—8, 1984
Most Blocked Field Goals—4, 1970
Most TDs off Blocked Kicks—6, 1984
Most TDs off Blocked Punts—5, 1984
Most TDs off Blocked Field Goals—1, many years, latest 1984

FUMBLES

Most Fumbles Caused—45, 1979
Most Fumbles Recovered—26, 1957

Year-by-Year Leaders

TOTAL OFFENSE

Year	Name	Plays	Yards	TD
1955	Len Swantic	116	595	6
1956	Lee Corso	147	725	8
1957	Bobby Renn	148	680	6
1958	Fred Pickard	122	602	4
1959	Joe Majors	227	1141	10
1960	Ed Trancygier	152	695	9
1961	Eddie Feely	181	722	7
1962	Eddie Feely	165	982	7
1963	Steve Tensi	169	852	9
1964	Steve Tensi	215	1635	15
1965	Ed Pritchett	325	1455	7
1966	Gary Pajcic	290	1735	9
1967	Kim Hammond	297	2074	17
1968	Bill Cappleman	349	2342	26
1969	Bill Cappleman	417	2135	14
1970	Tommy Warren	259	1713	12
1971	Gary Huff	386	2653	24
1972	Gary Huff	429	2770	26
1973	Billy Sexton	168	765	4
1974	Ron Coppess	215	909	3
1975	Clyde Walker	241	1424	11
1976	Jimmy Black	308	1836	11
1977	Wally Woodham	195	1263	13
1978	Jimmy Jordan	224	1330	15
1979	Jimmy Jordan	202	1107	13
1980	Rick Stockstill	272	1282	17
1981	Rick Stockstill	292	1247	11
1982	Kelly Lowrey	253	1670	15
1983	Kelly Lowrey	279	1686	20
1984	Eric Thomas	239	1277	14
1985	Chip Ferguson	161	976	13
1986	Danny McManus	126	903	9

RUSHING

Year	Name	No.	Yards	Avg.	TD
1955	Lee Corso	111	431	3.9	3
1956	Bobby Renn	105	596	5.7	2
1957	Fred Pickard	86	463	5.4	2
1958	Fred Pickard	122	615	5.0	4
1959	Fred Pickard	131	481	3.7	4
1960	Willie Whitehead	81	293	3.6	2
1961	Keith Kindermann	81	385	4.8	1
1962	Gene Roberts	75	299	4.0	0
1963	Dave Snyder	107	500	4.7	3
1964	Phil Spooner	136	516	3.8	5
1965	Jim Mankins	85	326	3.8	1
1966	Bill Moreman	123	480	3.9	7
1967	Bill Moreman	94	439	4.7	5
1968	Tom Bailey	116	570	4.9	2
1969	Tom Bailey	144	630	4.4	2
1970	Tom Bailey	121	514	4.2	2
1971	Paul Magalski	106	516	4.9	3
1972	Hodges Mitchell	192	944	4.9	3
1973	Hodges Mitchell	171	669	3.9	2
1974	Larry Key	123	602	4.9	3
1975	Leon Bright	162	675	4.2	3
1976	Larry Key	144	712	4.9	4
1977	Larry Key	239	1117	4.7	3
1978	Homes Johnson	183	817	4.5	4
1979	Mark Lyles	225	1011	4.5	8
1980	Sam Platt	224	983	4.4	6
1981	Greg Allen	139	888	6.4	3
1982	Ricky Williams	134	857	6.4	3
1983	Greg Allen	200	1134	5.7	13
1984	Greg Allen	133	971	7.3	8
1985	Tony Smith	111	678	6.1	4
1986	Victor Floyd	129	654	5.1	6

PASSING

Year	Name	Att.	Cmp.	Int.	Yards	TD
1955	Len Swantic	73	37	5	576	2
1956	Lee Corso	59	32	5	369	5
1957	Bobby Renn	54	23	4	263	2
1958	Vic Prinzi	71	40	5	480	7
1959	Joe Majors	168	90	7	1063	7
1960	Ed Trancygier	97	38	10	552	6
1961	Eddie Feely	83	48	3	471	4
1962	Steve Tensi	121	60	2	796	6
1963	Steve Tensi	147	71	9	915	9
1964	Steve Tensi	204	121	10	1681	14
1965	Ed Pritchett	247	110	14	1225	5
1966	Gary Pajcic	232	125	9	1590	8
1967	Kim Hammond	241	140	10	1991	15

Year	Name	Att.	Cmp.	Int.	Yards	TD
1968	Bill Cappleman	287	162	11	2410	25
1969	Bill Cappleman	344	183	18	2467	14
1970	Tommy Warren	190	97	10	1549	11
1971	Gary Huff	327	184	18	2736	23
1972	Gary Huff	385	206	23	2893	25
1973	Billy Sexton	128	51	12	754	4
1974	Ron Coppess	145	78	7	817	2
1975	Clyde Walker	203	117	8	1619	10
1976	Jimmy Black	179	104	9	1535	9
1977	Wally Woodham	154	94	9	1270	8
1978	Jimmy Jordan	199	108	9	1427	14
1979	Jimmy Jordan	180	87	14	1173	13
1980	Rick Stockstill	201	121	8	1377	15
1981	Rick Stockstill	238	122	14	1356	11
1982	Kelly Lowrey	217	113	8	1671	11
1983	Kelly Lowrey	233	131	12	1720	12
1984	Eric Thomas	161	78	4	1218	14
1985	Chip Ferguson	130	70	8	990	11
1986	Danny McManus	112	65	2	872	7

RECEIVING

Year	Name	No.	Yards	TD
1955	Tom Feamster	18	258	1
1956	Joe Holt	16	140	3
	Ron Schomburger	16	140	0
1957	Bob Nellums	21	217	2
1958	Jack Espenship	18	200	1
1959	Willie Whitehead	31	320	2
1960	Willie Whitehead	23	212	1
1961	Jim Daniel	10	113	0
	Tom Hillabrand	10	66	0
1962	Keith Kindermann	21	275	2
1963	Fred Biletnikoff	24	358	4
1964	Fred Biletnikoff	57	987	11
1965	Max Wettstein	24	365	3
1966	Ron Sellers	56	874	3
1967	Ron Sellers	70	1228	8
1968	Ron Sellers	86	1496	12
1969	Jim Tyson	49	720	4
1970	Rhett Dawson	54	946	5
1971	Rhett Dawson	62	817	7
1972	Barry Smith	69	1243	12
1973	Mike Shumann	21	280	2
1974	Mike Shumann	43	515	3
1975	Mike Shumann	38	730	5
1976	Ed Beckman	37	521	3
1977	Roger Overby	38	626	5
1978	Jackie Flowers	43	757	7
1979	Jackie Flowers	37	622	7
1980	Michael Whiting	25	203	0
1981	Michael Whiting	29	211	2
1982	Tony Johnson	30	500	2
1983	Weegie Thompson	31	502	3
	Jessie Hester	31	576	6
1984	Jessie Hester	42	832	9
1985	Hassan Jones	34	738	5
1986	Herb Gainer	27	441	5

SCORING

Year	Name	TD	PAT	CV	FG	PTS
1955	Len Swantic	4				24
	Buck Mets	4				24
1956	Bob Nellums	5	1-2			31
1957	Bob Nellums	5	2-3			32
1958	Bobby Renn	7		1		44
1959	Fred Pickard	7		1		44
1960	Bill Whitehead	3				18
	Ed Trancygier	3				18
1961	Eddie Feely	3				18
1962	Keith Kindermann	5				30
1963	Larry Brinkley	5		1		32
1964	Fred Biletnikoff	11		1		68
1965	Gene Roberts		10-14		7-12	31
1966	Jim Mankins	10				60
1967	Grant Guthrie		26-27		9-14	53
1968	Ron Sellers	12				72
1969	Grant Guthrie		15-17		11-18	48
1970	Frank Fontes		22-24		14-27	64
1971	Frank Fontes		30-31		13-24	69
1972	Barry Smith	14		1		86
1973	Ahmet Askin		8-9		4-9	20
1974	Ahmet Askin		14-15		4-14	26
1975	Rudy Thomas	6				36
	Larry Key	6				36
1976	Dave Cappelen		16-20		9-17	43
1977	Dave Cappelen		27-29		13-20	66
1978	Dave Cappelen		39-40		7-12	60
1979	Dave Cappelen		29-30		14-22	71
1980	Bill Capece		39-39		22-30	104
1981	Mike Rendina		25-27		9-15	52
1982	Greg Allen	21				126
1983	Greg Allen	13		1		80
1984	Derek Schmidt		42-42		17-24	93
1985	Derek Schmidt		44-44		18-25	98
1986	Derek Schmidt		41-42		15-24	86

Season Leaders

TOTAL OFFENSE

Name, Year	Plays	Yards
1. Gary Huff, 1972	429	2770
2. Gary Huff, 1971	386	2653
3. Bill Cappleman, 1968	349	2342
4. Bill Cappleman, 1969	417	2135
5. Kim Hammond, 1967	297	2074
6. Jimmy Black, 1976	308	1836
7. Gary Pajcic, 1966	290	1735
8. Tommy Warren, 1970	259	1713
9. Kelly Lowrey, 1983	279	1686
10. Kelly Lowrey, 1982	253	1670

RUSHING YARDAGE

Name, Year	Carries	Yards
1. Greg Allen, 1983	200	1134
2. Larry Key, 1977	239	1117
3. Mark Lyles, 1979	225	1011
4. Sam Platt, 1980	224	983
5. Greg Allen, 1984	133	971
6. Hodges Mitchell, 1972	192	944
7. Greg Allen, 1981	139	888
8. Ricky Williams, 1982	134	857
9. Homes Johnson, 1978	183	817
10. Greg Allen, 1982	152	776

RUSHING TOUCHDOWNS

Name, Year	TD
1. Greg Allen, 1982	20
2. Greg Allen, 1983	13
3. Kelly Lowrey, 1983	8
4. Mark Lyles, 1979	8
Jim Mankins, 1966	8
Greg Allen, 1984	8
7. Mark Lyles, 1978	7
8. Bill Moreman, 1966	7
9. Sam Platt, 1980	6
Rudy Thomas, 1975	6
Michael Whiting, 1980	6
Roosevelt Snipes, 1984	6
Victor Floyd, 1986	6

PASSES COMPLETED

Name, Year	Attempts	Completed
1. Gary Huff, 1972	385	206
2. Gary Huff, 1971	327	184
3. Bill Cappleman, 1969	344	183
4. Bill Cappleman, 1968	287	162
5. Kim Hammond, 1967	241	140
6. Kelly Lowrey, 1983	233	131
7. Gary Pajcic, 1966	232	125
8. Rick Stockstill, 1981	238	122
9. Steve Tensi, 1964	204	121
Rick Stockstill, 1980	201	121

PASSING YARDAGE

Name, Year	Yards
1. Gary Huff, 1972	2893
2. Gary Huff, 1971	2736
3. Bill Cappleman, 1969	2467
4. Bill Cappleman, 1968	2410
5. Kim Hammond, 1967	1991
6. Kelly Lowrey, 1983	1720
7. Steve Tensi, 1964	1681
8. Kelly Lowrey, 1982	1671
9. Clyde Walker, 1975	1619
10. Gary Pajcic, 1966	1590

TOUCHDOWN PASSES

Name, Year	TD
1. Gary Huff, 1972	25
Bill Cappleman, 1968	25
3. Gary Huff, 1971	23
4. Kim Hammond, 1967	15
Rick Stockstill, 1980	15
6. Jimmy Jordan, 1978	14
Steve Tensi, 1964	14
Bill Cappleman, 1969	14
Eric Thomas, 1984	14
10. Jimmy Jordan, 1979	13

RECEPTIONS

Name, Year	Catches
1. Ron Sellers, 1968	86
2. Ron Sellers, 1967	70
3. Barry Smith, 1972	69
4. Rhett Dawson, 1971	62
5. Fred Biletnikoff, 1964	57
6. Ron Sellers, 1966	56
7. Rhett Dawson, 1970	54
8. Gary Parris, 1972	49
Jim Tyson, 1969	49
10. Mike Shumann, 1974	43
Jackie Flowers, 1978	43

RECEIVING YARDAGE

Name, Year	Yards
1. Ron Sellers, 1968	1496
2. Barry Smith, 1972	1243
3. Ron Sellers, 1967	1228
4. Fred Biletnikoff, 1964	987
5. Rhett Dawson, 1970	946
6. Ron Sellers, 1966	874
7. Jessie Hester, 1984	832
8. Rhett Dawson, 1971	817
9. Jackie Flowers, 1978	757
10. Hassan Jones, 1985	738

TOUCHDOWN CATCHES

Name, Year	TD
1. Barry Smith, 1972	13
2. Ron Sellers, 1968	12
3. Fred Biletnikoff, 1964	11
4. Jessie Hester, 1984	9
5. Ron Sellers, 1967	8
6. Rhett Dawson, 1971	7
Jackie Flowers, 1978	7
Sam Platt, 1978	7
Jackie Flowers, 1979	7
Hassan Jones, 1984	7

TACKLES

Name, Year	Tackles	Assists	Total
1. Aaron Carter, 1977	82	99	181
2. Reggie Herring, 1980	92	78	170
3. Dale McCullers, 1968	102	61	163
4. Henry Taylor, 1984	80	79	159
5. Jimmy Heggins, 1977	67	90	157

TACKLES FOR LOSS

Name, Year	No.
1. Ron Simmons, 1979	17
2. Ron Simmons, 1977	13
3. Alphonso Carreker, 1983	12
Scott Warren, 1977	12
Paul McGowan, 1985	12
6. Arthur Scott, 1979	10

QUARTERBACK SACKS

Name, Year	No.
1. Ron Simmons, 1977	12
2. Willie Jones, 1978	10
3. Alphonso Carreker, 1982	8
Gerald Nichols, 1984	8

SCORING

Name, Year	TD	PAT	CV	FG	PTS.
1. Greg Allen, 1982	21				126
2. Bill Capece, 1980		38-38		22-30	104
3. Derek Schmidt, 1985		44-44		18-25	98
4. Derek Schmidt, 1984		42-42		17-24	93
5. Barry Smith, 1972	14				86
6. Derek Schmidt, 1986		41-42		15-24	86
7. Greg Allen, 1983	13		1		80
8. Ron Sellers, 1968	12				72
9. Dave Cappelen, 1979		29-30		14-22	71
10. Philip Hall, 1982		52-53		6-7	70

Career Leaders

TOTAL OFFENSE

Name, Years	Plays	Yards
1. Gary Huff (70–72)	921	6086
2. Bill Cappleman (67–69)	777	4499
3. Jimmy Jordan (76–79)	678	3764
4. Wally Woodham (75, 77–79)	573	3531
5. Kelly Lowrey (80–83)	450	3429
6. Steve Tensi (62–64)	525	3294
7. Larry Key (74–77)	627	2953
8. Kim Hammond (65–67)	433	2890
9. Gary Pajcic (66–68)	479	2681
Rick Stockstill (77, 79–81)	572	2630

RUSHING YARDAGE

Name, Years	Carries	Yards
1. Greg Allen (81–84)	624	3769
2. Larry Key (74–77)	625	2953
3. Mark Lyles (76–79)	515	2218
4. Tom Bailey (68–70)	381	1714
5. Ricky Williams (79–82)	320	1625
6. Hodges Mitchell (72–73)	363	1613
7. Fred Pickard (57–59)	339	1546
Michael Whiting (78–81)	355	1485
9. Bobby Renn (56–58)	268	1455
10. Roosevelt Snipes (83–84)	214	1385

RUSHING TOUCHDOWNS

Name, Years	TD
1. Greg Allen (81–84)	44
2. Mark Lyles (76–79)	20
3. Bill Moreman (65–67)	14
4. Kelly Lowrey (80–83)	13
Larry Key (74–77)	13
6. Michael Whiting (78–81)	12
7. Bobby Renn (56–58)	11
8. Fred Pickard (57–59)	10
Rudy Thomas (73–76)	10
Roosevelt Snipes (83–84)	10
Victor Floyd (85–86)	10

PASSES COMPLETED

Name, Years	Attempts	Completed
1. Gary Huff (70–72)	796	436
2. Bill Cappleman (67–69)	636	349
3. Jimmy Jordan (76–79)	594	297
4. Wally Woodham (75, 77–79)	476	273
5. Kelly Lowrey (80–83)	464	252
Steve Tensi (62–64)	472	252
7. Rick Stockstill (77, 79–81)	447	250
8. Kim Hammond (65–67)	351	196
9. Gary Pajcic (66–68)	383	195
10. Eddie Feely (60–62)	279	159

PASSING YARDAGE

Name, Years	Yards
1. Gary Huff (70–72)	6378
2. Bill Cappleman (67–69)	4904
3. Jimmy Jordan (76–79)	4144
4. Wally Woodham (75, 77–79)	3550
5. Kelly Lowrey (80–83)	3469
6. Steve Tensi (62–64)	3392
7. Kim Hammond (65–67)	2777
8. Rick Stockstill (77, 79–81)	2739
9. Gary Pajcic (66–68)	2451
10. Jimmy Black (74, 76)	1920

TOUCHDOWN PASSES

Name, Years	TD
1. Gary Huff (70–72)	52
2. Bill Cappleman (67–69)	39
Jimmy Jordan (76–79)	39
4. Steve Tensi (62–64)	28
5. Rick Stockstill (77, 79–81)	26
6. Kelly Lowrey (80–83)	24
7. Wally Woodham (75–79)	22
8. Kim Hammond (65–67)	19
9. Blair Williams (79–82)	16
10. Chip Ferguson (85–86)	15

PASS INTERCEPTIONS

Name, Years	No.
1. Monk Bonasorte (77–80)	15
2. Lee Corso (53–56)	14
3. James Thomas (70–72)	12
Curt Campbell (50–52)	12
Keith Jones (78–80)	12
Brian McCrary (81–84)	12
7. Bobby Butler (77–80)	11
8. Walt Sumner (66–68)	11
9. Bobby Jackson (74–77)	10
Bill Brown (55–58)	10
Eric Williams (84–86)	10

RECEPTIONS

Name, Years	Catches
1. Ron Sellers (66–68)	212
2. Mike Shumann (73–75, 77)	134
3. Rhett Dawson (69–71)	128
4. Barry Smith (70–72)	122
5. Jessie Hester (81–84)	107
6. Jackie Flowers (76–79)	101
7. Hassan Jones (82–85)	98
8. Fred Biletnikoff (62–64)	87
9. Gary Parris (70–72)	82
10. Mark Lyles (76–79)	81

RECEIVING YARDAGE

Name, Years	Yards
1. Ron Sellers (66–68)	3598
2. Barry Smith (70–72)	2392
3. Mike Shumann (73–75, 77)	2306
4. Jessie Hester (81–84)	2100
5. Rhett Dawson (69–71)	1915
6. Hassan Jones (82–85)	1764
7. Jackie Flowers (76–79)	1697
8. Fred Biletnikoff (62–64)	1463
9. Kurt Unglaub (76–80)	1260
10. Jim Tyson (68–70)	1204

TOUCHDOWN CATCHES

Name, Years	TD
1. Barry Smith (70–72)	25
2. Ron Sellers (66–68)	23
3. Jessie Hester (81–84)	21
4. Hassan Jones (82–85)	17
5. Mike Shumann (73–75, 77)	16
Fred Biletnikoff (62–64)	16
7. Jackie Flowers (76–79)	14
8. Kent Gaydos (69–71)	12
Rhett Dawson (69–71)	12
Hardis Johnson (79–80)	12

SCORING

Name, Years	TD	PAT	CV	FG.	PTS.
1. Greg Allen (81–84)	46		1		278
2. Derek Schmidt (84–86)		127-128		50-73	277
3. Dave Cappelen (76–79)		111-119		43-71	240

4. Barry Smith (70–72)	27		1	164
5. Grant Guthrie (67–69)		72-76	28-50	156
6. Ron Sellers (66–68)	23			138
7. Jessie Hester (81–84)	22		2	136
8. Mark Lyles (76–79)	22		1	134
9. Frank Fontes (70–71)		52-55	27-51	133
10. Philip Hall (82–83)		90-98	11-16	123

TACKLES

Name, Years	No.
1. Aaron Carter (74–77)	512
2. Ron Simmons (77–80)	483
3. Reggie Herring (77–80)	452
4. Ken Roe (80–83)	373
5. Henry Taylor (81–84)	344

TACKLES FOR LOSS

Name, Years	No.
1. Ron Simmons (77–80)	44
2. Scott Warren (76–79)	22
3. Paul McGowan (84–86)	21
4. Willie Jones (75–78)	20
Isaac Williams (82–85)	20
6. Alphonso Carreker (80–83)	19
Arthur Scott (76–80)	19

QUARTERBACK SACKS

Name, Years	No.
1. Ron Simmons (77–80)	25
2. Alphonso Carreker (80–83)	20
Willie Jones (75–78)	20

Best Single-Game Performances

TOTAL OFFENSE

Player	Opponent	Year	Yards
1. Bill Cappleman	Memphis State	1969	490
2. Bill Cappleman	South Carolina	1968	431
3. Tommy Warren	Virginia Tech	1970	384
4. Gary Huff	Houston	1972	383
5. Jimmy Black	Southern Mississippi	1976	372
6. Gary Huff	South Carolina	1971	369
Joe Majors	Tampa	1959	369
8. Bill Cappleman	Wake Forest	1968	367
9. Gary Huff	Virginia Tech	1971	357
10. Eric Thomas	Auburn	1984	352

YARDS RUSHING

Player	Opponent	Year	Yards
1. Greg Allen	Western Carolina	1981	322
2. Greg Allen	Arizona State	1984	223
3. Victor Floyd	South Carolina	1985	212
4. Sammie Smith	Indiana (All-American Bowl)	1986	205
5. Greg Allen	Louisiana State	1981	202
6. Greg Allen	Louisana State	1983	201
7. Sam Platt	Memphis State	1980	188
8. Greg Allen	Louisville	1982	173
9. Larry Key	Auburn	1977	170
10. Keith Ross	South Carolina	1985	163

YARDS PASSING

Player	Opponent	Year	Yards
1. Bill Cappleman	Memphis State	1969	508
2. Bill Cappleman	South Carolina	1968	437
3. Gary Huff	Houston	1972	409
4. Gary Huff	Virginia Tech	1971	374
5. Bill Cappleman	Tulsa	1969	372
6. Kim Hammond	Mississippi State	1967	369
7. Gary Huff	South Carolina	1971	366
8. Bill Cappleman	Wake Forest	1968	365
9. Kim Hammond	Penn State (Gator Bowl)	1967	362
10. Eric Thomas	Auburn	1984	357

YARDS RECEIVING

Player	Opponent	Year	Yards
1. Ron Sellers	Wake Forest	1968	260
2. Ron Sellers	South Carolina	1968	259
3. Ron Sellers	Virginia Tech	1967	229
4. Ron Sellers	Memphis State	1968	218
5. Ron Sellers	Houston	1968	214
6. Fred Biletnikoff	Oklahoma (Gator Bowl)	1965	192
7. Fred Biletnikoff	Virginia Tech	1964	182

8. Jackie Flowers	Louisiana State	1979	174
9. Tony Johnson	Southern Mississippi	1982	166
10. Jackie Flowers	Houston	1978	165

PASS ATTEMPTS

Player	Opponent	Year	Passes
1. Gary Huff	Florida	1972	58
2. Kim Hammond	Penn State (Gator Bowl)	1967	53
Gary Pajcic	Virginia Tech	1966	53
4. Gary Huff	Houston	1972	51
5. Bill Cappleman	Memphis State	1969	50
6. Gary Huff	Arizona State (Fiesta Bowl)	1971	46
7. Chip Ferguson	Oklahoma State (Gator Bowl)	1985	43
Jimmy Jordan	Mississippi State	1978	43
9. Gary Huff	Kansas	1972	42
Bill Cappleman	South Carolina	1968	42
Bill Cappleman	Florida	1969	42

PASS COMPLETIONS

Player	Opponent	Year	Passes
1. Kim Hammond	Penn State (Gator Bowl)	1967	37
2. Bill Cappleman	Memphis State	1969	31
3. Gary Pajcic	Virginia Tech	1966	28
Kelly Lowrey	East Carolina	1983	28
5. Gary Huff	Houston	1972	27
Gary Huff	Florida	1972	27
7. Gary Huff	Kansas	1972	26
Gary Huff	South Carolina	1971	26
9. Gary Huff	Auburn	1972	25
Gary Huff	Arizona State (Fiesta Bowl)	1971	25
Bill Cappleman	South Carolina	1968	25

PASS RECEPTIONS

Player	Opponent	Year	Passes
1. Ron Sellers	South Carolina	1968	16
2. Ron Sellers	Wake Forest	1968	14
Ron Sellers	Penn State (Gator Bowl)	1967	14
Ron Sellers	Houston	1968	14
5. Kent Gaydos	Houston	1969	13
Ron Sellers	Memphis State	1968	13
Ron Sellers	Alabama	1967	13
Ron Sellers	Virginia Tech	1966	13
Fred Biletnikoff	Oklahoma (Gator Bowl)	1965	13
10. Bill Moreman	Penn State (Gator Bowl)	1967	12

Longest Plays

LONGEST RUNS FROM SCRIMMAGE WITHOUT SCORING

1. 76 yards by Roy Thompson vs. Stetson, 1951
2. 66 yards by Greg Allen vs. Louisiana State, 1981
3. 65 yards by Wayne Giardino vs. Oklahoma (Gator Bowl), 1965
   65 yards by Dennis McKinnon vs. West Virginia (Gator Bowl), 1982
5. 64 yards by Nelson Italiano vs. Troy State, 1951
6. 60 yards by Jim Mankins vs. Texas Tech, 1966
   60 yards by Nelson Italiano vs. Tampa, 1950
   60 yards by Lee Corso vs. North Carolina State, 1956

LONGEST TOUCHDOWN RUNS FROM SCRIMMAGE

1. 97 yards by Larry Key vs. Virginia Tech, 1976
2. 81 yards by Fred Pickard vs. Virginia Tech, 1957
   81 yards by Greg Allen vs. Arizona State, 1984
4. 80 yards by Phil Spooner vs. Houston, 1965
5. 78 yards by Buck Metts vs. Stetson, 1964
6. 77 yards by Jessie Hester vs. Miami, 1984
7. 74 yards by Bobby McKinnon vs. Memphis State, 1973
8. 68 yards by Bobby Fiveash vs. Tampa, 1958
9. 66 yards by Dave Snyder vs. Furman, 1963
10. 62 yards by Sammie Smith vs. Southern Mississippi, 1986

LONGEST TOUCHDOWN PLAYS

1. 100 yards by Leon Bright vs. Virginia Tech, 1974 (KO return)
   100 yards by Bill Moreman and T.K. Wetherell vs. Kentucky, 1965 (lateral on KO return)
   100 yards by Deion Sanders vs. Tulsa, 1985 (interception return)
   100 yards by Keith Ross and Dexter Carter vs. Miami, 1986 (pass on KO return)
5. 99 yards by Ted Hewitt vs. Stetson, 1948 (pass interception return)
   99 yards by Fred Biletnikoff vs. Miami, 1963 (pass interception return)
7. 97-yard run by Larry Key vs. Virginia Tech, 1976
   97 yards by Billy Allen vs. Louisiana State, 1981 (KO return)
9. 96-yard pass from Jimmy Jordan to Kurt Unglaub vs. Virginia Tech, 1976
   96 yards by David Snell vs. Virginia Tech, 1970 (KO return)
11. 95-yard pass from Jimmy Black to Rudy Thomas vs. Southern Mississippi, 1976

95 yards by Greg Allen vs. Western Carolina, 1981 (KO return)
95 yards by Billy Allen vs. West Virginia (Gator Bowl), 1982 (KO return)
14. 94 yards by Bill Moreman and T.K. Wetherell vs. Miami, 1966 (lateral on KO return)
15. 93 yards by Eddie McMillan vs. Memphis State, 1970 (KO return)
   93 yards by Larry Key vs. Texas Tech (Tangerine Bowl), 1977 (KO return)
17. 92 yards by Phil Abraira vs. North Carolina State, 1969 (punt return)
18. 91-yard pass from Jimmy Black to Kurt Unglaub vs. North Texas State, 1976
19. 90 yards by Eddie McMillan vs. Miami, 1971 (KO return)

LONGEST FIELD GOALS

1. 54 yards by Derek Schmidt vs. Miami, 1984
2. 53 yards by Grant Guthrie vs. Miami, 1969
   53 yards by Derek Schmidt vs. Louisville, 1986
4. 52 yards by Derek Schmidt vs. Arizona State, 1984
   52 yards by Mike Rendina vs. Ohio State, 1981
6. 51 yards by Derek Schmidt vs. Memphis State, 1985
   51 yards by Derek Schmidt vs. Memphis State, 1985
   51 yards by Derek Schmidt vs. North Carolina, 1985
   51 yards by Grant Guthrie vs. Virginia Tech, 1969
10. 50 yards by Bill Capece vs. Pittsburgh, 1980
   50 yards by Dave Cappelen vs. South Carolina, 1979

LONGEST TOUCHDOWN PASSES

1. 96 yards from Jimmy Jordan to Kurt Unglaub vs. Virginia Tech, 1976
2. 95 yards from Jimmy Black to Rudy Thomas vs. Southern Mississippi, 1976
3. 91 yards from Jimmy Black to Kurt Unglaub vs. North Texas State, 1976
4. 88 yards from Gary Huff to Barry Smith vs. Kansas, 1971
5. 86 yards from Gary Pajcic to Ron Sellers vs. Wake Forest, 1966
6. 83 yards from Blair Williams to Dennis McKinnon vs. South Carolina, 1982
7. 82 yards from Gary Pajcic to Ron Sellers vs. Maryland, 1968
8. 80 yards from Bill Cappleman to Don Pederson vs. Memphis State, 1969
   80 yards from Nelson Italiano to Eddie Gray vs. Newberry, 1950
10. 78 yards from Clyde Walker to Mike Shumann vs. Iowa State, 1975

LONGEST PUNT RETURNS

1. 92 yards by Phil Abraira vs. North Carolina State, 1969 (TD)
2. 80 yards by Robert Jackson vs. Virginia Tech, 1974 (TD)
   80 yards by Bill Odom vs. Stetson, 1954 (TD)
4. 75 yards by Walt Sumner vs. Alabama, 1967 (TD)
   75 yards by Ralph Claudron vs. Whiting Field, 1949 (TD)
6. 71 yards by David Snell vs. Louisville, 1970 (TD)
7. 70 yards by Bill Campbell vs. Wake Forest, 1965 (TD)
8. 65 yards by Gary Henry vs. Southern Mississippi, 1979 (TD)
9. 60 yards by Lee Corso vs. North Carolina State, 1956
10. 58 yards by Tommy Brown vs. Jacksonville Navy, 1951
    58 yards by Deion Sanders vs. Florida, 1985 (TD)

LONGEST KICKOFF RETURNS

1. 100 yards by Leon Bright vs. Virginia Tech, 1974 (TD)
   100 yards by Bill Moreman and T.K. Wetherell vs. Kentucky, 1965 (TD, lateral)
   100 yards by Keith Ross and Dexter Carter vs. Miami, 1986 (TD, lateral)
4. 97 yards by Billy Allen vs. Louisiana State, 1981 (TD)
5. 96 yards by David Snell vs. Virginia Tech, 1970 (TD)
6. 95 yards by Greg Allen vs. Western Carolina, 1981 (TD)

   95 yards by Billy Allen vs. West Virginia (Gator Bowl), 1982 (KO return)
8. 94 yards by Bill Moreman and T.K. Wetherell vs. Miami, 1966 (TD, lateral)
9. 93 yards by Eddie McMillan vs. Memphis State, 1970 (TD)
   93 yards by Larry Key vs. Texas Tech (Tangerine Bowl), 1977
11. 90 yards by Eddie McMillan vs. Miami, 1971 (TD)
12. 89 yards by Bill Odom vs. Virginia Tech, 1955 (TD)
13. 84 yards by Fred Pickard vs. Tampa, 1958
14. 80 yards by Keith Ross vs. Tulsa, 1985
15. 72 yards by Bobby Renn vs. Florida, 1958

LONGEST INTERCEPTION RETURNS

1. 100 yards by Deion Sanders vs. Tulsa, 1985 (TD)
2. 99 yards by Ted Hewitt vs. Stetson, 1958 (TD)
   99 yards by Fred Biletnikoff vs. Miami, 1963 (TD)
4. 86 yards by Tom Hillabrand vs. Auburn, 1960 (TD)
5. 81 yards by Bud Whitehead vs. Wake Forest, 1959 (TD)
6. 74 yards by Dale McCullers vs. Houston, 1967
7. 69 yards by Howard Ehler vs. Oklahoma (Gator Bowl), 1965 (TD)
8. 66 yards by Bill Dawkins vs. Wofford (Cigar Bowl), 1959
9. 62 yards by Martin Mayhew vs. North Carolina, 1985 (TD)
10. 51 yards by Tracy Ashley vs. Southern Illinois, 1982
    51 yards by Eric Williams vs. Southern Mississippi, 1986

THE BOB CRENSHAW AWARD

Given in memory of Robert E. (Bob) Crenshaw, 1955, Florida State football captain and student leader who was killed in a jet crash in 1958, the plaque's inscription reads: "To the Football Player With the Biggest Heart." The recipient is chosen by his teammates as the man who best exemplified the "qualities that made Bob Crenshaw an outstanding football player and person."

1958—Al Ulmer, Guard
1959—Ramon Rogers, Center
1960—Abner Bigbee, Fullback
1961—Paul Andrews, Fullback
1962—Jim Sims, Tackle
1963—Larry Brinkley, Fullback
1964—Dick Hermann, Linebacker
1965—Howard Ehler, Defensive Back

1966—Ed Pope, Guard
1967—Kim Hammond, Quarterback
1968—Billy Gunter, Running Back
1969—Stan Walker, Guard
1970—Bill Lohse, Linebacker
1971—Bill Henson, Defensive Tackle
1972—Allen Dees, Center

1973—Steve Bratton, Defensive End
1974—Jeff Gardner, Offensive Guard
1975—Lee Nelson, Defensive Back
1976—Joe Camps, Defensive Back
1977—Aaron Carter, Linebacker
1978—Scott Warren, Defensive End
1979—Greg Futch, Offensive Tackle

1980—Monk Bonasorte, Defensive Back
1981—Barry Voltapetti, Offensive Tackle
1982—Blair Williams, Quarterback
1983—Tom McCormick, Center
1984—Todd Stroud, Noseguard
1985—Pete Panton, Tight End
1986—Greg Newell, Free Safety

OVERALL BOWL RECORD

Bowl	W	L	T
All-American	1	0	0
Bluegrass	0	1	0
Cigar	1	0	0
Citrus*	1	0	1
Fiesta	0	1	0
Gator	3	0	1
Orange	0	2	0
Peach	1	1	0
Sun	0	2	0
Totals	**7**	**7**	**2**

*Formerly the Tangerine Bowl

NATIONAL GEOGRAPHIC KiDS

weird but true!

2019

Published by Collins
An imprint of HarperCollins Publishers
Westerhill Road
Bishopbriggs
Glasgow G64 2QT
www.harpercollins.co.uk

In association with National Geographic Partners, LLC

First published 2018

ISBN 978-0-00-829438-0

10 9 8 7 6 5 4 3 2 1

A catalogue record for this book is available from the British Library

Printed and bound in China by RR Donnelley APS Co Ltd.

If you would like to comment on any aspect of this book, please contact
us at the above address or online.
natgeokidsbooks.co.uk
collins.reference@harpercollins.co.uk

Paper from responsible sources

NATIONAL GEOGRAPHIC KiDS

weird but true!

2019

wild & wacky facts & photos!

contents

Every year, around **8 million tonnes** of rubbish is thrown into **our oceans.**

Water pollution is a growing concern. Turn to pages 20–21 to find out why students in Taiwan are making lollies from polluted water sources.

100%純污水
製冰所

amAZiNg EaRTh

The COOLEST HOLIDAY EVER!

Ever dreamed of going on holiday to Antarctica – THE COLDEST CONTINENT ON EARTH?

Well, now it's easier than ever before! In 2018, the first tourist flights launched between Argentina and Seymour Island, Antarctica. Here's what to expect when you get off the plane. (Don't forget to pack your thermals...)

99% of Antarctica is covered by **ICE** – on average, **2.16 km** (1.3 miles) **THICK** – or five-and-a-half times the height of the **EMPIRE STATE BUILDING!**

Antarctica is officially a **DESERT** – although you won't find sand dunes and cacti there! It has this status because so **LITTLE WATER (IN THE FORM OF SNOW)** falls there – in the centre, only **50 MILLIMETRES** (2 inches) a year. That's less than the **SAHARA DESERT!**

Antarctica has towering **MOUNTAINS**, up to **3000 m** (9000 ft) high – and yet they're totally **INVISIBLE!** Why? Because they're **HIDDEN** under thick sheets of **ICE.**

The most **SOUTHERLY VOLCANO** in the world, **MOUNT EREBUS,** is found in Antarctica.

ANTARCTICA is the only place on Earth that **DOESN'T BELONG** to any **ONE COUNTRY.** Instead, responsibility for the continent is **SHARED** between the nations of the world, who have agreed to protect it as a site of **RESEARCH** and **SCIENCE.**

The **COLDEST TEMPERATURE** ever recorded on **EARTH** was in Antarctica – a bone-chilling **-89 ºC** (-128 ºF). **BRRRR!**

Nobody **LIVES** on Antarctica **PERMANENTLY.** The only humans there keeping the **PENGUINS** company are temporary colonies of **SCIENTIFIC RESEARCHERS.**

HEAVEN SENT

We often say 'IT'S RAINING CATS AND DOGS' meaning it's raining hard – but sometimes, strange things really DO rain down out of the **SKY!**

FROGS

Throughout history, there are tens of thousands of reports of frogs raining down from the sky. Some scientists think the poor creatures get sucked into the sky by a tornado or waterspout, then fall to Earth when the winds drop.

SQUID

In 1997, a frozen squid fell on top of a Korean fisherman called Kim Ho and knocked him unconscious. Nobody has ever been able to explain how this happened.

SPIDERS

In 2015, people in Southern Australia reported that they had been 'invaded' by tiny spiders falling from the sky. It was all down to how the spiders migrate: they climb to the top of tall trees, then launch themselves into the air using special webs that act like parachutes.

MEAT

In 1876, chunks of meat rained down on the town of Olympia Springs, Kentucky, USA. Some curious townsfolk even tasted the meat to try to determine what it could be! Nobody knows for sure how it happened, but the best guess is that the meat was vomited up by vultures flying overhead. Talk about bad manners...

FISH

The townspeople of Yoro, Honduras, hold a 'Rain of Fish' festival every year to mark the annual showers of tiny silver fish that they claim fall from the sky. They celebrate, naturally, by eating plenty of fish! As with frogs, scientists suspect waterspouts are to blame.

WORMS

In April 2015, thousands of tiny earthworms rained down from the clouds in Norway. The biology teacher who first spotted the phenomenon reported that the worms had survived their fall – and were still wriggling away!

GOLF BALLS

In 1969, people in the town of Punta Gorda, Florida, USA, reported that hundreds of golf balls dropped out of the sky onto their heads! The area is full of golf courses: waterspouts probably sucked the balls up and out of the lakes and ponds where they had ended up.

10 MARVELLOUSLY MONSTROUS

SOCKEYE SALMON
swim up to **3,800 KM**
(2,350 MILES)

MONARCH BUTTERFLIES
flutter **4,800 KM (3,000 MILES)**

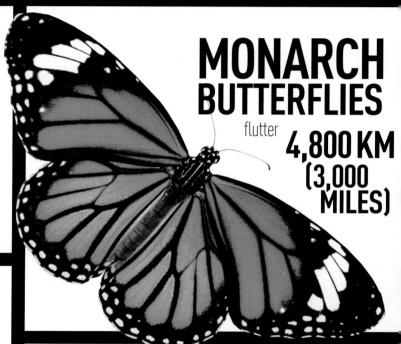

CARIBOU
travel **3,000 km**
(1,900 miles)

SEMIPALMATED SANDPIPERS FLY
5,300 KM (3,300 MILES)

Leatherback TURTLES
swim **20,000 km (12,400 miles)**

Dragonflies travel 17,000 km (10,500 miles) – but they **tag-team** it, like **relay runners,** because no single dragonfly lives long enough to make the journey.

MIGRATIONS

CHECK OUT THESE AMAZING ANNUAL ANIMAL MIGRATIONS

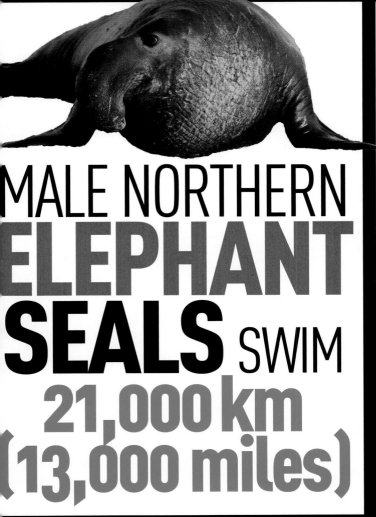

MALE NORTHERN **ELEPHANT SEALS** SWIM **21,000 km (13,000 miles)**

The **SOOTY SHEARWATER** flies **65,000 KM (40,400 MILES)**

HUMPBACK WHALES travel 15,000 KM (13,600 miles)

The **MIGRATION CHAMPION** is the **ARCTIC TERN.**

This bird makes the longest migration of any creature on Earth – **71,000 KM** (44,100 miles). That adds up to **2.4 million km** (1.5 million miles) in a lifetime – the equivalent of going to the **MOON** AND **BACK... THREE TIMES!**

A GLOWING REPORT?

SOME BEACHES GLOW BRIGHT BLUE IN THE DARK!

This **GLOWING LIGHT** might look like magic, but it's actually a natural phenomenon called **'BIOLUMINESCENCE'**.

You'll find these **INCREDIBLE** scenes worldwide, including certain bays in the **MALDIVES, PUERTO RICO** and southern **CALIFORNIA, USA**.

The light is given off by **TINY CREATURES** that live in the sea, called **PLANKTON**. These microscopic animals emit their **GLOW** as a cunning **SURVIVAL** technique. The **LIGHT** helps **PROTECT** them from fish and other **PREDATORS** that might eat them, by attracting bigger predators that then **EAT** those fish – leaving the plankton **SAFE!**

FANTASTIC FOSSILS

FOSSILS are the remains or other traces (like footprints) of PREHISTORIC ANIMALS and PLANTS that have been PRESERVED for MILLIONS of YEARS in MUD and ROCK.

Without fossils, we would have no idea that DINOSAURS had ever existed! The only EVIDENCE that they ever stalked the Earth comes from fossils.

The OLDEST FOSSILS ever found date back 4.2 BILLION YEARS. That's about 300 MILLION YEARS after the Earth was formed.

YUP – YOU CAN EVEN FIND FOSSILISED POO. THIS ONE CAME FROM A DINOSAUR!

MEET SUE! One of the **LARGEST,** most **COMPLETE FOSSILS** ever found. 'Sue' is a fossilised **TYRANNOSAURUS REX:** over **90%** of the dinosaur has been **RECOVERED.** You can find Sue on display at the **FIELD MUSEUM OF NATURAL HISTORY** in **CHICAGO, ILLINOIS, USA.**

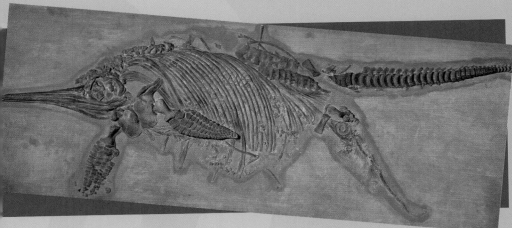

Sometimes fossils **CAPTURE INCREDIBLE MOMENTS** frozen in time—like this **ICHTHYOSAUR** (an extinct sea creature) giving **BIRTH!**

The **JURASSIC COAST** is a stretch of the **SOUTH** coast of **ENGLAND** where **MILLIONS** of **FOSSILS** have been **FOUND.**

DID YOU KNOW?

MOST **FOSSIL SITES** ARE EXTREMELY **FRAGILE** AND CAREFULLY PROTECTED. PLACES WHERE IT'S OK TO GO **HUNTING** FOR FOSSILS ARE SOMETIMES CALLED 'FOSSIL BEDS' — ALTHOUGH THEY WOULDN'T BE VERY COMFY SPOTS TO TAKE A **NAP**...

A really RUBBISH Island

Tiny, remote
HENDERSON ISLAND,
in the Pacific Ocean, doesn't have a single person living on it — but it's still covered in millions of pieces of
PLASTIC RUBBISH.
In fact, it's one of the most
POLLUTED PLACES
on the planet. How can that be?

The **38 MILLION** bits of rubbish on the island (and counting) have been thrown into the sea from all over the world. They've been carried across the ocean to the island's otherwise perfect, white sandy beaches by sea currents.

All in all, the rubbish weighs nearly
18 TONNES (20 tons) — that's about the same as

20 CARS

Sadly, it shows no sign of stopping: scientists estimate that another
13,000 PIECES
of rubbish arrive with the waves every day.

POLLUTED POPSICLES

HAVE YOU EVER BEEN TOLD, 'DON'T EAT SO MUCH RUBBISH'?

THREE STUDENTS IN **TAIWAN** TOOK THAT TO EXTREMES, BY MAKING **BEAUTIFUL ICE LOLLIES** OUT OF **POLLUTED WATER** THAT THEY COLLECTED FROM DIFFERENT LOCATIONS ACROSS THE **COUNTRY.**

THEY TOOK THE **WATER,** COMPLETE WITH BITS OF **RUBBISH** FLOATING IN IT, AND **FROZE** IT ON A STICK – JUST LIKE AN **ICE LOLLY.** BUT THESE **CONCOCTIONS** WEREN'T **DESIGNED** TO BE EATEN (THANK GOODNESS). THE STUDENTS WANTED TO DRAW ATTENTION TO THE **DANGEROUS** LEVELS OF **POLLUTION** IN THEIR COUNTRY'S WATER, AND **100** OF THEIR CREATIONS WERE PUT ON **DISPLAY** IN AN **ART GALLERY** IN **TAIPEI.**

100％純污水
製冰所

YES!
That is a
toothbrush!

DON'T BELIEVE YOUR EYES

Have you ever seen water flow uphill, or a parked car roll up a hill? At a few special places around the world, known as 'gravity hills', you see just that. Or at least, it looks like you can.

GRAVITY HILLS have particular characteristics that create optical illusions and play tricks on our eyes, making it look like, for example, a car is rolling up a hill, when it's actually not.

Before scientists explained what was going on, local people thought that the odd phenomenon they were 'seeing' was actually taking place, and assumed it was caused by magic, or that strange magnetic fields were causing objects to behave in unusual ways. That's why a lot of these places are still called things like 'Magic Hill', 'Mystery Hill', or 'Magnetic Hill' today.

SUNDOGS – where two **extra suns** seem to appear in the **sky** either side of the real one – are a kind of **illusion** caused by **ice crystals** in the **air.**

MIRAGES are another kind of **natural optical illusion.** They can make what look like lakes or ponds appear on the ground ahead of you – but it's just a **trick of the light.**

The **HORSETAIL WATERFALL** in **Yosemite National Park, USA,** looks like a **stream of fire** – but it's an **illusion** caused by **sunlight** hitting the water at a particular **angle.**

Yo-yos weren't made from **plastic** until the 1960s. Before that, they were made from **wood** and often **spun unevenly** because the **density of the wood** varied so much.

Some toys like the yo-yo have been around for years and years. Have a look at pages 30–31 for some other toys that have been around longer than you might think.

Step bACK iN timE

Eating for VICTORY

It's 65 years since rationing ended in Britain. Rationing is a system often introduced by governments during wartime, when some foods and other goods become hard to get hold of. It means everyone gets their fair share – but usually much less than they're used to.

Rationing for many basic foods such as butter, eggs, sugar, cheese and meat lasted from 1940 to 1954 in Britain – nine years after the end of World War Two! So, craving the foods they loved, people got very creative, using what they had to hand. Some of the results sound more appetising than others...

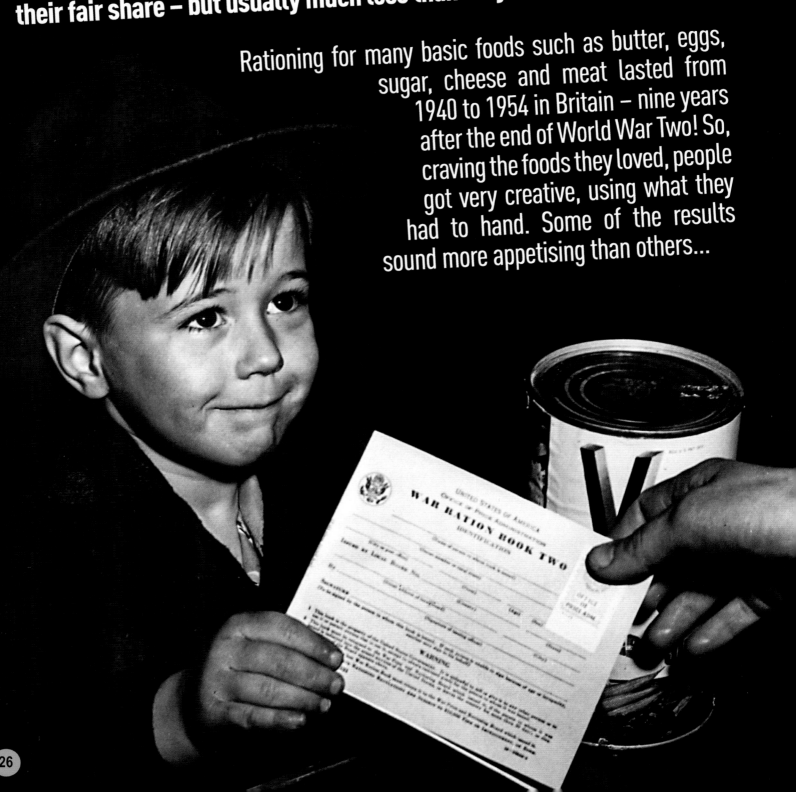

NOT SO HOT CHOCOLATES

Do you like homemade chocolate truffles? Who doesn't? But maybe not the wartime versions, which were made with cocoa powder, margarine... and mashed potato!

AS SURE AS EGGS IS EGGS

Unless you kept your own chickens, eggs were scarce. Instead, powdered eggs, to which you had to add water, were more widely available. They weren't too bad in cakes – but they put a lot of people off scrambled eggs for life!

A BIT FISHY

'Mock fish' could be made from ground rice, mashed potato and powdered eggs.

THAT'S BANANAS!

Instead of real bananas, people tucked into mashed parsnips mixed with banana essence.

IN A JAM?

Instead of real fresh fruit, jam and marmalade recipes often used a combination of carrot and beetroot along with some fruit jelly. Wooden pips were sometimes added to mimic the real pips from strawberries and raspberries!

FEELING CRABBY?

Recipe writers claimed that home cooks could recreate the taste of fresh crab with a 'mock crab' mixture mostly made of cheese and tomatoes.

FLOUR POWER!

Flour was scarcer than potatoes, so many puddings and pastries were made with mashed potato instead – then served with sweet jam and custard!

TEA OR COFFEE?

Instead of tea, which became difficult to import from overseas, people made do with herbal tea made from local herbs such as nettles or parsley. And if you preferred coffee, you might have found yourself drinking a cup of something made by roasting acorns – or even parsnips!

August 1887

December 1887

August 1888

December 1888

March 1889

Present day ...

The EIFFEL Tower

The **EIFFEL TOWER** was **BUILT IN 1889** and is one of the most **FAMOUS STRUCTURES** in the world. But did you know it was only meant to stand for **20 YEARS?**

The tower was built by **GUSTAV EIFFEL**, and it was the main attraction at the **1898 PARIS WORLD'S FAIR,** which celebrated the anniversary of the French Revolution. Back then, at **324 M** (1,062 ft), the Eiffel Tower was the **TALLEST MAN-MADE STRUCTURE** in the world—a title it held until **1930.**

But when it was first built, the **PICKY PARISIANS** declared they **HATED** it. Before long, though, they'd changed their minds—and it has been a beloved **SYMBOL OF THE CITY** ever since. It was left in place because it proved so useful as a radio transmitter! But maintaining the tower for so long hasn't been easy: it has to be **REPAINTED** every **7 YEARS** using **60 TONNES** (66 tons) of **PAINT.**

Today, over **7 MILLION TOURISTS** visit the Eiffel Tower each year. Some choose to climb the **1,665 STEPS** to the top... but most decide to take the lift. **OOH LÀ LÀ!**

CHILD'S Play

YO-YOS are a very **ANCIENT** toy, invented around **500 BCE** or even earlier: you can find images of people playing with them on **POTTERY** from Ancient **GREECE!**

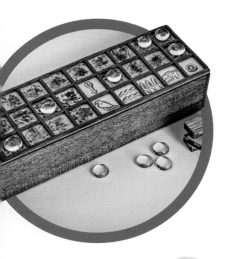

BOARD GAMES were first played by Ancient **EGYPTIANS** over **5,000 YEARS AGO.**

ROCKING HORSES became popular in the **1700s** to help children learn to **BALANCE**, so they would learn to **RIDE REAL HORSES** more quickly.

JIGSAW PUZZLES were created in **1767**, to help teach **GEOGRAPHY.**

DOLLS have been played with by boys and girls for **THOUSANDS OF YEARS.** The most famous doll of all – **BARBIE** – was first sold in **1959.**

LEGO was invented in **1932.** The name comes from the **DANISH 'LEG GODT'**, which means **'PLAY WELL'.**

Simple **VIDEO GAME CONSOLES** were first sold in **1972.**

The **fiendishly** difficult **RUBIK'S CUBE** puzzle was invented in **1974.**

FIDGET SPINNERS became popular in **2017**, but similar toys have been around since the early 1990s. They can help **RELIEVE STRESS** and anxiety.

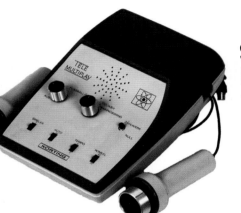

You've got (WEIRD) mail!

You might be happy to get a postcard in the post – but much weirder things could turn up on your doormat if history is anything to go by! Ever since the creation of proper postal systems in the 19th century, mischievous types have enjoyed testing the limits by sending the strangest things they could think of...

In the 1890s, a jar of live **SCORPIONS** turned up at the Returned Mail Office in London, UK.

In 1909, **SUFFRAGETTES** –women protesting for their right to vote–decided to post themselves to 10 Downing Street! They wanted to deliver a message to the Prime Minister, Herbert Asquith, but an official refused to sign for the 'human letters'.

CRYPTIC PUZZLES

Illustrator Harriet Russell sent dozens of postcards with the addresses disguised as cunning puzzles—join-the-dots, crosswords, illustrations and much more. Amazingly, almost all of them arrived: the postal workers who solved the puzzles clearly enjoyed the games!

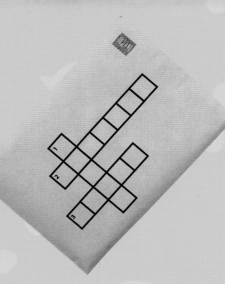

U. N. Derpants
22 Boxers Road
Pantstoun
Pd4 5NT

A PAIR OF PANTS with the address written on them (with three first-class stamps stuck in the top right-hand corner, of course!) were sent by author David Bramwell—just one in a long series of his postal pranks.

THE CULLINAN DIAMOND

This is the largest gemstone-quality diamond ever found —it is the size of a man's fist! In 1905, to transport it from South Africa, where it was discovered, to London, UK, the diamond was simply sent by regular (registered!) post. Meanwhile, a fake diamond was sent on a ship, guarded by detectives, to fool any would-be thieves!

ALWAYS CHECK THE
SELL-BY DATE

WOULD YOU EAT A 106-YEAR-OLD FRUIT CAKE?

That's what **CONSERVATORS** in the **ANTARCTIC** found in 2017. The cake was intact and **STILL WRAPPED** in paper, showing that it was made by **BRITISH MANUFACTURERS** Huntley & Palmers.

The cake is thought to be from **SUPPLIES** taken to Antarctica by the **EXPLORER ROBERT FALCON SCOTT,** who led an expedition to try to reach the **SOUTH POLE** for the first time in 1910–1913. Tragically, his attempt failed, and Scott, along with four of his men died before they could be rescued. What's more, Scott was beaten to the pole by a few weeks by his **COMPETITOR,** the Norwegian explorer **ROALD AMUNDSEN.**

Because the **ICY CONDITIONS** of the Antarctic **PRESERVE** things so well (think of it as a **GIANT FREEZER!),** the conservators could report that the cake looked and smelled almost **EDIBLE.**

THEY WERE SENSIBLE ENOUGH NOT TO TASTE IT THOUGH...

Carsten Borchgrevink's Huts at Cape Adare, where Scott's Northern Party were based.

Weird WARS

Nations go to **WAR** for many reasons – but some wars are much **WEIRDER** than others!

THE COD WARS weren't fought using **FISH** – they were fought over fish. **ICELAND** and the **UK** came to blows several times from the **1950s** to the **1970s** over who had the right to fish where in the **NORTH ATLANTIC OCEAN.**

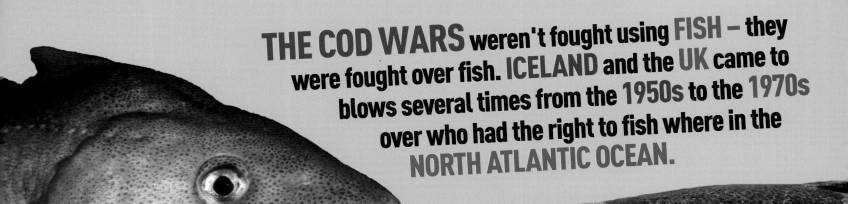

THE WAR OF THE OAKEN BUCKET was fought between the **ITALIAN CITIES** of **BOLOGNA** and **MODENA** in 1325, when both were **INDEPENDENT STATES**. It broke out when **SOLDIERS** from Modena **STOLE** a bucket from a **WELL!**

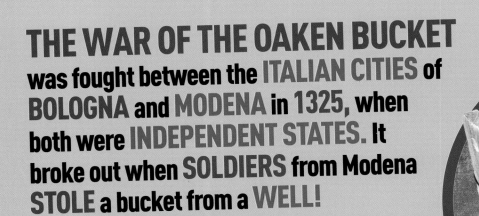

THE EMU WAR was fought in **AUSTRALIA** in 1932 between the Australian military and – yes – **EMUS!** Huge numbers of the **LARGE BIRDS** caused lots of **DAMAGE** to farmland and the **GOVERNMENT** had to intervene.

CRAZY castles

NEUSCHWANSTEIN CASTLE'S fairytale looks are the creation of King Ludwig II of Bavaria, which is now part of Germany. He borrowed **a fortune** to build himself this **extravagant** home during the 1870s and 1880s... but only spent **11 nights** there!

EDINBURGH CASTLE in Scotland has overlooked the city from the top of a long-extinct **volcano** since the **12th century.**

MEDIEVAL BRAN CASTLE, in Transylvania, Romania, attracts thousands of tourists every year because it's said to have been the inspiration for **Count Dracula's castle.** Yet there's no evidence that the author of *Dracula*, **Bram Stoker,** ever visited it.

ST MICHAEL'S MOUNT, off the coast of Cornwall, UK, is a **tiny island** topped with an **ancient castle.** When the tide is low, you can **walk** to the island... but when the tide rises, the castle is completely **cut off!**

PENA PALACE in Sintra, Portugal must be the **most colourful** castle in the world! The bright **yellow, pink and red buildings** were constructed by the **Portuguese royal family** in the 1840s and 1850s as a **summer home.**

The 'Crystal Palace',
London, UK, 1851.

Roll up! Roll up!

THE FIRST WORLD'S FAIR WAS THE GREAT EXHIBITION, HELD IN LONDON, UK IN 1851.

The SPECTACULAR GLASS BUILDING that housed it was nicknamed the CRYSTAL PALACE. SIX MILLION people visited – almost a QUARTER of BRITAIN'S TOTAL POPULATION at that time!

The TRADITION of World's Fairs is STILL ALIVE: the next one will be held in DUBAI, UAE, in 2020.

Each COUNTRY that takes part in a World's Fair creates its own PAVILION – a special EXHIBITION SPACE designed to represent its UNIQUE NATIONAL CULTURE and STYLE.

Usually, the INCREDIBLE BUILDINGS and attractions of a World's Fair are only TEMPORARY – so at World's Fairs AMAZING CITIES full of FANTASTICAL buildings appear... then DISAPPEAR almost without a trace after a few months!

INNOVATIONS that have DEBUTED at World's Fairs include the FERRIS WHEEL (Chicago, USA, 1893), the ZIP (Chicago, USA, 1893), the modern electric PLUG and WALL OUTLET (St Louis, USA, 1904), the VIDEO PHONE (New York, USA, 1964), and IMAX FILM screenings (Osaka, Japan, 1970).

You can still visit an attraction from the 1964 World's Fair, which was held in NEW YORK CITY. The CAROUSEL OF PROGRESS celebrates the advancements in people's lives created by technology – especially ELECTRICITY. WALT DISNEY loved it so much he wanted people to be able to enjoy it forever. He had it installed at DISNEYLAND in California, USA, then moved to WALT DISNEY WORLD in Florida, USA, where it remains today.

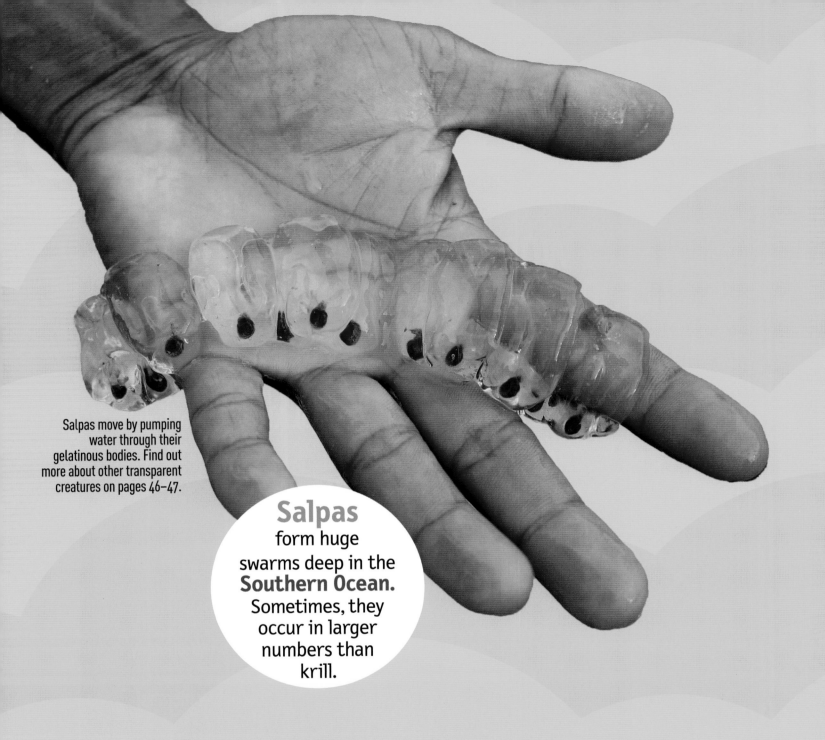

Salpas move by pumping water through their gelatinous bodies. Find out more about other transparent creatures on pages 46–47.

Salpas form huge swarms deep in the **Southern Ocean.** Sometimes, they occur in larger numbers than krill.

inCRediBlE CreatURes

Looking SHARP

HEDGEHOGS are an ENDANGERED SPECIES in the United Kingdom: there used to be **30 MILLION** hedgehogs in the country, but there are now **ONLY 1 MILLION.**

Let's find out more about our prickly pals...

A hedgehog has about **5000 – 7000 SPINES.** If **THREATENED**, it will **CURL** into a **SPIKY BALL** to **PROTECT** itself.

DID YOU KNOW?

Hedgehogs have a **TOP SPEED** of **6.4 KM/H (4 MPH)** – pretty **FAST** for a creature with such **SHORT LEGS!** However, they can't keep up that speed for very long. (The average **HUMAN** walking **PACE** is just over **4.8 KM/H (3 MPH)**).

▲ A **BABY** hedgehog is called a **HOGLET.**

A **GROUP** of hedgehogs is called an **'ARRAY'** of hedgehogs.

Hedgehogs **SLEEP FOR 18 HOURS A DAY!** As if that's not enough time **SNOOZING,** the hedgehog is one of several **SPECIES NATIVE** to the British Isles who **HIBERNATE** – that is, they go into a **DEEP SLEEP** for the whole of **WINTER.**

Crocodile ice fish

Glass octopus

I CAN SEE RIGHT THROUGH YOU!

Jellyfish

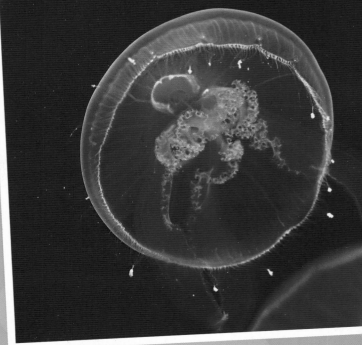

AMAZING see-through creatures float like **GHOSTS** through the waters of our seas and oceans. Their **TRANSPARENT** nature helps **HIDE** them from **PREDATORS.**

HERE ARE SOME OF THE STRANGEST...

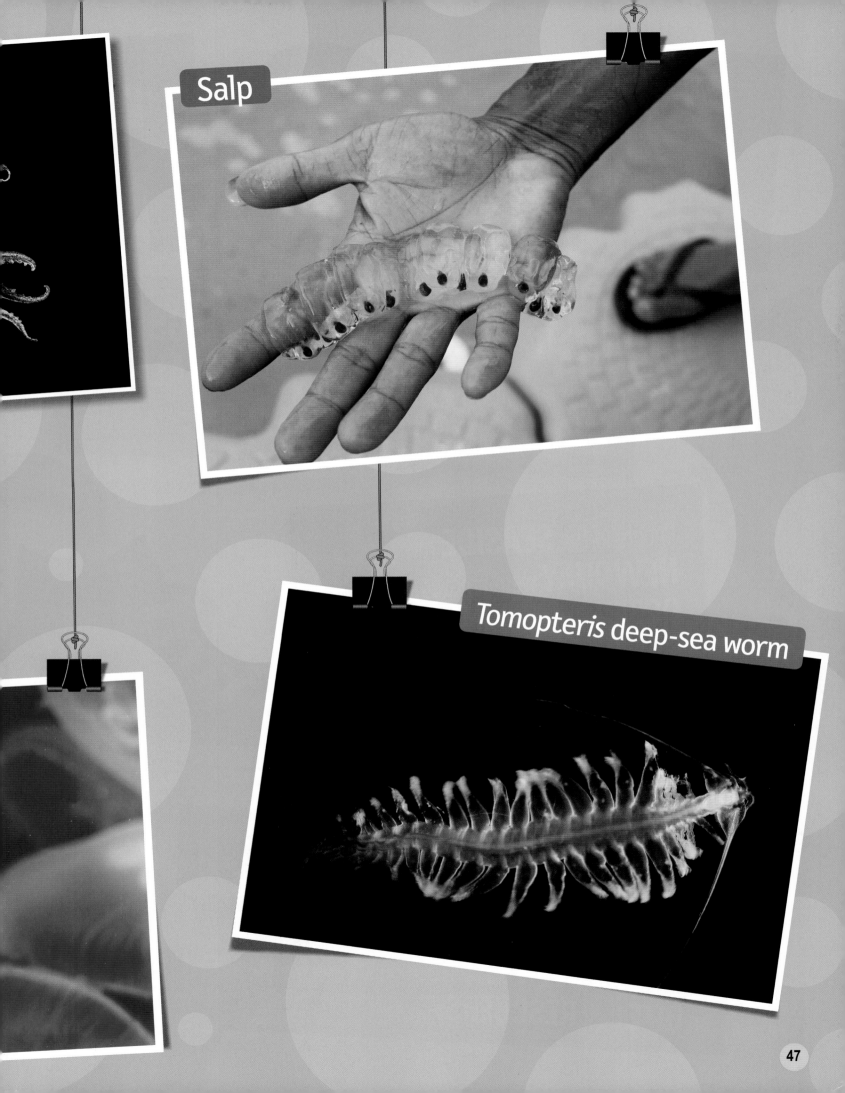

Salp

Tomopteris deep-sea worm

POOR

OCTOPUSES might have **EIGHT LEGS,** but they don't usually use them to take a **WALK...** **EXCEPT IN 2017,** in **WALES!**

People in the **SEASIDE** town of **NEWQUAY** were amazed to see **DOZENS** of the **TENTACLED** sea-creatures **WALKING** out of the sea and the beach – **THREE NIGHTS IN A ROW!**

LOCALS RUSHED to **RESCUE** the confused animals by **SCOOPING** them up and **DROPPING** them back into the sea from the end of the **PIER –** only to **DISCOVER** that the octopuses had a tendency to **BITE** their **RESCUERS.**

suckers

SCIENTISTS COULDN'T EXPLAIN why the octopuses had decided to take their NIGHTLY WALKS – so the MYSTERY of the WALKING WELSH octopuses REMAINS UNSOLVED.

HORSING AROUND

Can HORSES do SUMS?

CLEVER HANS was a horse who lived in Germany in the early 20th century. He got his name because it was said that he could do arithmetic, tell the time, read, spell and understand complex sentences (in **GERMAN**, of course).

Hans would respond to questions posed by his owner, **WILHELM VON OSTEN**, by tapping with his hooves up to whatever number the answer was.

Clever Hans became a **STAR**, touring the country to show off his abilities. But people were **SUSPICIOUS**, and an official committee was formed to investigate whether there was any trickery involved.

The **COMMITTEE** eventually **DISCOVERED** that Hans was carefully interpreting the behaviour of humans around him as he tapped his hoof. Without realising it, people would act differently as Hans's tapping approached the **CORRECT ANSWER.**

Hans could **RECOGNISE THESE SIGNALS**, and that's how he knew it was time to stop tapping. If the people near him didn't know the answer to the question Hans was asked, Hans wouldn't get any answers right either.

So it turns out that **HORSES CAN'T DO SUMS**, after all. But they *are* very good at interpreting human behaviour!

Das lesende und rechnende Pferd. mit seinem Lehrer HERRN von OSTEN

PIGGING OUT?

2019 is the **Chinese year of the pig**. The Chinese zodiac has **12 signs**, each named after an animal. The pig is the **LAST SIGN IN THE ZODIAC,** and in China pigs represent happiness, good fortune and honesty –pretty cool! Here are some more fun facts just in time for the year of the pig...

1 Pigs are **VERY INTELLIGENT –** by some estimates, as intelligent as a **HUMAN TODDLER!**

2 Most pigs actually like to **EAT SLOWLY** and **SAVOUR** their food – the expression **'PIGGING OUT'** isn't fair at all!

3 Pigs were among the **FIRST ANIMALS** to be domesticated for **FARMING,** around 7,000 BCE, in **CHINA.**

DID YOU KNOW?

The expression **'SWEATING LIKE A PIG'** is misguided. Pigs can't **SWEAT** much, which means they need to find other ways to **COOL DOWN** – including wallowing in lots of lovely **COOL MUD!**

4 Mother pigs 'SING' to their PIGLETS while they are NURSING.

5 Pigs DREAM, just like HUMANS!

6 Pigs can easily get SUNBURNED, because they have very LITTLE HAIR and very FAIR SKIN – just like some people! Farmers use SPECIAL SUN CREAM to protect pigs from the SUN.

DID YOU KNOW?
The **BIGGEST PIGS** in the world are a kind of **WILD BOAR** called the **'GIANT FOREST HOG'**. They can grow up to 2.1 m (6.9 ft) long! The **SMALLEST PIGS** are **PYGMY HOGS,** a kind of wild pig that lives in **INDIA**. They grow to about 55 – 71 cm (21.5 – 28 in) long, and weigh just 6.6–11.8 kg (15–26 lb).

7 Pigs have 15,000 taste buds: HUMANS ONLY HAVE 9,000!

MASTERS of DISGUISE

ANIMALS USE CAMOUFLAGE to blend into their ENVIRONMENTS and hide from PREDATORS who might hunt and eat them if they weren't so hard to spot.

◀ **STICK INSECT:** it's not hard to see how this **CREATURE** got its name! It's almost **IMPOSSIBLE** to tell the difference between it and the twigs it's found on.

▼ **OWLS:** owls hunt at **NIGHT**, and hide by day – many species are almost impossible to spot against the trees they **SNOOZE** in. Owls can also puff themselves up or slim themselves down to better match the **background** they're against!

◀ **DEAD LEAF MANTIS:** what could be less interesting to a predator than a **dead leaf?** Little do they know that it might actually be this **cunning insect...**

LEAFY SEA DRAGON: ▼ these delicate sea **creatures** look exactly like strands of **seaweed** gently floating in the water.

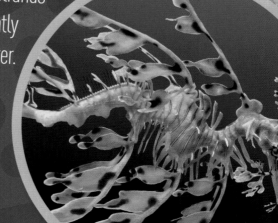

◀ CUTTLEFISH: these molluscs are the **CHAMELEONS** of the sea, able to **change colour** at will to blend into their **background** – and for even sneakier purposes! **MALE CUTTLEFISH CAN CAMOUFLAGE** themselves as a female to sneak past rival males and **BEAT** them to the female they want to mate with.

▶ LEOPARD: their **beautiful**, unusual coat allows these big cats to pass **UNNOTICED** through the dappled light and shade of their habitat.

▲ CHAMELEON: lots of species of chameleon **can change colour**, but **CAMOUFLAGE** is only one reason why. They also use colour changes to **communicate** with other chameleons, and to keep themselves at a comfortable temperature!

Here to HELP

'MAN'S BEST FRIEND' may be a dog but all kinds of **ANIMALS** do **INCREDIBLE** things to help their humans out. **SERVICE ANIMALS** are specially trained to **SUPPORT PEOPLE** who have **REDUCED SIGHT** or **HEARING, LEARNING DIFFICULTIES,** or other needs.

SERVICE ANIMALS ONLY BEYOND THIS POINT

Service animals are allowed in places that other animals aren't, such as restaurants, and even on aeroplanes! Check out this pooch in a supermarket.

Dogs are the most common service animals, but monkeys, birds and even ferrets have been trained to help humans! This monkey is helping wash a human's face.

Therapy animals support people emotionally and in their development, helping to put them at ease and express themselves more easily than they might usually be able to. There are therapy cats, dogs, rabbits, pigs and even llamas!

Miniature horses can be trained to guide the blind and pull wheelchairs!

DID YOU KNOW?
Dogs can be trained to recognise when their human companion is having a seizure, and seek help.

EURASIAN BEAVER: these large brown rodents live on and around the **WATER.** They have recently been reintroduced to Britain, and there aren't many around – so if you spot one, consider yourself **VERY LUCKY!**

HOUSE MOUSE: these little grey-brown rodents like to move into people's **HOUSES –** even though they're not welcome. A female mouse can have up to **150 BABIES** in a year! ▼

RATS! ...AND OTHER RODENTS

What do squirrels, beavers and mice have in common? **THEY'RE ALL KINDS OF RODENT!** Here are some rodents you might spot in Britain, and how to recognise them if you do.

GREY SQUIRREL: much **LARGER** and less colourful than native red squirrels, these **CRITTERS** also have white tummies, but a duller grey-brown coat. They **INVADED** the red squirrel's territory, and there are more than **2.5 MILLION** grey squirrels scurrying around Britain's woods and parks.

WATER VOLE: these **CHUBBY-CHEEKED** creatures live for up to two years in the wild. You can tell them apart from rats because even their ears, paws and tail are **COVERED WITH FUR.**

BROWN RAT: these **DULL-COLOURED** rodents like to live where people live, so they can feed on **RUBBISH** and waste. They grow up to 25cm (10″) long, with tails as **LONG** as their bodies!

RED SQUIRREL:

these small, brightly-coloured rodents are **ENDANGERED** because of competition from larger grey squirrels which were introduced from North America. They have **BUSHY EAR TUFTS, WHITE TUMMIES,** and are found in woodland, especially in **SCOTLAND.** ▶

HARVEST MOUSE: these reddish-brown mice are **EUROPE'S SMALLEST RODENT.** Harvest mice like to live in round nests, which they attach to stems above the ground. Conservation experts help them out by creating **ARTIFICIAL NESTS** using old Wimbledon **TENNIS BALLS!**

59

MIND your MANNERS!
EXTRAORDINARY
animal EATING habits

SOME **BEES** AND **BUTTERFLIES** LIKE TO **DRINK** THE **TEARS** OF OTHER ANIMALS – INCLUDING **HUMANS,** IF THEY GET THE CHANCE! TEARS CONTAIN **MINERALS IMPORTANT** TO THEIR **DIET** – ESPECIALLY **SALT.**

COWS WHO **SHARE** A **FIELD** LIKE TO TURN AND **FACE** THE SAME WAY WHILE THEY MUNCH ON **GRASS** – GENERALLY IN LINE WITH THE **NORTH POLE! SCIENTISTS** AREN'T QUITE SURE WHY THEY LINE UP LIKE THIS.

OSTRICHES SWALLOW **STONES,** WHICH SIT INSIDE A **SPECIAL** SECOND **STOMACH** CALLED A **GIZZARD.** SINCE OSTRICHES HAVE **NO TEETH,** THE ROCKY TREATS HELP **GRIND** UP THE FOOD THE BIRDS HAVE **SWALLOWED.**

GIANT ANTEATERS' TONGUES GROW UP TO 60 CM (2 FT) LONG! THEY USE THEM TO 'LAP UP' 35,000 ANTS AND TERMITES A DAY, SWALLOWING THE INSECTS WHOLE.

JAPANESE MACAQUE MONKEYS LIKE TO WASH SWEET POTATOES BEFORE THEY TUCK INTO THEM. THE MONKEYS CAREFULLY RINSE THE SAND OFF THEIR FOOD USING RIVER WATER.

10 VERY VENOMOUS CREATURES

CONE SNAILS might look harmless—but these tiny **SEA-SNAILS** are actually some of the **MOST VENOMOUS** creatures on the planet! Victims are **INSTANTLY PARALYSED** when the cone snail injects its poison from a **TOOTH** that it can propel from its head.

The **DEATHSTALKER SCORPION** got its name thanks to the huge doses of venom it can **INJECT** using the end of its **TAIL.** It lives in the deserts of North Africa and the Middle East.

BLUE-RINGED OCTOPUSES live off the coast of Australia and are one of the **MOST VENOMOUS** animals in the **OCEANS.** Each octopus carries enough venom to **KILL 26 HUMANS** in just a few **MINUTES!**

The **AUSTRALIAN KING BROWN SNAKE** can deliver **HUGE DOSES OF VENOM** in a single bite.

The **GOLDEN POISON FROG** contains enough venom to kill **MORE THAN 10 HUMANS!** It lives in tropical rainforests in Central and Southern America. Local people have long used the frogs' poison on the end of their **BLOW DARTS** —to help them **KILL** animals.

Not only is the **BRAZILIAN WANDERING SPIDER** incredibly venomous, but it likes to **HIDE** under clothes, in shoes, and in dark corners of rooms— **WATCH OUT!**

The **BOX JELLYFISH** may look delicate and beautiful, but its **LONG TENTACLES** pack a nasty punch.

It uses its venom to **CATCH AND STUN** the small fish it likes to eat.

PUFFER FISH are a **DELICACY** in some countries... but have to be prepared by a **HIGHLY-SKILLED CHEF**, as some parts of their bodies are so venomous they could **KILL** diners.

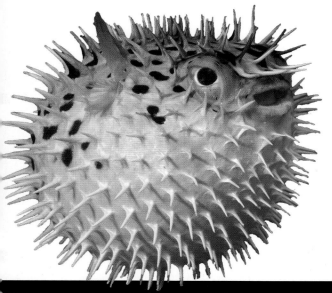

PLATYPUSES aren't just **STRANGE-LOOKING:** they're venomous too! There aren't many **VENOMOUS MAMMALS**, but these furry, duck-billed, egg-laying creatures use **SPURS** on their hind legs to **INJECT** other males with venom when they're **COMPETING** for a mate.

The **KING COBRA** is the **LONGEST** venomous snake in the world. It can grow up to **5.5 M (18 FT)** long—about twice as long as a **DOUBLE BED.**

Adopt-a-pet

We're all familiar with the amazing service animals that help humans who have disabilities or special needs. But the system works in reverse, too! Here are some of the most heart-warming tales from the wonderful world of disabled animal adoption.

- **DEAF DOGS ROCK** is an American charity that helps **HARD-OF-HEARING** pooches find **LOVING HOMES!** They also work to **EDUCATE** people everywhere on how to give dogs with **HEARING DIFFICULTIES** the best possible lives.

- The **SENIOR DOGS PROJECT** and **OLD DOG HAVEN** are both charities that help home **OLDER ANIMALS.** Just because a dog is older, doesn't mean they don't deserve a **LOVING HOME** to live out their final years.

- The **BLIND DOG RESCUE ALLIANCE** believes that 'blind dogs see **WITH THEIR HEARTS'.** They take in dogs who've lost their sight and help them to find owners who can cater to their very **SPECIAL NEEDS.**

- **PETS WITH DISABILITIES** support and home animals who need **EXTRA HELP** getting around—whether they've lost a limb, have back problems, or even need to use a wheelchair!

- **HEATH'S HAVEN RESCUE,** in the USA, takes in dogs with **SEVERE INJURIES** who might otherwise have been put down, and helps them to live **FULL AND HAPPY LIVES.** The dogs in their care even get **ACUPUNCTURE** and **HYDROTHERAPY TREATMENTS!**

- It isn't always physical disabilities that mean animals need **EXTRA-SPECIAL CARE.** Some poor creatures have special **EMOTIONAL NEEDS** because of **TRAUMAS** they've lived through. With patience, skill and the right know-how, **LOVING OWNERS** can help them live **CALMER, MORE CONFIDENT** and **HAPPIER LIVES.**

Dogs can be trained to sniff out illnesses, like certain types of **cancer.**

Sniffer dogs can sniff out all sorts of things – see pages 68-69 for more.

briGHT ideAs

SNIFFED OUT!

We all have our own unique scent – and one woman from Florida, USA, was found when she went missing because **SHE HAD BOTTLED HER SCENT!**

In 2017, local police reported that the lady suffered from DEMENTIA, meaning she would often FORGET WHERE SHE WAS and what she was doing.

Several years before, she had bottled her own scent with a special SCENT PRESERVATION KIT that captured her own smell. This was done by rubbing a SWAB under her arm, then sealing it in a sterile jar. When she went MISSING, police gave the scent sample to TRAINED SEARCH DOGS who tracked her down... WITHIN MINUTES!

Dogs have a very HIGHLY DEVELOPED SENSE OF SMELL: they can smell many more smells, in much greater detail, than humans can. Police and law enforcement officials work with TRAINED SNIFFER DOGS all over the world, using dogs' amazing ability to TRACK DOWN missing people or wanted criminals, as well as to identify the presence of illegal substances or explosives.

Fancy FOOTWORK

Nobody likes **CHORES**—especially **VACUUMING.** So next time your parents tell you you need to hoover your room, you might want to try out a **NEW INVENTION** from a Japanese company — **VACUUM SHOES!**

The shoes use the energy generated by walking to **SUCK UP DUST AND DIRT** from the floor as you go—so they're **ECO-FRIENDLY,** as well as a fun way to tidy the house!

In the heel is a **SMALL PEDAL** that gets pressed when the wearer takes a step. Gears connected to the pedal drive a **VACUUM MOTOR,** and the dirt is captured in a small box in the **SOLE.**

The shoes are only a **PROTOTYPE,** and you can't buy them yet. Perhaps it's not such a shame—they can only pick up a small amount of dirt at a time, and need **EMPTYING REGULARLY.**

What's more, they have very **THICK SOLES** to hide all the machinery, so they might not be to everyone's **FASHION TASTE...**

71

PILES OF **PLASTIC**

EVERY DAY OVER 38.5 MILLION PLASTIC BOTTLES ARE USED IN THE UK – THAT'S MORE THAN 1 FOR EVERY 2 PEOPLE!

ONCE IT'S THROWN AWAY, PLASTIC TAKES UP TO **500 YEARS** TO BREAK DOWN.

ALL THAT PLASTIC ENDS UP IN **LANDFILL** OR WORSE, IN THE **ENVIRONMENT,** WHERE IT CAN **POISON** AND **INJURE** WILDLIFE.

SO WE SHOULD ALWAYS TRY TO FIND AN **ALTERNATIVE,** LIKE **GLASS,** BUT IF WE REALLY HAVE TO USE PLASTIC, WE SHOULD **RECYCLE** IT WHEN WE'RE FINISHED WITH IT. THIS MEANS THAT IT CAN BE USED AGAIN INSTEAD OF BEING LEFT TO **POLLUTE THE PLANET.**

PLASTIC OBJECTS LIKE BOTTLES CAN BE **TRANSFORMED** INTO ALL KINDS OF NEW THINGS...

Here's how many plastic bottles can be recycled to make...

2 PENS ×1

×7 T-SHIRT

×48 QUILT

×15 JUMPER

×2 WATCH

OOPS! 8 ACCIDENTAL INVENTIONS

KEVLAR —an extremely high-strength material—was invented by research chemist, Stephanie Kwolek in 1965. She only discovered it by accident as a by-product of something else that was usually **THROWN AWAY** and it was initially used to improve the efficiency of tyres. Her accidental discovery was later developed by others, however, to be used in **BULLET-PROOF VESTS** which is what kevlar is best known for today.

PENICILLIN —the first antibiotic—was invented by Alexander Fleming in 1928. But it would have never existed if Fleming hadn't left his lab in a **MESS** over the summer. When he got back, he noticed a particular mould had **INFECTED** the Petri dishes where he was growing bacteria, stopping it from growing properly. The amazing bacteria-killing mould was called *Penicillin notatum*... and the rest is medical history.

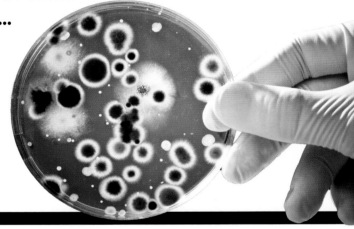

MATCHES were invented by British pharmacist John Walker in 1826, when he tried to scrape a lump of **DRIED CHEMICALS** off the end of the stick he had been using to stir them... and it **CAUGHT ALIGHT!**

PLAY-DOH was first sold in the 1930s as a **WALLPAPER CLEANER!** Back then, the coal fires used to heat homes left walls sooty. In the 1950s, coal fires became less popular, but the manufacturers realised their product made a great **CHILDREN'S TOY!**

VELCRO was invented with the help of a **DOG!** George de Mestral, from Switzerland, was fascinated by the way burrs from plants stuck to his dog's **FUR** using tiny hooks, when they went on a walk. He used the same approach to invent Velcro in 1955, but it didn't 'take off' until the 1960s, when **NASA** began using it in **ZERO-GRAVITY ENVIRONMENTS!**

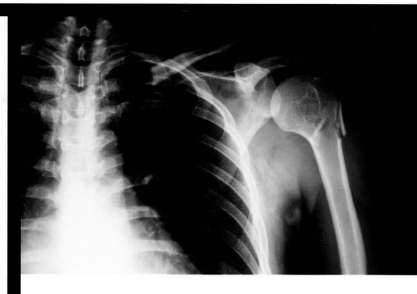

X-RAYS were accidentally discovered in 1895 by German scientist Wilhelm Röntgen. He had no idea what these strange, invisible rays that could **PASS THROUGH** all kinds of substances were, so he called them **'X'** because they were a **MYSTERY.** By 1897, X-rays were being used on battlefields to find bullets and broken bones in **INJURED SOLDIERS.**

NON-STICK PANS use a slippery substance called **TEFLON** to stop food sticking. Teflon was accidentally invented by Roy Plunkett in 1938, while he was trying to improve **REFRIGERATORS!** Teflon was originally put to military and industrial use; it wasn't until the early 1950s that the wife of a French engineer, Marc Grégoire, realised how useful it could be in the **KITCHEN.**

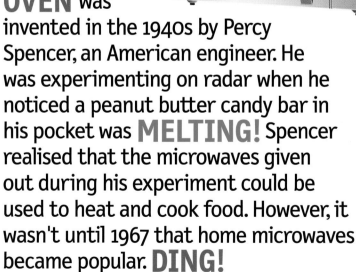

THE MICROWAVE OVEN was invented in the 1940s by Percy Spencer, an American engineer. He was experimenting on radar when he noticed a peanut butter candy bar in his pocket was **MELTING!** Spencer realised that the microwaves given out during his experiment could be used to heat and cook food. However, it wasn't until 1967 that home microwaves became popular. **DING!**

YOU'VE GOT TO BE KIDNEYING!

OUR KIDNEYS are the **organs** that act as the **rubbish processing plants** of the human body. They're responsible for getting rid of **toxins** that would otherwise build up inside us and make us very **ill.**

But **MILLIONS** of people have kidneys that aren't working properly. These patients have to undergo a process called **'dialysis'** three times a week to clear their **blood** of toxins and keep them **alive,** while they wait for a replacement **kidney** to be found from an organ donor.

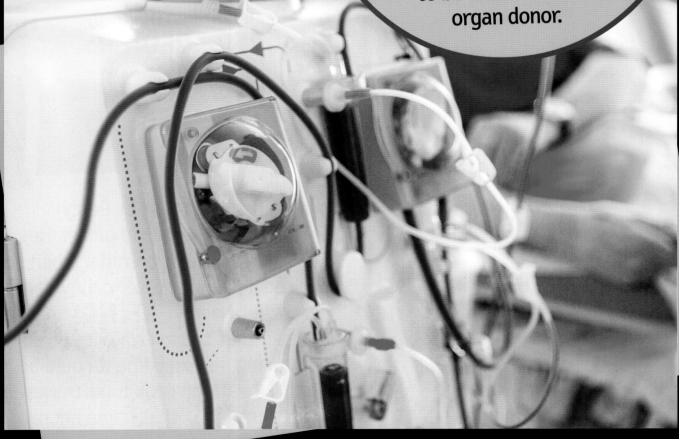

a dialysis machine

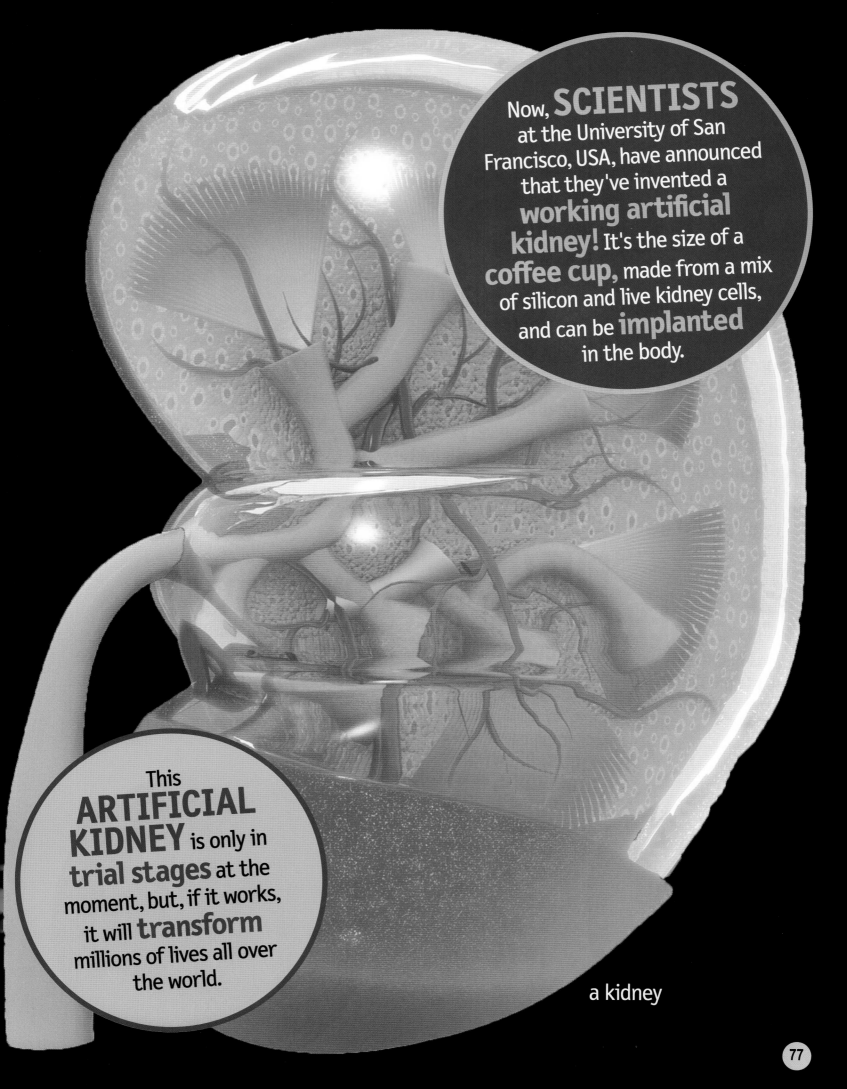

Now, **SCIENTISTS** at the University of San Francisco, USA, have announced that they've invented a **working artificial kidney!** It's the size of a **coffee cup,** made from a mix of silicon and live kidney cells, and can be **implanted** in the body.

This **ARTIFICIAL KIDNEY** is only in **trial stages** at the moment, but, if it works, it will **transform** millions of lives all over the world.

a kidney

HAPPY Snaps

2019 is the 180th anniversary of the launch of the daguerreotype – a process that used to be one of the most popular ways to take photographs. It was named after its Parisian inventor, Louis-Jacques-Mandé Daguerre. The process used a range of chemicals (including some very poisonous ones!) to fix an image onto a polished silver-plated copper plate, which had to be stored carefully under glass to protect it.

THE FIRST KNOWN PHOTOGRAPH

was taken in 1826 or 1827 by Joseph Nicéphore Niépce. It shows a view from his window in **Burgundy, France** – although you'd hardly know, it's so **blurry!**

PUT ON A SERIOUS FACE

You might hear that people **didn't smile** in early photos because pictures took so long to take. But that's not the case – it was just not 'the done thing' to smile. Having your photograph taken was a **serious, expensive procedure**, almost like having a portrait painted, so people adopted serious expressions, just as people do in **painted portraits.**

The BOX BROWNIE

camera went on sale in 1900, priced **$1.** It changed the world by making it possible for **ordinary people** to take snapshots themselves, at an affordable price. For the first time, everyone could be a **photographer!**

The first DIGITAL CAMERA was invented in 1975 by Steve Sasson. It weighed 3.6 kg (8 lb) – much heavier than the modern digital camera shown here – and took nearly a minute to take a photo and display it on a screen!

The first POLAROID-STYLE camera that could instantly print out the photos it took went on sale in 1947.

The first COLOUR PHOTOGRAPHS were taken in the 1850s and 1860s, but it wasn't until nearly 100 years later that technology made colour photography practical and widely available.

The first mobile phones to have cameras built-in went on sale in 2002. The rise of phones with TOP-QUALITY cameras has made it easier to take and share photos than ever before. It's estimated that OVER 1.7 TRILLION digital photos are now taken every year – most of them on phones!

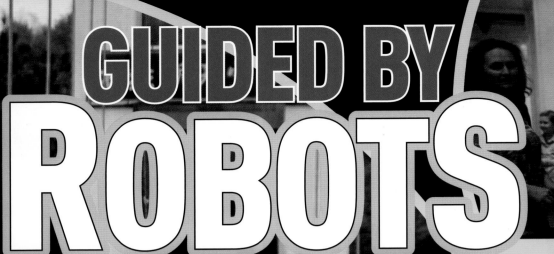

GUIDED BY ROBOTS

Would you trust a **ROBOT** to show you around a museum? **MUSEUMS AND GALLERIES** all around the world are experimenting with **ROBOTS** who are programmed to help visitors get the most out of their time – or even experience the exhibits without needing to visit at all!

The **SHCHUSEV MUSEUM** in **MOSCOW, RUSSIA** introduced a robot guide in **2016** at its 'MOSCOW METRO' exhibition. The robot welcomes visitors, answers their queries, and can even **CRACK JOKES!**

A cute child-sized robot can be found interacting with visitors to the **SHIYAN LAKE SCENIC AREA** in **CHINA**. The robot roams the picturesque landscape **24-hours a day**, chatting to tourists – and even giving them a **little dance!**

A robot at the **GREAT WAR MUSEUM** in northern France helps visitors explore re-creations of the trenches where so many soldiers lived and died.

#роботми

The **TATE BRITAIN GALLERY** in **LONDON, UK,** experimented with robot guides in 2014. People who wanted to tour the **MUSEUM REMOTELY** could log in via the website and direct the robots to show them whatever they wanted to see! The biggest issue? The robots couldn't cope with **STAIRS...**

The **QUAI BRANLY MUSEUM** in **PARIS, FRANCE,** held an exhibition in 2016 featuring a robot art critic! The robot observed visitors' reactions to the artworks, then used the data to make up its own **'MIND'** about the works on display.

Have a look at pages 86–87 for why unicorns are so popular in mythology.

The unicorn is the **national animal** of Scotland.

mYtHs & Legends

MONSTERS
of the depths

The ocean is full of VERY REAL DANGERS and PECULIAR CREATURES. It's no wonder people throughout history have believed in the existence of all kinds of mythical SEA-MONSTERS.

The **HYDRA OF LERNA** was an Ancient Greek sea-monster with many **VICIOUS HEADS** and poisonous breath. According to legend, each time one of its **HEADS WAS CUT OFF,** two more would grow in its **PLACE!**

The **KRAKEN** is a mythical **GIANT OCTOPUS**-like monster that is said to lurk in the waters off the coast of **NORWAY** and **GREENLAND,** where it attacks and **SINKS SHIPS.**

TEN OF CUPS
LEVIATHAN

The **LEVIATHAN** is a **TERRIFYING BEAST** named multiple times in Jewish holy texts and said to live in the **MEDITERRANEAN SEA.** It's said that, if it was angry, the sea around the **LEVIATHAN** would boil.

The **UMIBOZO** is a terrifying **JAPANESE** sea-spirit with huge black eyes. It's **BELIEVED** to appear on **CALM NIGHTS,** when it whips the sea into a sudden storm, destroying ships and drowning sailors.

NESSIE is the nickname of the **LOCH NESS MONSTER,** a mysterious creature believed to live in the deep waters of this Scottish loch. There are even photographs said to be of the **MONSTER** – although many have been proven to be **HOAXES.**

An IMPORTANT POINT about UNICORNS

UNICORNS are **MYTHICAL CREATURES** a lot like a horse, but with a single long **SPIRALLED HORN** in the middle of their heads.

Mentions of **UNICORNS** appear in the writings of **ANCIENT GREEKS** — but not as a myth. Unicorns were considered to be **REAL ANIMALS** that lived in **DISTANT LANDS**.

There are some real **ANIMALS** with unicorn-like horns, for example the **NARWHAL** — and most of the **HORNS** that were said to be from **UNICORNS** actually came from these creatures.

Unicorn horns were thought to be made of a **MAGICAL** substance called 'ALICORN'. Fake 'ALICORN POWDER' was sold in medieval times as **MEDICINE** to cure almost every **DISEASE!**

It was said that a cup made from unicorn horn could **NEUTRALISE POISON.**

The **THRONE CHAIR OF DENMARK**, created in the **17TH CENTURY**, is said to be made of unicorn horns. In reality they're **NARWHAL TUSKS.**

The unicorn is traditionally a symbol of **PURITY** and **GRACE**. It's also a **SYMBOL OF SCOTLAND**, which is why there's a unicorn in the **UK'S ROYAL COAT OF ARMS.**

According to legend, only someone who was 'PURE OF HEART' could capture a unicorn. The unicorn would approach them without fear and fall **ASLEEP** with its head in their lap!

A BIT FISHY?
MARVELLOUS
MERMAIDS
AND
MERMEN

A **MERMAID** is mythical creature who's half **woman,** half **fish.**

It's thought that legends about **MERMAIDS** might have started when sailors **SPOTTED CREATURES** such as **manatees** and **sea lions**, and let their imaginations get the better of them!

The **ANCIENT GREEKS** believed that beautiful but deadly creatures called **SIRENS** lured sailors to their deaths on rocky reefs with their enchanting **singing voices** – it's where we get our modern word '**siren**'!

Ancient folklore also tells of female water-spirits called **UNDINES**, who didn't have souls, but could be granted one if they **MARRIED A HUMAN MAN**.

FAKE MERMAIDS have been created by **fraudsters** keen to make money from curious people, and were displayed in museums during the 19TH CENTURY

THE LITTLE MERMAID, a fairytale by the **DANISH WRITER Hans Christian Andersen**, tells the story of a mermaid who falls in love with a human prince. It was first **PUBLISHED** in **1837**, and today you can find a Little Mermaid statue in the Danish capital of **COPENHAGEN**.

Even now, people come forward with videos and photos that they claim are evidence that **MERMAIDS AND MERMEN EXIST** – including one filmed in **MINNESOTA** as recently as 2017!

Ever dreamed of becoming a mermaid?

LAURA EVANS, from the coast of **Cornwall, England,** has done just that – she's a professional mermaid! She performs for tourists in the sea wearing a specially made tail.

► The **Theatre Royal**, in London, UK, is said to be the world's most haunted theatre. The most famous ghost is the Man in Grey, who has even been seen telling staff to 'Shhh!' during performances!

▲ **Skirrid Mountain Inn**, in Wales, dates from 1100, and is said to be haunted by hundreds of ghosts, including prisoners. It was once a courthouse and executions took place there. A prison cell has been converted into a bathroom for guests!

8 GHOSTLY GOINGS-ON

Not all spectres come in human form!

The **Tower of London** is said to be haunted by ghostly bears, as well as dozens of ghostly folk. ▼

ENTRY TO THE TRAITORS GATE

The **Winchester Mystery House**, in California, USA, was built to be haunted! Sarah Winchester's family fortunes were made selling rifles. She believed she needed to provide a home for the ghosts of everyone who had been shot using one. Eventually, her rambling house grew to 160 rooms, 10,000 windows, 2,000 trap doors, spy holes, mysterious staircases that lead nowhere, and secret passages galore. ▶

There really are dozens of **'ghost trains'** in Britain... but these aren't ghostly at all! They're real, normal trains that run without anyone knowing, and without any passengers on board, just so train companies can say that the route they follow technically still exists.

The fittingly named **Chillingham Castle** in Northumberland is said to be the most haunted castle in the UK. ▼

Dragsholm Castle in Denmark is now a hotel, but is said to be home to nearly 100 ghosts. It's amazing there's any room for guests! ▼

THE YETI: HAIR TODAY, GONE TOMORROW?

The **YETI** is a **MYSTERIOUS**, mythical monster who's long been said to live in the **HIMALAYAN MOUNTAINS**.

The Yeti is also known as the Abominable **SNOWMAN**.

The Yeti features in the ancient **FOLKLORE** and **MYTH** of communities in the Himalayan Mountains, usually as a way of teaching children not to venture far from their village!

Yetis are usually described as being about the height of a **TALL MAN**. They stand on **TWO FEET,** and are covered with dark **REDDISH-BROWN** hair.

When the Greek king **ALEXANDER THE GREAT** conquered the **INDUS VALLEY** in **326 BCE**, he demanded to meet a Yeti. Local people told him that the creature couldn't survive at such low altitudes. How convenient...

Monks in a Nepalese monastery used to claim they had the preserved finger of a Yeti — but eventually, **DNA ANALYSIS** proved it was a **HUMAN FINGER!**

SCIENTISTS have also analysed the DNA of other body parts, fur, and traces claimed to be proof of the **YETI'S EXISTENCE**. All have been shown to come from well-known animals — particularly, **BROWN BEARS**.

BROWN BEARS are incredibly powerful **PREDATORS** whose mannerisms can appear surprisingly human when standing on their **TWO HIND LEGS**. So it's hardly surprising that, in the end, the myth of the Yeti probably evolved from encounters with this real-life creature.

A RIGHT PAIN IN THE NECK! – VAMPIRE LORE AND LEGEND

Tales of **BLOOD-SUCKING MONSTERS** have existed around the world for centuries. They were often a way for people to try to make sense of **DISEASES** and events that they couldn't otherwise explain.

COUNT DRACULA, the world's most famous **VAMPIRE,** was invented by Irish novelist Bram Stoker in 1897.

Vlad Dracula, or Vlad the Impaler, is one of the origins of the **VAMPIRE MYTH.** This aristocratic ruler in what is now **ROMANIA** was infamous for his **BRUTALITY,** but otherwise had little in common with Bram Stoker's character.

VAMPIRE BATS are among the animal species who feed on **BLOOD** directly from other animals. They may have helped inspire the vampire myth.

Another inspiration for the **VAMPIRE** myth is thought to be **ELISABETH BÁTHORY,** a 16th-century **HUNGARIAN** countess who was said to bathe in **BLOOD** to try to keep herself looking young!

Traditionally, vampires can't come into contact with **SUNLIGHT,** or they'll **BURN** as if on **FIRE.**

Legend has it that a **VAMPIRE** can only be killed using a **SILVER BULLET,** or a **WOODEN STAKE** through the heart!

Vampires are said to **HATE GARLIC** — it was once given out in **CHURCHES** to check that no vampires had **SNEAKED IN!**

ALL GREEK TO ME?
GREEK MYTH'S WEIRDEST CREATURES

The Ancient Greeks believed the world was ruled over by a vast number of gods, monsters and other strange creatures, whose actions shaped humans' lives.

The **MINOTAUR** had the head of a bull on the body of a man. He lived at the centre of a dark and tricky labyrinth, and ate humans who were sacrificed to him.

The **CHIMERA** had three heads — a lion's, a goat's, and a snake's (instead of a tail). She could breathe fire. Seeing her was said to be a bad omen... no kidding!

CERBERUS was a creature with three dogs' heads, the claws of a lion, and a serpent for a tail. He was said to guard the entrance to Hell.

CYCLOPES were a kind of giant with a single eye in the middle of their foreheads.

The **GRIFFIN** had the back half of a lion but the head, claws and wings of an eagle.

The **SPHINX** had the head of a human, the body of a lion, and an eagle's wings. She liked to ask people fiendishly difficult riddles, then eat them if they didn't guess the correct answer. Charming!

PEGASUS was a beautiful white horse with wings. It was said that wherever his hoof landed, a spring would bubble up.

The **GORGONS** were three sisters with snakes for hair who were said to turn anyone who gazed into their eyes to stone!

Turn to pages 112–113 for more weird facts about the requirements of black cabs and their drivers.

Black cab drivers in London, UK have to pass **a test** in which they are expected to memorise **more than 25,000 roads** and around **20,000 landmarks!**

CHAPTER 6

GeT a mOVe On!

THAT SINKING FEELING

SINKHOLES are huge CRATERS that suddenly appear in the ground – sometimes swallowing ROADS, CARS and HOUSES as they do!

HEAVY RAIN OF 20 MM (0.7 IN) IN THREE HOURS helped create a sinkhole in MANCHESTER'S MANCUNIAN WAY in 2015.

The left-hand image shows a MASSIVE SINKHOLE measuring around 30 M (98 FT) wide and 15 M (49 FT) deep that appeared in a bustling, five-lane street in Fukuoka, JAPAN in 2016. Crews worked night and day to restore the street to its former glory, and, after 1 WEEK, it had been fixed as shown in the RIGHT-HAND IMAGE.

ROME'S BALDUINA DISTRICT in Italy saw parked cars sucked into an enormous sinkhole in 2018. As well as causing DEVASTATION to the road network, 22 LOCAL FAMILIES had to be evacuated from their HOMES. Thankfully no injuries were reported.

ANIMAL HITCHHIKERS

A pet **GOAT ESCAPED** its owners and hitched a ride on a **BUS** in Oregon, USA, in 2008! Wonder if officials took the animal into custody for not having paid the correct fare? ▼

Wall St Station ④ ⑤
Enter with MetroCard at all times or see agent across Broadway

▲ In **NEW YORK CITY, PIGEONS** are known to catch the **SUBWAY** around town. They board the trains **LOOKING FOR FOOD** and end up riding for several stops – all without a ticket, of course!

SAUSAGES

RATTY the dog became famous in 2006 for regularly catching a bus in **NORTH YORKSHIRE**, England. Ratty often made the journey to his favourite pub and back—to get a plate of his favourite sausages.

A huge **PYTHON** caught a lift with an unsuspecting driver in **QUEENSLAND**, Australia, in 2017! The man found the snake coiled under his car bonnet—it had probably **TRAVELLED** for 28 KM (17 MI) in his car!

◄ **MONKEYS** often like to ride public transport in **INDIA**. They've become quite a menace – **STEALING FROM PEOPLE** and damaging property. But it's hard for city authorities to crack down on their behaviour because they're considered **SACRED CREATURES!**

◄ Police in Colorado Springs, USA, were stopped on their way to an incident by a **RACCOON** who decided to hitch a **LIFT!** The animal clung to the police **CAR'S WINDSCREEN** as it raced to the scene of a car crash.

MAGNIFICENT METROS

In **TOKYO,** Japan, people are specially employed to push commuters into packed trains. Mind the doors! ▼

The NEW YORK CITY subway in the USA has the HIGHEST number of STATIONS of any network in the world: 472. ▼

The world's fastest metro train is **SHANGHAI'S MAGLEV** in China. It carries passengers to and from the airport at a top speed of 431 kmph (268 mph).

BEIJING'S subway system in China is thought to be the **BUSIEST** in the world, carrying people on over 3.6 bn journeys a year. That's equivalent to half the people in the world taking the train in Beijing! ▶

◄ The **LONGEST ESCALATOR** on a metro is in **MOSCOW, RUSSIA** at Park Pobedy. It's over 125 m (413 ft) long – that's almost two-and-a-half Nelson's Columns!

The deepest underground station in the world is Arsenalna Station in **KIEV, UKRAINE**. It's 105.5 m (346 ft) below ground level – that's even higher than Big Ben! ►

◄The Moscow underground in Russia is considered the most **BEAUTIFUL** in the world – its stations look like ornate palaces. One train even contains replica copies of famous **PAINTINGS**, to create an art gallery for commuters!

The oldest underground railway system is in **LONDON, UK**. It opened in **1863** – with steam trains and passengers in **TOP HATS!** ►

A BRIDGE TOO FAR?

◄ The **HIGHEST BRIDGE** in the world is the **DUGE BRIDGE** in China. You might want to avoid it if you suffer from vertigo. There's a **565 M (1,853 FT)** drop from the road to the river below. That's one-and-a-half Empire State Buildings!

The road between Seattle and Medina in the **USA** crosses Lake **WASHINGTON** on a **FLOATING BRIDGE!** The lake proved too deep to allow for a typical bridge to be built, so engineers came up with this ▼ solution instead.

The Gateshead Millennium Bridge in north-east **ENGLAND**, is a **'TILT BRIDGE'**, which rotates to let boats underneath. As the bridge moves, it looks like a ▼ **GIANT BLINKING EYE!**

▲ The world's longest bridge is the **DANYANG–KUNSHAN GRAND** Bridge in China. It carries high-speed trains, and is **164.8 KM (102.4 M)** long. The bridge took **10,000 PEOPLE FOUR YEARS TO BUILD!**

The longest suspension bridge in the world is the **AKASHI KAIKYO** Bridge in Japan. It spans nearly **2 KM (1.25 MILES)** between its towers!

ALL ABOARD! THE WORLD'S MOST EPIC TRAIN JOURNEYS

◄ **The TRANS-SIBERIAN RAILWAY** runs from **MOSCOW** to **VLADIVOSTOK**, in the far east of Russia. The journey is **9,289 kilometres (5,772 miles)** long, takes eight days, and passes through **eight time zones!**

► The **LEGENDARY ORIENT EXPRESS** once ran regular services between Paris and Istanbul. Now it's a luxury train that's more like a **5-STAR HOTEL ON WHEELS!** The journey takes **5 DAYS,** with a full restaurant, bar and staff to wait on passengers' every need.

▶ The **BLUE TRAIN** in South Africa carries passengers 1,600 kilometres **(994 MILES)**, with spectacular views over Table Mountain and across the countryside between **PRETORIA** and **CAPE TOWN.**

◀ The **GHAN** is a train that runs for **2,979 KILOMETRES (1,851 MILES)** between Adelaide, on **AUSTRALIA'S** south coast, and Darwin on its north coast. The journey right across the country takes **54 HOURS!**

▶ The **TREN A LAS NUBES (TRAIN TO THE CLOUDS)** in Argentina needs 29 bridges, 21 tunnels and 13 viaducts to travel across the steep **ANDES MOUNTAINS!**

◀ The **CANADIAN TRAIN** takes **3.5 days** to cross the country and the Rocky Mountains between **TORONTO** and **VANCOUVER.** Some of the carriages have domed glass roofs so passengers don't miss any of the **SPECTACULAR SCENERY!**

▶ The **SCHWYZ FUNICULAR** in **SWITZERLAND** opened in **2017** and is the steepest passenger railway in the world. It goes up **744 METRES (2,441 FT)** in just 4 minutes!

BLACK CABS need to be TALL enough to accommodate individuals wearing a BOWLER HAT.

There are around 21,000 'BLACK CABS' in London.

Despite being known as 'BLACK CABS', London taxis come in various colours including BLUE, YELLOW and RED, and despite sometimes being referred to as 'London taxis', they're found ALL OVER THE UK.

The first MOTORISED CABS were introduced to London in 1897. They had electric motors and were called 'HUMMINGBIRDS' because of the sound they made.

The name 'TAXI' comes from 'TAXIMETER' – a device used to calculate fares.

TAXI!

BLACK CABS are famous all over the UK, but particularly in London. Here are some facts about the LONDON BLACK CAB.

WATER WAY To live!
CITIES BUILT ON WATER

AMSTERDAM is the capital of the Netherlands and is famous for its CANALS. Like much of the country, it's built on land reclaimed from the sea using complicated systems of dams to keep the sea WATER BACK.

The Dutch city of NAARDEN is built in the middle of double star-shaped moats. From the air it looks like a SNOWFLAKE!

The Russian city of ST PETERSBURG was created out of marsh at the mouth of the river Neva by Emperor Peter the Great. Its elegant canals mean it's sometimes called 'THE VENICE OF THE NORTH'.

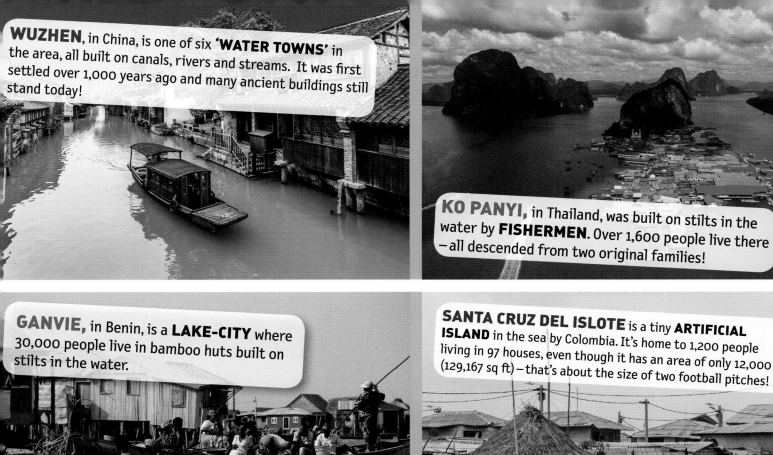

WUZHEN, in China, is one of six **'WATER TOWNS'** in the area, all built on canals, rivers and streams. It was first settled over 1,000 years ago and many ancient buildings still stand today!

KO PANYI, in Thailand, was built on stilts in the water by **FISHERMEN.** Over 1,600 people live there – all descended from two original families!

GANVIE, in Benin, is a **LAKE-CITY** where 30,000 people live in bamboo huts built on stilts in the water.

SANTA CRUZ DEL ISLOTE is a tiny **ARTIFICIAL ISLAND** in the sea by Colombia. It's home to 1,200 people living in 97 houses, even though it has an area of only 12,000 m² (129,167 sq ft) – that's about the size of two football pitches!

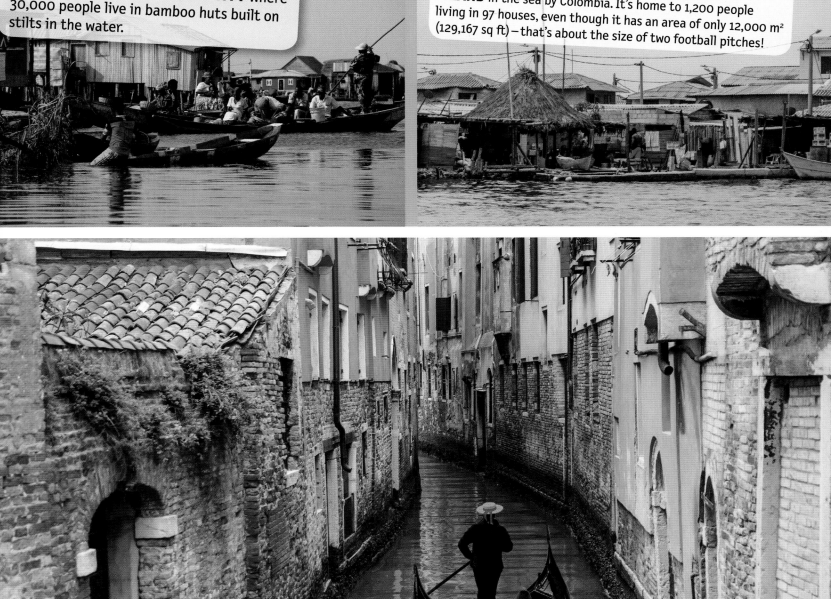

The Italian city of **VENICE** was an independent country for centuries. It's built on wooden foundations connecting **118 ISLANDS** and has almost no roads, only canals and footpaths – if you want to get around, you have to either walk or take a **BOAT!**

UFOs have formed part of **Wycliffe Well's folklore** since World War Two.

CAUTION
Proceed With Care
U.F.O
Landing Site Ahead

UFO sightings happen all over the world. Have a look at pages 120–121 for other places where they have been spotted.

CHAPTER 7

Out Of this WORLd!

WANT TO BE AN ASTRONAUT?

Here's how to planet...

▶ To stand a chance of being selected, you'll need a university **DEGREE** in **MATHS, ENGINEERING, BIOLOGY, PHYSICS OR COMPUTER SCIENCE.**

▶ And you'll need perfect **20/20 VISION** – although if you need to wear glasses or contacts to correct your sight, that's ok.

▶ Astronauts have to be able to **SPEAK ENGLISH.**

▶ The average age of astronauts is **34 YEARS OLD** when they're selected.

▶ Once selected, astronauts go through **TWO YEARS** of **INTENSIVE SPECIAL TRAINING.**

▶ Astronauts need to master subjects such as **FIRST AID** and **ENGINEERING.** They also learn languages, especially **RUSSIAN,** so they can communicate with their space colleagues from all around the world.

▶ Astronauts have to take classes in **PUBLIC SPEAKING** because they are often expected to appear on **TELEVISION,** the **INTERNET** or **RADIO** talking about their experience of space travel!

▶ Trainee astronauts also do a lot of **SCUBA DIVING!** Even though they'll be heading into space, not under the sea, scuba diving is a great way to simulate the experience of being in a **GRAVITY-FREE ENVIRONMENT.**

In **FEBRUARY 2018**, a car was fired into space from **CAPE CANAVERAL, FLORIDA, USA.**

It was fired into space by its manufacturer, **SpaceX**, as a publicity stunt to show off their new **SPACE ROCKET,** called **FALCON HEAVY.**

CAMERAS MOUNTED on the car sent back **AMAZING** views of Earth for a few hours before the screens went black.

The car was complete with a dummy driver, **NAMED STARMAN** after the famous **DAVID BOWIE** song *Star Man.* Bowie's song *Space Oddity* was playing on repeat on the car's stereo when the **ROCKET** was launched.

ROCKET

The car is a bright red Tesla Roadster, with a price tag of nearly £74,000 ($100,000).

The **CAR** has messages on it in case its travels bring it into contact with any **ALIEN** civilisations. The dashboard reads **'DON'T PANIC'**, while the circuit board reads **'MADE ON EARTH BY HUMANS'**.

Where will the car's journey end? **SPACE EXPERTS** think that eventually it might **CRASH** into the **SUN**... but not for tens of **MILLIONS OF YEARS**. It's got a **LONG DRIVE** still ahead!

space rocket, **FALCON HEAVY**

ROADSTER

WYCLIFFE WELL: this tiny VILLAGE CALLS itself the UFO capital of AUSTRALIA! Sightings here are so common that locals say you'd be unlucky NOT to spot a FLYING SAUCER...

SAN CLEMENTE, CHILE: the site of so many UFO SIGHTINGS that the government has even opened an official UFO TOURIST TRAIL through the area.

EXTRAORDINARY EXTRA-TERRESTRIALS

For thousands of years people have been CLAIMING that they have spotted STRANGE VISITORS from OUTER SPACE in the SKY. If you want to spot a UFO—that's an 'UNIDENTIFIED FLYING OBJECT'—here are some of the best places in the world to visit!

AREA 51: this site in the NEVADA DESERT, USA, is the location for top-secret MILITARY ACTIVITIES. It's long been RUMOURED that some of those activities might involve aliens...

WARNING
RESTRICTED AREA
NO TRESPASSING
VIOLATORS WILL BE PROSECUTED
NRS 207.200

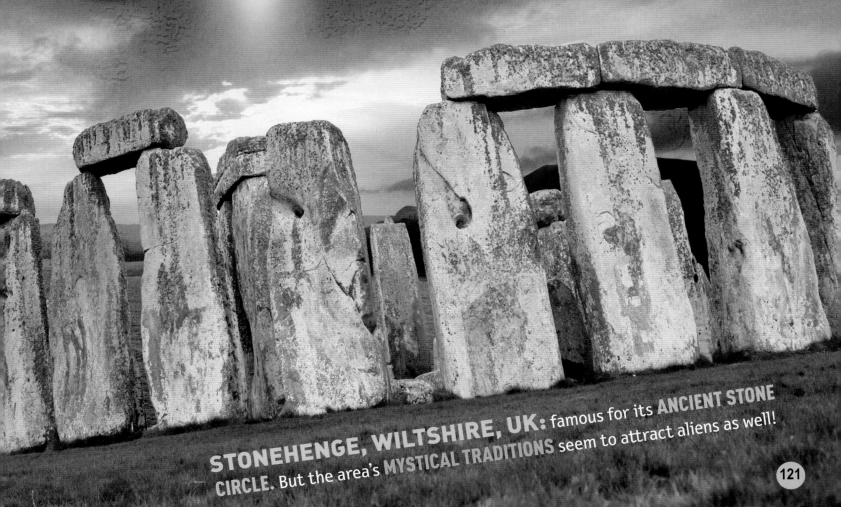

NAZCA, PERU: the **GIANT LINE DRAWINGS** in the ground here can only be appreciated from the air, but predate the **INVENTION OF AEROPLANES** by thousands of years! People have suggested they might be **ALIEN** landing strips...

FALKIRK, SCOTLAND: often called the **UFO** capital of the world, with over **300 SIGHTINGS A YEAR!**

ALTO PARAISO, BRAZIL: this tropical paradise has attracted **MYSTICS** and **PHILOSOPHERS FOR YEARS**...and aliens, too, apparently!

STONEHENGE, WILTSHIRE, UK: famous for its **ANCIENT STONE CIRCLE**. But the area's **MYSTICAL TRADITIONS** seem to attract aliens as well!

ANIMAL
ASTRONAUTS

Before **HUMANS** ventured into **SPACE, ANIMALS** got there **FIRST!** In the early days of **SPACE FLIGHT,** a huge range of **DIFFERENT CREATURES** were fired into **ORBIT** so that scientists could study **HOW** it affected them.

In 1949, a **RHESUS MONKEY** named **ALBERT** became the **FIRST ANIMAL** in space when he was blasted off in a **V2 ROCKET.**

Technically, the **FIRST ANIMALS** sent into **SPACE** were tiny **FRUIT FLIES** in 1947.

ABLE (left), a **RHESUS MONKEY,** and **MISS BAKER** (right), a **SQUIRREL MONKEY,** were launched together on 28 May, 1959 and returned unharmed. Miss Baker went on to live to the age of 27 – the oldest known monkey of her **SPECIES!**

In 1966, two **RUSSIAN DOGS** called **VETEROK** and **UGOLYOK** made the longest **SPACE FLIGHT** by dogs ever undertaken. They orbited for **22 DAYS**—a record not beaten by humans until 1971!

In 1957, the **SOVIET UNION** sent the first **DOG**, nicknamed **LAIKA**, into **ORBIT.**

The **FIRST CAT** didn't make it into space until 1963, when **FRENCH SCIENTISTS** launched **FÉLICETTE** into orbit. Félicette was found alive and well after a parachute returned her safely to earth!

Ham the **CHIMP** was trained to carry out tasks while in flight by rewarding him with **BANANA PELLETS.** His space flight in 1961 made him the **FIRST CREATURE** to interact with a **SPACECRAFT** rather than just travel in it.

In **1960**, the **SPUTNIK 5 CAPSULE** was fired into orbit by the Soviet Union, with **40 MICE, TWO RATS, A RABBIT, FRUIT FLIES** and **TWO DOGS** called **BELKA** and **STRELKA** on board. These were the **FIRST ANIMALS** to reach orbit!

A STAR IS BORN

Ever wondered how stars like our Sun come to exist? Here's how stars are born, live and die – a process that takes between 2 billion and 10 billion years!

NEBULAE are huge clouds of space dust and gas in which stars form.

A PROTOSTAR is a baby star. They're formed from nebula by complex gravitational forces.

After about 100,000 YEARS, most protostars become main sequence stars. At this stage in their lifecycle, stars can reach a temperature of 15,000,000 °C (270,000,032 °F)!

As stars age they turn into red giants. Some large stars become SUPERGIANTS – growing to 1,000 times BIGGER than the SUN!

SMALLER STARS eventually become WHITE DWARVES, shrinking and giving out less and LESS ENERGY until they fade out altogether.

BIGGER STARS produce a giant explosion called a SUPERNOVA. These make a brighter light than anything else in the sky.

Supernovas produce heat of 100 BILLION DEGREES CELSIUS!

There are about TWO SUPERNOVAS A YEAR in our galaxy and one every two seconds in the Universe in total.

After a supernova, some very LARGE STARS can even become BLACK HOLES.

Others will become incredibly dense stars called NEUTRON STARS. These are so dense that a teaspoon of neutron star material would weigh

PROTOSTAR

NEBULAE

BLACK HOLE

SUPERNOVA

WHITE DWARF

SUPERGIANT

BONKERS BLACK HOLES

The name 'black hole' was coined by American physicist John Wheeler in the 1960s. Read on for some more interesting facts about them.

Black holes are areas of space so massive that nothing can escape being pulled into them by **gravity** – **not even light!**

That means that you can't ever see a black hole. **Astronomers** can detect them by the particular kind of **radiation** they give off, and by the way they bend and shape light around them.

Black holes are formed by **huge stars** as they collapse in on themselves at the end of their lives.

If you were travelling at the speed of light, it would still take you **thousands of years to reach the nearest black hole to Earth.**

The existence of BLACK HOLES was suggested by ALBERT EINSTEIN (below) in the early 20th century. The first black hole was finally discovered in 1971 – proving Einstein's theory correct.

What happens **inside a black hole?** Well, physicists aren't completely sure. We're still a very long way from knowing exactly how these **mysterious black holes work!**

The gravitational pull of black holes even disrupts time: the **closer** you get to a black hole, the **slower** time runs!

It's thought that particularly large black holes, called **supermassive black holes,** lie at the centre of almost every galaxy.

There are about **100 million** black holes in our **galaxy** alone.

PLANETS AND THEIR Mad MOONS

Here on Earth we're used to having one, silver-grey, moon orbiting our planet. But other planets in our solar system often have many more, much weirder moons!

🌙 **JUPITER,** the largest planet in our solar system, has 53 official moons!

🌙 One of Jupiter's moons, **EUROPA,** is one of the largest in the solar system and is covered with a huge ocean beneath its icy crust.

🌙 Another of Jupiter's moons, **IO,** is covered with more than 400 active volcanoes!

🌙 As Io orbits Jupiter, huge eruptions of gas shoot from its surface. They can reach up to **480 KM (300 MI) HIGH** – that's almost a flight from **LONDON** TO **EDINBURGH!**

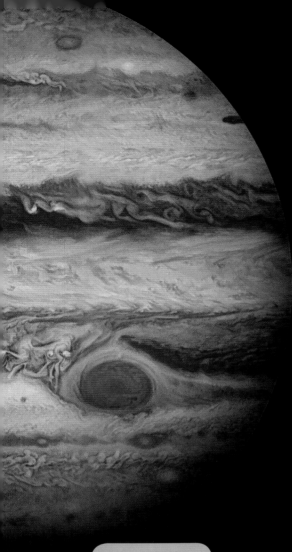

JUPITER

EUROPA
– a moon of Jupiter

IO
– a moon of Jupiter

VENUS

MERCURY

☽ SATURN has a moon called PHOEBE that orbits in a different direction to its other moons, and gives off a dust that creates a huge, DARK RING AROUND THE PLANET.

☽ Saturn has a pair of moons known as 'THE DANCING MOONS' – JANUS and EPIMETHEUS. Every four years, they swap places!

☽ Saturn's largest moon is called TITAN. It has a huge river on it that looks strangely like our own River Nile! But we know this river can't contain water – TITAN IS TOO COLD FOR IT TO REMAIN LIQUID.

☽ IAPETUS is only visible for half its orbit around Saturn, because it's almost exactly half black and half white!

TITAN – Saturn's largest moon

SATURN

Quidditch is now becoming a popular sport! Check out pages 142–143 for more on how it's played.

A game of quidditch is played with 4 balls: a Quaffle, a Golden Snitch, and 2 Bludgers.

CHAPTER 8

SPoRTiNG SuPeRStaRS

Goal DEFENCE

When a man became violent near the NORTH HARBOUR NETBALL COURTS in NEW ZEALAND in July 2017, little did he know that FIVE of the PLAYERS on court at the time were OFFICERS in the local WAITEMATA POLICE FORCE!

The women HALTED their match immediately and STEPPED IN to break up the disturbance, ARRESTING the offender ON THE SPOT.

Then, they went back onto the court... AND WON THE MATCH 40–34.

TALK ABOUT CHAMPIONS!

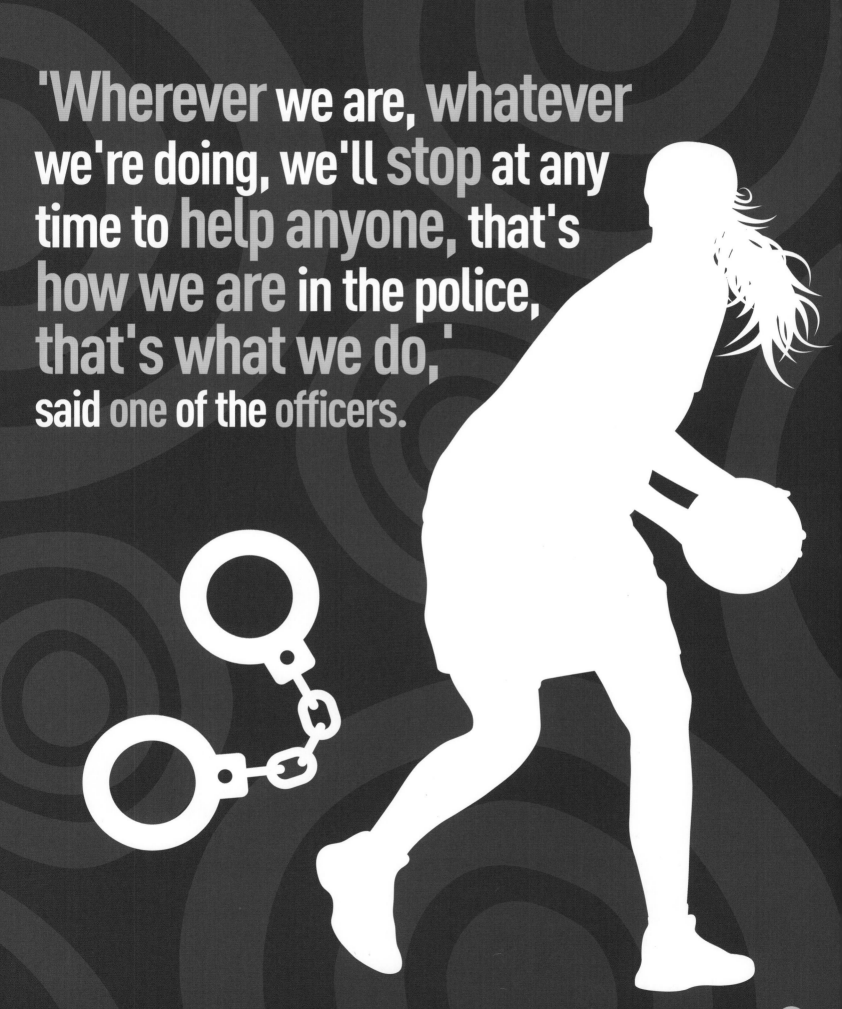

'Wherever we are, whatever we're doing, we'll stop at any time to help anyone, that's how we are in the police, that's what we do,' said one of the officers.

133

~~Pitch~~ POOCH
Invaders
AND OTHER SURPRISE SPORTS STARS

A GOLDEN LABRADOR interrupted the 2008 Tour de France by running in front of Marcus Burghardt, causing him to crash. Luckily, man and dog were both fine!

TWO DEADLY SNAKES appeared at one match and a swarm of bees held up another England cricket match in Sri Lanka!

A **MOUSE** invaded the pitch during a football match between Manchester United and Southampton in 2016. The game was so uneventful that fans called it the only interesting thing to happen!

The **ANFIELD CAT** is a stray tabby who became a TV star when he strolled onto the pitch during a match between Liverpool FC and Tottenham Hotspur FC.

A **CHICKEN** interrupted a European Cup Winners' Cup match between Dynamo Kiev and Atletico Madrid in 1986. Talk about fowl play!

A **FOX** wandered onto the pitch before a 2011 Six Nations game between England and Scotland. Maybe he just wanted a better view before the action started!

What's in a Name?

The world's strangest sporting team names

The **GRASSHOPPER** Club, Zurich, is a Swiss football team surely known for their bouncing energy! ▶

YOUNG BOYS of Bern is a Swiss football team. Their funny name goes way back to 1898, when they played a match against the Bern Old Boys Association, and the name stuck. ▶

BSC YOUNG BOYS
YB
1898

HAMILTON ACADEMICAL FC, from Scotland, sound like they spend more time in the **LIBRARY** than on the pitch! ▼

BOSTON

◀ The **BOSTON RED SOX** baseball team is named after the most famous part of their **UNIFORM** – their bright **RED STOCKINGS**.

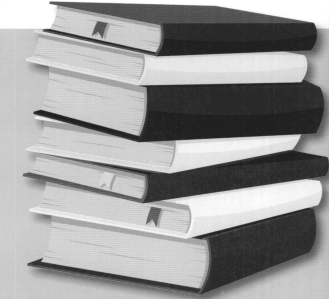

HOKKAIDO NIPPON-HAM
Fighters don't fight ham... they're a Japanese baseball team! ▼

◄ The **NEW ORLEANS BABY CAKES** changed their name from the **ZEPHYRS** in **2017**. This baseball team's 'sweet' new name was chosen in a 'name the team' competition!

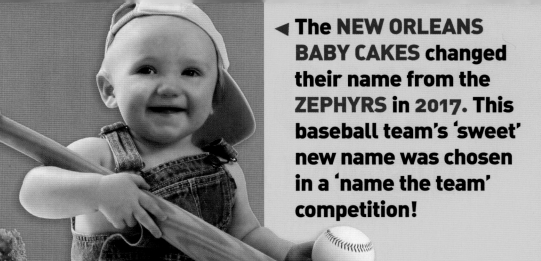

INSURANCE MANAGEMENT BEARS FC play in Nassau, Bahamas. Today they prefer to go by the snappier name of **BEARS FC.** ▼

FC SANTA CLAUS are from Finland – naturally. Now we know what **FATHER CHRISTMAS** does for the rest of the year! ►

SHEFFIELD WEDNESDAY FC got their weird name because... they used to **PLAY** on a **WEDNESDAY!** ►

WEDNESDAY

WED

137

KNOCKED OUT!
DISCONTINUED OLYMPIC SPORTS

Not every sport played in the **OLYMPICS** since the first **MODERN GAMES** in 1896 features in **TODAY'S GAMES**. Here are some of the stranger sports from **OLYMPIC HISTORY** that have been quietly forgotten...

TUG-OF-WAR: last featured in 1920. This event was only open to members of the **GREEK ARMY.**

100 M RUNNING DEER: **COMPETITORS** had to shoot at a moving **DEER-SHAPED TARGET** from **110 YARDS!** Last seen in **1948.**

CROQUET: this **GENTLE LAWN GAME** featured in the 1900 Olympics. **CUCUMBER SANDWICH,** anyone?

SWIMMING OBSTACLE RACE: this combination of a **SWIMMING RACE** and **OBSTACLES** was held in 1900 — competitors had to clamber over poles suspended above the water andswim under a row of ships.

ART COMPETITIONS: between 1912 and 1948, **OLYMPIC MEDALS** were awarded in **ARCHITECTURE, MUSIC, PAINTING, LITERATURE** and **SCULPTURE!**

UNDERWATER SWIMMING: no wonder this sport only featured once, in 1900. Without **UNDERWATER CAMERAS**, there can't have been much for the spectators to watch!

JEU DE PAUME (OR 'REAL TENNIS' IN THE UK) a sort of ancestor of **TENNIS**, this ancient sport featured in the **1908 GAMES.**

Game ON!
THE RISE OF
ESPORTS

In **2018,** Esports appeared in the Asian Games for the first time as a demonstration sport – in 2022, they will be played competitively alongside more traditional sports such as **athletics, cycling** and **gymnastics.**

In Esports the **world's top videogamers battle** it out to see who is the **ultimate champion** of some of the world's most popular games.

Esports emerged in **South Korea** in the late 1990s. Its appearance in the **Asian Games** is one of the biggest signs that it's becoming a **fully-fledged sport.**

Nearly **400 million people** a year tune in **online** around the world to watch different **Esports championships.**

Esports players are more like traditional athletes than you might think! They have **personal trainers, special diets** to keep them in peak playing condition, and **brand sponsors** – plus, of course, adoring fans.

It's quickly gone from a hobby to a **billion dollar industry.** The world's biggest Esports stars make millions of dollars in winnings, just by playing their **favourite games!**

KILLCAM FIN DE MANCHE

Although **South Korea** is the birthplace of Esports, the **Polish city of Katowice** hosts some of the most important tournaments in the calendar. It's all thanks to a forward-thinking **city councillor** who realised that Esports was going to be the **next big thing.**

TERRIFICTEAM SPORTS

SEPAK TAKRAW

Originating in Southeast Asia, this **VOLLEYBALL-LIKE** sport has been around since the 15th century. Players use their **FEET, KNEES, CHEST** or **HEAD** to get a small ball over the net.

QUIDDITCH

This **HARRY POTTER-INSPIRED** sport mixes rugby, dodgeball and handball. Teams are made up of keepers, beaters, seekers and chasers— all on **BROOMSTICKS!**

KORFBALL

A cross between **BASKETBALL** and **NETBALL,** korfball is a mixed gender sport popular in the Netherlands, Belgium and Taiwan. Teams of 8 (4 men and 4 women) score points by **THROWING** a ball through their opponents' basket.

UNICYCLE HOCKEY

Teams of 5 compete in this **FAST-PACED, ONE-WHEELED** contest. Both feet must be on your **UNICYCLE** when in contact with the ball and **NO CONTACT** is allowed, except between sticks. **FANCY TAKING PART?** There are 11 registered teams in the UK.

RIVER FOOTBALL: every year, the villagers of **Bourton-on-the-Water, UK** live up to their name by playing a game of football in the **River Windrush,** which flows through the village. The aim of the game isn't just to score as **many goals** as possible – it's to get as **wet as possible, too!**

Sporting

Not every sport takes place in a traditional arena. Here are some of the **chilliest, darkest** and **dampest** places that have seen **SPORTING ACTION.**

FOOTBALL ON ICE: in 2018, a **crew of scientists** took a break from their research work in the **Arctic** to play football on a **GIANT block** of ice.

CRAZY COLD GOLF: the World Ice Golf Championships swaps the neat lawns of most golf courses for the snows of **GREENLAND!**

Adventures

CAVE CRICKET: in the Lake District, UK in 2013 **two local cricket teams** faced off inside a slate mine – deep within **a mountain!**

Harbin's ice and snow festival in China is the biggest in the world. Turn to pages 150–151 to find out more about it.

Ice sculptures at **Harbin's ice and snow festival**, in China, are usually made using **blocks of ice** cut from the Songhua River. However, sometimes, **deionised water** is also frozen if a sculptor wants perfectly clear ice.

coolly creative

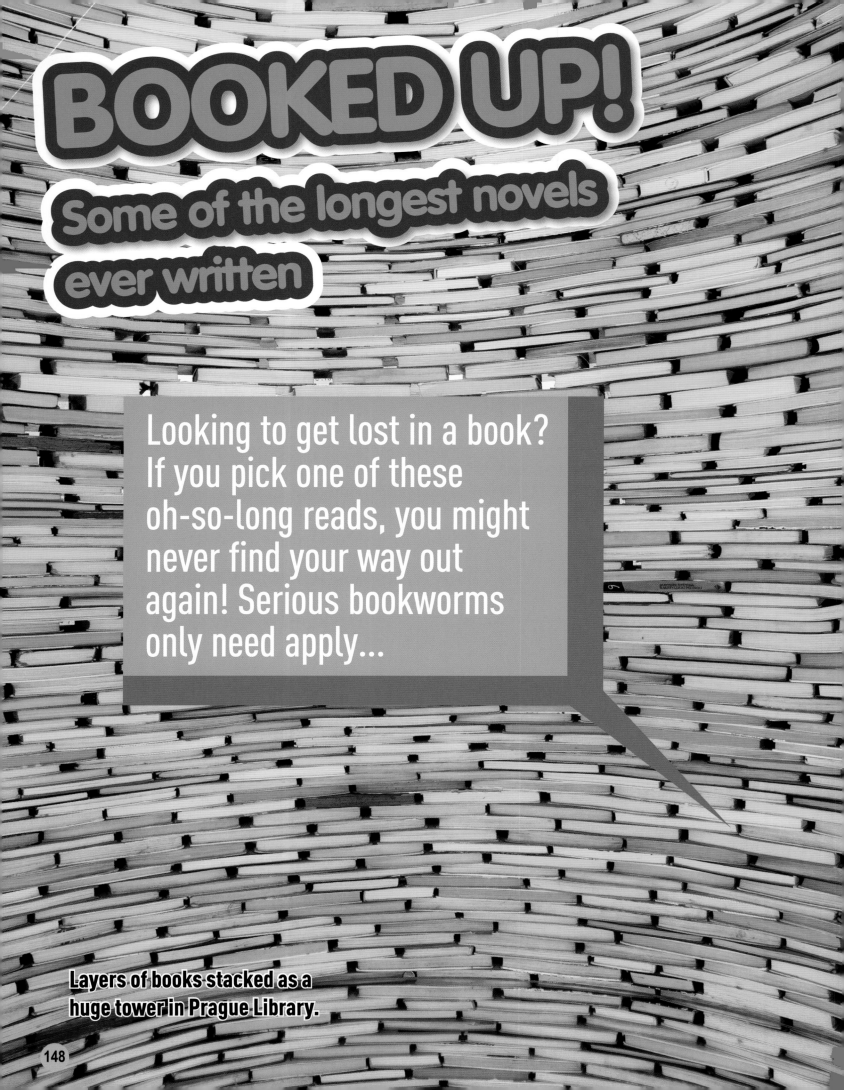

BOOKED UP!

Some of the longest novels ever written

Looking to get lost in a book? If you pick one of these oh-so-long reads, you might never find your way out again! Serious bookworms only need apply...

Layers of books stacked as a huge tower in Prague Library.

1. **Artamème, or Cyrus the Great**
   by Madeleine and Georges de Scudéry
   13,095 pages

2. **My Struggle**
   by Karl Ove Knausgård
   3,600 pages

3. **In Search of Lost Time**
   by Marcel Proust
   3,031 pages

4. **Kelidar**
   by Mahmoud Dowlatabadi
   2,836 pages

5. **The Son of Ponni**
   by Kalki Krishnamurthy
   2,400 pages

6. **Zettels Traum**
   by Arno Schmidt
   1,536 pages

7. **Clarissa, or the History of a Young Lady**
   by Samuel Richardson
   1,534 pages

8. **Joseph and his Brothers**
   by Thomas Mann
   1,492 pages

9. **My Poor Fellow Country**
   by Xavier Herbert
   1,466 pages

10. **A Suitable Boy**
    by Vikram Seth
    1,349 pages

THE WORLD'S COOLEST FESTIVAL

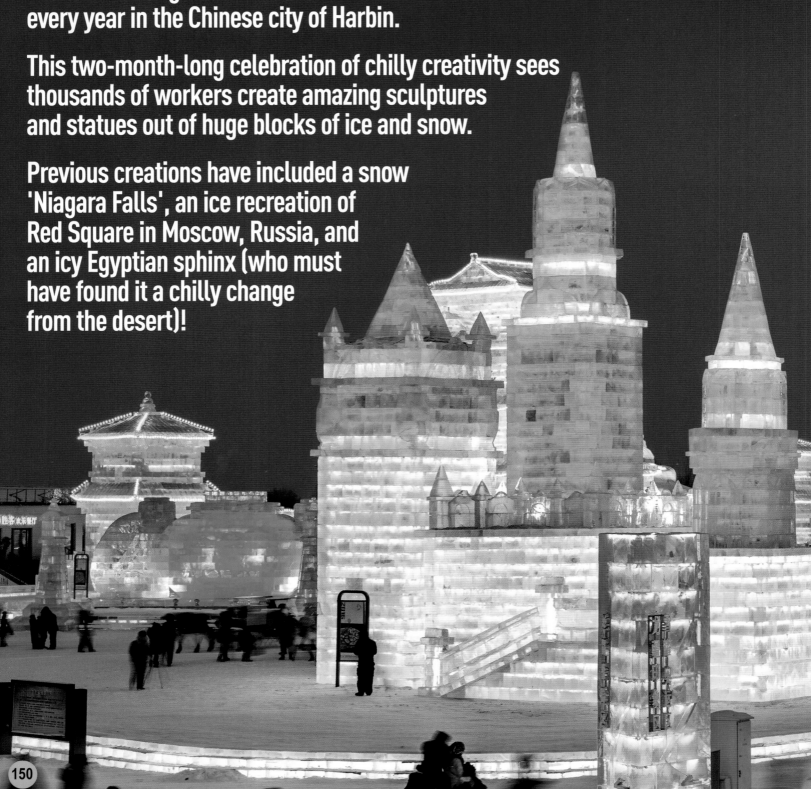

The world's largest ice and snow festival is held every year in the Chinese city of Harbin.

This two-month-long celebration of chilly creativity sees thousands of workers create amazing sculptures and statues out of huge blocks of ice and snow.

Previous creations have included a snow 'Niagara Falls', an ice recreation of Red Square in Moscow, Russia, and an icy Egyptian sphinx (who must have found it a chilly change from the desert)!

At night, **thousands of LED lights** illuminate the exhibits with a **magical light show.**

Because Harbin is one of the coldest cities in China, with winter temperatures as low as **-18 °C (-1.4 °F),** the icy creations often last much **longer than a month.**

The festival site is larger than Disneyland, and around **100,000 people visit** every day.

But of course, they can't last forever, and eventually all that work melts back to water...

151

BLOOMING MARVELLOUS

Talk about **flower power!** Artists around the world have been using the **colourful beauty of flowers** to transform their neighbourhoods using a form of **guerrilla art.**

Guerrilla gardening in Berlin, Germany

GUERRILLA ARTWORKS are installations that **pop up without warning** —and without permission!

But who could **object to the blooming beautiful sight** of Lewis Miller Design's **floral displays?** Locals have become used to seeing gorgeous flower displays appear **overnight in old rubbish bins** on street corners in New York City, USA. They've nicknamed them **'FLOWER FLASHES'.**

Meanwhile, in the Belgian capital of Brussels, florist Geoffroy Mottart has been **transforming statues** around the city. Locals wake up to find the **historical figures** in their parks and gardens have sprouted **BRIGHT, FLOWERY BEARDS AND HAIRSTYLES.**

Very fetching!

INSTRUMENTS OF NOTE
Peculiar musical instruments

Do you play the piano? Maybe the violin, or the guitar? Well, you've not seen (or heard) anything yet. Here are some of the WACKIEST instruments ever made.

Franklin's Glass Harmonica: in 1761, Benjamin Franklin created the first pedal-operated instrument based on the old trick of 'playing' water-glasses by rubbing your finger around the rim. There are more than 100 pieces of music composed for glass harmonicas!

Octobass: this huge version of the double bass is 3.48 m (11.4 ft) tall. Performers have to stand on a stool to play it!

Hyperbass Flute: this giant flute produces much lower notes than the standard instrument – some notes are too low for most humans to even hear!

Great Stalacpipe Organ: an ingenious inventor in Virginia, USA, realised that the stalactites in a local cave made different notes when tapped, so created an organ that 'plays' them as if they were organ pipes!

Theremin: performers play this futuristic instrument by moving their hand through the space between sensors – no physical contact needed! It sounds even stranger than it looks.

Sharpsichord: this huge pin-barrel harp is a giant version of the mechanisms that play music in old-fashioned music boxes.

The Vegetable Orchestra: carrot recorders? Aubergine clappers? Pumpkin drums? You name it, if it's a vegetable, Austria's Vegetable Orchestra have probably made an instrument out of it.

Sea Organ: this instrument turns the sea itself into a musician! Large pipes under a set of steps leading into the Adriatic Sea make musical notes as the waves move through them.

FAKE IT TILL YOU MAKE IT?
ART'S BIGGEST FORGERIES

Precious works of art from long ago can command huge prices from galleries, museums and collectors. No wonder some unscrupulous people have created fakes and forgeries to trick the world – sometimes very successfully indeed!

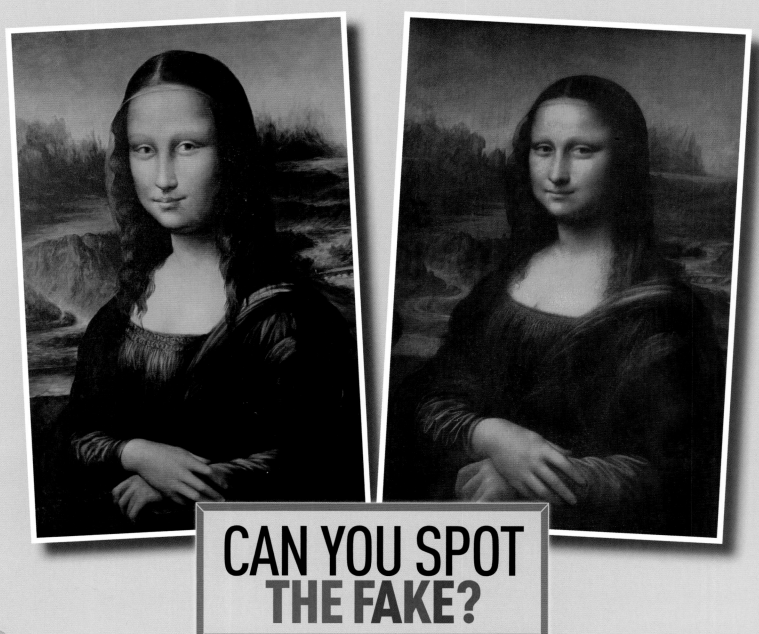

CAN YOU SPOT
THE FAKE?

The fake painting is the one on the left.

MICHELANGELO is one of the **greatest artists** to have ever lived, but he began his career in 1496 with a **marble statue** he passed off as being from **Ancient Rome!**

THOMAS KEATING was a **British forger** who became so famous that his known fakes themselves **still** sell for **thousands of pounds!**

HAN VAN MEEGEREN was a **forger** who became a **national hero** in his native Netherlands! After the Second World War, he was charged with the crime of selling a painting by the famous Dutch artist, Vermeer to an **enemy leader.** But Van Meegeren confessed that he hadn't done any such thing... because he had actually **painted the 'Vermeer' himself!**

JOHN MYATT forged and sold **more than 200 paintings** between 1986 and 1994. He was found out when his partner-in-crime's ex-girlfriend went to the police **in revenge,** however, **120** of his fakes are **still** out there, without anyone knowing where they are!

ELY SAKHAI used to buy real paintings, have them copied, then sell the real and the fake versions to different people... netting him **double the profits!** He was found out when the 'same' painting by the French artist **Gauguin** went up for auction at two separate auction houses **at the same time.**

WOLFGANG BELTRACCHI is a **German forger** who made more than **$100 million** during his 'career'! He and his wife were sentenced to **years in prison** for their crimes.

MUD, MUD, glorious mud?!

Everyone knows it isn't a REAL FESTIVAL without a little MUD —it's all part of the FUN! BORYEONG MUD FESTIVAL, in Boryeong, South Korea, takes that to EXTREMES.

First held in 1998, the ten-day festival promises revellers MUD GAMES, MUD SLIDES, a MUD MASSAGE and, for those looking for a more-than-muddy challenge, a MUD OBSTACLE MARATHON.

People in New Zealand loved the idea of a mud festival too, so MUDTOPIA FESTIVAL was created. But local people were SHOCKED to discover that the council organisers had spent THOUSANDS OF DOLLARS of taxpayers' money IMPORTING MUD FROM... SOUTH KOREA!

Organisers claimed the imported mud had SPECIAL PROPERTIES that the local mud just COULDN'T match.

They purchased 5 TONNES (5.5 TONS) of 'MUD POWDER' from a specialist producer in the town of... BORYEONG!

Just think of THE LAUNDRY!

Boryeong Mud Festival
Boryeong, South Korea

CARROT-GOLD RINGS

In 2017, a Canadian woman was **ASTONISHED** to find her **LONG-LOST ENGAGEMENT RING** in her back garden... **ON A CARROT!**

Mary Grams had lost her precious **DIAMOND RING** back in 2004, but had been too **SAD** to admit the loss to her husband.

13 YEARS LATER, her daughter-in-law was pulling up **CARROTS** for dinner from the back garden — and found one of them **'WEARING' THE RING!**

The jewellery had fallen into the soil and, eventually, the vegetable had grown **STRAIGHT THROUGH IT** — just waiting to be found.

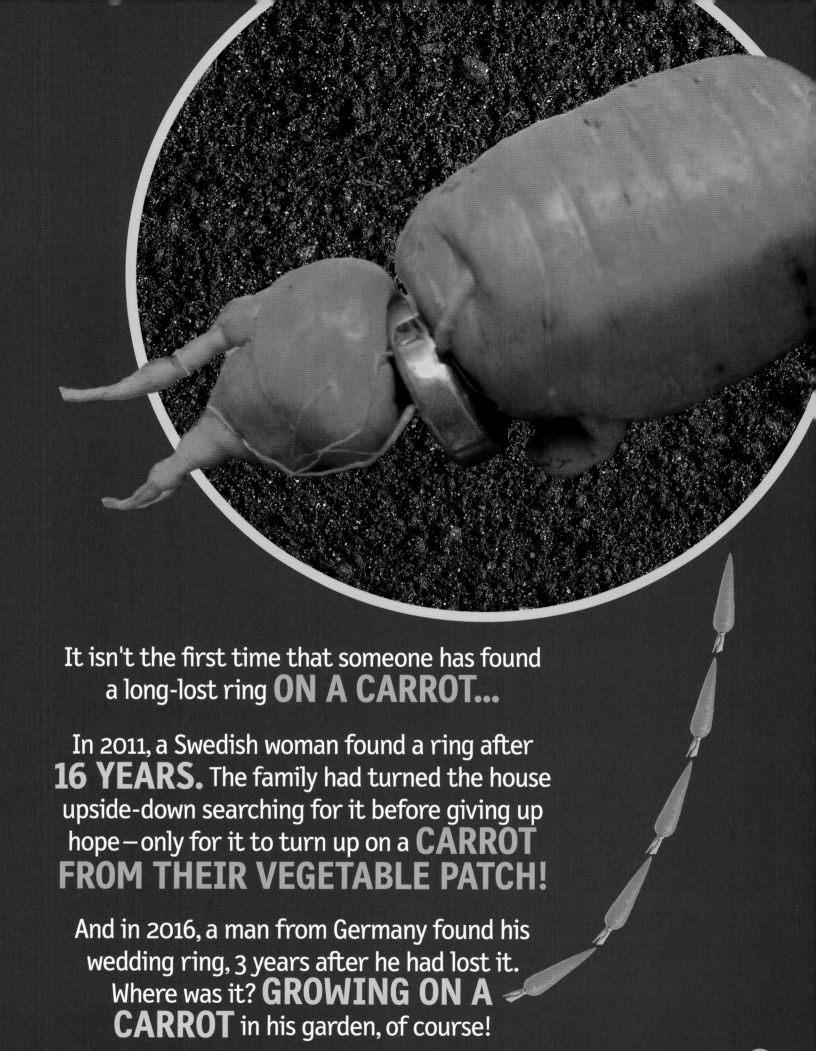

It isn't the first time that someone has found a long-lost ring **ON A CARROT...**

In 2011, a Swedish woman found a ring after **16 YEARS.** The family had turned the house upside-down searching for it before giving up hope—only for it to turn up on a **CARROT FROM THEIR VEGETABLE PATCH!**

And in 2016, a man from Germany found his wedding ring, 3 years after he had lost it. Where was it? **GROWING ON A CARROT** in his garden, of course!

FRUIT–STOPS!

Ever caught a bus from inside a TOMATO – or an ORANGE – or a STRAWBERRY?

If you ever find yourself in the Japanese town of **KONAGAI**, you might just do that!

The town's roads are brightened with **14 BUS STOPS** in the shapes of **GIANT FRUIT**.

All the bus stops have benches inside, and shelter travellers from the weather as they wait – so they're **PRACTICAL** as well as **FUN** to look at.

162

The bus stops were originally created for a festival in **celebration of travel**, held in the city of Osaka back in 1990.

They were such a hit that they were **transported to Konagai**, where they remain today.

And, nearly **30 years later**, they haven't even gone mouldy!

163

LEGENDARY
Leonardo da Vinci

NAME: Leonardo da Vinci

BORN: 15th April 1452, in Tuscany, Italy

DIED: 2nd May 1519, in France

Da Vinci's paintings are considered some of the **greatest ever produced**—including *The Last Supper* and the *Mona Lisa*.

However, Leonardo **never completed** the Mona Lisa—he died **before** it was finished.

His painting *Salvator Mundi* broke the record for the **most expensive painting** ever sold at an auction: in 2017 it went for $450.3 million!

He is one of the greatest **geniuses** that Europe has ever known. He was also an **architect, mathematician, writer, engineer, botanist, archaeologist, inventor...** the list goes on!

Among his **inventions**—many of which were only created long after his death—are the **first-ever designs** for a parachute, helicopter, aeroplane, tank, motor car, rifle, robot... **and many more!**

Leonardo was one of the **leading figures** in the period known as **the Renaissance,** which means 'rebirth' in French. The Renaissance shaped the whole of Europe, but was at its peak in Italy in the 14th to 17th centuries. It was a time when arts and culture **flourished** and people looked back to the great civilisations of **Ancient Greece** and **Rome** for inspiration.

Leonardo liked to write **backwards,** so you can only read many of his dense notebooks by **holding a mirror** up to the page!

You can still visit the **chateau** in France where this master spent his **final years**—and of course, if you're lucky enough to visit one, you'll still find some of his **masterpieces** in museums.

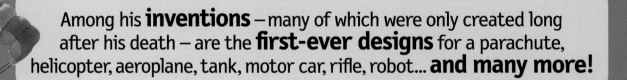

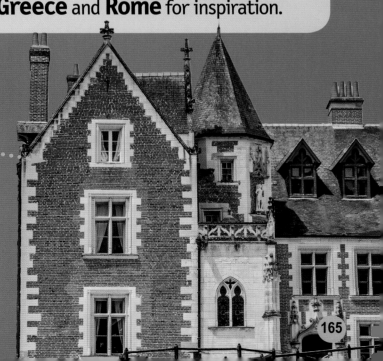

Animal
ARTISTS

Humans aren't the only creatures that express themselves through art. Here are some of the world's most amazing creative creatures!

▼ **A pot-bellied pig** in America **painted using a brush held in his mouth.** His owner took him on **tours** of America and would **sell his paintings** to onlookers.

▲ Buschi, **an orangutan** living in a German zoo, took up **painting** after his mate died.

▶ The owners of **Metro Meteor**, a retired racehorse, gave him **paints, brushes and canvas** and sold the paintings he created. They put the money towards caring for other **retired horses.**

◀ **A chimp** that was a former resident at London Zoo, UK was one of the world's **most famous animal artists.** Picasso was said to be a **great fan** of his abstract paintings!

▶ **A cat** in the USA wears a **tiny camera round his neck** that snaps photos as he roams his house and garden. The prints are sold complete with a **'paw-tograph'** signature on the reverse!

Food mash-ups such as the 'bronut' —**a donut-brownie hybrid** — are becoming increasingly popular.

Would you try a cronut? Or a pizookie? Head over to pages 170–171 to find out what they are.

gRUB'S UP!

Franken-foods

In 2013 in New York City, USA, pastry chef Dominique Ansel created a craze when he launched a new pastry called a 'CRONUT' – a cross between a flaky, buttery French croissant, and an iced American ring doughnut.

New Yorkers queued for hours to get their hands on this delicious treat – and the bakery had to limit the number each customer could buy. At one point, services sprang up offering cronut delivery, so you could skip the queues... if you were willing to pay $100 for a single pastry.

But the cronut isn't the only 'food mash-ups' made by combining two existing treats into a new monster meal.
Here are some other Franken-foods from around the world...

a cronut

piecaken
a pie baked into a cake

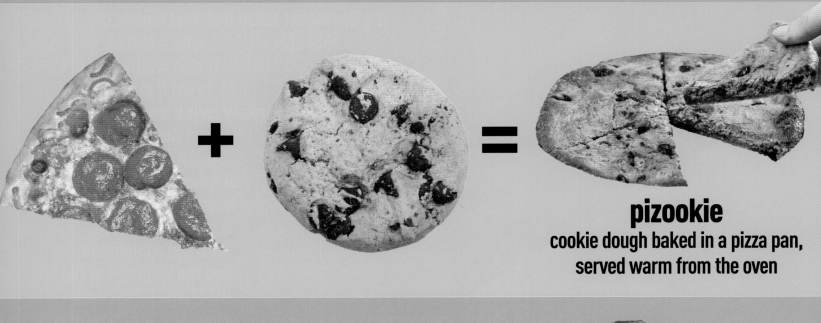

pizookie
cookie dough baked in a pizza pan,
served warm from the oven

duffin
a doughnut crossed with a muffin

tacro
a taco
made from
croissant
dough

171

HOLD YOUR NOSE!
The world's whiffiest foods...

DURIAN
is a Southeast Asian fruit that smells of **ROTTEN MEAT...** with a hint of **CUSTARD!** It's so whiffy that it's **ILLEGAL** to eat it in public in many countries. In 2018, a library in Australia was **EVACUATED** because of a suspected gas leak. It turned out that someone had left a durian in a cupboard, and the **STENCH** of the **ROTTING FRUIT** had been **MISTAKEN** for the smell of gas!

SURSTROMMING
are **FERMENTED HERRINGS** popular in Sweden. They smell like **USED NAPPIES AND RUBBISH** according to some people. Swedes think they're **DELICIOUS!**

ÉPOISSES DE BOURGOGNE
is a French cheese that's so pongy it's **BANNED FROM PUBLIC TRANSPORT.**

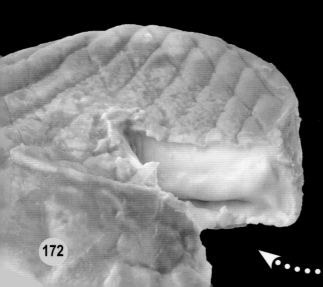

ROTTEN SHARK

(known as kæstur hákarl) is a delicacy in Iceland. It's buried for up to 12 weeks to ferment and then hung to dry for five months and has an unforgettable ROTTEN FISHY SMELL (AND TASTE!) – with a hint of WEE!

CENTURY EGGS

are a delicacy of PICKLED EGGS that are popular in China. The eggs are packed away in a special preparation for SEVERAL WEEKS until they turn BLACK and smell like HORSE URINE – at which point they're considered PERFECT to eat!

STINKY TOFU

is a Southeast Asian delicacy that smells like ROTTING PILES OF RUBBISH. It's made by bathing tofu in fermented meat, milk, vegetables and seafood brine until it takes on A PUTRID ODOUR. Yum!

We all scream for
ICE CREAM!

Nobody knows exactly **WHO** invented ice cream, but there are tales of **ROMAN EMPERORS** ordering snow to be brought from the mountains, which was **FLAVOURED WITH FRUIT AND HONEY.** Chinese records of frozen dishes a little like ice cream also exist from 200 BCE.

The world's **MOST POPULAR FLAVOUR** is **vanilla.**

Would you eat **BACON, CHEESEBURGER, OR SMOKED SALMON ICE CREAM?** They've all been made by chefs and ice cream parlours **around the world.**

It takes **50 LICKS** to **devour** an average scoop of ice cream.

Prime Minister **MARGARET THATCHER** was one of the scientists on the team that invented **soft scoop ice cream,** before she became a politician!

NEW ZEALANDERS love ice cream more than anyone else – eating an average of **28.4 litres (50 pints) each a year!**

The oldest surviving handwritten **ICE CREAM RECIPE** is from 1665. It's flavoured with **'ambergris'** – an unusual ingredient made from **whale vomit!**

Two **AMERICAN ICE CREAM PARLOURS** hotly contest the claim to have invented the **ice cream sundae:** Two Rivers' parlour in Wisconsin (in 1881), and Platt & Colt Pharmacy, in Ithaca, New York (in 1892).

175

HOT Stuff!
The world's hottest chillies

The **HEAT** of a **CHILLI** is measured using a rating system called the **SCOVILLE SCALE.** A **JALAPEÑO CHILLI**—the kind found on pizzas—measures around **10,000 SCOVILLE UNITS.**

The **CHEMICAL** in chillies that causes a **BURNING** sensation is called **CAPSAICAN.** It tricks the body's **PAIN SENSORS** into thinking they are **BURNING.**

If your mouth is **TINGLING** after eating spicy food, one of the best things you can do is **DRINK SOME MILK** or **HAVE A MOUTHFUL OF YOGHURT.** Dairy products contain **A PROTEIN** that helps **NEUTRALISE** capsaican.

FunFACT

The hottest chilli in the world is Pepper X, created by self-described mad scientist, 'Smokin'' Ed Currie.

Pepper X measures up to 3,180,000 on the Scoville scale!

Competitions are regularly held around the world to see who can eat the **HOTTEST CHILLIES.**

But eating these **SUPER-HOT** chillies can be very **DANGEROUS,** as well as extremely **PAINFUL!** One contestant in an eating competition in San Francisco, California, USA ended up **IN HOSPITAL** with a **COLLAPSED LUNG** after eating a burger laced with **GHOST PEPPERS** (which clock in at around **A MILLION** Scoville units).

a ghost pepper

The PASTA-bilities are endless...

Did you know there are more than 350 pasta shapes in Italy?

Many are local to specific regions, and they're all designed to go with different sauces and dishes. Some are tiny, to be added to broths and soups. Some are large sheets, used to prepare dishes like lasagne.

Here are some of the strangest pasta shapes – and their even stranger meanings in Italian!

 **lumaconi** 'big snails'

 **linguine** 'little tongues'

 **farfelle** 'butterflies'

 **orecchiette** 'little ears'

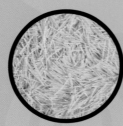 **vermicelli** 'little worms'

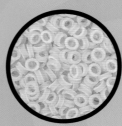 **anelli** 'rings'

 **creste di galli** 'cockerel's combs'

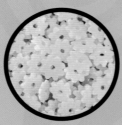 **stelline** 'little stars'

 **radiatori** 'radiators'

But the **STRANGEST-NAMED** pasta of all must be **STROZZAPRETI,** which means **'PRIEST STRANGLER'!**

This pasta dates from a time when the Catholic Church directly **GOVERNED LARGE PARTS OF ITALY,** and local people **RESENTED** the taxes and control that the **CLERGY EXERTED OVER THEM.**

9 AMAZING VENDING MACHINES

A **'CUPCAKE ATM'** in Beverly Hills, California, USA provides cupcakes complete with **SPRINKLES** —of course!

Parisians love their **BAGUETTES** and now they can even get them from a **VENDING MACHINE.**

...a pizza vending machine

CAVIAR vending machines, Los Angeles, USA: for those **LATE-NIGHT LUXURY** snack emergencies.

ITALIAN PIZZA

INGREDIENTS OME FROM:

Friuli Venezia Giulia

Mozzarella

Trentino / Alto Adige

Ham

www.buttonmeal.com

tomatoes

ITALIAN PIZZA

by BUTTONMEAL
italian dishes

10 inch Pizza ready in only 3 MINUTES

SERVATIVES and OURANTS FREE

→ flour

mozzarella

PIZZA vending machines, found across **EUROPE,** even make the dough **FROM SCRATCH!**

HOT DOG vending machines in the **STATES** will even **TOAST THE BUN** before dispensing your dinner.

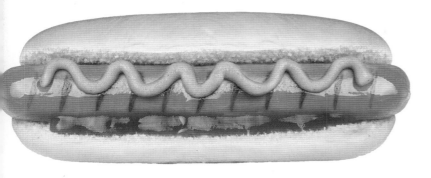

FRESH EGG vending machines are used by **JAPANESE FARMERS** to sell their **PRODUCE** on the roadside.

A **MASHED POTATO** vending machine in Singapore serves up the tasty treat topped with **LASHINGS OF GRAVY.**

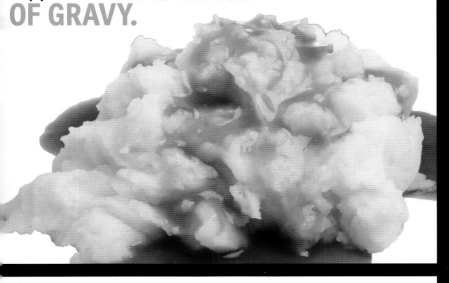

BANANA vending machines in **JAPAN** offer a **HEALTHY ALTERNATIVE** to a chocolate bar.

Australians can turn to **FRENCH FRIES** vending machines when they have a **CRAVING** for a **SALTY SNACK.**

MUSEUMS GOOD ENOUGH TO EAT!

HUNGRY FOR SOME CULTURE?

Why not take a trip to one of these **weird and wonderful food museums** around the world, all dedicated to a beloved **local dish.**

The Dutch Cheese Museum
Alkmaar, The Netherlands

>>> **SPAM© Museum**
Minnesota, USA

kimchi

>>> **The Kimchi Museum**
South Korea

>>> **Mustard Museum**
Norwich, UK

mustard

>>> **Belgian Fries Museum**
Bruges, Belgium

>>> **Ramen Museum**
Yokohama, Japan

ramen

>>> **Currywurst Museum**
Berlin, Germany

>>> **Canadian Potato Museum**
O'Leary, Canada

currywurst

>>> **Jell-O Museum**
Le Roy, New York, USA

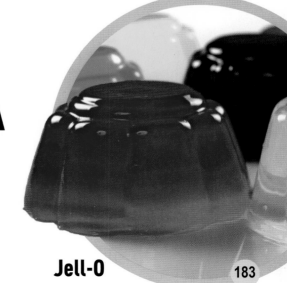

>>> **Cadbury World Chocolate Museum**
Birmingham, UK

Jell-O

183

BIG EATERS

The World Stinging Nettle-Eating Championship, Dorset, UK.

184

Think you've got a **BIG APPETITE,** or strange **TASTE IN SNACKS?** Competitive eaters around the world face off to see who can **EAT THE MOST** of some **VERY PECULIAR FOODS...**

The **OYSTER-EATING WORLD CHAMPIONSHIP** is held annually in New Orleans, Louisiana, USA—contestants often slurp down over 500 oysters each in one sitting!

The **NATIONAL FRIED MUSHROOM COMPETITION** takes place in Pennsylvania, USA. Mushrooms are breaded and deep-fried, and the record sits at over 5 kg (11.5 lb)!

A **PEANUT BUTTER AND BANANA SANDWICH COMPETITION** is often held in Biloxi, Mississippi, USA, to remember Elvis Presley—it was his favourite snack.

An annual **CURRY-EATING CONTEST** is held in Edinburgh, Scotland, each year: the contestants have to devour an especially spicy dish known as 'Killer Curry'!

The **WORLD PICKLE-EATING CHAMPIONSHIPS** is held annually in the USA. Patrick Bertoletti is the current record holder: he devoured over 2.5 kg (5 lb 11 oz) of gherkins in 6 minutes in 2010.

RAW ONIONS are a popular choice for competitive eaters, who compete to see who can finish one the fastest. Record holder Yusuke Yamaguchi gobbled his in a time of 29.56 seconds!

Don Lerman holds the record for the **MOST BUTTER** eaten in 5 minutes: nearly 800 g (1 lb 12 oz)!

An **ELVER-EATING COMPETITION** was historically held in the Gloucestershire village of Frampton-on-Severn, UK, each year, and recently revived. Never heard of an elver? They're a kind of tiny, worm-sized eel!

The record for **MINCE PIE-EATING** is held by Sonya Thomas, who is known as 'The Black Widow' by her fans. She munched 46 of them in just 10 minutes.

The **WORLD STINGING NETTLE-EATING CHAMPIONSHIP** takes place in Dorset, England, every year. Owww!

index

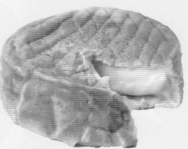

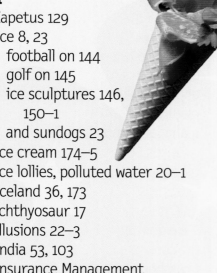

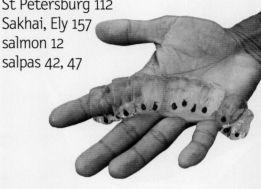

image credits

Subscribe TODAY!

Visit our new website natgeokids.com or call 0333057707272

Love National Geographic Kids? Well, sign up to the magazine, iPad edition or BOTH today and save money!

PRINT ONLY

£30

A subscription to *National Geographic Kids* magazine is the perfect gift for boys and girls aged six and over. Packed with features about nature, science, geography, history and popular culture, Nat Geo Kids gets children excited about the world. It helps with their homework, too!

Regular price £50
QUOTE CODE NGKWBT

FULL SUBSCRIPTION

PREMIUM

£40

This premium package will keep kids entertained for hours while teaching them about the amazing world we live in. Subscribe to both *National Geographic Kids* magazine and the interactive Nat Geo Kids iPad app and you'll save £40!

Regular price £80
QUOTE CODE NGKWBTB

DIGITAL ONLY

£15

The National Geographic Kids iPad app is jam-packed with videos, games, sounds and extra interactive content that really bring *National Geographic Kids* magazine to life! Engaging and exciting, Nat Geo Kids' iPad edition makes learning more fun than ever!

Regular price £30
QUOTE CODE NGKWBTD

NATIONAL GEOGRAPHIC KiDS

© 2017 National Geographic Partners, LLC